Effective Selling
Through Psychology:

DIMENSIONAL SALES AND SALES MANAGEMENT
STRATEGIES

Effective Selling Through Psychology:

DIMENSIONAL SALES AND SALES MANAGEMENT STRATEGIES

V. R. Buzzotta, Ph.D.

R. E. Lefton, Ph.D.

Manuel Sherberg

Psychological Associates, Inc., St. Louis
Behavioral Science Systems Division

WILEY INTERSCIENCE, a Division of John Wiley & Sons, Inc.
New York · London · Sydney · Toronto

Acknowledgment

We wish to express our gratitude to the following business colleagues, all of whom extended significant help and encouragement in the early development of Dimensional Sales Training: Benjamin F. Edwards III, Ronald E. Buesinger, and Charles D'Arcy Fox of A. G. Edwards & Sons; W. C. Fish, W. A. Lewis, J. H. Ebbeler, D. B. Noland, and E. P. Messenger of Eli Lilly and Company; and Donald E. Nickelson of Paine, Webber, Jackson & Curtis.

V.R.B.
R.E.L.
M.S.

Contents

Effective Selling
Through Psychology:

DIMENSIONAL SALES AND SALES MANAGEMENT
STRATEGIES

INTRODUCTION

Salesmen are lucky people. At a time when many discussions of work focus on such dismal topics as alienation, dehumanization, and boredom, salesmen do work that brings them into contact with other people, lets them establish productive human relationships, and is seldom repetitious or dull. At a time when many people feel estranged from or indifferent about their jobs, salesmen do work that can be engaging and engrossing. And, at a time when many people feel that their jobs lack challenge and exhilaration, salesmen do work that can be deeply satisfying and fulfilling.

Selling has always been associated with human gratification. The bazaars and marketplaces of the ancient world were colorful, exciting places that one visited with high expectation, and the men and women who tended the stalls and booths (who were the forerunners of modern sales people), coming from great distances to vend their wares, were often stimulating and cosmopolitan figures. In colonial and frontier America the itinerant peddler, braving bad weather and danger to take his wagonload of merchandise into the backwoods, was considered not only a seller of goods, but a source of news and a link with the outer world; his arrival was an event of real importance. And in rural America a few dacades ago the proprietor of the general store, a salesman whose "line" included everything from thimbles to plows, was a pivotal figure in the community, a man whose stove-warmed store was a haven from the loneliness and austerity of life on the farm. Since almost the beginning of recorded history, selling has meant much more than a simple exchange of goods; it has meant companionship, intellectual stimulation, and the person-to-person gusto without which life would have been much more barren.

Much the same is true today. For most people, a "shopping trip" still has an element of expectation and adventure about it; the meeting with

1

a salesman or saleswoman is still looked upon as a gratifying human encounter. For many businessmen, the visit of a salesman is still considered
an opportunity to learn, to discover, to be brought up to date. For most
of us, the buying and selling process is still uniquely *personal*, something
we look foward to. At its best, it is characterized by lively, satisfying give-
and-take. This is not to deny that selling is sometimes humdrum, that it
has moments, even hours, of frustration, or that after a call on a cantan-
kerous customer any salesman may momentarily wish he could trade his
job for one less demanding. But, admitting all this, we can still say that
selling offers opportunities for stimulation and satisfaction that many jobs
lack. The reason, of course, is that selling is a profoundly human activity.
No matter what a man sells, he sells it to people. No matter what else he
does during his working day, he spends a significant amount of time working with people. And no matter how successful he becomes his success is
always, in the last analysis, inseparable from his relationships with people.

We can say the same of sales managers. They enjoy most of the satisfactions their salesmen enjoy; in addition, they experience the special
gratification that comes from helping men develop and grow. More than
many jobs, sales management is deeply fulfilling because, like selling, it
is inseparable from relationships with people.

This book is about the human aspects of selling and sales management.
It takes a searching look at the interpersonal aspects of sales and sales
management success. And it does so realistically and candidly. Throughout, we have tried to talk about the real world of selling and management,
as we know it from our personal experience and as we have learned about
it from thousands of salesmen and sales managers with whom we have
worked over the years. We have ignored the fascinating but false folklore
of selling, and concentrated on the even more fascinating facts. And, although we write as behavioral scientists, we have tried to keep scientific
jargon and ivory-tower obscurity out of the book. This is, then, a full and
frank look at the human aspects of selling—the lively, zesty, perpetually
intriguing interpersonal aspects—written for salesmen and sales managers
by behavioral scientists who are themselves salesmen and sales managers.
It is a book about people who sell, their triumphs and tribulations, their
frailties and foibles, their ambitions and achievements, their strengths
and successes. It is, finally and most importantly, a book to help salesmen
and sales managers become better salesmen and sales managers. It is a
how-to book, a manual of interpersonal effectiveness and, we fervently
hope, a guidebook to sales success.

The authors' intellectual debts are enormous, far too numerous to be
listed completely. We are indebted to many behavioral scientists from
whom we acquired so many of the insights and ideas that form the theoret-

ical basis of this book. Many of these scientists are named in our first chapter; unfortunately, it is manifestly impossible to list all the researchers whose work has influenced ours over the years.

One note of caution: books, as the great English book-lover, Samuel Johnson, once wrote, are useless without the knowledge of life, a thought that Robert Louis Stevenson confirmed when he said that "Books are good enough in their own way, but they are a mighty bloodless substitute for life." This applies with special force to books about selling. By itself, this book can be no more than a provocative intellectual experience (at best); *applied in the field*, it can be a potent instrument of change. By itself, it can only be a bloodless substitute for the real world of selling and sales management; *applied in the field*, it can open new avenues to success. Only the *reader* can lend blood and bone and sinew to this book.

The authors hope the reader brings his own vitalizing knowledge of life to the otherwise inanimate pages of this book, and that he enlivens its principles by putting them to use in his daily work. If he does, he is almost certain to be pleased with the results.

1

Salesmanship
THE BEHAVIORAL SCIENCE PERSPECTIVE

Back in the eighteenth century, a German poet by the name of Friedrich Klopstock wrote poems that many people found impossible to understand. The story goes that one day he was asked to explain the meaning of one of these poems and, shrugging his shoulders, he replied: "Once, God and I both knew what it meant. Now God alone knows."

When it comes to *salesmanship*, most of us are Klopstockians. If the man who first coined the word were around today, chances are he'd have a difficult time explaining what it was originally intended to mean. Over the years, the word has become so encrusted with legend, myth, and pure bunkum that it now means almost anything that anyone wants it to mean. In this chapter, we're going to explore some of the more common definitions of salesmanship, and explain what *we* mean by it in this book. In the process, we'll also describe some of the basic ideas of the behavioral sciences, the ideas that form the bedrock of this book.

SOME POPULAR MYTHS ABOUT SELLING AND SALES MANAGEMENT

Perhaps the best way to understand the behavioral science perspective is to compare it with other ways of looking at selling and sales management.

4

So let's begin by examining some popular notions about selling and sales management. We call these notions myths because, according to Webster, a myth is "an ill-founded belief," and the behavioral sciences have shown each of these notions to be ill-founded.

"Salesmen are born, not made."   This is one of the most popular legends about selling. The idea is that some people come into the world with an inherited ability to sell things. This implies that while some people can *acquire* some selling skills, they will never be as successful as the man with salesmanship in his genes; since most people are born without selling skills, they cannot hope to succeed in selling. This is ridiculous, but it is an idea that finds surprisingly wide acceptance.

The truth is simple: There is no such creature as a "born salesman." There are people with traits that make them better fitted for selling than other people might be; we'll describe these people at length in this book. But, *and this is crucial*, most people who want to sell can *acquire* many of the traits that will make them successful; if a man knows what the characteristics of a successful salesman are, and if he *wants* to be a successful salesman, he can set about *developing* the characteristics and improving his selling skills. Some people, of course, have more of these traits at the outset than other people have; some acquire more of these traits through diligence than other people. But, we repeat, most people who want to sell *can* acquire many of the traits that will make them successful salesmen.

The notion that salesmen are born, not made, is not merely false; it is harmfully pessimistic. It says there's no point in *trying* to become a good salesman if you don't have inborn selling skills. Such pessimism, as this book will show, is unjustified. The entire approach of this book, based not on myth but on the behavioral sciences, is *optimistic*.

"Selling is a mystery."   This is widely believed, even among people who have been selling for many years. According to this idea, we cannot understand what makes the difference between a successful and an unsuccessful salesman, because the "secret" of successful selling is mysterious and impenetrable. All we know is that some men succeed at selling, while others don't. It is useless to analyze selling scientifically, since selling eludes analysis. Sales result from interaction between people, and people are an unsolvable puzzle. There is, therefore, no hope of understanding what really happens when a sale is made.

This notion predates modern behavioral science. It should have been laid to rest at the turn of the century when behavioral scientists began to show that much of what happens between people *can* be understood by proven scientific methods. While it is perfectly true that many aspects of the human mind do remain a mystery to us, it is equally true that the behavioral sciences have been slowly but surely penetrating these mysteries for at least the past fifty years. We *do* know what makes a successful salesman; we *do* understand what happens during a sale.

"Selling is a set of rules."   This is more plausible than the ideas we've considered so far, but it's nonetheless false. According to this very popular myth, anyone can become a successful salesman, or at least more successful than he is at present, if he masters a fairly simple set of rules. Anyone who has ever read a traditional book on "How to Sell," or sat through a traditional sales training course, knows what the rules are: always dress neatly, know your product line, be able to answer objections, have a well-practiced presentation, manage your time well, keep your prospect list replenished, always ask for the order . . . . These are a few of the more common rules. Follow these and you'll succeed.

Now, we don't for a minute suggest that these rules are bad. In fact, each of them makes good sense. But it's a gross oversimplification to suggest that these rules, or any others, *by themselves*, will make a man a success at selling. The unhappy truth is that thousands of men have memorized rules like these and put them into practice, only to fail miserably at selling. These rules are externals, *important* externals but nevertheless externals, that fail to get to the *heart* of salesmanship. Underlying all these externals are patterns of *sales behavior,* and, as we will show in detail, these patterns of sales behavior, along with other recommended practices, determine sales success.

To succeed in selling, a salesman should know the principles which govern *why* people (salesmen, customers, sales managers) interact with one another as they do. These principles are the subject of this book.

"Salesmen are different."   On the surface, this idea seems so reasonable that many people readily believe it without thinking about it. According to it, every salesman differs from every other salesman, so much, in fact, that no useful comparison can be made between them. Selling, it contends, is a highly individualized process; generalizations about salesmen are futile, since each salesman has his own personal selling strategy, his own work habits, and his own techniques for making sales. So it is useless to talk about salesmen as a group.

There's a large measure of truth in this, combined with a large measure of falsehood. The truth is that salesmen *are* individuals, and no two are exactly alike. But this does not mean we cannot generalize about salesmen. The behavioral sciences are based on the premise that, while people differ from one another, certain characteristics are basic to *all* people or to *large groups* of people, and these characteristics make it possible to talk about people in *general* terms. This premise does not overlook the differences between people; it simply emphasizes their many similarities. It does not wipe out individuality; it simply insists that we can best understand individuals if we first understand how people are alike.

Time and again, in talking about sales behavior, we will emphasize that real salesmen vary from our descriptions in one way or another. But there are, nevertheless, typical behaviors that are more or less shared by large numbers of salesmen.

In a phrase, the "salesmen are different" myth, reasonable though it may sound, is unscientific.

There are as many erroneous ideas about *sales management* as about selling. In fact, all the common mistakes about selling have, at one time or another, been applied to sales management. It's still quite common to hear people (including some sales managers) say that sales managers are born, not made; that managing is a baffling puzzle that no one can hope to understand; that anyone can be a reasonably successful sales manager if he follows certain hard-and-fast rules; or that each sales manager is unique, unlike anyone else in the world of business, and it is therefore useless to talk about sales managers in general. There is little or no basis in fact for any of these ideas.

Briefly, the facts are these:

Men can learn to be good sales managers, just as they can learn to be good salesmen. Managerial skill is not inherited—like the color of one's eyes; nobody comes into the world as a sales manager. The "born-not-made" idea is about as realistic as the "flat-earth" idea.

Sales management is *not* an imponderable mystery. The behavioral sciences have done a great deal to help us understand the managerial process. We have a wealth of research findings that cast light on what management is all about. To say there is no hope of understanding sales management makes no more sense than to say we cannot understand yellow fever or bubonic plague. In each case, understanding comes from science.

There are *no* easy-to-memorize rules that will make a man a good sales manager. As we will see, effective sales management largely depends on *interactional skills*, and these depend upon understanding, insight, and practice, not on formulas. Managing salesmen is something like marriage: it's basically a matter of the way people interact with one another. There is no rulebook for motivating salesmen or for getting along with your wife.

As with salesmen, it's possible, and profitable, to talk about sales managers in *general terms.* Each sales manager *is* unique, of course, but so is each sycamore tree and each dachshund. In spite of this, the science of botany has acquired vast amounts of information about sycamore trees in general, and the science of zoology has no qualms about discussing dachshunds as a group. The behavioral sciences enable us to do the same about sales managers.

BEHAVIORAL SCIENCE: WHAT IT IS

In this book, we define selling (and sales management) as an *applied behavioral science.* Behavioral science is the science that studies, among other things, the *how* and *why* of human interaction. Its findings, which are increasing at an accelerating rate, can be applied in workaday situations to help people interact more effectively and more productively.

In fact, behavioral science is probably best defined as the study of human interaction, of the ways people interrelate, either face-to-face or in groups. For the salesman or sales manager, this means behavioral science is interested in the things *he* is interested in: the problems of human communication; how people are motivated; how they learn and develop; how attitudes are formed; how creativity is stimulated; how human conflict can be managed productively; and a host of other topics that clarify human interaction. Behavioral science has much to contribute to our understanding of such practical matters as how salesmen can be more persuasive, what customers really want when they buy, how managers can manage for better results, how organizational innovation can be increased, or how an organization's goals can be made meaningful to the people in the organization.

Where does the behavioral scientist get his data? Mainly from psychology, sociology, and social psychology, but also from economics, anthropology, linguistics, education, and political science. In fact, behavioral scientists draw their information and ideas from any field that can throw scientific, verifiable light on human behavior. They combine findings from all the so-called "behavioral sciences" into a single science of human conduct. And, significantly, behavioral scientists are *not* especially interested in "abnormal" or "pathological" behavior. They don't ignore such behavior, but the *primary* focus of their research is the practical, everyday behavior of people in practical, everyday settings.

In the all-important area of communication, for example, behavioral scientists have done work of fundamental importance to managers and salesmen. They've studied the factors that make new ideas acceptable or unacceptable to listeners (the listener's emotional commitment to his present ideas, for example, or his trust in the person who is presenting the new idea); they've analyzed the ways in which speakers can get and hold the attention of listeners; and they've studied the techniques by which speakers can get their ideas across clearly (for instance, it was behavioral scientists who discovered that the typical speaker's tendency to "bunch" his ideas, to hurl them at the listener in a rapid-fire, nonstop way, is a much less effective technique for making the ideas understandable than "spacing" the ideas and leaving time between them, time in which the listener can mull them over and master them). Behavioral scientists have investigated what happens to ideas that lack personal meaning for the listener, what happens to ideas that don't fit in with the listener's current ideas, and what causes listeners to distort or confuse certain ideas, and why. These are a few (actually, a *very* few) of the down-to-earth topics that behavioral scientists have researched in their continuing effort to throw light on communication.

Or take *motivation*, a subject of equal significance to managers and salesmen. Here, too, the focus of the behavioral scientists' work has been practical and useful. They've done intensive research into human needs, the basic drives that underlie motivation; they've explored what happens to people's motivation once their needs are satisfied, and how motivation can be redirected to other needs; and what happens to motivation when opportunities to fill needs are blocked or thwarted. This has led to studies of the impact of frustrated needs on productivity, of ways in which needs can be identified and responded to, what happens when individual needs and organizational needs are in conflict, and how such conflicts can be reconciled.

All of this research, it should be stressed, attempts to meet the rigorous criteria of *science*. All of it is conducted by rigorous scientific standards which can be checked out and confirmed. The behavioral scientist, like the physicist or biologist, demands hard, empirical *proofs*, not hunches, guesswork, or intuition. In this way, behavioral science is replacing generations of folklore with fact.

SELLING AND SALES MANAGEMENT: APPLIED BEHAVIORAL SCIENCES

In *applying* behavioral science, we put it to work for practical purposes. Selling and sales management are activities in which the findings of the behavioral sciences are (or should be) put to use to achieve practical results. They are applied behavioral sciences in the same way that electronics is an applied physical science and medicine is an applied biological science. In each instance, the idea is the same: to *use* scientific data to attain a given practical outcome.

The Behavioral Science Perspective

What it means to think of selling and sales management as applied behavioral sciences will become clearer if we look a little more closely at some of the basic ideas of behavioral science.

  1. *Behavioral science is primarily interested in everyday behavior.*

So-called "abnormal" or "pathological" behavior is not its basic concern. Behavioral scientists don't ignore deviations from "normal" behavior, but their *primary* focus is on what must be called, for lack of a better word, "ordinary" behavior, the things people do in routine, workaday interaction. In studying communication, for instance, behavioral scientists are largely interested in how people get through to one another in familiar, typical situations. This means that most of the data about communication that behavioral scientists have amassed are pertinent to people in familiar pursuits: salesmen, for example, or sales managers. For the most part, behavioral science is interested in the world most of us know and are interested in.

  2. *Behavioral science stresses the importance of human interaction.*

One of its basic premises is that human behavior cannot be understood unless human *interaction* is understood. Most behavior is shaped in situations involving two or more people; even when alone, we shape many decisions by our estimates of the way other people will respond to them. Because it emphasizes interaction, behavioral science has much to say to salesmen and sales managers, whose very livelihood depends upon successful interaction. Throughout this book, we'll use the word *interaction* repeatedly; most of what we have to say about it will come from, or be based upon, behavioral science.

  3. *Behavioral science is optimistic about people.*

This does not mean it is naive. Behavioral scientists recognize that people can be, and frequently are, self-defeating and destructive; they know that the human record is tarnished by many episodes of cruelty and stupidity. Yet behavioral science is essentially optimistic about man because he has the capacity to learn, develop, and grow. People can initiate significant improvement in their behavior; they are capable of change and progress.

Behavior is not unalterable; we are not forever condemned to act the way we act now. (Many people, admittedly, change very little after reaching maturity, but this is because of circumstances, not because they lack the capacity to change.) For the salesman or sales manager, this means there is no reason to despair of becoming more effective or more successful. Nothing in behavioral science indicates that human behavior is frozen, petrified, or beyond hope.

4. *Behavioral science views human behavior as dynamic.*

This is closely related to our last point. Human behavior is formed in interaction, in *activity* between people, so it is always dynamic, not static. In all interaction, something *happens*; even in a momentary meeting between two people, something occurs. Salesmen and sales managers are, of course, very much aware of this. Any salesman realizes, for example, that merely by introducing himself to a customer he causes some kind of response from the customer which in turn causes some kind of response from himself, and so on in a constant exchange. The reader is urged to keep this in mind throughout this book. While many of our descriptions will, unhappily, make selling and sales management sound static, the *reality* that these descriptions try to come to grips with is always *dynamic*.

In applying behavioral science to selling, then, we are applying principles that are relevant to what actually happens out in the field. In its emphasis on everyday behavior, human interaction, optimism, and dynamism, behavioral science is particularly suited to the realities of the salesman's world.

Applying behavioral science principles will not by itself, however, make a successful salesman or sales manager. To say that selling and sales management should be applied behavioral sciences is not to say that that is all they should be. In addition to applying behavioral science principles, the successful salesman must apply product knowledge, time management, and self-discipline. And the successful sales manager must apply a host of technical skills, ranging from budgeting to product training. Without technical skills, fiscal skills, and physical energy, a salesman or sales manager can make good use of behavioral science and still fail. An enormous number of skills that are *not* interpersonal must be mastered and applied by any salesman or sales manager who wants to succeed and grow. The brutal but inescapable fact is that a wizard at applying the behavioral sciences will still starve if he fails to get out of bed in the morning

We cannot stress this last point too strongly. Nothing in this book should be interpreted to mean that interpersonal skills *by themselves* will lead to success in sales or sales management. Interpersonal skills are vital, but they can never take the place of product knowledge, of hard work, of diligent prospecting, of skill at organizing, of good speaking skills, of intelligence, and all the many other skills that are essential to long range success in selling or managing. Interpersonal skills are an essential adjunct to these skills, not a substitute for them.

THE DIMENSIONAL SALES AND SALES MANAGEMENT MODEL OF BEHAVIOR

The behavioral scientist faces a situation no other scientist faces. Physical and biological scientists deal mainly with *uniformity* and *repeatability* (two hydrogen molecules combined with one oxygen molecule at temperatures between 0 and 100 degrees centigrade always produce water; the circulatory system of one normal frog functions like the circulatory system of all other normal frogs under similar conditions; and on and on). But the behavioral scientist deals with *diversity*. Even in similar situations, different people always behave at least somewhat differently, and many of them behave in widely different ways. Human behavior is not uniform and repeatable; it is widely varied. But although we cannot observe strict uniformity in human behavior, we can observe numerous similarities and resemblances, and, on the basis of these, we can build a science of human behavior. These similarities do not make for identical behavior, but they do make for roughly parallel behavior. Without these parallels, there would be no behavioral science.

The behavioral scientist does far more, however, than merely observe and record the similarities in human behavior; he tries to *arrange* his observations into a system that *explains* human behavior (or at least some part of it). This arrangement of observations into a systematic description is called model-building. (Physical and biological scientists also build models, but, because they deal with uniformities, their models are much more precise. An astronomer's model of the universe, for example, may be so exact that it can be expressed entirely in mathematics. The models prepared by behavioral scientists generally lack this kind of precision.) Without models, behavioral science would be like a jigsaw puzzle that nobody had ever bothered to put together; the individual pieces of the puzzle might be interesting or attractive in their own right, but they would not form a unified picture. Models are the behavioral scientist's way of uniting items of information into a coherent, meaningful description.

The Dimensional Sales and Sales Management model which is the basis of this book *organizes* selling behavior by focusing on certain similarities in the way salesmen behave. The model systematizes selling behavior without ignoring its enormous variety. By using the Dimensional model, or some comparable model, we can understand selling behavior much better than we could otherwise do, yet we do not distort reality by oversimplifying it. The Dimensional model, it should be pointed out, is not the only model which could be used to analyze sales and sales management behavior, but the authors feel it is an especially valuable one because it is both scientifically well-founded and easily used.

While the Dimensional model is the creation of the authors, it has its roots deep in the behavioral sciences, and would have been unthinkable without the work of numerous researchers in the field. It is impossible to acknowledge all the scientists whose work in interpersonal psychology, group dynamics, motivation theory, and psychotherapy laid the groundwork for our model, just as it is impossible to mention the many researchers in communications, learning theory, and systems analysis whose insights were so useful in other sections of the book. But surely the groundbreaking work of S. E. Asch, Robert F. Bales, Chester Barnard, Alex Bavelas, Warren Bennis, Robert Blake, John Dollard, Amitai Etzioni, Leon Festinger, Mason Haire, Frederick Herzberg, Karen Horney, Carl Hovland, Paul Lazarsfeld, Timothy Leary, Harold Leavitt, Rensis Likert, A. H. Maslow, David McClelland, Douglas McGregor, Jacob Moreno, Gardner Murphy, Henry Murray, William Schutz, and Muzafer Sherif has had a significant impact on our thinking at many points.

What follows, then, is an analysis of selling and sales management as applied behavioral sciences built upon foundations laid by other men. It is written in full awareness that the behavioral sciences are the youngest of all sciences, and that there is still much we do not fully understand about interaction between people. Nevertheless, there is a great deal we *do* understand, and that we can use. In the chapters that follow, we will describe much of what is now understood about selling behavior and later, sales management behavior, and we'll describe how this understanding can be used. The rest must be up to the reader.

SUMMARY

In this book, we define selling and sales management as applied behavioral sciences. Behavioral science is the study of human interaction; in applying behavioral science, we put it to work for practical purposes.

Some of the basic ideas of behavioral science that are especially important for selling and sales management are:

1. Behavioral science is primarily interested in everyday behavior.

2. It stresses the importance of human interaction.
3. It is optimistic about people.
4. It views human behavior as dynamic.

The basic principles of behavioral science are thus relevant to what salesmen and sales managers actually experience in their daily work.

The application of behavioral science principles will not, by itself, make a successful salesman or sales manager. Interpersonal skills are a vital adjunct, but not a substitute for, physical energy, product knowledge, business and fiscal skills.

Unlike the physical and biological scientists, the behavioral scientist does not deal with either uniformity or repeatability, but with diversity. Nevertheless, while strict uniformity is lacking in human behavior, numerous similarities do exist, and these form the basis of behavioral science. These similarities can be arranged into systems, or models, that help explain human behavior. The Dimensional Sales and Sales Management model which is the basis of this book, is one such system. The Dimensional model is the creation of the authors, whose debts to numerous researchers are profound; without the labors of these scientists, the Dimensional model would have been impossible.

The authors will describe the Dimensional model and, later in the book, the "how-to-do-it" techniques suggested by the model. It is up to the reader to put the model and the how-to-do-it techniques to use.

2

Dimensional Sales and Sales Management

PUTTING BEHAVIORAL SCIENCE TO WORK

In this chapter, we describe the Dimensional model of sales behavior and the behavioral science principles on which it is based. The reader is urged to remember that the function of the model is not to make human behavior seem simpler than it is, but to make human behavior more easily understandable.

It may help to think of the Dimensional model as a specialized vocabulary for describing human behavior. The purpose of any vocabulary, of course, is to help us think and talk about diversity. Just as we can use the word *book* to describe every kind of book, from comic books and paperbacks to leather-bound volumes to medieval tomes with parchment pages, we can use the phrase *dominant-hostile* to describe (as we shall soon see in detail) every salesman whose behavior is essentially domineering and power-oriented. And, just as we never make the mistake of thinking all books are identical just because they're all called books, we need never make the mistake of thinking all dominant-hostile salesmen are identical (in fact, no two are) just because they're all called dominant-hostile. Vocabulary is an invention that *arranges* variety so it can be

15

understood. The Dimensional model is nothing more than a specialized vocabulary that arranges the varieties of selling behavior so *they* can be understood.

BEHAVIOR DEFINED

In its broadest sense, behavior is *everything* a person does. As we use the word, however, it has a somewhat narrower meaning. We are primarily concerned not with *personal* behavior (how a salesman knots his necktie, how many newspapers he reads each week, or whether he prefers comedies to whodunits on TV) but with *interpersonal* behavior (how he thinks about and relates to other people). We are interested in the attitudes, assumptions, and conduct that determine how a salesman interacts with customers. Our concern is person-to-person behavior, the kind that leads customers to say "Harry's too pushy, he tries too hard for the order and never gives me a chance to say anything," or "Al's a strange guy, he always seems to be going through the motions without really caring whether he makes a sale or not," or "Wally's a wonderful fellow, always willing to spend time shooting the breeze and clowning around," or "Steve's a terrific salesman, a real businessman who always helps me out with new ideas; he always seems to have my best interests at heart."

Put another way, this book is not especially interested in superficial behavior (whether George orders milk or martinis when he's lunching with a customer, or whether Dave wears loud sport coats or conservative suits) even though this behavior may have some impact on interpersonal relations. Our major interest is in fundamental person-to-person behavior (whether Charlie is blatantly aggressive or painfully remote with his customers, or whether Bob controls his presentations or simply reacts to his prospect's lead). This behavior plays a *crucial* role in shaping interpersonal relations. It is *decisive* behavior.

BEHAVIOR IS GENERALLY CONSISTENT

Salesmen, like other people, are not robots that mechanically repeat the same behavior. Nevertheless, any salesman's behavior follows a generally consistent pattern over a period of time. Inconsistent or exceptional behavior is usually short-lived. Thus, once a salesman's basic behavior is understood, his behavior in a specific selling situation can usually be predicted with reasonable accuracy. This is true simply because people with certain traits usually behave in a certain way; if they didn't, life would be impossibly frustrating.

This doesn't mean a saleman's behavior can ever be predicted with precision. It means only that any salesman behaves in a fairly unsurprising way most of the time. When he doesn't, when he deviates from his typical behavior, the fact is usually noted by those who know him well. "Joe's not his usual self today," they'll say, implying that Joe *has* a "usual" way of behaving. This is what we mean by saying that human behavior follows a generally consistent pattern. To say this is not to deny that human behavior is sometimes unpredictable.

TWO PRINCIPLES OF HUMAN BEHAVIOR

This book is based on two principles of behavior that are familiar to every reader. Like most familiar facts of everyday experience, however, they are usually taken for granted and ignored. Our purpose is to get the reader to think about them, deeply and at length, because an understanding of these principles is basic to an understanding of the Dimensional model. The principles themselves have been validated by numerous behavioral scientists; we are merely building on their work by adapting the principles to salesmen.

1. *Every person tends to be either warm or hostile.*

We shall define *warmth* and *hostility* in a minute. First we want to emphasize the word *tends*; we are saying that each of us is inclined or prone to be either warm or hostile, *not* that each of us is invariably and always warm or hostile. Behavior cannot be described in absolute terms. Nevertheless, we can speak of individuals as either basically warm or hostile; in each person, one trait outweighs the other. Let us look at each trait in its pure form, keeping in mind that nobody consistently displays either trait in the ideal form that we describe.

Warmth. Warmth is *regard for others*. It involves awareness of the worth and dignity of other people, and sensitivity to their needs. It implies that the gratification of one's own needs is bound up with the gratification of other people's needs.

The warm person is characteristically interested in and responsive to others. He is frequently outgoing and good-humored, although warm persons are sometimes shy and retiring. He is optimistic and willing to place confidence in others. The warm person is certain that his self-interest is entwined with that of other people, so competition must always take place in a framework of mutually respected rules.

Hostility.   Hostility is *lack of regard for others,* the attitude that other people matter less than oneself, and therefore deserve less care. It implies indifference to others, insensitivity to their needs and ideas, resistance to collaboration, and, in some cases, outright animosity. Hostile people are often cold and manipulative.

Hostility is self-seeking behavior. It has its roots in egoism, the doctrine (frequently unconscious) that self-interest should be the final goal of one's actions. Hostile people often disdain others. Not surprisingly, they frequently provoke dislike in others, and then complain that they are surrounded by unfriendly people. The hostile man's view of the world is self-fulfilling; he stimulates hostility in others which in turn reinforces his own hostility, enabling him to say, "I told you so."

Once again, we emphasize that these are extreme descriptions of *warmth* and *hostility.* Many people manifest one or the other of these traits in diluted form, and virtually no one is hostile or warm *all* the time.

2.   *Every person tends to be either dominant or submissive.*

Both key terms are defined below. At the moment, we again want to stress the ideal quality of our descriptions; pure dominance or pure submissiveness, as we describe them, are seldom found in life. Nor is any person likely to be totally dominant or totally submissive all the time. All we are saying is that each of us tends to be *predominantly* one or the other.

Dominance.   Dominance is the *drive to take control* in face-to-face situations. It includes a cluster of traits: initiative, forcefulness, and independence. It implies leadership in personal encounters, control of situations, and a wish to be paramount.

Dominance is an *active* trait found in people who believe they can mold, control, and master situations. Whatever his real worth, the dominant person *thinks* he has something valuable to contribute to others, and he acts on that belief. He is invariably ambitious, with a strong desire for personal independence.

Submission.   Submission is the disposition to *let others take the lead* in personal encounters. It includes traits like dependence, unassertiveness, and passiveness. It implies willingness to be controlled, avoidance of personal confrontations, and compliance with other people's wishes.

In brief, submissive people would rather be led than lead. They feel tense or uneasy when called upon to take charge; they prefer the secure knowledge that someone else is responsible for things. Submissive people, often characterized by self-doubt, are sometimes slow to assert themselves in their own behalf.

Recapitulation

Let's recap the points made so far:

1. The behavior we talk about in this book is interpersonal behavior; it has to do with fundamental characteristics like warmth, hostility, dominance, and submission, which determine the ways in which people relate to one another.

2. Nearly every salesman's behavior follows a generally consistent pattern over a period of time; behavior is not random.

3. Warmth and hostility are opposite poles of one *dimension,* or measure, of behavior; while no two salesmen are identical, we can speak of any salesman as predominantly warm *or* hostile.

4. Dominance and submission are opposite poles of another dimension of behavior; once again, we can describe any salesman as basically dominant *or* submissive, although no two are ever identical.

A VISUAL DEPICTION OF THE BEHAVIORAL DIMENSIONS

The two dimensions or measures of behavior can be depicted visually. Such a depiction will help us to make some further important points.

> Hostility———————————————Warmth
>
> Dominance————————————————Submission

In thinking of these dimensions in visual terms, the reader should keep several points in mind:

1. *Each dimension is a continuum without specific ends.*

Human behavior cannot be thought of in terms of endings or *ultimates.* If we could speak of ultimate hostility as a clearly specified degree of hostility, as we can speak of the freezing point of water as a clearly specified degree of temperature, we could then represent that degree of behavior as an endpoint on the dimension. If we could identify ultimate warmth, as we can identify the boiling point of water, as a precise degree of behavior, we could plot that as the other endpoint on the dimension.

But behavior cannot be quantified in this way. So, in spite of the fact that the lines drawn above do have specified ends, the reader is urged to remember that the dimensions should be thought of as *open-ended* continuums.

> **2.** *The more extreme an individual's behavior, the farther from the middle of the line it should be graphed.*

Thus *exceedingly* submissive behavior would be depicted by a point quite distant from the middle of the dimension; *slightly* submissive behavior would be plotted by a point much closer to the center.

> **3.** *The reader should not be misled by the idea of plotting points on a dimension.*

Graphing behavior in this way is useful for analysis, but it does not mean behavior is so rigid that it can always be described by a single point. Actually, as behavior shifts in intensity, it can only be plotted by a *series* of points. Most of the time, these points are in the same general area, but, as we shall see later, not always. Even if we use a point to describe behavior at a given moment, the point is only a *general* indicator of behavior; it is not, and cannot be, a precise description. Behavior is far too complex to be reduced to a point on a line.

A Musical Analogy

The above remarks may strike the reader as so abstract that they are meaningless, so let's try to breathe life into them by an analogy from music. Suppose you were invited to a concert at which an unusual variety of music was played: The Eroica Symphony, Stardust, a rock-and-roll tune, a Buddhist liturgical chant, a concerto "written" by an electronic computer, and the Washington Post March. Imagine that at the end of the concert you were asked to rate the amount of pleasure you derived from each piece on a scale like this:

Pleasure————————————————————//————————————Displeasure

The mid-point of the scale would represent a neutral reaction, in which the listener had no discernible feelings about the music one way or the other. Now, for the sake of example, imagine that you rated the music this way:

Pleasure———/———/———/———/——//——/———/————Displeasure
       Eroica Rock Star- March Chant Electronic
             and   dust   Music
             Roll

Two points are immediately clear:

The rating scale is obviously an open-ended continuum. Since nobody can say he experienced "absolute" pleasure or "ultimate" displeasure from a piece of music (nobody knows what "absolute" or "ultimate" means in this context), it is clear that the endpoints of the rating scale are arbitrarily drawn. For all we know, the line should be infinitely extended in both directions.

Your reactions to the music would not have been nearly as precise as the points on the line indicate. The points merely depict a reaction that would probably go something like this: "I enjoyed the Eroica symphony most of all, a great deal in fact. And I strongly disliked the electronic music; it sounded weird and made me feel uncomfortable. I didn't care much for the Bhuddist chant, either; it bored me. I liked the rock-and-roll a lot, but not as much as the symphony. I enjoyed Stardust, although I wasn't really enthusiastic about it. As far as the march was concerned, I could pretty well take it or leave it."

Behavior can be plotted in the same way as musical preferences, without implying that the measures are precise. While not exact, the resulting graph is, in either case, both meaningful and useful.

THE DIMENSIONAL SALES BEHAVIOR MODEL

The Dimensional Sales Behavior model (Figure 1) is a visual presentation of the fact that both dimensions exist *simultaneously* in the behavior of every salesman. A salesman may, for example, be warm and dominant or hostile and submissive at the same time. There are four possible combinations of traits, as shown in Figure 1. (A similar model will be used later to describe sales managers' behavior.)

Since salesmen (and other people) occupy positions on both dimensions of the model, any salesman's behavior can be described by the way his traits coordinate on the dimensions. This means selling behavior can be described as one of four basic types. We emphasize once again that not all the salesmen who fit one of the types are identical—far from it. *Everyone* in each of the four categories is different; there are as many distinctions as there are salesmen. But, *in general,* every salesman belongs *basically* to one of the four groups.

Q1. The Dominant-Hostile Strategy
Customers seldom buy willingly; the salesman must impose his will on the customer by superior determination and strength. Selling is a struggle that the salesman must win.

Q4. The Dominant-Warm Strategy
Sales are made when customers become convinced they can satisfy a need by buying. The salesman's job is to demonstrate to the customer that his product will best satisfy the customer's need, thus benefiting the customer, the salesman's company, and himself.

HOSTILITY ———————————————————————————— WARMTH

Q2. The Submissive-Hostile Strategy
Customers buy only when they are ready to buy. Until that time, the salesman can do nothing to get them to buy. Since persuasion does not work, the salesman's only option is to take the order when the customer is ready to give it. There is no other way for a salesman to survive.

Q3. The Submissive-Warm Strategy
People buy from salesmen they like. Once a prospect becomes a friend, its only reasonable that he should also become a customer. The salesman's job is to make every prospect a friend.

SUBMISSION

FIGURE 1. The Dimensional Model of Sales Behavior.

Throughout this book, we refer to these categories interchangeably as *behaviors* or *strategies*. The four basic behaviors are:

Quadrant 1 (Q1)—Dominant-hostile
Quadrant 2 (Q2)—Submissive-hostile
Quadrant 3 (Q3)—Submissive-warm
Quadrant 4 (Q4)—Dominant-warm

Three Critical Points About the Dimensional Model

Three critical points should be kept in mind in considering the model:

1. Human beings cannot be neatly pigeonholed. Most of us, surely, know hard-driving, domineering salesmen who could accurately be described as dominant-hostile, but who occasionally display ingratiating flashes of warmth and conviviality, just as most of us know genial, pleasant submissive-warm salesmen who, to our puzzlement, sometimes lash out in a caustic, biting manner. The fact that selling behavior is generally patterned does not mean it is machine-like in its consistency.

2. Behavior frequently varies with role. A man who's dominant-hostile in the role of salesman may be submissive-warm in the role of father, displaying few or none of the coercive traits to his children that he shows to his customers, and he may be submissive-hostile in the role of husband, aloof and withdrawn from his wife in contrast to his overbearing behavior on the job. Such shifts are common. Selling behavior, it must be remembered, is not the *whole* of a man's behavior.

3. A behavioral strategy is not simply the sum of two behavioral traits added together. In fact, the concept of single character traits is artificial, useful for analysis but not realistic. Human qualities do not exist in isolation; there is no such thing as freestanding hostility or warmth. In life, behavioral traits are combined, and the combination is always more than the sum of its parts. A dominant-hostile salesman, for example, is not a mere aggregate of dominance and hostility. He is, as we shall see in the next chapter, something different, a person whose combined traits interact and modify one another. Behavioral strategies can be compared to plant grafts, in which the new plant, while displaying characteristics of both the plants from which it was blended, is really a new growth with traits found in neither parent.

The Interactional Nature of Behavior

We should pause here to make a point that we will make repeatedly in this book: the Dimensional model is *interactional*. It describes behavior in terms of interpersonal relationships, in terms of what happens *between* people. The idea of warmth or hostility has no meaning apart from interaction; it is useless to talk about a salesman being warm or hostile unless there is another person toward whom he is warm or hostile. The same is true of dominance and submission. Our key concepts are inconceivable in isolation from other people.

A Note on Typologies

In the next five chapters, we present *typologies:* extreme descriptions of *types* of selling behavior. Typologies, one of the most useful tools used by behavioral scientists, are never intended as descriptions of real people in the real world; they are too farfetched for that. They are intended as verbal *caricatures,* in which certain behavior that distinguishes groups of people is accentuated and exaggerated. By writing such overstated descriptions, we can more easily understand how the group is *distinctive,* how it differs from other groups with other behaviors. Everyone sharing the distinctive traits, even though not as extreme as in the caricature, can be placed somewhere in the group. This helps us to systematize our descriptions of human behavior. Without typologies, we would be unable to talk about *categories* of human behavior, and would be forced to talk only about separate, individual behaviors. For this reason, typologies are an unusually useful device for replacing confusion with order.

But a word of caution is required. The behaviors described in our typologies are rarely, perhaps never, seen in the real world. *Real* behavior is always more complex, varied, and intricate than that in typologies. The reader may know a salesman with many of the traits, in one degree or another, that we ascribe to the Q3 salesman. If so, that salesman's behavior can be described as Q3 behavior. But this does *not* mean that a perfect fit can be established between the real-life salesman and our caricature. In fact, perfect fits are exceedingly rare or nonexistent. The real-life Q3 salesman probably displays some elements of *other* kinds of behavior. He may display some of the traits in the typology in extreme form. He may manifest other traits in the typology in diminished form. And he may lack some of the traits in the typology completely.

It is important, then, to remember that the next five chapters draw deliberately extreme portraits that are probably never exactly duplicated in the real world. These caricatures increase our understanding by reducing a huge mass of characteristics to manageable terms. But they are still *only* caricatures. (In like manner, political cartoons are useful for making simple, clear-cut points about exceedingly complicated political issues. But no one, not even the cartoonist, pretends that they are genuine descriptions of the real political world.) In later chapters, we will try to show how *real* selling behavior is more complex, more diverse, and more fascinating than the caricatures.

A Note on Dimensions

The Dimensional model uses two dimensions of behavior that research has shown to be critical in sales and managerial behavior. But these are by no means the only dimensions that are important in selling and sales management. Dimensions measuring the need for achievement, or intelligence, or verbal skills, could, among others, be included in a model. We have focused on two highly significant dimensions, but the reader should keep in mind that other dimensions do exist.

SUMMARY

The Dimensional model is comparable to a specialized vocabulary for describing human behavior. Like a vocabulary, it helps us to arrange variety so that we can more easily understand it.

This book is concerned with interpersonal behavior, the kind that plays a decisive role in shaping relationships between salesmen and customers. Such behavior can be arranged in the form of a model because it follows a generally consistent pattern over a period of time. This in no way denies that interpersonal behavior is sometimes unpredictable.

The two principles of human behavior on which this book is based are: (*1*) every person tends to be either warm or hostile, and (*2*) every person tends to be either dominant or submissive. Warmth is regard for others, and the realization that the gratification of one's needs is bound up with the gratification of other people's. Hostility is self-seeking behavior, and the belief that self-interest should be the final goal of one's actions. Dominance is the drive to take control in face-to-face situations. Submission is the disposition to let others take the lead.

Hostility and warmth can be depicted as two poles of a dimension, or measure, of behavior. Dominance and submission can be pictured as two poles of still another dimension. These dimensions are continuums without specified endpoints; they do not imply that we can talk about ultimates in human behavior. In plotting any person's behavior on one of the dimensions, the more extreme the behavior, the farther from the middle it should be graphed. Such graphing is useful for analysis, but it does not mean that behavior is so rigid that it can always be described by a single point.

The Dimensional Sales Behavior model is a visual presentation of the fact that both dimensions exist simultaneously in the behavior of every salesman. No two salesmen in any one quadrant of the model are identical, but, in general, every salesman's behavior places him basically in one of the quadrants. The quadrants are: Q1 (dominant-hostile), Q2 (submissive-hostile), Q3 (submissive-warm), and Q4 (dominant-warm).

Three key points should be kept in mind when considering the model: human beings cannot be neatly pigeonholed, behavior is not machine-like; behavior often varies with role; and a behavioral strategy is always something more, and different from, the sum of the behavioral traits that comprise it; behavioral traits, in life, modify one another.

The Dimensional model is interactional; it describes behavior in terms of what happens between people.

In the next five chapters, we present typologies of each of the four basic selling strategies; these will be verbal caricatures that are rarely or never duplicated exactly in the real world. The two dimensions that comprise the Dimensional model are critical to sales and sales management behavior, but they should not be thought of as the only important dimensions.

3

The Basic Selling
Beliefs

HOW SALESMEN LOOK AT THEIR JOBS

Before we look at typologies of the four basic selling strategies, we should understand the basic beliefs that underlie and support each strategy. Behavior, after all, doesn't "just happen." It reflects certain beliefs, attitudes, assumptions, and viewpoints. There are *reasons* why people believe as they do. A salesman who is consistently overbearing and domineering with his customers reflects, in his behavior, certain beliefs about his customers as people; the same can be said about the salesman who is usually friendly and easygoing. Behavior is based on assumptions or viewpoints; it is governed by beliefs about *the way things are*. If we understand these beliefs, we will find it much easier to understand the various selling strategies. In this chapter, we want to come to grips with the fundamental assumptions each type of salesman makes about people and about selling.

These assumptions are not always voiced; many salesmen never bother to phrase them clearly and coherently. In many cases, the beliefs can only be deduced from the salesman's behavior, which, unlike his beliefs, is clearly observable. But, put into words or not, these beliefs undergird what the salesman does on the job. Unless they are understood, his behavior itself is not wholly comprehensible. For this reason, we'll examine these basic assumptions carefully.

THE SOURCE OF SELLING ATTITUDES AND BELIEFS

A salesman's beliefs about people and his assumptions about how to make sales to them, are learned as he goes through life. He learns them primarily in interactions with other people, beginning at a very early age. Childhood experiences with parents, teachers, other youngsters, neighbors, and relatives give a person insights (which may or may not be valid) into how to interact with people. Not all these experiences are equally important, of course; those people who are closest to a child and spend the most time with him usually do most to mold his interpersonal beliefs. As he grows and meets different people in new situations, he may modify or even change these beliefs. By adulthood, he has had countless experiences in which he has learned certain attitudes about people and about human interaction. (Beliefs are not formed entirely by direct interaction with others; indirect or imagined interaction—with a public hero, a storybook figure, an athletic idol, and so forth—also plays a part in shaping attitudes and beliefs.)

Not surprisingly, by the time the individual becomes a salesman, his beliefs and assumptions are deeply ingrained. They are part of the person himself. They condition and influence his selling behavior. He seldom thinks or talks about his assumptions because they seem so natural that he feels no need to do so. Even more significant, he seldom feels any reason to question them. They become basic truths, like the belief the sun will rise tomorrow. The typical Q3 salesman, for instance, who believes people buy from salesmen they like, believes this almost as firmly as he believes the world is round. A series of contradictory experiences, in which a number of customers repaid his friendliness by buying from someone else, might shake his Q3 belief, just as a series of reports of ships falling off the edge of the earth and hurtling into space might shake his belief in a globe-shaped world. But, on the other hand, he might rationalize both experiences and stick with his original beliefs. Basic assumptions and attitudes are hard (but not impossible) to change.

In the rest of this chapter, we'll describe each basic selling belief in some detail. In each instance, we'll first talk about the salesman's assumptions about people, then his assumptions about how to sell to people.

The Basic Q1 Beliefs

About People. The dominant-hostile salesman sees other people as essentially self-serving, seeking their own advantage without much concern for others. He sometimes describes this attitude by such cliches as: "It's a dog-eat-dog world" or "It's every man for himself." He's fond of phrases like: "In business, the law of the jungle prevails," or "It's a hard world, and only the fittest survive." He sees the interpersonal world in the same way that the early supporters of the theory of evolution saw the animal world: filled with incessant strife in which the strong win and the weak lose.

The Q1 salesman considers himself a stern realist who sees things as they really are, without sentimentality or wishful thinking. "Everyone's out for himself," he says, "so a guy has to fight for everything he gets in this world." Then he quickly adds, "Don't get me wrong, I'm not saying that's the way things *should* be. I'm just saying that's the way things *are.*"

Sometimes, though, the Q1 salesman tries to justify the way things are. "Why shouldn't everyone look out for himself?" he asks. "Nobody gets anything in this world unless he grabs it for himself. If a man doesn't grab, he deserves to get nothing. Everyone ought to stand on his own two feet, instead of acting like some kind of parasite." Thus the Q1 salesman often advocates a doctrine of rugged individualism in which self-interest is a virtue.

The Q1 salesman, in a phrase, sees the business world as a huge arena in which each man is pitted against every other man in a relentless win–lose struggle for success, money, prestige, promotions, and so forth. He never forgets that the other people in the arena are antagonists who must be overcome, before they overcome him.

About Selling. The dominant-hostile salesman believes that customers are resistant and often unwilling to buy. In the salesman-customer encounter, this means that the customer can seldom be expected to buy willingly. To do so would require more trust and more confidence than any intelligent person willingly places in another. So customers must be *made* to buy. The sale must be *imposed* upon them by a salesman with superior determination and superior strength. Selling, in effect, is simply a specialized form of the survival of the fittest.

The Q1 salesman, then, assumes that customers who know what is good for them are likely to resist him or any other salesman. They know, as he knows, that the sales presentation is a struggle which only one man can win. Selling is arduous work in which both salesman and customer strive for dominance. The secret of success in selling is to come out on top of the strife.

Even those customers who have no stomach for the battle are regarded as adversaries by the Q1 salesman. He assumes that very few customers *want* to buy, not even the pleasant and friendly ones who show no signs of belligerence. Most customers, no matter what their outward behavior, resist salesmen. So customers in general must be regarded as foes, and all sales presentations as a form of combat.

The Basic Q2 Beliefs

About People. The submissive-hostile salesman, like his dominant-hostile counterpart, sees other people as essentially self-serving, seeking their own advantage without much concern for others. But, starting from this premise, the Q2 salesman arrives at much bleaker conclusions than the Q1. The difference between their conclusions is as broad as the difference between dominance and submissiveness.

Although the Q1 has a dim view of other people, he interacts with them with gusto. He enjoys competition; he relishes the chance to pit himself against an adversary and win. Not so the Q2. He has none of the Q1 salesman's self-confidence, nor his zest for combat. The Q1 sees people as land-mines which must be cleared out of the way so that he can proceed to his destination. The Q2 sees people as land-mines which must be avoided, lest he be blown to bits. To the Q2, people are menacing. There is no exhilaration in his attitude, only apprehension.

The great psychologist and philosopher William James once said that man is the "most formidable of all the beasts of prey . . . the only one that preys systematically on its own species." Both the Q1 and the Q2 salesman would agree. But the Q1 insists that he is formidable enough to *overcome* his fellow predators, while the Q2 fears he will *become* their prey. And prey always ends up getting devoured. No wonder the Q2 salesman's basic beliefs about people are so bleak.

About Selling. The Q2 salesman believes close interaction with people is risky, so the intelligent man maintains a certain measure of interpersonal distance from others, and refuses to become more involved with them than he must. This means there is a certain passivity and aloofness about his approach to selling. The Q2 *chooses* to be somewhat remote in sales presentations.

He realizes, of course, that salesmen are *supposed* to be dynamic and involved during presentations, not remote and aloof. So he justifies his behavior by insisting that it is sensible in view of the way *customers* behave. Customers, according to this rationalization, buy only when they're ready to buy; when they have a need or desire that can only be satisfied by a purchase. Until that time, the salesman can do nothing to get them to buy. Customers cannot be persuaded, or induced, or prevailed upon to buy. They know their needs and will buy when ready, not before.

This negative, almost defeatist, attitude is obviously very useful to the Q2 salesman. It enables him to make sales calls in which he passively *waits* for the order instead of actively *developing* it, without feeling that he is falling down on the job. Given his basic beliefs about selling, his behavior is logical, reasonable, and sensible.

The Basic Q3 Beliefs

About People.   To the submissive-warm salesman, William James' melancholy description of man is not worth taking seriously. The Q3 salesman sees people not as hungry beasts of prey, but as cooperative social beings. He is convinced that the Jamesian view (which is also the Q1 and the Q2 view) is a cynical misreading of the facts. People, he insists, are basically helpful, not exploitative; outgoing, not threatening. The Q3 is cheerful and optimistic about others.

While his critics charge him with being naive or foolish about people, the submissive-warm salesman insists that *he* is the realist who sees things as they are. He readily admits that people are sometimes belligerent or downright mean, but he insists that these are reactions to provocative behavior. "Treat people warmly," he argues, "and they'll treat you warmly. Life is a two-way street. You only get out of it what you put into it." He likes to cite the Golden Rule. "Look," he says, "the secret of success in life is to act toward people exactly the way you want them to act toward you. People want to be friendly and responsive, but sometimes they're afraid they'll be rebuffed. So I always take the first step myself. If I start out by being friendly to them, they're always friendly to me."

Of course, even the Q3 salesman has to admit that this is something of an exaggeration, that people don't *always* respond to friendliness by being friendly. When they don't, he rationalizes their behavior: "He's probably under terrific pressure today," or, "Maybe he's not feeling well," or, "I probably caught him at a bad time." But he sticks doggedly to his belief that people are inherently warm, good-natured, and obliging.

About Selling.   The Q3's basic belief about selling is that people buy from salesmen they like. Buying is simply one way in which people display their natural tendency to be friendly and helpful. Once a prospect becomes a friend (and the Q3 salesman believes every prospect can be made into a friend), it is only reasonable that he should manifest his friendliness by becoming a customer. What better way for him to prove his friendship?

At first, this attitude may strike the reader as manipulative. But the Q3 salesman does not make friends of his prospects and customers so that he can make sales to them. He makes friends of them because this seems to him the right way to behave, and because he has a deep need for acceptance. If sales follow, so much the better. But the Q3's friendliness is not a trick for finagling a sale out of the customer; it is an honest expression of his interpersonal outlook.

The Q3, in brief, believes that love does conquer all. He is hardheaded enough to know that there may be pitfalls and snares on the way to the conquest, but, in the end, warmth and affection are sure to prevail. Nothing could be further from the bleak, gloomy attitude of the Q1 and Q2.

The Basic Q4 Beliefs

About People.   The dominant-warm salesman has a more complex attitude about people than the other salesmen we've considered. He sees them as self-concerned but not necessarily selfish; cooperative, but not often self-sacrificing; seeking their own advantage, but not usually at someone else's expense. He considers them neither beasts of prey nor angels of love, but, for the most part, as human beings trying their best to get along in a difficult world, helping themselves without hurting others. Beyond this, the Q4 salesman refuses to generalize. Realizing that people are a mixed lot whose behavior ranges from the saintly to the devilish, with most of them somewhere in-between, he prefers to take them on a one-by-one basis. Instead of approaching them in an overcontrolling way (like the Q1) or guardedly (like the Q2) or gladhandedly (like the Q3), he approaches them openly. He assumes they are both self-interested and well-meaning, and sticks with this assumption unless experience proves him wrong.

Another significant difference is that the Q4 is the only salesman who doesn't view people mechanically. To the Q1, Q2, and Q3, people can be compared to automobiles coming off an assembly line. Superficially, each may vary from the others. One may be a two-door hardtop, another a convertible, and still another a sports car. But *basically* they are all the *same*; each has the same general function, each is powered by an internal combustion engine, and each can be driven by the same methods. Not only is each car essentially the same, each car is also *fiinished*. True, minor modifications might be made later on some of them. One may get white-wall tires to replace its black ones, another may get a different color of paint, and still another may have a stereo radio added. But as far as fundamental features are concerned, each automobile coming off the line is *completed*; it is what it will always be.

This is pretty much the way the Q1, Q2, and Q3 look at people: as basically the same and basically finished. The Q1 would concede that people differ in shallow, unimportant ways, but he would insist that, on matters that really count, they are all essentially the same: grasping, self-centered, opportunistic. The degree of self-centeredness and opportunism may differ from person to person (just as horsepower may vary from car to car) but it is always there, in everybody. And it is there to stay. People don't change, except in unimportant ways. On matters that really count, they stay what they are: grasping, self-centered and opportunistic. That's just the way things are, says the Q1, and the smart man recognizes the fact. The Q2 and the Q3 agree that people are fundamentally alike and fundamentally unchangeable.

Not the Q4. His view of people is not *mechanistic*, but *humanistic* (even though he may never use the word). Humanism insists that people *do* differ from one another in significant ways, so that most generalizations about them are apt to be wrong. There is one generalization, however, on which all humanists agree: people have the potential to *change* and to *grow*. To the humanist, the assembly-line analogy is wrong. People are not machine-like copies of one another, but singular, unique individuals. As long as they live, they are never finished, completed, or closed off. They are always capable of change.

So Q4 is slow to generalize about people, but convinced of the truth of one generalization: people can grow, learn, develop, improve. Unlike the legendary King Sisyphus, who had to spend eternity rolling a boulder up a steep hill only to have it roll to the bottom each time, none of us is condemned to persist in one mode of behavior. King Sisyphus's punishment took place in Hades; to the Q4, a world in which behavioral change was impossible would be a living hell.

About Selling.   The Q4 salesman believes that sales are made when customers become convinced they can satisfy one (or more) of their needs by making a purchase. Thus, when a salesman conclusively demonstrates to a customer that his product or service will best satisfy the customers' need, he does something simultaneously for the customer's self-interest, for his own self-interest, and for his company's self-interest.

This assumption is a direct outgrowth of the Q4 salesman's humanistic beliefs about people. He takes it for granted that because people differ, their needs are likely to differ, so that successful salesmanship depends, in part, on the ability to identify needs. He believes that, because people are capable of change, they can be taught and persuaded, so that successful salesmanship depends, in part, on the ability to teach and persuade. Because people are not all alike, the Q4 refuses to use rigid, unchanging selling behavior. And, because people are not closed to new ideas, he does not believe they must be bludgeoned (verbally) into buying.

CONCLUSIONS

Our descriptions are, of course, considerably oversimplified. Probably few Q1 salesmen are as predatory as the one we've described, few Q2s as apprehensive, few Q3s as friendly, and few Q4s as flexible. Real behavior is always mixed, like the threads on a piece of plaid cloth. Nevertheless, some of the threads are so much more striking than the others and so frequently repeated that they create a discernible pattern. We can draw the following conclusions about the pattern we have discerned in this chapter.

1. Q4 beliefs are the least restrictive. Because the Q1, Q2, and Q3 assume that most customers are pretty much alike, their range of responses is more limited. This is logical, of course. If every customer has essentially the same aspirations, attitudes, and outlook, then every customer should respond favorably to the same sales strategy, provided the strategy exploits his aspirations, attitudes, and outlook. The Q4 does not quarrel with this logic; he quarrels with the premise on which it's based, insisting that customers are not essentially the same, and do not respond to one and only one strategy.

2. Selling attitudes and beliefs are often remarkably unchanged by experience. A Q1 salesman may believe that nearly all customers are resistant even though he meets quite a few customers who are clearly not. A Q3 salesman is likely to be perturbed by a persistently cold, antagonistic customer, but he will probably continue to reassure himself that the customer is a pleasant fellow who is "under terrific pressure." Attitudes do change, but they do not change easily or quickly. Basic selling beliefs are deeply ingrained, and they are sometimes completely unaffected by contrary experience.

3. Only the Q4 responds to experience without undue reliance on preconceived beliefs. Or, to be more accurate, he is considerably more

open to experience than the Q1, Q2, and Q3. His conviction that people should be evaluated on a one-by-one basis makes it easier for him to be open to experience, to form judgments on the basis of what actually happens between him and the customer, rather than what he expects to happen. He is more influenced by direct observation and facts than are other salesmen.

In the next four chapters, we draw much fuller pictures of the basic selling behaviors, and of the assumptions and beliefs that underlie them. Once again, we urge the reader to remember that these chapters are typologies, useful caricatures not intended as portraits of people in the real world. They are merely devices to help the reader organize and comprehend his *own* experience in the real world of selling and sales management.

4

The Quadrant 1 (Dominant-Hostile) Salesman

"MAKE 'EM BUY"

Let us imagine a salesman named Bob Hawthorne: 38 years old, married, the father of two children, and a salesman for the past 16 years. For the past year and a half, Bob has worked for a manufacturer of automobile parts, calling on service stations and parts suppliers. He has a broad line, but hoses, filters, and fan-belts account for most of his sales. Bob is a consistently high producer; his sales manager is generally pleased with his performance, and frequently says, "I only hope Hawthorne doesn't decide to pick up and leave one of these days." The boss has some doubts on this score, however, because Bob has never worked for one company longer than three years. His record shows eight different employers in sixteen years, and there is evidence that he was quite successful in each of the eight jobs.

Now, imagine that we have just interviewed three people who know Bob well: his district sales manager, one of his customers, and a fellow-salesman who works out of the same district office, and that in our interviews, we asked each man the same questions: "What's your reaction to Bob Hawthorne? How do you see him? How does he come across to you?" Here are the answers we got:

Customer (the owner of a large automobile parts store). "Bob Hawthorne? There's only one word that really describes the guy: hard-nosed. He's an aggressive, two-fisted salesman who doesn't know how to take 'no' for an answer. I admire him for that. I built this business with the same sort of qualities, so I respect a man who knows what he wants, and then goes out and gets it . . . . At times, I must admit, Bob's a little bit overwhelming. He comes on real strong, like a boxer going for a first-round knockout. Of course, that doesn't bother me. I'm as tough as he is, and I kind of enjoy sparring with him. But pity the poor guy who isn't strong enough to stand up to Bob. Why, Bob would flatten him out like a steam roller. Yes sir, he's one tough salesman."

District Sales Manager. "Bob's a spirited, assertive salesman who always hangs in there until he gets the order. I only hope I can hold on to him. He's sort of footloose . . . always going from one job to another. I guess he's one of those people who figure the grass is always greener on the other side. I don't think he'd have a minute's trouble finding another job. He's got everything a sales manager would want: he works hard, prospects like crazy, and never lets up on the pressure. 'Unrelenting' is the word that describes him, I guess. Of course, he's not perfect . . . not by a long shot. He's terrible on paperwork . . . argumentative . . . and he has no respect for systems. But when he's in front of a customer, watch out! The man's a human bulldozer."

Fellow Salesman. "I've got very mixed feelings about Hawthorne. On the one hand, I've got to admit that he knows how to sell. His record proves it. But he's a hard guy to get along with. It seems that he's always accusing somebody in the office of raiding his territory and trying to steal his accounts . . . he's constantly screaming that there's a mistake on his commission statement . . . and he refuses to abide by company rules if he thinks he can get away with it. He seems to think company policies apply to everyone but him. This may sound like sour grapes, but I really believe that if I ignored my paperwork the way Hawthorne does . . . and if I worried less about doing things the way the company prescribes, I'd have more time to make sales . . . just like Hawthorne. But mind you, now . . . I'm not belittling the man. As I said at the beginning, he *can* sell."

Bob Hawthorne, as the reader no doubt guessed a few paragraphs ago, is an example of a dominant-hostile (Quadrant 1) salesman. In this chapter, we'll look at dominant-hostile behavior in some detail, to better understand Bob Hawthorne and his many real-life counterparts. Our typology will probably impress the reader as extreme, lacking nuances and subtleties. Nevertheless, such a portrait will be useful at this point; fine distinctions can and will be added later.

A GENERAL DESCRIPTION OF THE Q1 SALESMAN

The Q1 salesman is a man with strong needs for self-esteem and independence, needs he can readily satisfy on the job. To the Q1, a sale is far more than a business transaction; it is proof that he is able to control and dominate the buyer, to bend the customer's will until it coincides with his own ("One of us *has* to give . . . him or me. And it's not going to be me"). Because the sale demonstrates his power and ascendancy over the customer, it gratifies his self-esteem. Making a sale bolsters the Q1's image of himself as a strong, dominant person who controls his own destiny by controlling his customers. Selling thus satisfies both his need for self-esteem and his need for independence.

Because each sale is so important to him, the Q1 pushes very hard to make each one. And because he considers failure to make a sale a sign of personal inadequacy, he is especially determined not to let his customers say "no." He is aggressive, hard-hitting, and stubborn; making the sale counts more than the means used to make it.

The Q1 Salesman's Relationship to Himself

WHAT HE IS

Let's look now at some of the Q1 salesman's personal qualities (we'll do this in our other typologies as well), so as to get a full picture of what he is and what makes him that way.

On the surface, the Q1 is confident he can control situations; he's assertive, self-assured, perhaps even cocky. He likes to compete, to be in the middle of things, and to voice his views; he is frequently described as "coming on strong." Energetic and dynamic, he places a high value on getting things done. Like a skilled hunter who senses game even when it's well hidden, he is alert to opportunities others might miss, and he seizes them eagerly. Seldom satisfied to follow someone else's lead, he quickly assumes roles which involve directing other people ("There are two kinds of people in the world: leaders and followers. There aren't too many leaders, but, to be perfectly frank, I think *I'm* one"). His admirers describe him as a doer or go-getter; others call him pushy.

Modesty is seldom a Q1 virtue. He has strong opinions on most matters and can be extremely stubborn. He likes to be the center of attention, and sometimes "hams things up" to attract notice. He prides himself on being decisive, and is impatient with people who seem unsure of themselves.

The Q1 salesman is exploitative, sometimes openly, sometimes subtly, and will manipulate others to achieve his ends if he thinks he must. Deeply aware that "time is money," he often works long hours, and seldom wastes time. He has little use for the idea that "it pays to relax once in a while," and is often scornful of people who like to sit back, stare at the ceiling, and think. He believes time should be spent in clearly productive ways ("Time is money").

These characteristics tell only part of the story, however. Beneath his concern with time and efficiency is a strong desire not to look weak; the Q1 tries hard not to seem indecisive, incompetent, or lacking forcefulness. He fears failure, and sometimes feels less confident than he appears. His striving, his ambition, his steady hard work, all bolster a sometimes shaky image of himself. He has a need to prove himself—to himself as well as to others.

Not surprisingly, the Q1 usually considers close cooperation a sign of weakness. He thinks of himself as a rugged individualist, and prefers to work alone to demonstrate that "I've got what it takes." He dislikes taking instructions from or reporting to his superiors. Only by being unfettered, he believes, can he prove that he really does have what it takes. ("Any salesman who needs close supervision shouldn't be in selling. This is a sink-or-swim profession. There's no room in it for weaklings who can't swim.")

It may help to think of the Q1 as a man walking along the edge of a steep cliff which drops precipitously to a deep abyss. As long as he keeps walking steadily, he knows he is unlikely to fall. But he dare not relax or look around to enjoy the scenery, and he dare not lend a helping hand to others walking along the edge; if he does, he may hurtle into the abyss. For the same reason, he is afraid to link hands with others; he feels safe only as long as he walks alone. Of course, it might be safer for him to get down on his hands and knees and crawl along the edge, but he fears this would make him look weak and cowardly. So he continues to stride ahead, forcefully and alone. This is the Q1 salesman; he spends his days on the edge of the cliff, fully aware that the abyss of failure awaits him if he slips.

WHAT HE THINKS HE IS

Most of us see ourselves somewhat differently than other people see us, as Robert Burns complained in his famous lines: "O wad some power the giftie gie us, to see ourselves as others see us." This is especially typical of the Q1.

He is largely unaware that he seems overbearing and manipulative to others. He sees himself as a strong man surrounded by weak, indecisive people, but certainly not as an exploitative man.

When, on occasion, he hears about his true impact, he becomes defensive. He is a master rationalizer who persuades himself that he is not the kind of person other people think ("I am *not* domineering. I'm only looking out for myself, just like everybody else. I don't really have any choice; that's the kind of world it is"). He remains self-satisfied, and sees no good reason to change. After all, why should a "winner" change?

WHAT HE WOULD LIKE TO BE

The Q1 salesman wants to be on top because that is where he can best enhance his self-esteem and lay to rest any nagging doubts about himself. For him, being on top means controlling others; it means power. He wants admiration and believes he can gain it by mastery over others. Power implies obedience, and, he hopes, obedience implies respect. If others hold him in esteem, he is sure he can hold himself in esteem.

The Q1 Salesman's Relationship to Others

PEOPLE IN GENERAL

Preoccupied with enhancing his own position, the Q1 spends relatively little time thinking about others. Much of the time, his own welfare and advancement are at the center of his thoughts. Not surprisingly, he is frequently insensitive to others' needs and feelings. He is sometimes abrupt and brusque, unaware of, or unconcerned about, his impact. His relationships often seem brittle; many people are unable to feel completely relaxed in his presence. His insensitivity sometimes hurts people, but it would be wrong to imply that he deliberately inflicts these hurts. Most of the time, they are caused by his thoughtlessness and rashness. ("Look, I don't have time to weigh every word before I utter it. Sure, I may be a little bit outspoken at times, but what else can I be? I'm too busy making a living to worry about these things.")

Because he is so eager to dominate and control others, the Q1 salesman often clashes with other forceful people. He gets along best with docile people who let him have his way. Basically, he interacts with others in two ways: with forceful people, he is shrewd and manipulative; with submissive people, he is assertive and overbearing. With nearly everyone, he provokes either resentment or discomfort. Many of his relationships have a "cold war" quality marked by tension and muted antagonism.

None of this means that the Q1 is a friendless man. As we said much earlier, behavior often varies with roles. A Q1 salesman who manifests many of the traits we've described *on the job* may be a much warmer person when playing poker with friends, when chatting with his youngsters, or at a party. The bold strokes in which our typology is drawn should not obscure this fact.

The reader ought not to think of the Q1 as a monster who, like the ogres of folklore, devours people. He is a thoroughly understandable human being, impelled, like all of us, by needs. His most compelling needs, those with the greatest impact on his behavior, are needs for *esteem* and *independence*. By appearing strong, decisive, self-reliant, and unshackled, he maintains a satisfactory image of himself, and sets to rest any fears about his competence or worth. He believes a man is measured largely by his independence of others, so collaboration is weakness and autonomy is strength. He tries to do nothing that will make him appear indecisive or hesitant. As he sees it, a man must be headstrong and tough in an essentially hostile world. Viewed in this way, his behavior is not at all monstrous. For emphasis, our portrait of the Q1 is drawn in sweeping, somewhat harsh strokes, but, with empathy, the reader should be able to see him as an understandable human being.

HIS RELATIONSHIP TO HIS FAMILY

We have emphasized that behavior may vary from role to role, so that a dominant-hostile salesman is not necessarily a dominant-hostile husband or father. To draw a consistent picture, however, we describe in this and the following sections a Q1 salesman who is dominant-hostile in *all* his roles: as a family man, citizen, and jobholder. The reader is cautioned *not* to assume such consistency is always the case; sometimes it is, sometimes not. When all our typologies are completed, the reader will be able to put together his own portrait of salesmen whose behavior differs from role to role.

When a Q1 salesman is also a dominant-hostile husband and father, we find strong resemblances between his selling relationships and his family relationships. He is likely to place his own needs and interests above those of his family, behaving as if his wife and children exist primarily to satisfy him. Not deeply involved in family activities, he derives few deep-rooted pleasures from them. He expects strict compliance and respect from his family, insisting that they behave according to his rules ("Somebody has to be boss around here. What kind of a family would it be if everyone did whatever he pleased?"). There is little give-and-take between him and the rest of the family.

He almost literally believes a man's home is his palace, and expects his wife to share this belief and treat him like a king. If his wife rebels, friction and outright conflict will probably result. When this happens, the Q1 may withdraw, abdicate many of his family responsibilities, and expend more time and energy on his job.

Once again, we emphasize that a Q1 salesman who is dominant-hostile at home as well as the office is seldom a heartless tyrant, although he may be inconsiderate, demanding, insensitive, or self-centered. Our portrait is, again, a caricature rarely seen in real life. Actually, the dominant-hostile husband is often willful, domineering, and overbearing, demanding excessive attention and respect, but rarely an unrelenting autocrat.

HIS RELATIONSHIP TO THE COMMUNITY

The Q1 salesman who is also a dominant-hostile citizen (and not all are: once again, behavior is not always consistent across roles) usually displays the same power-drive in the community as on the job.

A Q1 who has attained some success may begin to expand his horizon, to look for areas where he can enlarge his self-esteem by enlarging his influence and control. So he begins to participate in community affairs with all the single-mindedness and drive that he brings to his job.

In general, the Q1 who participates in community affairs is likely to seek out roles in which he can gain public notice, applause, and praise. He doesn't object to wielding power behind the scenes, but he enjoys being widely-known. To the man in search of esteem, public acclaim is an invaluable reinforcer. ("I'm not a glory-seeker, but I admit that I like attention. Doesn't everyone?") Some Q1 salesmen, however, are not involved in public affairs at all, and don't want to be. Some believe they stand to gain personally from civic involvement, while others consider it a waste of time with little or no personal payoff. Some of the more cynical contend that leadership in community projects bestows the appearance of power, not the substance. In either instance, he seldom acts for disinterested reasons.

The Q1 Salesman's Relationship to His Company

HIS RELATIONSHIP WITH OTHER PEOPLE IN HIS COMPANY

Although he knows better, the Q1 sometimes behaves as if his company exists for only one reason: to help him achieve his personal goals, like a tool to be used and, if necessary, discarded. He usually feels little loyalty; phrases like "company spirit" or "team effort" mean little to him. (There are exceptions to this statement. Some Q1 salesmen are loyal employees with years of experience in a single company.)

The Q1 salesman's basic attitude to his superiors is hostile; he considers them obstacles who must be hurdled. His superiors have the power to make him feel weak, and to judge him a failure. They constrain him and threaten his cherished independence. Since he knows, however, that he cannot openly oppose his bosses, the Q1 usually chooses to manipulate or circumvent them. He wants their approval, without which he cannot hope to succeed, but he wants no interference from them in his affairs. He wants to please his boss without coming under his thumb. In fact, one reason the Q1 selects sales as his life's work is that in sales he is largely free of direct pressures from superiors ("I'd probably go out of my mind if I had a boss looking over my shoulder all the time").

While astute enough to disguise the way he feels about his superiors, the Q1 sees no need to do so with his peers. At worst, he sees his relationship with his fellow salesmen as "dog eat dog"; at best he lives with them in an uneasy truce. He thinks of them as competitors for preferential treatment by superiors, competitors for preferential delivery of orders, and competitors for available business. If the Q1 thinks a fellow salesman has hurt him in some way, he may become openly abusive. No wonder many of his peers feel vaguely uncomfortable in his presence.

The Q1's relationships to the nonselling departments in his company are shrewd. Accountants, production people, and administrators are considered necessary evils ("Sure, I admit we need these people. But let's be honest about it: the *salesman* is the real heart and soul of this business. He's the guy who *really* makes things go"). Generally, his relationships with nonselling people fluctuate from intense praise (to win favorable treatment) to intense criticism (to deflect blame from himself when things go wrong). When he has problems in the field, he may become especially critical of his nonselling associates. ("If those guys would deliver on time, I wouldn't be losing all these customers.") Actually, he is often vaguely aware that he is the cause of many of his own problems, but he dare not admit this, so he often displaces his anger onto the nonselling staff. These people, innocent of the accusations, are used as scapegoats.

HIS ATTITUDE TOWARD REGULATIONS

His strong need for independence makes the Q1 salesman especially disdainful of policies and procedures. He resents rules and regulations as stumbling blocks between him and success ("Rules only get in the way of initiative. They hinder more than they help"). He is seldom willing to admit that policies might exist for his benefit, or that they might be useful guidelines for staying out of trouble. As far as he is concerned, all rules restrain him from doing the kind of job that will bring him the greatest reward.

To the Q1, then, rules and policies are made to be circumvented. Like the pedestrian who glances in all directions to make sure no policeman will see him cross the street against a red light, the Q1 asks himself only one question before doing as he wants: "Can I get away with it?" If he fears punishment, he usually obeys the rule.

If the Q1 had his way, he would be entrusted with policy-making authority, and would make up rules to fit situations as they occur. Confident of his ability to be his own policy-maker, he is sure he can do better than "those guys in the home office who don't really know what's going on out here in the field." The smart salesman, in his estimation, "plays it by ear" and makes policy on the spot. The Q1 dignifies this approach by calling it "sales flexibility." Most other people would call it sales anarchy.

The Q1 resents expense reports because they force him to account for his activities; they are another managerial device, he feels, to deprive him of his freedom. For the same reason, he dislikes reports of any kind. Few subjects, in fact, fill him with such fervor. He considers all reports, no matter what their function, a misuse of time and energy. ("We'd all be a lot better off if I were allowed to spend all my time making sales calls. I'm a salesman, not a clerk.") Worse than that, he suspects that his company deliberately contrives some of its reports to transform its people into robot-like creatures without initiative. ("All this paperwork is just management's way of keeping people in line. If you ask me, it's a waste of time.") Frequently, he vents his disdain by failing to file reports; if forced to submit them, he spends as little time on them as possible and often files them late. He may even distort his reports, so that the information he writes down reflects what he wants his company to think rather than what he has actually been doing.

HIS ATTITUDE TOWARD HIS PRODUCT

"Give me anything and I can sell it" is a claim the Q1 salesman frequently makes. This is not an idle boast either; he really believes he can sell anything. As a result, he's not deeply concerned with the quality of his product, since he believes the sale depends upon his selling skill rather than what he's selling.

With customers or prospects, the Q1 praises his product to the skies, no matter how he really feels about it; with people from his own company, he downgrades it. He wants his company to know that "Without me, you wouldn't be able to sell this product." By talking down what he sells, he tries to increase his own stature and importance.

The Q1 salesman seldom understands how people really react to him; when he does learn of their negative reactions, he insists the fault is theirs, not his, so there is no need for him to change. In fact, to the Q1, change is an admission of weakness. If a man is strong and successful, as he thinks he is, why should he change?

This does not mean the Q1 never changes. He does, but only when something seriously upsets his usual way of doing things, so that he begins to doubt himself. Then, to quiet the doubt, he may consider doing things differently. But he seldom goes very deep in diagnosing his dilemma. Like the patient who goes to a doctor for some cough medicine to relieve a bad cough, but is unwilling to let the doctor discover why he is coughing, the Q1 is willing to treat symptoms, but seldom underlying causes.

Intensely proud of his selling ability, the Q1 does not want to learn anything that might shatter his self-esteem. He is unhappy when his manager suggests ways in which he can improve his selling (even though he is ready and eager to advise others), and he sometimes tries to avoid training sessions in which he will hear critiques of his selling skill.

A good salesman, he believes, needs little or no training; training is for inferior or inadequate salesmen, not for him. He is critical of formal sales training courses; his idea of sales training is to send the trainee into the field to do a day's work. If he has what it takes, he will get by; if not, he will be better off in some other field. This, of course, is a modern version of the "survival of the fittest" doctrine.

It is never easy to get the Q1 to embark upon a course of self-improvement, but it can be done if he can be persuaded that training will help him. He sometimes welcomes change at the outset of his sales career or when he realizes that other salesmen are doing better than he. Since he hates taking a back seat to anyone, he may undertake retraining if fellow salesmen begin to make more money or attract more attention than he. Or he may be jolted into change by missing several important sales in a row, or by failing to make quotas for a sustained period, or by losing a number of key accounts ("I hate to admit it, but I've lost three of my five biggest accounts in the last year. Maybe the boss is right. Maybe I *do* need to try a new approach. Just between you and me, for the first time in my career, I'm starting to worry about myself").

In general, the Q1 resists change unless he is shown that his present selling techniques are costing him money and success, and that another strategy will help him make money and attain success. An appeal to these factors, if skillfully handled, can cause him to change his selling technique, even though he strongly dislikes change.

HIS ATTITUDE TOWARD COMPETITION

The Q1 is an eager and aggressive competitor who relishes the opportunity to win out over other salesmen. In a competitive situation, he fights hard with everything at his disposal. And he fights zestfully. To the Q1, selling is far more exciting and far more satisfying when a competitor is involved; making a sale in a noncompetitive situation is much less gratifying.

To hear his competitors tell it, the Q1 seldom fights fairly, a charge the Q1 vigorously denies ("Sour grapes! I got the order for only one reason: because I'm a better salesman. He knows it, but he won't admit it"). The fact is that most Q1s, in their eagerness to make the sale, do bend facts and exaggerate claims. But it is impossible to generalize about *all* Q1s in this regard.

JOB SATISFACTION

The Q1 is seldom happy about his income, about the amount of appreciation he gets, and about other salesmen who are more successful than he. His company loyalty is usually conditional; when business is good, he may feel fairly loyal; if business declines, he may begin thinking about getting a job somewhere else. Because his self-image is closely tied to the amount of money he makes, he does not usually stick with a company that's in a protracted slump. Some Q1 salesmen do stay in one job for a long time, perhaps because of loyalty, or perhaps because they believe they cannot do better anywhere else.

It is typical of the Q1 that he is dissatisfied with being "merely a salesman," and the longer he remains one the more dissatisfied he is likely to become. He really wants to become a manager, and to move up the managerial ladder quickly ("I know I've got what it takes. All I need is a chance to prove myself"). His ambition is based less on a desire to work with other people than on what management can mean to him—more money and more power. Few things appeal to the Q1 more than exerting control over others.

When a Q1 is promoted to a sales manager's job, he takes a bleak view of the salesmen who work for him. He assumes the men under his control are as self-interested and as self-concerned as he is. Naturally, he distrusts them, and fears them as potential competitors for his present job as sales manager ("I understand salesmen because I used to be one myself. Any good salesman is ambitious. And ambitious people have to be watched very closely"). So he institutes rigid controls, the very kind of controls, ironically, that he rebelled against when he was a salesman. All his talk about "sales flexibility" is quickly forgotten, and he becomes a demanding boss who insists that policies and rules be strictly adhered to. As a sales manager, the Q1 is a living contradiction.

The Q1 Salesman's Relationship to His Customers

With customers, the Q1 salesman is aggressive, forceful, and often overwhelming. He is a "take charge" person who tries to completely control the presentation. He is often so assertive that customers are unable to say "no" to him. As a result, he frequently has an excellent sales record.

Few things are as important to the Q1 salesman as making a sale. His entire image of himself, his pride, his self-respect, are wrapped up in his ability to sell. Only by making sales continually and repeatedly can he stave off the feeling of inadequacy and impending failure. It is important to understand this; the Q1 salesman has a profound emotional stake in his job. For him, selling is not only a means of acquiring money and power; it is a means of acquiring the sense of personal worth that money and power bring in their wake. For the Q1, making sales is of crucial psychological importance. And, because of his deep-rooted fear of failure, he cannot feel self-esteem unless he *continues* to make sales, day in and day out. Every sale is critically important to him ("A man *is* what he does. We're all measured by performance. After all, we don't have much regard for doctors who lose lives and lawyers who lose cases. How can anyone respect a salesman who loses sales?").

Because he measures his personal value by his sales record, the Q1 expends enormous energy and effort to make a sale. Generally, he takes a "hard-sell" approach, but is shrewd enough to adopt a "soft-sell" line as an expedient if it will help to get an order. Even when he "soft-sells," however, there is no doubt in anyone's mind that he controls the presentation; he dare not lose control for fear of losing the sale. If that happens, he also loses face—with himself.

PROSPECTING

The Q1 pursues prospects as tenaciously as a bloodhound in pursuit of its quarry. To maintain a favorable image of himself, he constantly seeks new opportunities to test himself; every new prospect is a challenge, and every challenge that's successfully met bolsters his self-image.

It is not much of an exaggeration to say that the Q1 eats, sleeps, and breathes selling. In a sense, he is always busy selling. Because he constantly thinks in terms of sales, he has a remarkable ability to ferret out sales opportunities. He seldom relaxes; even among friends or in a social situation, he is alert to clues that might lead to a sale.

In a way, prospecting is easier for the Q1 than for other salesmen. He talks about himself frequently, and his talk usually centers on his sales accomplishments, so he is able to introduce the subject of sales into most of his conversations. From this point, it is only a short step to developing prospects or obtaining sales leads. He considers everyone a prospect or as someone who knows a prospect.

The Q1 has one other advantage that makes him a formidable prospector: his relatively thick skin. He is not easily brushed off or discouraged. He refuses to take "no" for an answer without a struggle. If someone tells him, "You can't sell me," he digs in like a general preparing for a long siege, and tries to discover a sizable chink in his prospect's armor; because he considers *everyone* a prospect, he is neither selective nor analytic in his prospecting. He wastes much time and effort following up bad leads; he often gives poor prospects the same treatment as outstanding prospects. He is like a baseball player who swings at every ball thrown; naturally, he hits a lot of them, more than he would if he never took the bat off his shoulder, but, at the same time, he has an excessively high strike-out record.

On balance, the Q1 has unusual strengths and unusual weaknesses as a prospector. Because he's hard to discourage, and tries to sell every conceivable prospect, he does make some sales that most salesmen would regard as impossible. Many men have achieved success in many fields because they refused to believe that "it can't be done"; the world would be remarkably different if men always accepted the popular notion of what is or is not possible. On this score, the Q1 deserves full credit. At the same time, his unselective prospecting diminishes his returns on the time and energy he invests, and makes it very difficult for him to concentrate his best efforts on those prospects who deserve them. As a result, the Q1 may be more successful at selling high-volume, low-cost items of a relatively nontechnical nature than at selling more costly products that require well-planned, lengthy presentations and considerable technical background.

HIS PRESENTATIONS TO NEW CUSTOMERS

While the Q1 likes to think of himself as a masterful planner, he is really too rash and headstrong to adhere to any plan for very long.

Contrary to his self-image, he tends to do things on the spur of the moment. He seldom makes appointments to see prospects, but "drops in" unexpectedly, and, as a result, wastes time in waiting rooms and lobbies, frequently ends up talking to the wrong person, and then shows up late for those interviews that were scheduled for a specific time. He often annoys receptionists, secretaries, and even prospects themselves by his brash approach, although he can be both charming and disarming when the situation requires. Once he begins his presentation, he is forceful and direct, and makes a generally good initial impression. His no-nonsense air appeals to many people. While he may seem too forward and too over-bearing, his overall behavior is that of a man who intends to be business-like and not to waste time. Accordingly, he spends little time on social niceties, and states the reason for his call fairly quickly.

Like a boxer who hopes to weaken his opponent by landing several good punches in the opening round, the Q1 tries to gain an immediate advantage by describing himself, his company, and his product in glowing terms, making it clear at the same time that his competition is not com-parable in any way. The prospect may feel somewhat put off by the Q1's overpowering assertiveness, but he is probably impressed by his obvious control of the situation. Many Q1 salesmen, in fact, display such domi-nance at the start of the interview that the prospect feels somewhat help less.

Naturally, very few prospects capitulate immediately. Their most com-mon reaction is to realize that the salesman is very forceful and may over-whelm them unless they manifest some resistance quickly. This resistance can take several forms, ranging from vigorous argument to withdrawn silence. But some form of resistance almost always takes place.

Throughout the interview, the Q1 is a strenuous talker but a poor listener. The surest way to dominate the interview, he feels, is to do most of the talking ("Giving a customer a chance to talk is like giving up the football to the other team. You may never get it back"). The Q1 seldom really hears objections voiced by the prospect; he is usually too busy thinking up ways to distract the prospect or shift his attention. He is not interested in the underlying meaning, but only in answering the objection quickly.

Any sign that he does not know all the answers is, he fears, a sign of weakness, to be avoided at all costs. Even when he does not know the answer, he maintains an air of authority, usually by improvising an answer. He sometimes answers objections that have not really been raised; he sets up straw men and then knocks them down. Often, he does not really "answer" objections; he merely overpowers his prospect by his pre-sumably superior knowledge ("Whatever you do, never let a customer get the idea that you're not an expert. Once that happens, you're in real trouble. The customer has to understand that no matter how much he knows, the salesman knows *more*"). The Q1 always sounds self-assured and definite.

Typically, the Q1 has trouble closing effectively. The problem is that he monopolizes the presentation and gives the prospect little chance to voice objections. As a result, the objections are restrained until he tries to close; then, instead of agreeing to buy, the prospect raises a whole series of objections. The inexperienced Q1, in particular, tries to get the prospect to buy before the latter is ready; only after long experience does he learn to make trial closes at critical points.

Frequently, the Q1 tries to close by making the prospect ashamed not to buy. If the prospect still refuses, the Q1 pressures him to appoint a time to discuss the matter further, and, at the appointed time, he applies more pressure. Since he wants to avoid feelings of weakness, he is remarkably adept at avoiding blame if he fails to make a sale. Instead, he blames lost sales on the customer, or his company, or his product ("That customer is too stupid to know what's good for him," or "The company has assigned me an impossible territory," or "The product's lousy and everybody knows it").

Why does the Q1 so seldom learn from his mistakes? Because self-criticism is extremely difficult for him. Once he begins to examine himself, he may begin to feel weak and inept; his self-image may start to crumble; his self-respect, feelings of adequacy, and sense of superiority over others may begin to disintegrate. He prefers not to take this risk.

AFTER THE SALE

To the Q1 salesman, making the sale counts; follow-up is unimportant. As far as he is concerned, the most important follow-up is to submit the order quickly, so that he gets quick sales credit and commission. "Servicing the account" he considers impractical. Why spend time servicing existing accounts when you can spend it selling new prospects? If his company is dissatisfied with the terms of the order, he consoles himself with the thought that "Nobody appreciates me." If the customer complains that he hasn't received everything promised to him, the Q1 assures himself that "I've done everything I can, but people are never satisfied." If the customer persists, the Q1 usually tells him that, "There seems to be some misunderstanding. But don't worry—I'm on your side, and I'll do everything I can to get the company to give you what you've got coming." Blame is subtly shifted from salesman to company. Then he submits the customer's claim to the company and contends that the company should humor the customer in spite of his obvious misunderstanding of the terms of the sale. The salesman portrays himself as an innocent bystander who is only trying to keep peace between hostile factions.

The Q1's treatment of customers works better in the short run. In the long run, it is self-defeating, engendering distrust and resistance from customers. The Q1's strategy is very dependent upon the salesman's assertive presence; once his forceful personality is removed from the scene, the strategy begins to seem hollow. Unless the Q1 is on the scene to keep things going, his customers start to realize how they have been treated, and they slip away. His sales technique is like a delicate piece of stage machinery; unless well-oiled on a regular schedule, it begins to creak, and finally no longer provides illusion.

That is why there is often a considerable turnover among the Q1's customers. He seldom fully understands why his customers leave him, preferring to think that "Competition is sure tough," or "Those so-and-so's stole my customer by price-cutting." Because turnover is frequently high, the Q1 must work hard to replace lost business; he can seldom depend upon long-range customer loyalty. So the search for new customers to replace the old never ends. The problem is complicated by the fact that the Q1 is unlikely to get referrals from his present customers, once they begin to see through him. He is forced to get prospects from entirely new sources. As a result, he may "burn out" at a relatively early age. When this happens, he either changes jobs, hoping new surroundings will mean new opportunities, or he watches his income shrink, powerless to do much about it.

A Perspective on the Q1 Salesman

We're now better able to understand Bob Hawthorne, the fictional auto-parts salesman with whom we began this chapter. When his customer described him as a hard-nosed salesman who would flatten weak buyers like a steam-roller, he described a man with a strong psychological need to make sales and thereby prove that he is strong and capable, *not* weak and inept. When his district sales manager described him as terrible on paperwork, argumentative, and disrespectful of systems, he described a man with strong needs for independence who feels constrained by reports and regulations. And when his fellow salesman described him as a hard man to get along with, he described a salesman who views most people, including those in his own company, with some hostility and suspicion.

None of this will seem strange if we recall the attitudes and beliefs described in Chapter Three. Bob Hawthorne's behavior is what we would expect from a man who believes it's a dog-eat-dog world where only the fittest survive, where nobody gets anything unless he grabs it for himself, where rugged individualism and hard-nosed self-interest are the only sensible virtues. Nor is it surprising in a man who believes that, in a world where everyone is shrewdly wary of everyone else, customers seldom buy willingly; that sales must be imposed on customers by forceful, over-powering salesmen, and that, as a matter of simple self-concern, customer resistance must be split apart by jackhammer selling techniques. Given the Q1's basic belief that "it's either him or me," Hawthorne's behavior seems logical and practical. Readers can both understand and empathize with Q1 behavior if they remember three points:

1. The Q1 sees selling as a win–lose occupation. Every presentation is a contest from which both a winner and a loser must emerge. Every sales presentation is a struggle of wills to determine which of two men will prevail over the other. Even when the customer buys something that is good for him, that satisfies a need and provides a benefit, he still, in a sense, loses, because he *gives in* to the salesman. In the very act of buying (no matter how beneficial the purchase), the customer *submits*; he defers to the salesman. And conversely, in the very act of selling, the salesman *dominates*; he triumphs over a buyer who, in the very nature of things, is resistive. The idea of win–lose, victory–defeat, is thus built into the very structure of the sales presentation. Unless the reader understands this viewpoint, which all Q1s share to some degree, Q1 behavior will always seem a little strange.

2. The Q1 has very strong needs for esteem. If sales prove he is strong, as the Q1 believes they do, then he is forced to the reluctant conclusion that *failure* to make sales proves he is weak, or at least relatively weak compared to the customer. To a man who wants to be on top, who likes to be number one, this is a painful thought. If failures occur often enough, they can become very painful. In view of this, the Q1's tireless prospecting, his incessant hard work, his seemingly ceaseless drive to pile sale upon sale, are readily understandable. The Q1 is literally a man who keeps score on himself.

3. The Q1 has very strong needs for independence. To the Q1, external constraints of any kind are demeaning; they force him to subject himself to other people's thinking and wishes. Rules, directives, policies, all symbolize his subservience to control by others. They remind him of the fact that he is subordinate. At heart, every Q1 is a maverick who wants to be let alone to prove that he is his own man, strong and self-reliant.

All of these traits are manifest in the comments about Bob Hawthorne that opened this chapter. All of them are manifest, to some degree, in the behavior of all Q1 salesmen.

SUMMARY

In this chapter, we've developed a typology of the Quadrant 1 or dominant-hostile salesman. We've seen that he has strong needs for self-esteem and independence, and that making sales is important to him because sales demonstrate his power and they bolster his self-image as a man who controls his own destiny. On the surface, the Q1 is confident and assertive; he has strong opinions, works hard, and seldom fails to detect an opportunity to make a sale. Beneath the surface, the Q1 is afraid of failure, and eager not to appear weak or dependent.

To other people, the Q1 often seems overbearing and manipulative, although he does not see himself this way. Instead, he believes his behavior is demanded by the circumstances in which he finds himself. Q1s are often insensitive to the needs and feelings of other people, as is evidenced by a certain brusqueness in their behavior.

Those Q1 salesmen who are also Q1 family men, and not all are, usually guide their families with a firm hand, and expect their ideas to be dominant. There is little "democracy" in such families. Some Q1s avoid community work entirely, but others take on community responsibilities eagerly, in an effort to enlarge their personal power.

The typical Q1 is loyal to his company as long as business is good; if sales wane, he may quickly go elsewhere. Nearly all Q1 salesmen dislike rules and procedures of any kind, since these are restraints on their freedom. The Q1 maintains shrewd but seldom friendly relationships with nonselling people in his company.

Q1s are invariably strenuous competitors who enjoy a fight. They work hard to beat competition, and find victories especially gratifying.

When a Q1 is promoted to sales manager, he is frequently a hard-driving and distrustful boss, who sees his salesmen as duplicates of what he himself used to be.

Most Q1s resist training and development unless they are first convinced it will help them to increased earnings and success. As a rule, Q1s prefer not to examine their behavior closely and thus open themselves up to self-doubt. Typically, the Q1 sees himself as an excellent salesman who doesn't need and won't benefit from training.

Q1s are dogged prospectors and aggressive salesmen. They waste a good deal of time trying to sell unqualified prospects, and they usually have high turnover among their customers, who frequently resent their high-pressure tactics. But, at least in the short-run, the Q1 is usually quite successful because he is hard-hitting, forceful, dynamic, and hard-working.

5

The Quadrant 2 (Submissive-Hostile) Salesman

"WHATEVER WILL BE, WILL BE"

Let us begin by setting an imaginary salesman next to Bob Hawthorne. We will call him Steve Whittier: 43 years old, married, the father of one child now in college, a salesman for the past eight years. Before becoming a salesman, he was office-manager for a branch office of a life-insurance company; the company was acquired by a larger insurance company which closed the branch office and eliminated Steve's job. Steve then became, at the age of 35, a life-insurance salesman, a job he quit after a year or so because, as he put it, "I didn't like all those night hours." After leaving the insurance job, he became a salesman for a paint manufacturer, calling on paint and hardware stores. He has been in this job ever since, covering a territory that extends over the eastern half of the state.

As we did with Bob Hawthorne, we'll conduct imaginary interviews with three people who know Steve well: one of his customers, his district sales manager, and a salesman who works out of the same district office.

Once again, our questions are the same: "What's your reaction to Steve Whittier? How do you see him? How does he come across to you?"

Customer (paint buyer for a small chain of hardware stores): "Sometimes I wonder how people like Whittier ever get into selling in the first place. He's a decent enough guy . . . but he's just not what I think of as a salesman. He's always so reserved . . . so detached. It's funny . . . I've known the man for five, maybe six, years, and yet I don't really feel I know him at all. We've never had one really good talk . . . not that I can remember, anyway. Of course, I'd buy Radiant Glow paints no matter who was selling them. That's one of the finest paint lines on the market, and I couldn't afford to be without it. But I can't say that I buy it because of Whittier. In fact, I could just as easily order by mail. Oh, sure, it's convenient to have Whittier come by to take the order . . . but I'd never miss him if they took him out of the territory. Now, mind you . . . I'm not saying anything against the man personally. I just can't understand how he ever got into selling in the first place, that's all."

District Sales Manager: "Every sales organization has a few men like Steve Whittier. They don't set the world on fire, but they do their jobs, and they don't cause any trouble. Oh, sure, I'd like nothing better than a whole sales force full of world-beaters . . . but I'm realistic about these things. Every sales manager has to settle for a few guys like Steve. He's quiet . . . he takes orders . . . never gives me any back-talk . . . and usually manages to make his quota. I'd never put a man like Steve in a new territory . . . but he's in an old, well-established area where the product really sells itself. I guess you could say Steve's a marginal salesman . . . but you'll find a few marginal people in any sales office. After all . . . not everyone can be the world's heavyweight champ."

Fellow Salesman: "Steve's a strange guy. I've known him for years, and, in a way, he's sort of a stranger to me. Quiet . . . almost remote . . . kind of a loner. He minds his own business . . . never causes anybody any trouble . . . but never offers to help anybody, either. Steve's the sort of person who very seldom socializes with the other salesmen in the office. On the rare occasions when he does, he's not really very sociable. That's about all I can tell you . . . Steve's not exactly what you'd call a colorful character."

Steve Whittier is a submissive-hostile (Quadrant 2) salesman, a type we'll describe in detail in this chapter.

A GENERAL DESCRIPTION OF THE Q2 SALESMAN

The Q2 salesman is security-oriented. Safety and protection from life's uncertainties count more to him than adventure. He seeks not challenge but repose, not growth but stability, not stimulation but tranquillity. He considers other people potential threats, possible disrupters of the placid existence he tries so hard to maintain. He spends considerable time making sure that other people do not endanger his survival. How he builds psychological fortifications to protect himself from possible trouble from other people, becomes clear later in this chapter. The important point to keep in mind throughout is that the Q2 salesman is motivated largely by strong *security* needs; he wants to insure predictability in his work, and, even more, he wants to insure his own survival on the job.

The Q2 is seldom seen in this classic form, however. Most submissive-hostile salesmen are muted versions of the man just described. The classic Q2 is usually so busy digging protective trenches that he has difficulty functioning effectively as a salesman. But many Q2s *do* function adequately; at least, their work is regarded as "sufficient." They perform up to the minimum established standards; they perform well enough to "get by." They are far more security-oriented than other salesmen, but they are certainly not incapacitated by their search for stability.

The Q2 Salesman's Relationship to Himself

WHAT HE IS

The Q2, like the Q1, has a negative view of people in general. Most people, he feels, are self-centered, out to get what they can, and not very scrupulous about how they do it. So an intelligent man, the Q2 believes, must guard against them to make sure he does not become a pawn in the ceaseless struggle for survival. Because nearly everyone is out for himself, almost no one can be trusted or depended upon. The man who thinks he can find security in other people fools himself; a man must make his *own* security. In a world marked by constant struggle, each man must look out for himself.

Up to this point, the Q2 view is much like the Q1. But there are significant differences. The dominant-hostile salesman feels less endangered than the submissive-hostile salesman. The Q1 thinks most people are too apathetic or inept to hurt him directly; as long as he carefully controls them, they represent little or no danger. Some people, of course, do represent a *direct* threat to the Q1 by competing with him for sales and status. The Q1 willingly struggles with these people, using whatever practical means are necessary to eliminate them as potential dangers.

While the Q1 feels most people lack the ability to hurt him (or is confident of his own ability to neutralize their threat), the Q2 does *not* feel capable of controlling or overcoming others. So, while the Q1 enthusiastically joins the fight, the Q2 holds back, convinced that the best offense is a good defense. The Q2 prefers to avert trouble by maintaining a "low profile" and avoiding confrontation. "Nobody," he insists, "ever got hurt by staying out of a fight."

WHAT HE THINKS HE IS

The Q2 salesman considers himself a realist. He rejects the verdict that he is cynical or pessimistic, and insists that he sees things the way they are. As he puts it: "A guy has to look out for himself if he's going to survive."

Sometimes, however, he is aware of, and defensive about, his submissiveness. In a society that honors competitiveness and dynamism, he senses that he is noncompetitive and nondynamic. He may deny his submissiveness ("I'm as aggressive as the next person, only I don't make a lot of noise about it") or rationalize it ("Sure, I'm not a very aggressive person, but so what? I've survived, haven't I? And survival is what counts in this world"). But his lack of forcefulness sometimes bothers him, and in moments of candor he may acknowledge that assertive people are more secure. But he remains submissive nevertheless.

Sometimes, he sees himself as victimized by others. It is easy for a person who believes the world is a primitive place where only the fittest survive to blame his troubles on others, or on circumstances. But, underneath, he often realizes his shortcomings, and regretfully admits that he lacks the assertiveness so important in selling.

WHAT HE WOULD LIKE TO BE

The Q2 salesman wants a well-ordered, predictable, manageable existence, free of worry and anxiety. He wants to get by with a minimum of competing. As much as anything, he wants to be let alone. Why does a man who is withdrawn and detached choose to become a salesman? Because the Q2 doesn't believe that selling differs from any other kind of work. He believes anybody can survive in any job, including selling, if he only plays it safe, does as he's told, and stays out of trouble. As the Q2 often says, "A job is a job." The important thing, in selling or any other occupation, is to be prudent, to act only after weighing all the possible consequences, and always to select the safest course. The cautious salesman, he believes, *endures,* and endurance is what the Q2 wants most.

The Q2 Salesman's Relationship to Others

PEOPLE IN GENERAL

The Q2 tends to look down upon others. He often is willing to strike out at others with sarcasm and subtly veiled hostility. Other people sometimes think of him as cold; his manner often conveys superiority. His distrust and suspicion of other people increase the distance he tries to maintain between them and himself; he is generally aloof and uncommunicative. He is commonly a man with few, if any, intimate friends. Oddly enough, while the Q2 salesman strongly needs approval and admiration, he is unwilling to put himself on display. Unlike the Q1, he refuses to become the center of attention. He insists on staying on the fringes. When he does choose to associate with others, he selects people like himself, with whom he can share his hostilities and fears. He finds comfort in the fact that there are other people who feel about the world as he does.

The Q2 is especially careful not to get involved with aggressive people. He particularly dislikes the Q1 salesman, whom he regards as a "carnival barker." "The selling profession could do without these loud-mouths," he contends. The Q2 also feels disdain for people who are deeply concerned with others. They are, he believes, naive bleeding-hearts with a completely unrealistic view of things.

In general, then, the Q2 salesman is a "loner." He is not often capable of the reciprocal behavior on which friendship must be based; as a result, he has few close friends. Instead of the affection and respect he so badly wants, and that would make him feel more secure and less threatened, he frequently provokes rejection, resentment, and sometimes outright hostility. The Q2 is like a bricklayer who has built a unique wall; he stands on one side, and the rest of the world stands on the other. The wall is of his own making, yet he cannot understand why he is separated from everyone else.

HIS RELATIONSHIP TO HIS FAMILY

Once again, for illustration, we shall describe a Q2 salesman whose behavior in varying roles is consistent.

At home, he frequently lets his wife make major decisions, although he may feel sheepish about his own failure to assert authority. If, like him, his wife is indecisive, major decisions may be long delayed until one of them takes the lead; then the other usually goes along without argument. Submissive-hostile fathers seldom exert much authority over their children, whose independence they rationalize with observations like: "It's impossible to control kids these days; they don't get enough discipline in school." While both wife and children are largely independent of the father's control, they may go to elaborate lengths to disguise the fact. No one explicitly acknowledges his lack of authority; in some cases, no one even implicitly acknowledges it. Everyone pretends the head of the house is really in charge of things, while each goes about his business with little or no paternal control. The father's feelings are thus soothed and arguments and tension avoided.

HIS RELATIONSHIP TO THE COMMUNITY

The Q2 usually avoids participation in civic affairs. "Don't kid yourself," he admonishes, "these civic minded people are only feathering their own nests. Nobody does anything for nothing." His real reason for not getting involved is, of course, that he feels more comfortable on the sidelines.

The Q2 Salesman's Relationship to His Company

HIS RELATIONSHIP WITH OTHER PEOPLE IN HIS COMPANY

The Q2 salesman often feels quite loyal to his company because it is a haven from the outside world. It provides him with a paycheck, keeps him from having to look for another job, and helps him to feel secure. His company is a known quantity, and the Q2 fears the unknown. It is a safe port in a stormy world ("I'll never be able to understand how some guys can stand bouncing from job to job. When I wake up in the morning, I want to know *exactly* what to expect for the day. None of this job-hopping for me").

The Q2 "plays it safe" much of the time. His apprehensions about people extend to his sales manager as well as others; he is very cautious in dealing with him. He tries to keep as far from him as he reasonably can, since he fears his boss may make demands upon him that he cannot fulfill. He prefers not to attract his manager's attention; he wants to fade comfortably into the background (except when he thinks he can gain praise or favorable notice). He wants to be unnoticed and unnoticeable.

One kind of attention the Q2 wants from his superior is sympathy. To gain sympathy, he will, from time to time, complain, but not too loudly. But he is careful not to make unreasonable demands upon his manager, or to attract his critical attention. He wants sympathy, not scrutiny.

With peers, the Q2 is usually aloof. He prefers not to interact with them in any significant way, although he is willing to accept help from them. He does his share of team effort, but seldom more ("If you're not careful about these things, the other guys will think you're a chump. The first thing you know, you'll be carrying *everybody's* load"). He is usually neither popular nor unpopular with his fellow salesmen, who usually respect his desire to be let alone. He is often described as a "loner."

He is sometimes hostile to people in his company who are not in sales. They become scapegoats for his failures ("It's getting tougher to make sales every day. Those guys in production don't make the kind of product that's easy to sell").

HIS ATTITUDE TOWARD REGULATIONS

The Q2 sticks very close to company policies, since these make him feel secure. He likes the assurance that comes from well-defined guidelines. Companies very seldom have trouble getting their Q2 salesmen to follow rules. If anything, the Q2 follows them too closely; he sometimes makes the policies seem more rigid and inflexible than they are.

Company policies serve another purpose; they provide the Q2 with a ready-made rationale when things go wrong. "It's not my fault—I was only following the rules. You know me, I always play by the numbers. If things aren't working out right, maybe something is wrong with the numbers." At the same time, however, he frequently complains that the company's regulations are too restrictive; "I'd sell a lot more if it weren't for all those policies. Every time I turn around, the rule book is staring at me. No wonder I can't sell more than I do."

If someone thinks a set of rules is wrong, it would seem reasonable to expect him to suggest changes. But the Q2 does not see things this way. As long as the rules stay the way they are, he derives comfort from following them, and security from blaming them, rather than himself, for his mediocre sales performance.

The Q2 salesman's expense reports are models of exactness. He always stays within his budget, another tactic by which he remains "faceless." Spending too much money, he reasons, will bring the wrath of the company down upon him; spending too little will make it appear he isn't trying very hard. Either way, he will attract notice. He prefers to live within his budget and attract no attention. His other reports also have a faceless quality about them. The Q2 submits all reports on time, but the information he transmits is mechanical and unimaginative. He gives whatever is asked for, nothing more or less. He dares not antagonize his boss by failing to submit reports, but he realizes that by volunteering too much information, he may get out on a limb.

HIS ATTITUDE TOWARD HIS PRODUCT

The Q2 is usually superficially knowledgeable about his product's features. He memorizes all the product information his company feels he should know, and can usually discuss the features at some length, although he has great trouble translating them into customer benefits. However, he often explains his lack of sales success by blaming the product. "People recognize a faulty product," he says. "The best salesman in the world couldn't do a better job than I'm doing with the kind of product we've got."

HIS ATTITUDE TOWARD TRAINING

The Q2 needs training, but he resists self-development. Part of the problem is that he's not eager to change, and development is change. He prefers to stay as he is; training is a threat to his sense of stability and peace of mind ("I'm doing well enough to get by. I may not be setting the world on fire, but I am managing to survive. Why tamper with a sure thing?"). He seldom resists training openly, however. He goes along with any demands the company makes upon him, but seldom enters into the training experience wholeheartedly. He sits in the classroom, but does not get involved; he makes notes, but seldom looks at them again; he hears lectures, but doesn't really listen to what is said. His presence is more physical than mental.

The same is true of field training. When out with a trainer, the Q2 goes through the motions, but they usually lack meaning. The simple fact is that he is usually afraid to learn, and no trainer or training technique can get through to him until his fear is removed. Only when he realizes that training is not only not a threat, but that it will enhance his security, is the Q2 ready to get much out of training.

HIS ATTITUDE TOWARD COMPETITION

While the Q2 is unwilling to display hostility openly inside his company, he seldom feels inhibited when it comes to competition. He often does a better job of selling against competition than of selling in his own behalf. Some Q2 presentations are devoted largely to explaining why the customer should not buy from competition, but little time is spent explaining why he should buy from the Q2. Disparaging competitors is one way the Q2 works off some of the aggressiveness that he is otherwise unwilling to manifest.

JOB SATISFACTION

The Q2 is seldom really happy with his job. He tolerates it because it is something with which he is familiar, an accustomed refuge from the world outside ("This may not be the best job in the world, but at least it's a job. If I went to work for another company, I might find things a whole lot worse"). But he seems to have little zest for selling; he doesn't particularly enjoy meeting and talking with customers, he gets little delight out of making sales, and he doesn't have a strong need to prove himself. He prefers to avoid involvement and commitment, to remain on the sidelines as much as possible. As in football, life on the sidelines may be lonely, but it's also safe. Many times, Q2 salesmen enjoy long tenure on their jobs, hanging on year after year as marginal producers.

The Q2 Salesman's Relationship to His Customers

PROSPECTING

His lack of forcefulness makes prospecting very difficult for the Q2 salesman. Instead of seeking out prospects, and running the risk of rebuff, he prefers to wait for prospects to come to him. Consequently, his prospect list is small. The root of the problem is his fear of the word "no." Any refusal makes him feel inadequate. He rationalizes his failure to prospect by asking, "Why bother calling on people who aren't ready to buy? When they're ready, they'll let me know." As a rule, his new customers are referred to him by his company or by present customers; he seldom prospects for them.

Once he gets a referral, the Q2 approaches him in a lackluster way. If his company has a "canned" technique for qualifying prospects, he uses it; this is far preferable, in his opinion, to exercising his own initiative. If left on his own, he usually does a mechanical job of qualification, characterized by a lack of assertiveness and a lack of probing.

Part of his lack of enthusiasm stems from the conviction that he can't control the sale anyway, so why worry? After all, the prospect will buy if he's ready to buy. If he's not, he won't. It's that simple, so why spend a lot of time and energy qualifying him?

HIS PRESENTATIONS TO NEW CUSTOMERS

The Q2's presentations are usually colorless and uninspired. Instead of adapting his presentations to different prospects and different situations, he follows a set presentation. Because it is largely a rote performance, the presentation usually sounds unenthusiastic and unconvincing, as if the salesman himself hardly believes what he's saying.

Because he gets little pleasure out of selling, the Q2 sometimes procrastinates, idles, finds excuses for not making appointments. When he finally gets around to arranging an appointment, he submits easily to the prospect's wishes. No salesman is easier to put off or discourage than the Q2 ("Why force yourself on people? Either they're ready to buy or they're not. It doesn't do any good to push").

In the presentation, the Q2 is courteous but unsure of himself. He may make apologetic statements like "I won't take up too much of your time" or "It was nice of you to give me an opportunity to talk with you" or "I know you're busy, so I'll get right to the point." He is hesitant, almost reluctant.

Unlike many salesmen, the Q2 gets little pleasure from using words ("I've seen too many salesmen get themselves into trouble by talking too much. The smart thing is to say no more than you have to say"). He uses words sparingly in his presentations, and displays little verve or flair. His halting manner often makes prospects uncomfortable and embarrassed. To overcome this feeling, some prospects step in and help the Q2 complete his presentation. Although he doesn't plan it that way, the Q2 has a genius for evoking support and sympathy from some prospects.

One advantage of this limping style of presentation, from the salesman's point of view, is that it lowers the customer's resistance. The customer hesitates to ask many questions or voice many objections. In some cases, he actually ends up making the sale to himself. This situation seems implausible only if one forgets that the Q2's submissiveness strikes a responsive chord in many people; it arouses sympathy, pity, a desire to help. (This is certainly not always the case, however; in dominant people, the Q2's submissiveness will usually evoke lack of respect and perhaps even hostility.)

Although he makes sales, the Q2 seldom really "closes" them. Closing requires a degree of forcefulness he usually lacks. If he is lucky enough to have an excellent product or service, the sale is often closed for him by the customer. Or, the customer may close the sale out of sheer compassion. But if the customer fails to close for him, the Q2 is at something of a loss. He is hesitant to force the issue; everything about him rebels against taking the initiative. As a result, the presentation frequently ends inconclusively. The salesman grabs at any reason the prospect gives for not buying, relieved to have an excuse to leave without having to close.

Not unexpectedly, the Q2 seldom makes a follow-up call once he has lost a sale. Persistence is not a Q2 trait. Once he hears "no," he is satisfied.

He has no desire to try to convert "no" to "yes" ("It never pays to try to change a customer's mind. After all, a customer is a mature adult, he knows what he wants, and he doesn't need a salesman to tell him how to think").

AFTER THE SALE

The Q2 dislikes continued close contacts with people; there is too much risk in such contacts. So he does a routine job of follow-up after the sale, but doesn't put his heart into it. He fulfills any commitments he may have made, but seldom extends himself, seldom gives anything extra.

The Q2 is braced at all times for the worst, so he is not surprised when things go wrong. When he gets complaints from customers, he takes them in stride, shrugging his shoulders and asking, "What else can you expect? That's the way it goes." Complaints reinforce his belief that, try as you will, you can't please people.

The Q2 tries to handle complaints in the simplest way possible— by sending them through channels to the appropriate person in his company. He makes almost no effort to evaluate the complaint or suggest ways of solving it, unless the complaint is about *him,* in which case he tries hard to explain it. Generally, he tries not to get involved in complaints, preferring to let the home office handle them with the customer.

The Q2 rarely does much repeat business. Customers may buy from him once out of pity or embarrassment or because he walked in when their inventory was low, but they seldom repeat their orders. They recognize that he lacks interest in them, and that they can get better service from someone else. So the Q2 must constantly scrape for new customers to replace those he loses. But this is where he is weakest: prospecting. Consequently, his earnings seldom rise very high. Sometimes, of course, he does get some renewal business by continuing to evoke a customer's sympathy, or by luck, or because he has an unexcelled product. But, for the most part, he has little repeat business.

Even referrals from present customers are hard to get. Most buyers refuse to refer the Q2 salesman as a salesman, but some refer him because his product is good. In general, then, his career is a constant struggle to stay in one place, neither getting ahead nor slipping back. Oddly enough, he doesn't mind this treadmill existence. This is the penalty he is willing to pay for job survival, and survival is what counts most.

A Perspective on the Q2 Salesman

Steve Whittier's behavior, described at the start of this chapter, should seem less strange to the reader now. When the paint buyer for the hardware store chain described him as reserved and detached, a man that "I don't really feel I know," he described a man whose insecurity turns him away from close, meaningful interaction with customers. When his district manager described Steve as "quiet . . . never gives me any back-talk," he described a man too fearful of losing his job to speak out. And when a fellow salesman described him as "a loner . . . who never offers to help anybody," he described a man who believes the safest thing anyone can do for himself is mind his own business.

There is nothing mysterious about Q2 behavior. In fact, given the assumptions on which it's based, it is both reasonable and expectable. What is harder to explain is the Q2's choice of selling as a career. Perhaps "choice" is the wrong word. Many Q2s drift into selling after trying other work; they take a sales job to "try it out," without commitment. Years later, they are still in selling, still without commitment. They think of selling as "a way of making a living." And, while hardly happy in their work, they like the relative freedom from close supervision that selling gives them ("At least the boss isn't breathing down my neck all the time"). Many other Q2s deliberately choose selling as a career because they think it involves little more than order-taking. Years later, when experience should have proved how wrong they are, they still persist in the idea that people cannot be persuaded to buy and that the salesman's basic function is to record orders, not create them.

This will make more sense to the reader if he keeps the following points in mind:

1. The Q2 scoffs at the idea of "making" sales. The Q2 believes that, contrary to the popular misconception, salesmen are powerless to get customers to act. Salesmen, the Q2 feels, have far less impact on customers than most of them think. People buy when they are ready, and when *they* determine they are ready. At best, the salesman can show them what's available to buy, and give them information to help them choose. But he cannot stimulate or speed up the decision to buy. *That* decision is controlled entirely by the customer.

2. The Q2 believes that attempts to persuade can only lead to trouble. People, he reasons, don't like to be pushed. They want to make up their own minds in their own way. Any salesman who tries to pressure them into buying, or to accelerate their decision, is courting trouble; the customers are sure to respond with resentment, anger, or a stubborn refusal to buy anything at all. Assertive salesmanship is therefore self-defeating. In the long run, the salesman will be better off if he lets the customer take the initiative. The Q2 admits, somewhat grudgingly, that dynamic, assertive salesmen *do* make some sales that he would not make (a fact he has great difficulty explaining, and that he usually ascribes to "luck" or

"circumstances"). But he insists that *ultimately* his approach is safer.

3. There is a paradox in the Q2's behavior. On the one hand, the Q2 is dissatisfied with things as they are; he seldom seems happy in his job, or exhilarated by his work. His resigned observation that "a job is a job" conveys his lack of enthusiasm. On the other hand, he is strongly opposed to change, to anything that promises to make things different from what they are. This paradox is easily explained by the Q2's insecurity; to the insecure man, the *known* is preferable to the unknown. Bad as things are, change might make them worse. The present situation is at least familiar and predictable. So the Q2's resistance to change or anything that might bring change is hardly surprising.

Each of us has some Q2 traits; in the Q2, they are magnified, not different. Each of us (even the cocky Q1) sometimes backs away from major obstacles; each of us (even the self-assured Q4) sometimes worries about threats to his security; each of us (even the engaging Q3) sometimes feels that withdrawal is better than confrontation. In the Q2, these characteristics are elevated to a dominant position; they influence most of his thinking and most of his behavior. The Q2 is like all of us, only more so.

SUMMARY

In this chapter, we've presented a typology of the Quadrant 2 or submissive-hostile salesman, a security-oriented salesman primarily concerned with survival on the job. He has a generally negative view of people, much like the Q1, but he lacks the Q1's self-confidence and forcefulness. So, instead of neutralizing the threat he feels from people by trying to control them, he backs away from them. His basic strategy is self-protective.

The Q2 is sometimes bothered by his own submissiveness; at other times he sees himself as a victim. He wants a well-ordered, predictable existence with as little tension as possible. He seeks personal survival above all else. His lack of assertiveness often carries over into his family and community life.

He regards his company as a refuge from the harsh world outside. His dealings with others in the company are cautious and somewhat remote; he seldom gets closely involved with others. He is especially careful not to attract unfavorable attention from his sales manager. On occasion, he is hostile to nonselling people in the company, blaming them for his lack of sales. He seldom strays from company procedures or policies; he does nothing to endanger his position. His reports are models of precision, but seldom very useful. As a rule, he resists training unless he is first convinced that it is not a threat to his security, but will actually enhance his security. He is often openly hostile to competition. He is seldom really happy with his job, tolerating it because it provides security. Most Q2s have relatively long job tenure as marginal producers.

The Q2 does little active prospecting. His presentations are usually lackluster and mechanical recitations of product features and advantages with little attempt to establish benefits. Some prospects buy from the Q2 because they feel sorry for him, others buy because their inventory is low, and still others buy because the product is excellent. But the Q2 is convinced that he is powerless to persuade customers to buy, and that they will buy only when they are ready to do so. His approach is more passive than active. He does a routine job of follow-up and tries to avoid personal involvement in customer complaints.

The Q2 can best be understood if it is remembered that he does not believe a salesman can "make" a sale, that he believes attempts to persuade often lead only to trouble, and that he is strongly opposed to change. Each of us, of course, has some Q2 traits, but in the Q2 these traits are enlarged.

6

The Quadrant 3 (Submissive-Warm) Salesman

"YOU CAN'T SAY NO TO A FRIEND"

We call our third imaginary salesman Sam Melville. He is 35 years old, married, but without children. He has been a life insurance salesman for a large local agency for the last ten years. Before taking this job, he was in graduate school, majoring in accounting, a field he dropped because "I'd rather do things that involve people. I decided that I'd go out of my head if I had to sit at a desk for the rest of my life and stare at rows of numbers." Sam is considered a "better-than-average producer" although he is not one of the top salesmen in the agency. A hearty, lively man, he is very much involved in organizational work as vice-president of the local Life Underwriters' Association, president of two service clubs, and a participant in numerous charity drives. Last year, he spearheaded a drive for funds to build a hospital-wing for crippled children, and was so successful that a plaque in recognition of his efforts will be placed in the new wing, which is now being built.

Once again, we will conduct fanciful interviews with three people, all of whom know Sam well: one of his customers, the owner of the insurance agency for which he works, and another salesman in the same agency. We'll ask the same questions of each man: "What's your reaction to Sam Melville? How do you see him? How does he come across to you?"

Customer: "Sam's one of the most likable people I know. In fact, I don't really think of him as a salesman . . . I consider him a friend, even though we've never been together in a social setting. Sam's one of the few salesmen I know that I really enjoy talking to. He's always very interested in me and my family . . . and very willing to go out of his way to do us favors. If Sam's got any flaws, I guess one of them is that he talks a little too much. Sometimes, he'll come over to the house at eight o'clock in the evening to talk about insurance, and he'll still be going strong at midnight. Of course, I don't pretend to know how Sam stacks up as an *insurance* man . . . insurance is a pretty technical subject, and I'm not qualified to judge Sam's expertness in the field. All I know is that he's a great guy who's really concerned about me and the wife and kids . . . and that's what *really* counts in an insurance agent."

Owner of Insurance Agency: "Sam Melville is a joy and a despair . . . all at the same time. He's a wonderful man to have around . . . willing, cooperative, helpful. The guy's attitude is absolutely great. But, at the same time, he should be selling *more* insurance. After ten years with this agency, he's nowhere near realizing his potential. If you ask me, he wastes too much time. In this business, it's a good thing to like people, but Sam goes overboard. He's *too* friendly . . . *too* involved with his clients. I know he works hard . . . and I know he puts in long hours . . . but he doesn't make half the number of calls that my top producers make. It's heart-breaking, really . . . . The man's got plenty of ability, but he spends most of his time spinning his wheels. I'm really fond of the guy . . . but he sure can be exasperating."

Fellow Salesman: "Sam's too nice for his own good. He's the only man in the agency who will turn a lead over to another salesman if he's too busy to make the call right away. He's one of the most unselfish, outgoing people I've ever met. Never argues . . . never raises his voice . . . and never acts greedy. Everyone around here loves the guy . . . although none of us really understands him. If everybody was like Sam, this would be a great world. The only trouble is, people like Sam don't make nearly as much money as the rest of us. Just look at the record: being a nice guy is wonderful . . . but it doesn't pay off."

Sam Melville is a submissive-warm (Quadrant 3) salesman, a type we examine in detail in the following pages.

A GENERAL DESCRIPTION OF THE Q3 SALESMAN

The Q3 salesman is *people-oriented*. He would, quite literally, like to be everyone's friend. He dislikes divisions between people. Status, rank, and hierarchy make him uncomfortable; they are barriers to free-and-easy companionship. He has difficulty understanding competition or anything else that divides instead of unites people. He believes nice guys do win ball games, and, when they don't, that they have more fun playing than anyone else.

The Q3 Salesman's Relationship to Himself

WHAT HE IS

The Q3 is made very uncomfortable by hostility, in himself or others. He is very eager to protect himself from coldness, anger, resentment, and aggression. He tries to be constantly agreeable, friendly, and conventional. He lacks assertiveness, not only with others but with himself. He seldom vents his own hostility, and is reluctant to recognize hostility in others.

Of course, hostility cannot be denied forever. Even the most optimistic of men must sometimes admit it exists. When the Q3 comes face to face with hostility, he usually disregards it; he laughs it off, rationalizes it, or pretends it is less severe than it really is. He seldom sees anything but the bright side; he insists the world is friendly, that people are well-intentioned and decent if one is kind to them. On rare occasions when he "blows his stack" and displays aggression, he feels guilty and remorseful.

Many people would call the Q3 naive; he calls *them* cynical. He really believes that the world is basically warm and accepting. He rarely experiences the soul-searching and doubts common to most other people; he seldom feels anxious or apprehensive. "Just wait and see," is his motto, "everything will turn out for the best."

Sometimes, however, external pressures beyond his control build up to such a degree that he does feel tense. When this happens, he usually turns his anxiety on himself and develops vague and nagging physical symptoms—headaches, unusual pains, fatigue, a general "run-down" feeling, and so on. These symptoms help channel off the tensions he is unwilling to admit, and they attract sympathy and comfort from others, reinforcing his belief that people really are warm and sympathetic. Thus, while he seldom says, "I feel tense, worried, uncertain," he sometimes says, "Something's wrong with me; I just don't feel very good lately."

The Q3 is often pleasant to have around. People think of him as extroverted, friendly, understanding, encouraging, and positive-minded. He is a happy person who communicates his happiness.

WHAT HE THINKS HE IS

In part, the Q3 deludes himself; the world is not as hospitable, nor are people as friendly, as he believes. But he believes his view is realistic and honest ("I know a lot of people are pretty pessimistic about the prospects for the human race. They're entitled to their opinion, of course, but I think they're wrong. If they were a little more outgoing and friendly themselves, they'd get a lot more friendship in response. Believe me, people are hungry for a little human kindness").

Thus, like the Q1 and Q2, the Q3 sees himself as a realist who understands truths that elude others. Nobody, it seems, no matter what his outlook, views himself as out-of-touch with reality. Everyone believes his view corresponds to the real world.

WHAT HE WOULD LIKE TO BE

The Q3 wants to be liked, to feel that he belongs. He likes selling because it enables him to be easygoing, affable, and supportive, and receive plenty of warmth in response. He extends warmth to others, and he expects warmth in return. In a way, his behavior is an insurance policy that guarantees him regular payments of kindness and goodwill.

The Q3 Salesman's Relationship to Others

PEOPLE IN GENERAL

The Q3 salesman rarely expresses hostility or assertiveness toward others, and he refuses to recognize these traits in others. He views virtually everyone as sincere, dependable, and decent. Because he trusts others and is not assertive, he is willing to become dependent upon others; he frequently relies on other people for advice and decisions. In doing so, he assures himself of a certain measure of affection; if he were to assert himself and arrive at independent decisions, he might antagonize some people, but by accepting the advice of others, he also obtains their friendship, since people generally take a warm view of those who listen to them and follow them.

Not surprisingly, the Q3 is often exploited by more dominant or more hostile types. Other people often regard him as an easy mark, a pushover.

Easygoing and eager to please, he seems to invite exploitation from more assertive but less scrupulous persons.

It is important to understand, however, that the Q3 salesman usually gets what he wants: affection. In general, he is well liked, although not always respected. His presence is usually welcomed by others, since he brings no threats or hostility with him. As a rule, he gets along very well with other people; his relationships are largely free of conflict, tension, or antagonism.

HIS RELATIONSHIP TO HIS FAMILY

The Q3 who is submissive-warm at home (and not all are) probably enjoys a pleasant, or at least placid, family life, unless he has a strong wife who takes advantage of his submissiveness. A doting father and "pal" to his children, he believes that love conquers all ("Show a kid enough love and he'll grow up all right. Kids need affection, not discipline"). He makes very few rules and is casual about enforcing them. Of course, while affection is immensely important to children, it is not a cure-all for the problems of growing up; not surprisingly, the Q3's children do have some behavior problems, as do many children. But he either fails to recognize these or finds alibis for them. "Kids will be kids," he says. "They don't need discipline, they need warmth. Believe me, it's strict parents that have kids with real problems."

His relationship with his wife is usually equally relaxed. If tensions arise, he gives in rather than argue. Other women usually think of him as a model husband, but his own wife may doubt it; his lack of assertiveness may cause her some anxiety, particularly if she is not very forceful herself.

If the Q3 marries a dominant woman, he usually permits her to assume control of the family. Occasionally, an assertive wife tries to transform her husband, at least in his job; she urges him to become more aggressive, more ambitious. To make her happy, the husband blandly promises to try to change, but never does. Why should he? After all, change might stir up antagonism in others, the one thing he especially wants to avoid. Happy as he is, he sees no reason to change.

Of course, the Q3's family life is not invariably blissful. His wife may nag, scold, and exploit his submissiveness. If she does, he is likely to withdraw to maintain peace. He becomes aloof, distant, and uncommunicative, indistinguishable from the Q2.

HIS RELATIONSHIP TO THE COMMUNITY

The Q3 salesman is frequently a willing and tireless worker in community projects ("Somebody's got to do these things. Where would the world be if we all waited for the other guy to help the community?"). Sometimes, because of his idealism and willingness to serve, he wins high office in civic organizations, where he usually assumes a moderator's role, and tries to mediate conflicting views. He seldom seeks the best solution to a problem; rather, he seeks the most popular solution. In his view, the most popular solution is also the best.

In controversies, he stands firmly in the middle. He is not a moral coward by any means, but believes the right thing to do, the thing that shows the greatest moral strength, is to refuse to take sides. He believes people's intentions are good; if given a chance, they will work things out peaceably and in the best possible spirit. There is no need, as he sees it, to throw coals on the fires of controversy; the thing to do is stand aside and let the fires burn themselves out.

The Q3 Salesman's Relationship to His Company

The Q3 salesman has strong and enduring loyalties to his company. He thinks of it as "home," a place where he can gratify his need for belongingness. After a short while with a company, he begins to think of it as "my" company. The feeling is sometimes quite personal and emotional ("Why shouldn't I feel devoted to the company? It's been good to me. I intend to be good to it. That's what makes the world go 'round").

HIS RELATIONSHIP WITH OTHER PEOPLE IN HIS COMPANY

Whenever possible, the Q3 casts his sales manager in the role of a kind, benign boss, a source of comfort, encouragement, and warmth. He willingly defers to his judgment, even when he doesn't quite believe in his wisdom ("Look, I'm no fool. I've got a mind of my own. I know the boss isn't right all the time. But I'll bend over backwards to support him. After all, the man has a hard job, and he needs strong support from everybody who works for him. If anyone's going to take issue with the boss, let it be top management. That's their job, not mine").

With his peers, the Q3 resembles a man in a popularity contest; his words and actions are designed to "gain points." He is helpful, good-natured, friendly, and encouraging; he laughs readily at their jokes, and agrees quickly with their opinions (even though he may have private reservations). He rarely thinks of himself as competing with his peers; on the contrary, he considers the whole company one big family, with everyone working together toward a common goal. One of his favorite words is *teamwork*; he likes statements like: "Life is a game, and you have to play it by the rules," or "You can't beat a team in which every man knows his position and plays it well." These may sound like cliches, but to the Q3 they are simple truth.

The Q3's relations with the rest of his company are equally unruffled. If problems arise because of an error in some other department, he is quick to excuse them. He prefers to ignore problems rather than make a stir about them ("What's the use of getting excited? We're all human, and we all make mistakes. Getting riled up doesn't do anybody any good").

HIS ATTITUDE TOWARD REGULATIONS

The Q3 regards policies and rules as a natural extension of his superior's authority. Just as he readily accepts that authority, he accepts the procedures based upon it. He seldom grumbles or complains. He finds it difficult to think of policies as abstractions separate from the people who create them; instead, he takes a personal view of his company's regulations, and feels that an attack on them is equivalent to an attack on the people who created them. Thus he neither analyzes policies, nor makes suggestions for improving them. He accepts them as a natural part of things.

Loyal and devoted to the company, the Q3 is nevertheless unable to develop a deep commitment to the idea of profit. He appreciates the need for profit, but feels that its pursuit should never get in the way of good human relations. ("If you put profits before people, you're likely to lose all around. Unhappy people can't produce high profits. But if you put people before profits, you'll wind up with happy people *and* high profits. By giving priority to people, you also give priority to earnings").

Understandably, the Q3 is sometimes careless about expenses and budgets. Not money-oriented, he finds it difficult to be practical about money. He gives little thought to budgets, but accepts them as another fact of life, something he has to live with. His spending is often random and haphazard, and he may overspend on customers in an effort to make friends of them ("I admit I'm not a fiscal wizard. But every cent I spend is well-spent. I've made a world of friends for the company by spending a few dollars on my customers").

The same lack of concern applies to reports. He fills these out without much thought. He makes no effort to withhold information, but he makes no special effort to supply it either. His approach to his job lacks system, and this shows in his reports. As he puts it: "I like the *human* aspects of this job. Paperwork drives me crazy."

HIS ATTITUDE TOWARD HIS PRODUCT

The fervor and dedication that the Q3 feels for his company extend to his product. He is loyal to whatever he sells; his enthusiasm for his product results not from analysis of its worth, but from his tendency to see everything in a favorable light. Thoroughly convinced his product is good ("The people who run this company wouldn't dream of putting out anything but a good product"), he feels no need to know a great deal about it; he is content to believe that what he sells is as good as anything else on the market. As a result, he usually knows very little about its technical details, and is not especially interested in learning more.

To make a sale, the Q3 believes it is sufficient to communicate enthusiasm rather than facts. He reasons that a customer who really likes a salesman will accept his recommendation of the product without wanting to know more about it. This belief is often expressed this way: "The customer is really buying *me*. If he knows I'm a nice, honest guy, then he knows he can depend upon the product I'm selling. In this business, you really sell *yourself*."

HIS ATTITUDE TOWARD TRAINING

The Q3 displays great enthusiasm for self-development. He often says things like: "You never get enough training. All of us have to keep on learning to keep on growing." For the most part, however, this is lip service. Although he attends training classes faithfully and participates cheerfully, he seldom learns much that changes his selling behavior. As a rule, the Q3 changes only if he feels that he must change in order to retain affection or acceptance. Unless his boss makes it clear that he will think less of him if he fails to change, the Q3 sees no reason to change. Once it becomes clear to him, however, that he risks losing his boss's esteem unless he improves his behavior, he may change somewhat. Any threat of conflict with other people is a powerful goad to the Q3 salesman.

Even under such a threat, though, he finds it difficult to become more forceful or dominant, since these are qualities he equates with hostility. Even though he hears the familiar refrain "Be aggressive, be aggressive, be aggressive" in training, he still believes that making sales has nothing to do with forcefulness. The successful salesman, he is convinced, is well liked, and the surest way to close a sale is to get people to like you. Everything else is secondary.

HIS ATTITUDE TOWARD COMPETITION

By any standards, the Q3 is not a strong competitor. The idea of competition represents qualities he fears: hostility, aggression, forcefulness, and dominance. It is hardly too much to say that he is psychologically incapable of competing. Affectionate toward everything and everybody, he even likes his competitors.

To avoid getting himself in a bind, he avoids mention of competition in his sales presentation. If the customer brings up the subject, the Q3 makes generally favorable remarks about his competition: "There's plenty of room in this world for everybody. I don't believe in being greedy, and I don't believe in knocking anyone."

He sometimes goes even further and makes a determined effort to know and socialize with his competitors. He may even boast of the number of competitive salesmen he knows personally. By being friendly with his competitors, he relieves himself of the anxiety that comes from realizing that, when all is said and done, he really is competing. His thinking goes like this: "As long as I socialize with these men, I'm not really competing with them, so I'm not really being hostile. I like them and they like me, and that's all that really counts."

JOB SATISFACTION

The Q3 likes his job. He finds it hard to imagine working for another company, or in another job. Everything is as it should be, here and now. Occasionally, he may feel unappreciated, but these feelings are typically short-lived and then repressed. By and large, he likes the way things are, and is sure that appropriate recognition will come his way if only he makes himself likable enough. He is not avid to climb the managerial ladder, although he is attracted by the idea of being in a position where he can help others. If he is promoted, he becomes a managerial "pal" to his men.

The Q3 Salesman's Relationship to His Customers

To the Q3, the customer is neither adversary nor business associate, but friend. He pictures himself as the customer's "buddy," always within reach, ready to help. His job, he believes, is to maintain this friendship; a friendly customer is certain to buy from him ("Listen, if selling was simply a matter of giving product information to the customer, they wouldn't need me. The whole job could be done by mail. The only justification for a salesman is that a salesman introduces the *human* element. That's what selling is all about"). Salesmanship is a matter of establishing long-lasting friendships; the popular salesman is successful, and the unpopular one is not.

PROSPECTING

A prospecting Q3 can be compared to a campaigning politician; he constantly strives to add new friends to his list, to spread his popularity among more and more people. In a sense, he doesn't prospect for customers; he prospects for friends who will automatically become customers by virtue of their friendship. Just as a politician refuses to discriminate among voters, since one man's vote is as good as another's, the Q3 is uncritical about his prospects. He seldom asks himself if one prospect will buy more than another, or if one prospect offers better opportunities to make a sale than another. All he wants is to increase the number of his prospects, since every prospect is a potential friend, and every friend increases his feeling of security and well-being.

As a prospector, the Q3 wastes a good deal of time and energy. Rather than focus on key decision-makers, he tries to meet and be friendly with a broad spectrum of people within a company. Most of the people with whom he speaks are not in a position to buy, and some of them are not even able to influence purchases.

His profound need to be liked thus becomes a liability as well as an asset. It is an asset because it helps him meet many bona fide prospects among the people he calls upon; it is a liability because he would make more profitable use of his time if he concentrated on significant prospects. Because his prospect list is always much longer than it should be, it threatens to become unmanageable; as a result, he usually takes a long time to convert a prospect into a customer. In a new sales job, he is usually a slow starter who builds volume in small amounts over a relatively long period ("Believe me, I'll be around long after some of these high-pressure guys are gone. I'm building relationships that *last*").

HIS PRESENTATIONS TO NEW CUSTOMERS

It is often difficult to know when the Q3 has made a sales presentation, if "sales presentation" means an explanation of product features and advantages and benefits. In a sense, the Q3 never makes this kind of presentation. What he sells is himself, and this selling job goes on all the time, in every contact with the prospect. On his initial call, the Q3 might not even refer to the product, mentioning only his company's name and letting it go at that. In a non-Q3 presentation, the salesman says, in effect: "Here is my product, here is what it can do for you, here are the reasons why you should buy it now." The good sales presentation ought to give the prospect reasons to buy by translating product information into benefits the prospect can obtain by purchasing the product. However, in a Q3 presentation, the approach is completely different. The Q3 says, in effect, "Here I am, I'm a nice guy, you like me, so naturally you're going to buy from me." The product is pushed into the background; the salesman himself is what is being sold. "If *I* am pleasant, likable, trustworthy, honest, and dependable, then," he implies, " you'll want to buy my product as a matter of course."

When the Q3 does mention his product, he does so in very general and glowing terms. He ignores details, but talks ardently about its value. His enthusiasm, always sincere and infectious, seems unbounded. But, for the most part, the product always remains secondary to the salesman.

A Q3 presentation seldom follows a planned pattern. It is usually conversational, informal, almost rambling. Topics having nothing to do with the product may be touched upon, sometimes at great length ("Let me tell you what happened on the eighteenth hole Sunday . . . "). Answers to questions and objections are offhand and casual. The entire interchange is very friendly and, from one point of view, very unbusinesslike.

The Q3 uses vague closing techniques. Or he may use no closing techniques at all. Frequently, the customer seems to buy simply because it's the friendly, decent thing to do. There may be no trial closes, no subtle attempts to find out if the prospect is ready to buy. The whole presentation ends in a relaxed way, sometimes with a firm sale or commitment, and sometimes with no real understanding of what action (if any) has been agreed on.

But the question still remains: If the prospect buys, *why* does he buy? What has happened during the "presentation" to persuade him to make a purchase? In large measure, the answer is that the prospect *does* like the salesman, and would probably feel guilty if he didn't buy. Of course, many hard-headed buyers refuse to be persuaded by the Q3's friendly manner, but many others feel that "This is a nice guy. I think I'll give him some business." Sometimes, this feeling is so strong that the prospect gives the Q3 at least part of his business even though he could buy cheaper elsewhere. Sometimes, of course, the customer buys because he has determined, on his own, that the product will deliver a net gain to him; when this happens, the customer really makes the sale to himself.

Many times, of course, the presentation ends inconclusively, with the prospect saying, "I'll think about it." When this happens, the Q3 seldom exerts pressure or becomes discouraged. Confident that he will get the order sooner or later, he continues to call upon the prospect. He feels very little anxiety about a missed sale, unless he thinks the reason he didn't make the sale is that the prospect didn't like him. In general, though, his attitude is "Why worry? After all, the prospect likes me, and that's the important thing. When he feels the time is right, he'll buy. So why push?"

A more analytic salesman would ask himself how he can close sales faster; he'd think about changing his sales strategy to increase his sales efficiency. But not the Q3. He seldom sees any need for self-analysis or criticism. Even when he fails to make a sale, he is comforted by the thought that he has made a friend ("Making sales isn't the only thing in life. And it's not the most important thing either. I'd rather lose a sale any day than lose a friend").

AFTER THE SALE

The Q3 does a good job of service and follow-through. In fact, he may "overservice" the customer without stopping to consider either the customer's real needs for service or the cost of such overservice to himself and his company. Because he is dealing with a friend as well as a customer, he goes to great lengths to assure that the sale meets all expectations. If complaints arise, he promises complete and prompt satisfaction. Then he pleads for assistance from his company in a friendly and submissive way. "Don't reject a nice guy like me," is the general burden of his request. "I need help." And, as a rule, he gets it. In this way, he avoids conflict with either company or customer.

In making repeat sales, the Q3 salesman continues the approach he used in the initial sale. He calls back often, and, in the course of a long informal conversation, he asks the customer what he needs to bring his inventory up to its proper level. He becomes an order-taker, although order taking is not the basic reason for this call; the basic reason is to visit and chat. Because he seldom gathers up-to-date facts about the customer's problems and needs, the Q3 misses opportunities to increase his volume. His conversations are seldom structured enough to enable him to uncover new business opportunities.

By and large, the Q3 cultivates customers with traits like his, with whom he gets along very well. As we'll see in detail in a later chapter, dominant-hostile prospects usually regard him as a weakling, someone to be exploited. They often make unreasonable demands upon him, perhaps for special credit terms or other preferential treatment, certain that he won't say no. The Q3, unwilling to antagonize these customers by taking a firm stand, finds it extremely difficult to resist such requests. If he gives the customer what he wants, he is likely to get into trouble with his own company; situations like these create a good deal of tension for the Q3, who wants to make *everybody* happy, but isn't always able to do so.

The Q3 gets a good amount of repeat business. Often, though, his volume climbs to a certain point and then levels off, since his haphazard time-management habits make it difficult for him to sell new accounts after a certain point. The relaxed pace of a Q3 presentation is very time-consuming, and he frequently fails to get as much business from the customer as the customer has to give.

After he is well-established, however, the Q3 does get some new business, largely through referrals from present customers. He gets referrals much more frequently than a Q1 or Q2 salesman. Referring new customers seems the "friendly" thing for a customer to do, and the Q3 builds his entire career on friendliness. Generally, he profits from these referrals less than he should; his inability to channel his time and energy, coupled with his insistence upon making as many calls on as many people as he can, makes it very difficult for him to develop these prospects in depth.

In summary, the Q3 gains and loses from his easygoing, friendly approach. His likableness brings him customers, sales, commissions, and referrals, but his need for affection results in mismanagement of his time and efforts ("I'm a man, not a machine. It seems to me that people worry too much about schedules. We'd all be better off if we relaxed a little and stopped looking at the clock all the time").

A Perspective on the Q3 Salesman

The impressions of Sam Melville with which we began this chapter should now make more sense. Sam's customer admitted that he was unable to evaluate Sam's insurance expertise, but would continue to buy from Sam anyway, a response that many customers of Q3 salesmen would make. The Q3 generates a feeling of *concern*; many customers are convinced that a salesman who *cares* about them, as the Q3 obviously does, is sure to sell them only what's good for them. Sam's boss complained that Sam's lack of system kept him from realizing his potential. This, too, is typical; many Q3s sell less than they could because they are disorganized, lacking plan, order, or direction. Sam's fellow salesman commented on Sam's selflessness, a quality that the other men in the office considered impractical. This, too, is an expected comment; most other salesmen consider the Q3 a visionary who lacks an understanding of the hard realities of life.

The typical Q3 is all of these things: a good-natured man who shows concern for others; a somewhat disorganized worker; a man who ignores or minimizes many of the hard realities that absorb the energy and attention of other salesmen. All of these characteristics will be easier to understand if the following points are kept in mind:

1. The Q3 genuinely likes people. The concern the Q3 manifests is real. There is nothing phony or contrived about the warmth he displays, though it may be inappropriate at times. The Q3 is not a cynic who pretends to like people *in order to* make sales. But he does take it for granted that people will respond to his warmth in kind, that they will "naturally" buy from him because it is "normal" to buy from people you

like. So the Q3 does expect something in return for his friendship. But it is safe to say that he would be outgoing and friendly even if *no* sale could be expected.

2. The Q3 is bored by systems. He is a poor, even sloppy, organizer because the details of organization don't interest him. If he were to spend a few solitary hours each weekend carefully planning the next week's calls, he would become bored, restive, even fretful. Why waste precious hours on dull matters, he wonders, when the same hours can be spent with *people*? He blithely assumes that everything will take care of itself if a man only has enough friends.

3. The Q3 lacks forcefulness. It is extremely difficult for him to assert himself, to make himself the *dominant* party in an interaction. It is not so much dominance itself that bothers him as the possible *reaction* by the other person to such dominance. The Q3 worries that if he asserts himself, the *other* person may resent him, and that this resentment may cause him to view the Q3 with something less than affection. From the Q3 point of view, self-assertion is too risky to be worth the effort.

4. The Q3 pays a price for his popularity. The Q3 world is pleasant, but he works hard to keep it that way. The price he pays for his popularity is that some people consider him a "pushover," a "nice guy but something of a chump." Usually unaware of this verdict, he sees himself as both liked and respected, although, in fact, the affection usually outweighs the respect. The affection is not gained without effort, but he does not really care. Important things are worth working for, and nothing is more important to the submissive-warm salesman than affection.

SUMMARY

In this chapter, we've presented a typology of the Quadrant 3 or submissive-warm salesman, a people-oriented man who is made uncomfortable by hostility in any form. He usually ignores or denies aggression, preferring to see things in a warm, positive way. On the rare occasions when he does feel hostile, he is usually assailed by guilt or develops nagging physical symptoms. He is generally regarded as extroverted, friendly, and pleasant to have around.

The Q3 believes that kindness is almost always repaid by kindness, and that the world is basically pleasant. A man who is submissive-warm at home usually enjoys a placid family life, showering plenty of affection on everyone and making few demands. In community work, the Q3 is usually tireless and enthusiastic, doing his best, if he becomes a civic leader, to moderate differences and reconcile factions.

The Q3 is very loyal to his company, even devoted. He seldom openly doubts or disagrees with his manager. He enjoys working with others, and is usually easygoing and patient. He regards policies as an extension of the authority of his superiors, and usually accepts them without question. Profit is a somewhat abstract concept to him, and one that he feels should never get in the way of good relationships with people. He displays great enthusiasm for training, but does not often change very much as a result of training. Generally, he changes only when necessary to retain affection. The Q3 is very loyal to and enthusiastic about his product, although he believes that what a salesman really sells is himself. He is an unenthusiastic competitor who prefers to be friendly rather than antagonistic to other people in the same business. Although not terribly ambitious, the Q3 does like the idea of becoming a manager because managerial power can be converted into close relationships with others.

With customers, the Q3 tries to be, more than anything, a friend. When he prospects, he feels that he is simply making new friends. Because he is eager to be friendly, he wastes a good deal of time in presentations on small talk and socializing. His presentations are typically unplanned and meandering, without focus on the product itself. There is usually no formal close. Yet Q3 presentations often end in sales, largely because the customer does like the Q3 and would feel guilty if he didn't buy. Q3s do a good job of follow-up and handling of complaints.

The Q3 usually gets quite a bit of repeat business, but his lack of time-management usually makes it difficult for him to capitalize on his opportunities beyond a certain point.

The Q3 can best be understood if it is remembered that he genuinely likes people, he is bored by systems, and he is sometimes regarded as a pushover by some people.

7

The Quadrant 4 (Dominant-Warm) Salesman

"GET 'EM COMMITTED"

Joe Emerson is a sheet-steel salesman for a large steel manufacturer. Thirty years old, married, and the father of two children, he has worked for his present employer for four years. He calls on industrial users of sheet steel in two states. Two weeks ago, Joe was promoted to sales supervisor, a job in which he will train and work with young salesmen in seven states; he will begin this new job as soon as he has introduced his replacement to all major buyers in his present territory. Joe has worked in the metal fabricating industry for eight years, since his graduation from college: he spent four of those years as a salesman and sales trainer for a manufacturer of steel tubing, and lost his job when the company merged with another. Immediately after, he was hired by his present employer.

Let us hear what three hypothetical people who know Joe well think of him. We'll ask one of his customers, his district manager, and a fellow salesman in the same district, to describe their reactions to him.

Customer (purchasing agent for a company that manufactures truck bodies): "Emerson is a good man. It's that simple. He knows his business and . . . every bit as important . . . he knows my business. He's sharp . . . savvy and hard-working. In this industry, price is tremendously important . . . yet Emerson gets the lion's share of our business, even though his prices are sometimes a little high. Why? Because, in four years, he's the only salesman I know who's never caused me a minute of grief. The guy keeps his promises . . . he follows up like a bloodhound . . . and he's always here when I need him. He's bailed us out of some real inventory jams. A purchasing agent doesn't forget things like that. I guess the words that best describe Joe are *dynamic* and *dependable*. The man never lets you down. You've *got* to buy from someone like that."

District Manager: "Joe's a pro. That's why I promoted him a couple of weeks ago. The sales supervisor's job is mainly a training job . . . and there's *nobody* I'd rather have training my men than Joe Emerson. It's not just that he's a heckuva fine salesman with a great record . . . it's more than that. Joe *demands* more of himself than most of my men. He's got high standards . . . and he lives up to them. I never have to push Joe . . . he pushes himself. I don't think he could live with himself if he didn't believe he was doing a thoroughly professional job of representing this company. He's tough, forceful, strong . . . and a tremendous competitor who very much wants to make sales. Believe me, he's going to go places in this company."

Fellow Salesman: "Joe's one of the few salesmen from whom I've ever learned anything. He's not like some of these hot-shots. Joe lends a hand . . . he lets you know *how* he makes all those sales . . . he gives you ideas and tips. Don't get me wrong . . . Joe's no show-off. But if you ask him something, he gives you a real answer. I think the difference between Joe and most of the salesmen in this district is that Joe is really interested in the rest of us . . . he really *wants* everybody to succeed. I think the company made a great decision in promoting Joe. He deserves it."

Joe Emerson is our last typological salesman: the dominant-warm salesman. In this chapter, we try to discover why he's made such a favorable impression on so many people.

A GENERAL DESCRIPTION OF THE Q4 SALESMAN

Let's begin by making it plain that the Q4 salesman is not a paragon who embodies only virtues, no faults. Far from it. Like the rest of us, he is a human being, with his full share of idiosyncrasies, quirks, and frailties. If this chapter makes him sound impossibly righteous, the fault is due to the authors' caricature.

The Q4 salesman is largely motivated by a need for self-realization and independence. Self-realization is a stuffy but nevertheless useful term that literally means *making oneself* what one can be. A person becomes what he can be, or realizes himself, by transforming his *potential* into *reality*. Each of us who changes a latent, undeveloped ability into an actual, usable skill, realizes a portion of himself in the process. We all have dormant, submerged talents; in bringing these to the surface and activating them, we realize ourselves. Far from being an unusual or mysterious process, self-realization is a common and inescapable part of being alive.

What distinguishes the Q4 from his fellow salesmen is that his need to grow, to develop, to realize himself, is more compelling, more pronounced. He wants to work at the top of his form, to be the best salesman he is capable of being today, and to become an even better salesman tomorrow. He deplores the idea of standing still ("I hate to stagnate. There's too much to do in life, too much to achieve, for anyone to stand still for very long").

The Q4 then, can best be understood as a man in the process of developing, a man who is constantly enlarging his abilities. He wants to know: "How far can I go? What are my limitations and my limits?" He never stops asking these questions because he never finds final answers. Like all growth-oriented people, he is on a lifelong quest.

The Q4 Salesman's Relationship to Himself

WHAT HE IS

The French novelist Camus wrote that "To know oneself, one should assert oneself." Or, put another way, if you want to find out who and what you really are, the best way to do so is through *doing things,* through action. The Q4 salesman proves that this idea makes sense.

Basically, of course, selling is a way of making a living. But, as we have already seen, it is more than that. To the Q1, it is a way to prove his worth and bolster his esteem; to the Q2, it is a way to build security and long-range survival; to the Q3, it is a way to obtain affection and acceptance; and, to the Q4, it is a way to develop himself beyond what he already is. The Q4 learns how good he really is by pushing himself to be the best salesman he can. Selling is *his* way to transform his potential into actuality, to realize himself. In Camus' terms, he comes to know himself by asserting himself.

The reader who thinks all this sounds a little impractical and obscure should reflect back on his own experience. He should recall the deep, abiding satisfaction he has obtained from closing a really challenging sale; he should recall the profound insight into his own capabilities that he has obtained from overcoming a really tough sales problem. Most professional salesmen have experienced, not once but numerous times, the exhilaration that comes from successfully using their full range of talents—presentational skills, organizational skills, product knowledge, competitive insight, verbal and intellectual skills—to make a "breakthrough" sale to a new customer. These are the kinds of satisfactions the Q4 seeks ("I like the thrill of opening a major account, or winning a really tough competitive battle. I'm convinced that selling is one of the most fulfilling careers anyone can have").

So the Q4 is anything but unworldly. He is assertive and energetic, an ambitious man who wants very much to succeed, to get ahead, to make all the sales he is capable of making. But his ambition is tempered by warmth, by concern for others. This concern enables him to form warm, long-lasting relationships.

One of the Q4's chief characteristics is his ability to keep cool. A decisive man, he lives with his decisions without great anxiety. He keeps his composure under stress, and usually rolls with even the hardest punches.

Equally important, he is flexible. This does not mean he is a weathervane that shifts with every changing wind. It means simply that he is able to cope with change, even to encourage and welcome it. He sees change as opportunity, not threat, as opening up possibilities of growth and advancement ("One of the reasons I chose selling as my life's work is that it gives me so many opportunities for new experiences. No two customers, no two sales calls, are ever alike. A salesman always encounters the unexpected. I couldn't stand a job where everything was the same all the time").

Finally, he is open. He deplores manipulation. He is a candid man who solicits candor from others. He accepts honest criticism without defensiveness, and welcomes unorthodox viewpoints. And he tries to keep self-deception to a minimum; he prefers to know the truth about himself and the world.

The Q4 is reasonably objective about himself; he has few outright illusions about what he is. Nobody ever sees himself with complete objectivity, of course, but the Q4 comes closer than anyone else. He admits his virtues without embarrassment, and his limitations without alibi. He evaluates himself in a factual and tough-minded way ("Look, I make no apologies for what I am. I know I've got plenty of shortcomings, plenty of weaknesses. But experience has taught me that I've got quite a few strong points, too. It seems to me that as long as a man capitalizes on his strengths and tries to overcome his weaknesses, he's doing exactly what he should do. The important thing is to realize that there's always room for growth and improvement. Anybody who thinks he's grown as much as he *can* grow ought to have his head examined").

WHAT HE WOULD LIKE TO BE

The Q4 wants to be a self-realized person. He wants to use his talents to the fullest, to go as far and as fast as his ability will take him. He seeks situations in which to prove himself, to discover how good he really is. His openness to new experiences is tempered, however, by the realization that the more he attempts, the more he risks failure. He does not expect to succeed every time, but he enjoys trying, even when he fails. And he tries to learn from his failures, to make them productive. To the Q4, striving is a synonym for living.

The Q4 Salesman's Relationship to Others

PEOPLE IN GENERAL

The Q4 salesman usually maintains excellent relationships with others. He likes being with others, and has a real interest in their welfare. Naturally, people respond to this interest, and find him easy to like.

Usually, the Q4 is relaxed and informal with others; people feel comfortable with him. In appropriate situations, he is spontaneous, high-spirited, and enjoys being the center of attention. He rarely makes people fear him; he is seldom considered a threat. He is assertive, but not in a threatening way; his assertiveness is always tempered by his warmth. He is able to exercise considerable dominance without appearing hostile; he is able to get others to follow him without arousing their fear or resentment.

The way the Q4 assumes leadership is both simple and effective. By displaying a deep and genuine respect for others, by demonstrating that he considers them important and their feelings significant, the Q4 creates in other people a desire to work with him, to cooperate with him, and to do their bit to further his ends. This is not a manipulative technique on his part; he does not pretend respect so that others will follow him. His respect is real. People respond to it because they know it is free of hypocrisy and exploitation.

Equally important, people respond to the Q4's candor and openness. They know he listens attentively to their ideas and that he weighs their judgment and thinking. But they also know he accepts only those ideas he thinks are good. The Q4 does not pretend to accept everyone's thinking in order to keep everyone on his side. His respect for others is too genuine to permit this.

HIS RELATIONSHIP TO HIS FAMILY

If the Q4 salesman is also a dominant-warm father and husband, he usually has a good relationship with his family. He guides the family, but not autocratically. Decisions are reached with the involvement of those concerned. Each has a voice in what happens, yet the father remains the "head of the family."

The Q4 is a strong person with clear-cut standards, who evokes esteem as well as affection from his family. He respects each member, and accepts each one's oddities. He is understanding and flexible when one of the family deviates from its norms. He searches to understand why the deviations occurred and he tries to help solve the underlying problem. In the constant give-and-take of the family, he is a source of strength who in turn draws strength from the family.

Before painting too idyllic a picture, however, we hasten to add that Q4 domestic life is not inevitably serene. But when trouble develops, the Q4 usually handles it better than other husbands because he is better able to communicate. The same flexibility that helps him so much in sales presentations helps him through family difficulties as well.

HIS RELATIONSHIP TO THE COMMUNITY

Not all Q4s want to be involved in community work, but those who do frequently become community leaders. Their ability to work with people is as valuable in civic life as in selling. Those dominant-warm salesmen who take part in community activities usually do so because they want additional opportunities to grow. Many relish the idea of testing their skills on a different stage than the one provided by their jobs ("I'm

always intrigued by the idea of trying something new, something different from what I do most of the time. It's always exciting to discover a
talent you didn't know you had").

The Q4 Salesman's Relationship to His Company

The Q4 believes his personal growth is closely related to his company's.
His company's success is important to him. Without it, he realizes, his
own opportunities to succeed will be minimized. For this reason, he
eagerly utilizes the talents of everyone in the company; he understands
that total organizational effectiveness contributes to his own effectiveness.
To use a hackneyed but still meaningful phrase, he is a team player
("Look, I'm a human being, not Superman. I give help but I also *need*
help. Any salesman who thinks he can succeed entirely on his own is
fooling himself. Every successful salesman gets plenty of help from lots of
people, only some of them won't admit it. I'm not bashful about these
things; I *ask* for assistance and advice, just as I try to give it when other
people ask it of me").

HIS RELATIONSHIP WITH OTHER PEOPLE IN HIS COMPANY

The Q4 realizes that no organization can function without hierarchy;
there must be superiors and subordinates, lines of authority, and clearly
defined responsibility in any company. Somebody must issue policies,
and somebody must implement policies. But he does not follow other
people's thinking slavishly. He works best when he takes part in developing solutions to problems that affect his sales efforts. He wants to contribute to management's effectiveness.

Because he wants to become a better salesman, he welcomes critique
from his supervisors. He seldom resents suggestions about better ways to
do things. He likes to work with managers who talk things out with him,
rather than managers who gloss over problems. He prefers to face up
to difficulties rather than ignore them ("I learned long ago that every
time you bury a problem it returns to haunt you. And sometimes it haunts
you even worse than it did before it was buried. Believe me, I'd much
rather *settle* problems as they arise").

The Q4 is a realist who knows that supervisors must sometimes exercise authority on their own, without admitting him to their counsels.
He goes along with such exercise of authority if it is based on solid
knowledge and experience. But he dislikes authority exercised without
sufficient background, just as he dislikes authority exercised for its own

sake. If his manager makes demands the Q4 considers unrealistic or unnecessary, the Q4 tells his manager what he thinks. If he cannot modify the demands, he follows them to the best of his ability. But if the situation continues, and no change can be expected, he may eventually quit the organization or transfer to another manager. He is willing to go along with the autocratic exercise of authority on occasion, but not to subject himself to a constant flow of one-sided and unrealistic orders. Such authority stifles growth, and the Q4 is too concerned with growth to remain long in a situation where it is not possible ("I don't want a job where my manager does all my thinking for me. I refuse to be a puppet. If a manager's looking for a rubber-stamp, he'd better not look in my direction").

The Q4 maintains good relationships with his fellow salesmen. He values smooth personal relationships, but does not place them ahead of everything else. His chief concern is with his own and his company's progress. If he can further that progress while maintaining good personal ties with his associates, well and good. But he values performance higher than popularity, and respect higher than affection. He would rather be admired for what he achieves than be well liked ("I'm not willing to step on other people in order to get ahead. I don't want to succeed if somebody else has to get hurt. But sometimes you've got to take an unpopular or even a hard-nosed stand, for your own good and the company's good. I'm willing to do that, if I think it's right. That's the only way I can maintain my self-respect").

His relationships with other departments of the company are generally businesslike. He knows these departments are vital to his success; he respects them and expects them to do a good job. If they falter, he suggests methods of improvement, but without fault-finding and blaming.

HIS ATTITUDE TOWARD REGULATIONS

Once again, the Q4's attitude is practical. No business can operate without procedures, rules, and policies; he accepts these as facts of life, and does his best to follow them. But he does not follow blindly. He looks hard at his company's policies, and suggests alternatives to those which he thinks hamper his sales efforts. If he criticizes a policy, he tries to keep two guidelines in mind: first, don't criticize without suggesting alternatives, and, second, do your best to implement the policies anyway, since the only other course is chaos.

The Q4 respects reports. Management must have information to function, a fact he well understands. So he tries to provide sound information, and to make his reports prompt, clear, and complete. He often volunteers information not specifically requested: observations, opinions, suggestions. He knows he is a vital link in providing firsthand information about product acceptance, pricing trends, and competitive activity in his area. Since his position is unique and since management depends upon his knowledge, he tries to furnish as much information as he considers important.

The Q4 invests a good deal of time and energy in his reports, and he expects some return from management. He wants to know how they react to the information he supplies, and that the information is being used. He keeps his company informed, and he expects it to keep him informed ("Communication is a two-way process. You can't expect a guy to file detailed reports month after month if, for all he knows, they're going straight into the wastebasket").

HIS ATTITUDE TOWARD HIS PRODUCT

The Q4 knows he can make sales only if he understands his product. He does not try to sell by coercing his customers or gaining their affection. So his best hope is to make benefit-proving presentations based upon sound product knowledge. For this reason, he works hard to keep his knowledge at a high level. He sees his product realistically, as it is, not as he would like it to be.

When the Q4 believes his product is good, his enthusiasm carries over into his presentations. If he is not convinced his product is good, he may suggest changes in it, or he may leave the company. He never cons himself into believing that a good salesman can sell even a bad product, nor does he pretend to be enthusiastic if there is nothing to be enthusiastic about. He has too much pride to deceive either his customers or himself ("Let's just say that I'm not willing to make a sale unless it will do the customer some good. As I see it, my job is to produce a benefit and a net gain for everybody . . . the customer, my company, and me. If any one of us suffers as a result of the sale, then I haven't done my job").

HIS ATTITUDE TOWARD TRAINING

The Q4 is enthusiastic about training. He participates in all the training his company provides, and, if he thinks it necessary, even seeks training outside his company. He approaches most training critically; he expects it to be good. When it isn't, he feels his time and effort have been wasted, that he has been cheated. He wholeheartedly supports training programs, and he expects the same support from the people who run them ("I don't have much respect for second-rate training programs. When I go into a training program, I'm looking for training that will make me a better salesman, not a vacation from the field'').

The Q4 takes competition in stride. He realizes it is here to stay, that wishful thinking will not make it disappear, and that it is something he must live with. He does his best to outwork and outsell competitors.

This is not to say he is casual or unconcerned about competitors. He views them with utmost seriousness. He learns as much about them, their products, and their selling strategies as he can. And he constantly compares their products and strategies with his, so he can develop good competitive presentations.

Sometimes, he actually refuses to sell against competition. When it is clear that a customer will be considerably better off if he buys a competitive product, the Q4 may not try to sell his own. He understands that, in the long run, a salesman sometimes profits most by *not* making a sale.

The Q4 salesman gets deep satisfaction from his job: money, variety, stimulation, the knowledge that he fulfills customers' needs and contributes to his company's growth, and the knowledge that he performs an important role in the economy. If his company allows him to use his own sales strategies effectively, and if he feels he is growing on his job, he is a very loyal worker.

He may display low morale or dissatisfaction, however, if the organizational climate is not congenial to his strategy, if he feels thwarted or unable to progress. If this happens, he usually gets out of the company as rapidly as possible, and moves into one where he can find scope for his talents and opportunity for self-fulfillment ("Some years ago, when I was getting started in selling, I worked for a company that insisted that you *always* try to close on the first call, and that you *never* call back. I don't believe in operating that way. After a few months of frustration and argument, I left the company. It was a pretty depressing experience while it lasted").

The Q4 Salesman's Relationship to His Customers

Keeping in mind the Q4 salesman's two basic traits, dominance and warmth, we can easily understand how he successfully adapts his behavior to his customers. With either customers or prospects, he is forceful and direct; he leads and advises; he controls the sales interview through sound communication skills rather than coercion. He is competitive, sensitive, and responsive to the customer's needs. At the same time, he feels genuine concern for the customer. He wants the sale to benefit both the customer and himself (and, through himself, his company).

PROSPECTING

The Q4 consistently searches for new prospects. As a rule, he enjoys prospecting; sizing up the market and determining who his best prospects are makes him feel that he is master of his own fate ("That's one of the things I like about selling. In the final analysis, you're thrown on your own resources. You're responsible for picking your own prospects . . . for doing your own thinking. If you end up with a bunch of fourth-rate prospects, you've got nobody to blame but yourself").

He is a systematic and methodical prospector who wastes as little time as possible on people who are not in a position to buy. He evaluates potential prospects carefully, determines whether or not a need for his product might exist, and then arranges a call during which the prospect is further qualified, and, if possible, sold.

The Q4 often uses ingenious prospecting techniques. He may send out promotional pamphlets or institutional brochures before his first call; he may send letters designed to whet the prospect's curiosity for more information; he may even send out promotional "teasers" that relate to his product. Whenever possible, he tries to do two things in his initial call: find out if the prospect is in a position to buy, and, if he is, start to sell him ("I research my prospects carefully. But I'm a salesman, not a researcher, so I always try to go *beyond* qualifying the prospect to *selling* him. You can't always do this on a first call, but when you can, you should").

HIS PRESENTATIONS TO NEW CUSTOMERS

As a result of careful planning and spadework, the Q4 usually has little trouble arranging his initial call. Generally, he makes a strong first impression. Most customers admire his combined assertiveness and warmth. They are impressed by his no-nonsense attitude, his knowledge, and his interest in them. They usually recognize very early that he is a man who may be able to help them, and is therefore worth listening to.

After the *appropriate* social remarks, the Q4 begins the interview by explaining why he is there and what benefit he thinks the customer will get from the presentation. He wastes little or no time on joke-telling, pleasantries, or small talk. He makes it plain that he is a businessman who is aware of the value of time. (It should be pointed out that he varies his approach with Quadrant 3, submissive-warm, customers, who obviously *want* to socialize; with these customers, his opening is more casual, and may include a lengthier and more relaxed exchange of pleasantries. But even with Q3 customers he maintains a clear orientation toward the goal of closing the sale.) The prospect quickly realizes that the salesman is well-organized, confident, and knows his product. Most important, the customer quickly realizes this man talks his own language.

The entire presentation carries conviction; the Q4 obviously believes what he says. And the presentation is flexible; the Q4 is tuned in to the customer's feelings and needs, and adapts his strategy to these feelings and needs as he goes along. His success is largely based upon his sensitivity to his impact upon the customer; he is constantly alert to clues which indicate whether he is getting through.

A Q4 presentation is never a monologue, because a real meeting of minds is seldom achieved when one man does the talking. As the Q4 talks, he encourages questions, comments, even objections. He tries to keep the customer involved, so that he can size up his reactions and get feedback on his own performance. The customer appreciates this approach; he feels he is being talked *with*, not *at*.

Another advantage of involving the customer in the presentation is that the salesman can better estimate, before the presentation draws to a close, if a sale is going to be made. The Q4 is skillful at predicting the outcome of presentations. He knows that if he and the customer really understand one another, if he has correctly analyzed the customer's needs, and if he has persuasively shown how his product or service will fill these needs, a sale will almost surely result ("There's no mystery about why people buy. They buy because they think their purchase will make them better off in some way. If I've proven that a customer will be better off by buying from me, why *shouldn't* he buy?").

Of course a customer sometimes feels he needs more data or more time to think before he reaches a decision. When this happens, the Q4 summarizes his presentation, states clearly what both he and the customer need to do to arrive at a final decision, and sets a date for his callback. He leaves nothing to chance.

To the Q4, a sale is not a win–lose struggle, but a joint-venture between his customer and himself and his company in which everybody wins ("I never think of selling in terms of victory and defeat, just in terms of victory. Believe me, I've had plenty of experience, and I *know* that a good sale benefits everybody").

AFTER THE SALE

To the Q4, there are three critical elements in successful selling: intelligent prospecting, skillful presentations, and determined follow-up after the sale. He works hard to make sure the commitments he made during the sale are carried out. He calls back personally or by phone to learn whether the customer is satisfied with his purchase. He deals with complaints candidly and honestly. He tries to find out what really went wrong and how it can be corrected, looking for solutions that are mutually beneficial to customer and company.

This kind of follow-up results in repeat sales and steadily increasing volume. After his first few years on the job, the Q4 has a large and loyal group of customers who stick with him because they know he is good for them. As might be expected, the Q4 easily obtains referrals from present customers.

To summarize: The Q4 is assertive enough to control and guide presentations in the direction he wants them to go; at the same time, he is concerned enough about his customers to provide them with real benefits.

A Perspective on the Q4 Salesman

Let's go back to the comments about Joe Emerson at the beginning of the chapter. We can see now that his customer's description of Joe as a man who "knows my business," who is "dependable," and who is "sharp . . . savvy . . . and hard-working" applies to any Q4 salesman. Q4s are typically knowledgeable and insightful about their customer's business; this is the basis of their problem-solving skill. Q4s are typically dependable, working as hard *after* the sale as during the sale. And they are typically sharp and hard-working; their success is not a matter of luck, but of *diligently applied know-how.*

Similarly, we can see now that Joe's district manager was describing not only Joe, but all Q4s. His description of Joe as a man who "demands more of himself," who "has high standards and lives up to them," who "couldn't live with himself if he didn't believe he was doing a thoroughly professional job" describes all salesmen bent on self-realization. The Q4 pushes himself to become something more than he already is, to achieve higher and harder goals. And, when Joe's manager described him as "tough, forceful, strong . . . and a tremendous competitor," his description again applied to Q4s in general. In selling situations, the Q4 is an assertive leader who knows where he wants to go and how to get there, and a scrappy competitor who takes great delight in making sales.

The remarks by Joe's fellow-salesman are also pertinent to Q4s in general. His conviction that Joe is "really interested" is the way all kinds of people—fellow salesmen, managers, and customers—feel about the Q4. Q4 salesmen convey genuine concern. They come across as *intelligently* interested people who can translate their concern into help.

Once again, we urge the reader to remember that the Q4—Joe Emerson or any other—is no paragon. He is a human being with human shortcomings. If we have stressed his strengths in this chapter, that is because his strengths help us to understand his success, and it is his success that most interests us. The following points about the Q4 should be kept in mind.

1. The Q4 assumes people are both self-interested and well-meaning. We made this point in an earlier chapter; its importance cannot be overstressed. Believing that customers are self-interested, the Q4 knows that any successful sales presentation must appeal to this self-interest: this means he must talk not about himself or his product, but about what he and the product can do *for* the customer. The customer must be the pivot of the presentation, the pin on which everything else turns. But, because he believes the customer is well-meaning enough to buy if the product fits his needs, he doesn't feel he has to coerce the customer. The Q4 begins every presentation with the assumption that he and the customer want the same thing: mutual benefit ("Let's put it this way: I start out with the assumption that the customer wants to help himself, and that he has no desire to hurt me. If the sale makes me, the customer, and my company better off, that's fine with the customer, and it's certainly fine with me. I never assume that the customer and I are natural enemies").

2. The Q4 refuses to view people mechanically. He sees customers as differing from one another, and tries to adapt his presentations and his strategy to their particular needs. He knows that an approach that works with one customer may not work with another, that it is up to him to understand the customer and to tailor his approach to fit. To the Q4, there is no such creature as "the" customer; there are only separate, singular, unique customers. There are often detectable similarities between certain customers (we'll describe these in detail in a later chapter), but these similarities cannot be taken for granted before the presentation; they must be discovered in face-to-face interaction during the presentation. The Q4 never forgets he is selling to people, not to abstractions.

3. The Q4 is practical. Critics of Q4 behavior, mostly Q1s, often accuse him of being a soft-headed visionary, an impractical dreamer who does not see the world as it really is. Nothing could be further from the truth. The Q4 is *pragmatic,* basing his behavior not on dogma but on his own *experience.* He is *practical,* deeply concerned about sales, about commissions, about profits. And he is *realistic,* taking people as they are, not as he would like them to be. Q4 behavior is not the result of ivory-tower speculation, but of daily, down-to-earth grappling with the hard facts of selling. Anyone who doubts this need only look at the Q4's sales record.

SUMMARY

In this chapter, we presented a typology of the Quadrant 4 or dominant-warm salesman, a growth-oriented salesman seeking self-realization. His interest is in steady improvement, in becoming a better salesman than he is. He likes selling because of the chance it provides for satisfaction of his ambition and development of his skills. The Q4 is assertive, energetic, and ambitious, but also warm and concerned about others. He is flexible, able to cope with change, and open to criticism and feedback.

The Q4 is relatively free of illusions about himself. He admits both his weaknesses and his strengths. In family situations dominant-warm men guide their families democratically yet with authority. Q4s often seek roles in civic affairs so they can use their skills on a wider stage.

As a salesman, the Q4 has a strong sense of himself as a member of a team, who willingly gives help and asks for it. He respects the management of his company, but does not follow it slavishly. He wants to take part in developing solutions to problems that affect his sales efforts. He dislikes one-sided, arbitrary exercise of power. With his fellow salesmen, he maintains good ties, but is more concerned with earning their respect than their affection. He has stable, businesslike relationships with other departments in the company.

The Q4 does his best to follow his company's policies and procedures, but not blindly. He criticizes these when he feels he should, and suggests alternatives. He files detailed and informative reports on conditions in the field, seeing himself as a key source of marketing information. He understands the importance of profit, and works hard to maximize it.

The Q4 is enthusiastic about training, and seeks all he can get. He has solid product knowledge, and seldom stays long in a job where he is not able to sell the product with conviction. His attitude toward competition is realistic; he knows it is here to stay, and he does his best to outsell it, except when he believes a prospect will be considerably better off by buying from competition.

Deeply satisfied with his job, the Q4 is a loyal and long-lasting employee, except in those cases where his selling philosophy clashes with his company's, or where he is stymied in his efforts to grow. If either of these things happens, he usually goes to work somewhere else.

In presentations, the Q4 is forceful and direct, but also concerned and responsive. He is a diligent prospector who thoroughly studies and qualifies prospects. His openings are usually impressively businesslike, with, as a rule, little time spent on socializing. He is well-organized, knowledgeable, and confident. His presentations carry conviction; they are marked by sensitivity to the customer's needs and willingness to adapt to those needs. The Q4 tries to make each presentation a dialogue, a two-way communication in which the prospect is encouraged to speak and contribute. If he is unable to close, the Q4 sets up a call-back appointment to pursue the matter further. Throughout, he is methodical and systematic. After the sale, he provides conscientious follow-up.

The Q4 defines a good sale as one from which his customer, his company, and he all benefit. He tries to make every sale lead to mutual gain. To do this, he starts with the assumption that his customers are both self-interested and well-meaning, he refuses to view them mechanically, and he tries to be practical and result-oriented.

TABLE 1. How Salesmen Relate to Themselves and Other People

	Q1	Q2	Q3	Q4
Relationship to self	Largely unaware that other people see him as manipulative and overbearing; has strong need to be on top, where he can enhance his self-esteem and assert his independence; fearful of any signs of personal weakness or failure; sees self as forceful leader in a world comprised largely of submissive followers	Considers self realist whose bleak outlook is justified by the facts; but he is sometimes defensive about his submissiveness; his lack of forcefulness sometimes bothers him; seeks well-ordered, predictable existence; greatest concern is with endurance in a threatening world	Tries to ignore hostility in self and others by laughing it off, rationalizing it, or minimizing it; persists in believing that world is basically warm and accepting, and that things are sure to work out right in the end	Flexible, open, growth-oriented; objective about self; able to admit weaknesses and accept strengths; wants to use talents to go as far and as fast as he can; but his ambition is tempered by his concern and respect for others
Relationship to others	Frequently insensitive to others' needs and feelings; often clashes with other forceful people; gets along best with docile people; with people who are assertive, he is usually shrewd and manipulative; with those who are submissive, he is aggressive and overbearing; many of his relationships marked by tension and muted antagonism	Often looks down on others, and is regarded as cold; generally aloof, uncommunicative, distant; has few close friends; these usually reflect his own outlook; is especially careful not to get involved with aggressive people; cannot understand people who manifest deep concern for others; basically a "loner"	Views everyone as sincere, dependable, decent; very willing to trust and rely upon others; sometimes exploited by more aggressive people, who regard him as pushover; generally well-liked, but not always highly respected	Good relationships with others; rarely appears as threat to others, yet is assertive and forceful; exercises dominance without seeming hostile; displays candor and respect for other people's ideas; refuses to manipulate or exploit

99

TABLE 2. How Salesmen Relate to Their Companies

	Q1	Q2	Q3	Q4
Relationship to others in company	Disdains "company spirit" and "team effort;" sees superiors as obstacles to be hurdled; interacts manipulatively with them; sees his peers as competitors; relates to them in dog-eat-dog manner, or lives with them in uneasy truce	Regards his company as a haven from outside forces, a safe port in a stormy world; he "plays it safe" with others in the company, especially his sales manager, with whom he prefers to have little to do; tries to stay on fringes and attract little attention	Has strong company loyalty; sees most people as benign and helpful; often resembles man in a popularity contest, friendly, good-natured, encouraging; considers company "big happy family;" always cooperative, rarely competitive	Understands his role in the organization, and the organization's importance to him; relates to others reciprocally, trying to develop effective and mutual working relationships; gives all he's got and expects others to do same
Attitude toward regulations	Resents rules and regulations as stumbling blocks to his success; dislikes restraints of any kind; often tries to circumvent bothersome policies; very poor at preparing and filing reports; detests paperwork	Sticks very close to rules; well-defined guidelines make him feel secure and give him handy "I did it the way I was supposed to" alibi when things go wrong	Accepts rules without complaint, never deliberately breaks them; but he is generally loose and unstructured in his approach to things; considers warm human relationships far more important than abstract rules	Accepts rules and policies as facts of life but refuses to follow them blindly; criticizes and suggests alternatives when appropriate; respects need for good reports
Attitude toward training	Believes training is for inferior salesmen, not for him; cocky about his sales ability and fearful of learning something that might shatter his self-esteem; resists training unless he is convinced it will help him to more money and success	Resists self-development; prefers not to change; goes through motions of training but rarely gets involved; benefits from training only if he understands that it will enhance his security	Pays enthusiastic lip service to training; participates cheerfully but seldom learns much that changes his behavior; usually changes only if it will help him retain affection and acceptance	Enthusiastic about training; expects good training programs; accepts critiques readily and tries to effect changes on basis of what he's learned

TABLE 2 (Continued)

	Q1	Q2	Q3	Q4
Attitude toward competition	Eager, aggressive competitor; relishes opportunity to defeat other salesmen; fights competitors hard, using every available weapon; often bends facts and exaggerates claims in effort to beat down competition	Disparages competition; works off aggressiveness that he fears to display otherwise by telling customers of competitors' faults	Weak competitor; thinks well even of competitive salesmen; believes there's "room for everybody;" sometimes socializes with competitors; strongly dislikes idea of "beating" competition	Takes competition in stride; does his best to outwork and outsell competitors; studies competitive products and keeps abreast of competitive activity
Job satisfaction	Seldom deeply satisfied; usually wants to become manager and move up ladder quickly; constantly seeks more money and power, even if it means moving from company to company	Seldom happy with his job; has little zest for selling; tolerates his job because it provides security, not because he likes it	Likes his job; is not eager to climb managerial ladder, although he likes idea of being promoted to job where he can help others; generally contented	Gets deep satisfaction from job, as long as he feels he is growing; morale sags if he feels thwarted in his progress, and he may then leave the company

8

Secondary Sales
Strategies and
Sales Masks

THINGS AREN'T ALWAYS WHAT THEY SEEM TO BE

We made the point earlier that people behave consistently *over a period of time*. But, of course, not invariably; a Bob Hawthorne isn't hard-driving and overpowering *all* the time, and a Sam Melville isn't *always* good-natured and affable. Each of us, in fact, is a mixture of characteristics from all four quadrants. In this chapter, we explore the seeming *inconsistencies* in behavior, and show that they, too, can be understood by means of the Dimensional model. We shall see that inconsistent behavior is neither random nor impossible to explain, but understandable and frequently predictable by use of behavioral science principles.

PRIMARY STRATEGIES

Up to now, we described *primary strategies*, those most basic to each type of salesman. A primary strategy is the one a salesman (or anyone else) uses most often; it is his most frequent and fundamental behavior. When we say a salesman is Q2 or submissive-hostile, we mean the submissive-hostile strategy is his most characteristic strategy, the one that best describes him. There is nothing short-lived or temporary about a primary strategy; it is the one a man typically uses day in and day out, the strategy from which he may occasionally stray but to which he typically comes back. Primary behavior is a man's *principal* and most frequent behavior.

Variations in Behavior

In our typologies, we described each primary strategy in its purest, or most intense, form. But we emphasized that real behavior rarely resembles our descriptions in every respect or at least not continuously. Most people, as we've said, exhibit behavior that's a mixture of traits from all four quadrants. There are five reasons why selling behavior is rarely found in the pure, undiluted form we described. We will list these, and then look at them in detail.

1. A given bit of any salesman's behavior (a specific interaction between himself and another person) can be located at any point in any quadrant, and there are an infinite number of these points, each indicating a different intensity and quality of behavior, within each quadrant.

2. Behavior is often related to situations and to other people in these situations, and situations and people vary.

3. Salesmen may shift to secondary strategies, which are automatic or unconscious reactions to frustration or pressure.

4. Salesmen may shift to mask strategies, which are deliberate or conscious reactions to frustration or pressure.

5. Secondary strategies may become quasipermanent.

1. *A given bit of any salesman's behavior can be located at any point in any quadrant, and there are an infinite number of these points, each indicating a different intensity of behavior, within each quadrant.*

The Dimensional model is one on which coordinates are plotted graphically (admittedly with some imprecision). The coordinates signify the point at which any salesman's behavior is measured on either the dominance-submission or hostility-warmth dimensions. In our typologies, we have deliberately described salesmen with very high dominance or very high submission and very high hostility or very high warmth. But there are other possibilities. A salesman may have high dominance but only moderate warmth; his coordinates would intersect at a point in the fourth quadrant some distance from the point occupied by the salesman in our extreme Q4 typology.

Thus, in any quadrant, the *intensity* of any given bit of a salesman's behavior may vary somewhat from that of any other salesman. A Q2 salesman with a great deal of hostility and submissiveness is likely to be quite withdrawn, remote, and greatly concerned about job security; a Q2 with only moderate hostility and submissiveness is likely to be less aloof, not nearly so detached or anxious about job security. The first Q2 salesman would probably be considerably less effective than the second; he might be unable to function at all in certain selling jobs that the latter would handle at least adequately. So the *intensity* of a salesman's behavior is of real significance.

To make this point less abstract, let's imagine that Sam Melville, our prototype of the Q3 salesman, has a colleague who works out of the same district office, who can also be described as having a submissive-warm primary strategy. We'll call this second salesman Chuck Clemens. Let's see how Sam and Chuck compare.

Both are very *warm* people, ranking high on the warmth dimension. But Chuck is considerably less *submissive* than Sam. As a result, where Sam almost never examines customers' objections (he is afraid he will antagonize the customer), Chuck at least tries, on most occasions, to analyze objections, at least slightly. Where Sam almost invariably accepts customers' objections and then quickly changes the subject, Chuck makes some attempt to respond to them. In fact, in every part of the sales presentation, Chuck is a bit less submissive and therefore somewhat more assertive, somewhat more forceful. Not surprisingly, he manages to close a few sales that would prove too demanding for Sam; his sales record is somewhat better.

Both Sam and Chuck are clearly recognizable as Q3s. But they are not identical. If their primary strategies were plotted on the Dimensional model, each would be coordinated at a different point in the third quadrant. Here's how the graphs might look:

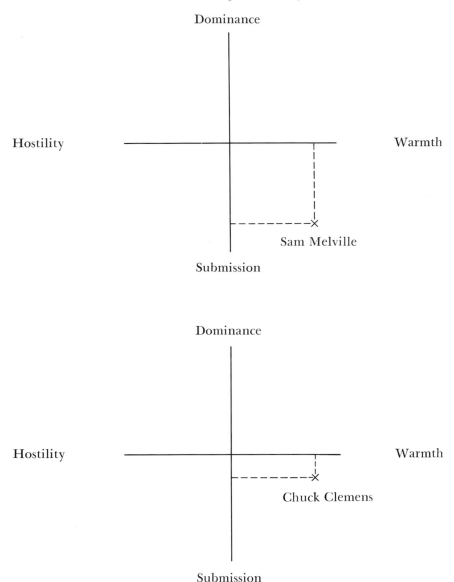

Now, the crucial point is this: theoretically, *every* Q3 salesman's traits could coordinate at a different point on the model. A third Q3 salesman might be *less* submissive than both Sam and Chuck, but somewhat warmer than either. A fourth might be both less warm and less submissive. And so on. *Similarity* in behavior never implies *identity* in behavior.

2. *Behavior is often related to situations and people in those situations, and situations and people vary.*

Let's assume that two salesmen do have identical amounts of submissiveness and warmth in their behavior (a most implausible assumption). Even then, their behavior would differ, since each would function in different situations. A Q3 who calls on a restrained, somewhat sullen customer behaves differently than a Q3 making a presentation to a man like himself, hearty, amiable, and sociable. In each instance, the situation molds the behavior (just as the behavior molds the situation).

Even an individual salesman's behavior varies from situation to situation. Our outgoing Q3 is considerably less hearty when making a call on a gloomy, sarcastic prospect than when calling on a warm, receptive customer.

The point, as we shall see repeatedly, is that it is not very meaningful to talk about behavior without considering the situation in which it occurs. Since situations are rarely if ever identical, behavior always fluctuates.

3. *Salesmen may shift to secondary strategies when frustrated.*

Sometimes a salesman's primary strategy fails to produce the result he wants, and he may become frustrated. In psychological terms, frustration is the dissatisfaction and tension a person feels when he is blocked from achieving a goal; the frustrated person feels hostile, uncomfortable, anxious, or uneasy, and tries in some way to overcome the obstacle keeping him from his goal. Sometimes, he does this by temporarily and automatically shifting his behavior; this happens without thought or premeditation. Such an automatic, unconscious shift in behavior to overcome frustration is known as a *secondary* strategy. Secondary strategies are usually short-lived and temporary, unlike primary strategies, which recur day-in and day-out. And secondary strategies are invariably spontaneous, involuntary, and without deliberation; they are not planned or contrived.

A secondary strategy, then, is an unintentional reaction to frustration. A salesman simply finds his basic strategy not getting him anywhere, and, without really thinking about it, he suddenly and automatically changes his behavior. We'll discuss these reactions in detail later in this chapter.

4. *Salesmen may deliberately shift to mask strategies.*

A mask strategy is a conscious and deliberate response to external pressures. When a salesman dons a mask, he intentionally tries to disguise or hide his primary behavior. A mask is worn to make someone think that the wearer of the mask is not the kind of person he seems to be. An over-bearing Q1 may find his manner causes a prospect to "freeze up" during the presentation; to overcome this situation, he may assume a Q3 ("I'm a nice, easygoing guy, and there's no need to be afraid of me") mask. A mask, like a secondary strategy, is a *temporary* form of behavior; when the mask has served its purpose, the salesman typically reverts to his primary strategy.

We examine masks in detail later in this chapter.

5. *Secondary strategies may become quasipermanent.*

Occasionally, a secondary strategy, adopted in frustration, becomes quasi-permanent because the frustration itself becomes permanent, or at least very long-lasting. Here's an example: Salesman Jones, in his late forties, whose primary strategy is dominant-hostile, has been aspiring to the sales vice president's job for many years. To everyone's surprise, when the position finally becomes vacant through retirement, Smith, in his late thirties, is brought in to fill it from another company. Jones is passed over for the job he has yearned for, a deep blow to his pride and his self-image. In frustration, he shifts to a secondary strategy; without planning it, he goes from his typical hard-driving behavior to quiet, withdrawn behavior. Those who have known him for years predict that "He'll be his old self again as soon as he gets over the shock." But, as it becomes evident to him that his situation is hopeless, that he is too old to quit and get a job somewhere else, that he has no chance of displacing Smith, who is doing an outstanding job, that he will, in brief, never become the sales vice president, his aloof, subdued behavior becomes fairly typical. Rarely does he display his old drive and aggressiveness; for the most part, he seems resigned and apathetic. As an old acquaintance puts it, "The fire seems to have gone out." In behavioral science terms, we would say that his secondary Q2 strategy has, in the face of continued and unalter-able frustration, become quasipermanent. A Q1 salesman has shifted to a Q2 strategy not through planning or contrivance, but through an auto-matic response to a highly unsettling situation.

Such responses are fairly common among people trapped in highly frustrating no-exit situations. By becoming more or less resigned, by refusing to batter their heads against brick walls, they diminish, if not eliminate, the great discomfort they feel.

The foregoing, then, are five reasons why behavior is never as pat or as stereotyped as our earlier chapters made it seem. Every salesman has a primary strategy, and this strategy makes his behavior generally consistent over a sustained period of time. But, on any given day, any salesman may vary his behavior in response to varying situations, shift to a secondary strategy when frustrated, or don a mask in an effort to relieve pressure. This explains why pushy Bob Hawthorne sometimes seems uncharacteristically relaxed and submissive, why quiet Steve Whittier sometimes surprises those who know him by a burst of self-assertion, why friendly Sam Melville occasionally loses his temper, and why determined Joe Emerson sometimes gives up during a presentation and lets a tough customer have his way. If we understand the situational nature of behavior, secondary strategies, and mask strategies, we can easily understand why our language has phrases like: "He doesn't seem to be himself today," and "He suddenly seems like a different person."

RECOGNIZING SECONDARY AND MASK STRATEGIES

It is often difficult to distinguish between secondary and mask strategies in real life. Unless the observer knows the person he is observing very well, he has little chance to determine whether a shift in behavior is automatic or planned, although he can sometimes make a good guess. Practically speaking, it is not always crucial to distinguish between secondary and mask behavior; the important thing is that the reader understand the mechanisms underlying behavioral shifts, especially his own. These shifts almost always indicate frustration or pressure; the person making the shift responds to discomfort, uneasiness, anxiety, or the simple feeling of getting nowhere. As long as a primary strategy produces the desired results, there is little impetus, conscious or unconscious, to change it.

Examples of Some Typical Variations in Strategy

Before we examine secondary and mask strategies more closely, let's look at some typical variations within each primary strategy. These will help us understand where certain salesmen who do not correspond to our typologies fit into the Dimensional model.

THE COERCIVE Q1 VERSUS THE INTELLECTUAL Q1.

In his most extreme form, the coercive Q1 salesman depends upon raw, blatant strength to get results. The message he conveys to customers (not in so many words, but by his overall behavior) is this: "Look, I intend to leave here with an order, and I'll be just as rough-and-tumble as I have to be to get it. Understand clearly, I'm not going to take no for an answer." He is a bully who relies heavily on intimidation and compulsion (he can't actually compel a customer to buy, but he can and does create an atmosphere in which the customer *feels* compelled to buy). If he thinks he can get away with it, he badgers and browbeats the customer, using words as verbal cudgels to beat down resistance. This is bare-knuckles selling, completely devoid of subtlety. Of course, very few Q1s are this coercive, but many, to one degree or another, are pretty uninhibited in the way they use their strength.

The intellectual Q1, on the other hand, is much more subtle. He overwhelms customers by a steady display of mental gymnastics, elegant language, and verbal agility. He is so articulate, so fast-thinking, so nimble in movement from idea to idea that he often leaves his customer feeling powerless to withstand him. Those who engage in mental combat with him often find themselves outreasoned and outmaneuvered; feeling helpless, they give in. The intellectual Q1 is a bright, fluent man who uses his intellectual skills to wear down customers. (Boxing fans can easily understand the distinction between the coercive and the intellectual Q1 by comparing the clumsy but powerful puncher to the elegant but equally dangerous boxer.) The intellectual Q1 is as much of a no-holds-barred salesman as his coercive counterpart, but he uses his strength in a different way. Few intellectual Q1s are as dazzling as the one we've described, but many come close.

It's important to stress that both types measure high in dominance and hostility. What distinguishes them is the way they *express* their basic traits. Both a wish to dominate and a lack of concern for other people can be expressed in different ways. What unites both men is their strong desire to *get the order* at whatever cost to the customer. They are joined by a common determination to *make the sale* no matter what the consequences for the buyer or, for that matter, for their own company. Both are poor listeners, both ramrod their ideas, both monopolize the presentation. Both have a strong need to bolster their self-esteem, to prove themselves to themselves, and to display their independence of other people. And both believe that only the fittest survive in the merciless business jungle; they differ only in the weapons they use to prevail.

THE INGRAINED Q2 VERSUS THE REACTIVE Q2

The ingrained Q2 falls into our second quadrant because his basic behavioral tendency *is* submissive-hostile; the reactive Q2 would ordinarily fall into some other quadrant, but is classified as a Q2 because he behaves in a submissive-hostile way *in reaction* to a situation he cannot cope with in any other way (the man we described earlier, who shifts from Q1 to Q2 behavior as a way of managing his chagrin at being passed over for promotion, is an example). At the risk of oversimplification, we can say that the ingrained Q2's strategy is *dimensionally* determined, whereas the reactive Q2's is *situationally* determined.

Reactive Q2s are more common in saleswork than might be supposed. A Q3 salesman, for example, who wants nothing more than to be accepted and outgoing, may find himself working for an autocratic boss who breathes down his neck, carps and criticizes constantly, and rebuffs the salesman's attempts to be friendly. The salesman, who lacks the assertiveness to confront this situation head-on, may, once he realizes there is nothing he can do to change it, respond by withdrawing, by keeping to himself, and by losing much of his enthusiasm and openness. Or a 50-year-old Q1 salesman, aggressive and hard-driving, may find himself working for a Q1 boss who is so domineering, so overbearing, that even the Q1 salesman becomes discouraged and reacts by withdrawing because he fears he is too old to find a job anywhere else. In each instance, a man who is not an ingrained Q2 reacts to a very difficult situation by becoming, for all practical purposes, *like* the ingrained Q2. The plight of the reactive Q2 is sad; it represents a waste, or at least a misuse of human potential that sales management should not permit. Reactive Q2s can often be recognized by the fact that they are very active outside of their jobs, whereas ingrained Q2s seldom are.

THE HEARTY Q3 VERSUS THE SOFT-SPOKEN Q3

The hearty Q3 is outgoing and exuberant, a man of gusto and vitality. At his most extreme, he is a back-slapper, joke teller, and nonstop socializer, a hail-fellow-well-met who is impossible to ignore. The soft-spoken Q3, on the other hand, is every bit as warm but much gentler in interaction. In extreme form, he may be shy and somewhat unsure of himself. Yet his obvious concern for others, his unfailing kindness and eagerness to help, his selflessness, make him very popular and well-liked. Both men want and get affection and approval, but each has a distinctively different bearing. Probably most Q3s are the *hearty* type, somewhat unrestrained in their good-nature. But not all.

THE COMPLEX Q4

Q4s are so complex, so individualized, that it is fruitless to talk of only a couple of types. Each is motivated by a need for self-realization, and no two selves are alike. The self is the focus of individual aspirations and individual ambitions. So each Q4 defines self-realization in his own way, and grows toward self-realization under his own terms. We will say much more about this later, in our chapter on motivation.

By now, it should be clear that each quadrant of the Dimensional model accommodates a much wider range of behavior than our earlier chapters indicated. And it should be very clear that most of us are a mixture of all four types of behavior.

A CLOSER LOOK AT SECONDARY AND MASK STRATEGIES

In this section, we explore the secondary and mask strategies most typically used by each salesman type when interacting with customers.

Secondary Strategies and Sales Situations

A secondary strategy is an unplanned reaction to frustration. Ordinarily, the reaction to frustration is *aggression;* if sufficiently frustrated, and if circumstances permit, a person will lash out, physically or verbally, at the source of his frustration. He may shout, hit, curse, slap, or display anger in any of dozens of ways. But, while aggression is the usual reaction to frustration, it is not always allowed by circumstances. In fact, most of us learn, from early childhood on, *not* to display hostility but to restrain it. So a salesman may feel very aggressive toward a frustrating customer, but not dare show it. Secondary strategies are always modified by the realities of the sales situation. Even though acting unconsciously, salesmen do not usually shift into secondary strategies that will permanently destroy their relationship with the customer. Within each of us, it seems, is a monitor that usually restrains us from dangerously impetuous behavior.

Theoretically, any salesman could shift from any primary strategy to any secondary strategy. Actually, however, each primary strategy leads to certain specific strategies more frequently than to others. As we shall see, this is not accidental.

THE Q1 SALESMAN

The Q1's most typical secondary is Q2; he is especially likely to become submissive-hostile if he finds himself frustrated. Usually, when a Q1 is thwarted in his sales efforts, it is because his domineering ways are not getting the results he wants; he is a "take-charge guy" who is unable to take charge. When a customer refuses to be dominated, the Q1's hostility and resentment increase. He may suddenly become submissive, which leads to a quick withdrawal from a frustrating and, for him, demeaning, situation. By temporarily becoming Q2 the Q1 says, "If I can't get my way, the hell with it," or "I don't really need him anyway." By pretending not to care about the outcome of the interview, he protects himself from psychological defeat.

Here's an illustration that may clarify how secondary strategies replace primary ones. Suppose an extremely hard-driving Q1 is trying to sell a life insurance policy to an equally aggressive prospect. After trying hard to close the sale, the salesman senses that his usual approach is not working; the prospect refuses to succumb. Without really thinking about it, the Q1 automatically begins to display more and more Q2 traits. His dominance melts and is replaced by a sullen submissiveness. This change in attitude may or may not help him make the sale; if it does not, it at least helps him to withdraw easily. If he withdraws, he can tell himself, in typical Q2 fashion, "I don't care. In fact, I didn't really need that sale anyway. I've already made the Honor Club this year, so I can do without that stupid guy. He doesn't know what's good for him."

Thus, when the Q1 fails to make a sale, we sometimes see what appears to be a paradox, a shift from pushing behavior to withdrawal, usually tinged with a heavy flavor of sour grapes.

THE Q2 SALESMAN

The Q2 rarely shows a dramatic shift to another quadrant when he displays a secondary strategy. He feels little emotional commitment to making a sale because he believes the sale is in the customers' hands anyway, not in his. So he seldom experiences sufficiently intense emotional pressure during a presentation to exhibit a secondary strategy. Instead, the obstacles he meets cause him to intensify his Q2 approach. If he finds himself in danger of losing the sale, he becomes that much more withdrawn and defeatist. This more intense Q2 behavior can be called his secondary strategy.

On rare occasions, the Q2 may exhibit secondary behavior that resembles Q1. Bursts of aggression may break through slightly if pressures mount so rapidly that his Q2 shell begins to crack. This is relatively unusual, however. As a rule, his secondary strategy is to become a more intense, a more withdrawn, Q2.

THE Q3 SALESMAN

The Q3 salesman seldom manifests a secondary strategy because he is seldom aware of sales obstacles. He sees things so optimistically that he is rarely aware that things are going badly. Incidents that would frustrate other salesmen pass by him unnoticed. He maintains his optimistic, unruffled manner with customer after customer often without becoming upset.

Sometimes, of course, severe frustrations may cause him to react with a secondary strategy. When this happens, he usually shifts to Q2 behavior, accepting defeat and withdrawing. This is his way of saying, "I'm beaten; it's impossible to make this sale." By adopting a Q2 attitude, he withdraws and avoids unpleasantness. Whatever indignation he feels is hidden under typical Q2 rationalizations, so he is not forced to the ultimate catastrophe, as he sees it, of displaying hostile Q1 traits. Nevertheless, there are times when even the Q3 salesman is so vexed that he does burst out with displays of Q1 aggression, but these are usually very brief.

THE Q4 SALESMAN

The Q4's strategy is usually so flexible that he is likely to experience fewer frustrations than other salesmen; he heads them off before they develop. Because he shares the dominance of a Q1, the warmth of a Q3, and an ability to keep his mouth shut that sometimes resembles Q2 behavior, he is able to roll with a greater variety of punches and to deflect more blows than other salesmen. His primary strategy is one of flexibility. If, however, he does experience pressures so severe that they exceed his high tolerance for frustration, he will be forced to a secondary strategy. When this happens, he usually demonstrates Q1 behavior. This is easy to understand if one similarity between the Q4 and Q1 is kept in mind: both men have a strong need to achieve. Both want very much to make sales. So it is easy to see why the Q4 falls back on Q1 behavior. If this behavior fails, as it often does, so that the pressures and frustrations continue, he is apt to move to a Q2 strategy and withdraw. Of course, if a Q4 salesman were a pure, 100% Q4, he would never display any secondary strategy, because a secondary strategy would be unnecessary; instead, he would maintain his primary, flexible Q4 strategy. But, as we have said before, the Q4 is never a pure, 100% Q4. He is a human being, and, like all human beings, is a mixture of characteristics.

Sales Masks

A sales mask, as we have said, differs from a secondary strategy in one very significant way. A secondary strategy is an automatic response to sales frustrations, neither planned nor worked out beforehand. A sales mask is a conscious and purposeful response to pressures from either a customer or from sales management.

A sales mask is *deliberate,* while a secondary strategy is not. A salesman who dons a sales mask makes an intentional effort to disguise or hide the motivation, beliefs, and behavior that characterize him most of the time.

Theoretically, any salesman can assume any mask. In practice, however, the Q3 is the most commonly chosen mask. This is understandable if we recall that masks are often worn to mislead a customer and gain one's own ends, and most salesmen believe that, if a customer is going to be fooled, he should be fooled into believing that the salesman is pleasant and likable. Warmth becomes a means of manipulation. A Q1 salesman, for example, whose aggressive manner frightens a customer into withdrawing, is likely to deliberately assume a Q3 mask. In effect, he says to himself: "I'll get this guy to relax by making him think I'm really good-natured and concerned about him."

The next most common sales mask is the Q1, particularly when management begins to pressure a salesman to "get out there and sell." The salesman may then respond by assuming a Q1 pose ("If they want me to be tough and forceful, I'll be tough and forceful"). Frequently, the chief purpose of inspirational speeches at sales meetings is to get salesmen to start behaving like Q1s; sales contests are often used in the same way. Many sales managers believe the tough, overpowering salesman is ideal, and they try to get their men to act as Q1s. Many salesmen then put on a Q1 mask to relieve pressure from management.

After the Q1, the Q4 is the most commonly worn mask. By pretending to be Q4, a salesman says, in effect, "Look, I'm a reasonable, rational person who's interested in your welfare as well as my own. You have nothing to fear from me. Let's sit down and talk, and we'll work out your problems." Almost any pressure, whether from company, customer, or sales situation, can create the conditions under which the Q4 mask is used.

Let's look at the masks most commonly worn by the various types of salesmen.

THE Q1 SALESMAN

A Q1 whose customer does not respond favorably to his tactics is most likely to don a Q3 mask (the "wolf in sheep's clothing" strategy). He pretends warmth and concern, while beneath the mask he remains self-interested, hostile, and eager to control the situation. In fact, he puts on the mask to make sure he does *not* lose control.

If the pressures on the Q1 come from his company, he will probably resort to a Q4 mask. Suppose, for example, a Q1's manager complains about reports from customers of misrepresentation and exploitation. "You're too aggressive," he charges "and your customers are beginning to resent it. You'll have to tone down." The natural response to this kind of pressure is a pose of reasonableness, and the Q4 mask is perfect for this purpose.

THE Q2 SALESMAN

The Q2 salesman doesn't believe a mask will accomplish much, since the customer will do whatever he wants to do anyway. So he seldom wears a sales mask with any real effect. His efforts are half-hearted and ineffective.

It must be remembered that wearing a sales mask requires real effort. If it is to succeed, the salesman must expend considerable energy playing a role in which he does not feel natural. But the Q2 sees no good reason to expend this energy. He plays the role, but his heart is not in it. If his customer or company exerts enough pressure, he may behave in a pseudo-dominant manner for a few days, and he may even have some slight increase in sales, but the change will not last long. Sooner or later, his belief that "it doesn't really matter" asserts itself.

THE Q3 SALESMAN

The Q3, much like the Q2, usually adopts a Q1 mask, but *only* under extreme provocation. Otherwise, he wears no mask at all. Sometimes, his customers or company, directly or by implication, may pressure him to become more aggressive, and if the pressures are sufficiently severe, he may assume a Q1 mask. But he does so only with great strain, since Q1 behavior violates all that he holds dear. If the pressures persist, he will probably look for another job rather than continue to act in a distressingly uncongenial way.

THE Q4 SALESMAN

The Q4 salesman's use of masks is a somewhat complicated topic, so we'll devote somewhat more space to it. To understand when and how the Q4 dons sales masks, the reader should keep three points in mind:

1. The Q4 does not don a sales mask until he experiences frustration that exceeds his frustration-tolerance level. This, of course, is true of all salesmen, not only the Q4. A mask strategy is, by definition, a strategy employed when a salesman finds himself unable to cope with frustration by means of his primary strategy. Or, to put it another way, a salesman puts on a mask when his frustration-tolerance level is exceeded. Up to that point, he usually maintains his primary strategy. But the significant point here is that the Q4 has a much *higher* tolerance for frustration than other salesmen because his primary strategy, being *flexible* to begin with, is *more* effective in *more* situations. This means that in any given selling situation, the Q4 is less likely to experience *unmanageable* frustration or pressure, so he is less likely to feel that he *needs* to don a mask. As a rule, he can go farther and longer with his primary Q4 strategy.

2. Up to his frustration-tolerance level, the Q4's behavior is flexible and adaptive, but he does not wear masks. This is a very important point. The Q4's *primary* strategy is one in which he *naturally* shifts his behavior to fit particular circumstances. This is why he is less likely than other salesmen to experience unmanageable frustration. The Q4 constantly adapts his sales approach to suit the individual needs of individual customers. When necessary, he can be as unyielding as the Q1, as quiet as the Q2, or as affable as the Q3. *But these are not masks.* They are simply differing aspects of his *primary* behavior.

One crucial distinction, then, between the Q4 and other salesmen is that the Q4 shifts and modifies his behavior even though he is not in the least frustrated. Because he shifts his behavior to suit his customer's needs, he heads off many situations that would otherwise *cause* frustration. And, as he adapts his behavior, he consistently works toward an outcome that benefits himself, his customer, and his company. As a rule, however, *other* salesmen shift their behavior only *after* experiencing frustration; their primary strategy is basically inflexible and unchanging. And their shifts are basically motivated by a concern for their own welfare rather than a concern for the customer and company as well. So, up to the level of his frustration-tolerance, the Q4 salesman may *seem* to be donning masks as he moves from one mode of behavior to another. *But he is not.* He is, quite simply, being a Q4, which means being flexible, adaptive, supple, and resilient.

3. Beyond his frustration-tolerance level, the Q4 may don masks, just like any other salesman. We've already made it plain that the Q4 *does*, at times, experience frustration that exceeds even his high level of tolerance. He may find himself in a situation where he is baffled, thwarted, confounded, and unable to cope. If so, he is, as we have already said, likely to exhibit automatic Q1 or Q2 secondary behavor. *It is at these times,* when he is functioning *not* as a primary Q4 but as a secondary Q1 or Q2, that he is likely to don sales masks. These are *not* the flexible, adaptive shifts described above; they are deliberate attempts to manipulate or mislead the customer. And they are motivated, like all masks, by a concern for himself rather than a concern for himself, his customer, and his company.

To summarize: as long as the Q4 is functioning as a Q4, he will probably feel no need for masks; when he is functioning in a secondary behavior, he may very well feel such a need. The reader should be especially careful, however, not to mistake the Q4's *ordinary* flexibility for masks. In his primary behavior, he may exhibit, in addition to Q4 traits, some behavior that resembles Q1, some that resembles Q2, and some that resembles Q3. This is the hallmark of Q4 selling; it is not mask behavior. In actuality, the Q4 is adapting his approach to meet the customer's personal and product needs.

A Final Note on Sales Masks

We ought not to leave the subject of sales masks without answering some questions that are probably perplexing the reader. Are sales masks always bad because they are manipulative? Don't they exploit the customer's readiness to believe? Aren't they at least slightly unfair?

Condemning the wearing of masks is something like condemning breathing. The wearing of masks, by *all* of us, not just salesmen, is so profoundly and inescapably human that it can accurately be called a fundamental part of the human condition. Each day, in countless ways, each of us tries to present himself to others to the best possible advantage; each of us tries to create favorable, positive impressions; each of us experiments endlessly with behavior that will, we hope, work to our benefit.

Furthermore, we can say that without masks there could be no change in human behavior. If a Q1 salesman, for example, has determined to change his behavior in the direction of Q4, he has no choice but to begin by putting on Q4 masks. After a while, if he does this skillfully and consistently, the Q4 masks will cease to be masks and will become part of his primary behavior. But, at the beginning, change can only be effected if he is willing to experiment with mask behavior.

Masking, quite simply, is a fundamental part of human interaction, *all* human interaction. To condemn it is futile; to understand it is important.

SUMMARY

Selling behavior is rarely found in the pure forms we have described in our typologies for five reasons: a given bit of a salesman's behavior can be located at any point in any quadrant, and there are an infinite number of these points, signifying varying intensities of behavior, in each quadrant: behavior is frequently related to situations, and situations vary; salesmen may shift to secondary (automatic) strategies when frustrated; they may shift to mask (deliberate) strategies when frustrated; and secondary strategies may become quasipermanent.

Within each primary strategy, there are several basic variations: the coercive versus the intellectual Q1, the ingrained versus the reactive Q2, and the hearty versus the soft-spoken Q3. The Q4 strategy is so complex that a very sizable number of variations can be discerned.

When automatically moving to a secondary strategy, the Q1 salesman usually displays Q2 behavior. The Q2 shows a deepened secondary strategy, usually shifting to more passive and withdrawn behavior when frustrated; on rare occasions, he may move to Q1. Similarly, the Q3 is seldom frustrated enough to show secondary traits; when he is, he usually lapses into Q2 withdrawal, although he may show Q1 aggressiveness on very rare occasions. The Q4's flexibility makes it possible for him to avert much frustration before it occurs; when he is frustrated, he usually displays Q1 traits, perhaps followed by Q2 withdrawal.

The nice-guy Q3 mask is the most common sales mask, followed by the tough-guy Q1 mask, and then the reasonable-guy Q4 mask. Q1 salesmen usually resort to Q3 masks with customers, and Q4 masks with pressures from their company. The Q2 seldom wears a mask effectively, although he may sometimes shift to brief Q1 behavior. Under extreme pressure, the Q3 may also don a Q1 mask. And the Q4 is most accurately described as consistently adaptable, flexibly modifying his behavior to suit particular circumstances, although he does don masks when frustrations become intolerable.

At times, all of us wear masks. They are not necessarily bad. Without them, behavior change and growth would be impossible. If a salesman dons masks in a deliberate effort to do a better job for himself, his customer, and his company, he may develop into a better salesman as a result. If he does this consistently, the masks may cease to be masks and become part of his primary strategy.

TABLE 3. Typical Secondary and Mask Strategies

Primary	Secondary	Mask
Q1	Q2 ("To hell with it; I can get by without an order from this guy.")	Q3 (Wolf in sheep's clothing.) Q4 (If company pressures him to moderate his behavior.)
Q2	Q2 (More intense withdrawal than is usual under his primary strategy.)	Q1 (Rarely, under pressure from his company.)
Q3	Q2 ("I give up; this man refuses to respond to my friendliness.")	Q1 (Only when under extreme provocation.)
Q4	Q1 (Under extreme frustration only; otherwise remains flexibly Q4.) Q2 (Withdraws when Q1 secondary fails to get results.)	Q3 (Adopts mask only when he is in a secondary strategy.)

9

Customer Strategies

TO BUY OR NOT TO BUY . . .

We have repeatedly made the point that selling is interactional, that it actively involves at least two people. But, for the most part, our previous chapters have talked only about one partner in the interaction: the salesman. This distorted emphasis may have given some readers the impression that the sales process can be understood simply by understanding salesmen's behavior. Nothing could be more wrong, or more damaging to the salesman who wants to improve his sales effectiveness.

The fact is this: the sales process cannot be understood until *both* the salesman's and the customer's behavior are understood. The customer—his beliefs, assumptions, attitudes, and actions—is every bit as important in determining the outcome of a sales presentation as the salesman. He is a full and equal partner in the interaction. What really controls the outcome of a sales presentation is not the salesman's behavior alone, but the meshing of his behavior with the customer's behavior. This interlocking of behaviors cannot be understood unless the behavioral strategies of customers are understood as well as those of salesmen.

In this chapter, then, we describe the basic customer strategies. In the next chapter we discuss how they mesh, or fail to mesh, with the various sales strategies.

119

THE DIMENSIONAL MODEL OF CUSTOMER BEHAVIOR

The dimensions we used to describe sales behavior pertain to *all* behavior, including that of customers. So we can depict customer behavior by means of a model like the one we used earlier:

Dominance

Q1 Salesmen are corrupt. Stay in control, or they'll take advantage of you.	Q4 Salesmen must understand my needs, and I must understand how their product fits my needs.
Q2 Salesmen always try to sell you something you don't want or need. Avoid them.	Q3 Some of my best friends are salesmen.

Hostility ————————————————— Warmth

Submission

In the pages that follow, we will describe each customer strategy by describing first the basic buying beliefs that underlie it and then the buying behavior itself. Once again, we caution that our typologies are verbal caricatures which cannot be exactly duplicated in the real world.

The Q1 (Dominant-Hostile) Customer

BASIC BUYING BELIEFS

Salesmen are untrustworthy. They're determined to sell me something I neither want nor need. As a matter of simple self-protection, I must control them by being tough, domineering, and resistant. Salesmen believe that all buyers are suckers who don't deserve an even break, so I can defend myself only by proving that I'm too shrewd to be duped and too strong to be bulldozed. Against salesmen, the best defense (in fact, the *only* defense) is an irresistible offense.

BASIC BUYING BEHAVIOR

The Q1 is a defiant, argumentative customer determined to prove to the salesman that "you can't put anything over on me." He virtually dares the salesman to sell him, and then makes his job difficult by disputing minor points, making snide remarks, and quibbling over details ("Always keep these guys off balance. That's the only way to beat them").

It should not be thought, however, that the Q1 customer regrets his behavior as a necessary evil. On the contrary. He relishes the struggle. He considers the sales presentation a battle of wills and wits, and he wages the battle with gusto. His aim is not to avoid buying (after all, no one can permanently avoid buying) but to buy on *his* terms after proving that he is stronger than the salesman. As he likes to boast: "I buy when *I'm* ready, not when some salesman thinks I should."

As with Q1 salesmen, we can point to two quite different styles of Q1 customer behavior. The *coercive* Q1 customer has an almost visible chip on his shoulder. Arrogant and overbearing, he impresses most salesmen as spiteful and unreasonable. Salesmen often walk away from an encounter with a coercive Q1 shaking their heads and muttering that "the guy never gave me a chance, he wouldn't even listen to me." The *intellectual* Q1 customer is less heavy handed but equally arrogant. The message he implicitly conveys is: "Look, I don't need you or anybody else to tell me about my business. I'm fully able to figure out my own needs and make my own decisions." He likes to dazzle salesmen with his business prowess, to tell boastful stories of his exploits (usually exaggerated) and his successes (usually inflated). He tries to come across as a man of rare business acumen, compared to whom the salesman is a rank amateur.

Neither the coercive nor the intellectual Q1 customer considers the salesman an equal with whom he can talk on terms of mutual respect. At the very least, they consider salesmen as questionable characters who must be kept in line. The crux of the Q1 customer strategy is to make the salesman realize that he is dependent upon the stronger will of the customer, that he is subject to the customer's decisions and the customer's choices. In making this point, the Q1 customer also makes the related point that *he* is superior to the salesman. Like his counterpart, the Q1 salesman, the Q1 customer is power-oriented and status-conscious.

The Q2 (Submissive-Hostile) Customer

BASIC BUYING BELIEFS

Salesmen are devious scoundrels whose goal is to sell me something I neither want nor need. In self-defense, I do all I can to avoid them. When a confrontation with a salesman is unavoidable, I remain as uninvolved and unresponsive as I can. Salesmen are experts at cunningly turning people's words against them; they are specialists at cleverly exploiting customers. I refuse to give them an opportunity to take advantage of me.

BASIC BUYING BEHAVIOR

The basic Q2 customer belief is not very different from the basic Q1 customer belief. Both men believe salesmen are dangerously tricky and shrewd. But the dominant Q1 is self-assured enough to think he can beat the salesman at his own game, whereas the submissive Q2 fears he is no match for the salesman. So, while the Q1 marches eagerly off to battle, the Q2 withdraws.

His withdrawal takes two forms. When he can, he avoids salesmen completely, refusing to grant appointments. When this is impractical, he assumes a passive, almost detached role in the presentation. A call on a Q2 customer can be frustrating and unsettling. He is likely to be listless and uncommunicative, keeping words to a minimum, expressing himself largely in grunts or nods, volunteering no information, and, in general, giving the salesman the uneasy feeling that he is talking to himself.

The Q2 customer also comes in two varieties: the ingrained and the reactive. The *ingrained* Q2 customer fears all salesmen. Insecure and uneasy in the presence of forceful, fluent people, he prefers to avoid every salesman, like the hesitant football player who knows that the best way to avoid getting mauled is to stay out of the game. The *reactive* Q2 may be reacting to pressures from his boss or his company. Or he may be a customer who has been badly treated by a particular salesman (or several salesmen) in the past, and who now avoids *all* salesmen who sell the same product that the offender sold. "You can't trust any of those guys," he complains. "They're all a bunch of connivers."

Both the Q2 and Q1 customer base their behavior mainly on stereotypes. Both have a standardized mental image of "the" salesman, who, beneath a dignified exterior, is really a combination side-show barker and patent-medicine man. Their interaction with salesmen is so colored by this view that they seldom get to know the *real* salesmen with whom they interact.

The Q3 (Submissive-Warm) Customer

BASIC BUYING BELIEFS

When you get right down to it, many competitive products and services are pretty much alike. Since it doesn't really make much difference which ones I buy, I might as well buy from salesmen I like. As long as I'm spending money, I might as well make a friend happy. After all, taking care of your friends is what makes the world go around.

BASIC BUYING BEHAVIOR

The Q3 customer is warm, friendly, and easygoing with salesmen. He not only believes in buying from friends, he believes in trying to make a friend of every salesman he meets. A benevolent, outgoing man, he enjoys sales presentations because he thinks of them as social occasions. During a presentation, he talks longwindedly about a host of topics, most of which have little to do with the salesman's product or service. Chatty, gossipy, and relaxed, he is reluctant to disagree with the salesman or even raise objections. At most, he may ask an occasional friendly (and easily answered) question, but in general he accepts, or seems to accept, most of what he hears. If he does feel any doubts about the product or service, he keeps them to himself. He assents readily, even when he has serious doubts. After the salesman departs, the Q3 customer may back out of the sale, justifying himself by amiable rationalizations that do not offend the salesman. He tries desperately not to endanger the cordial relationship between himself and the salesman.

We can distinguish two kinds of Q3 customer: the hearty and the soft-spoken. The *hearty* Q3 customer is sometimes exasperatingly talkative, often impossible to keep on the subject. Jokes, small-talk, and irrelevancies pour forth as he labors to convert the salesman into a friend. The *soft-spoken* Q3 is less talkative, but equally warm. Not as long-winded (and therefore not as wasteful of time) he is every bit as easygoing and agreeable, seldom arguing, doubting, or probing.

It might seem that the Q3 customer has no sales resistance at all, that he is a naive and easily fooled buyer who purchases anything any salesman offers him. Not so. Q3s are not necessarily gullible. Although more trusting than either the Q1 or Q2, they still offer plenty of resistance if they think resistance is justified. But they do not express resistance openly. Instead, they offer alibis for their unwillingness to buy, alibis that are both reasonable and inoffensive: "I'd really like to buy from you, but business has been slow, and I just can't afford the investment," "It sounds like a great idea, but I never make a decision about things like this without consulting my partner, and he's out of town," "It breaks my heart to tell you this, but I just placed a big order with another company." And so on. Q3 customers are fully able to take care of themselves without seeming unfriendly.

Nevertheless, the Q3 customer does sometimes buy things he doesn't really need because he wants to give the salesman a break, or because he feels sorry for the salesman, or simply because the salesman seemed "too nice a guy to say no to." Unlike the Q1 and Q2, the Q3 customer starts out with the assumption that the salesman is a decent fellow who wants to help him, and he maintains this assumption unless the salesman clearly disproves it. If he can find a plausible reason to buy, he is likely to buy. But, especially if he thinks the salesman is exploiting or cheating him, he can, in his own disarming way, be as resistant as any other customer.

The Q4 (Dominant-Warm) Customer

BASIC BUYING BELIEFS

When I buy something, I want to be sure it will benefit me (and my company). When I part with my money, I expect to get some advantage out of it. I'll buy from any salesman who proves to my satisfaction that he can help me get the benefit I need, and that he can help me get more benefit than any salesman of competing products or services can. The salesman's job is to produce a gain for me, and I expect him to do his job.

BASIC BUYING BEHAVIOR

The Q4 is hard-headed, pragmatic, skeptical. He wants *proof* that his purchase will produce results for him. He wants to do business with salesmen who have his interests in mind, who can analyze and solve his buying problems, and who are as hard-headed and pragmatic as he. He sees the salesman–customer relationship as a *partnership* in which both men work toward a single goal: a sale from which *both* profit.

The Q4 is one of the most difficult of all customers to sell to. He is demanding, challenging, exacting. He wants data and demonstration, not poetic puffery. He wants informed analysis of his problems ("That's what a salesman is paid to do," he insists, "analyze and solve my problems"). And he wants to emerge from the sales presentation knowing more about his situation than he knew at the beginning. The Q4 customer is tough-minded.

Maybe the best way to describe him is to say that he expects the same kind of knowledgeable, factual, resultful problem-solving from salesmen that he gets from his doctor and lawyer. This is not far-fetched. Here's how the Q4 customer would put it: "I'll do everything I can to cooperate with a salesman, just as I do with my doctor and lawyer. I'll give him all the information I can, answer his questions to the best of my ability, and give him as much of my time as he needs to do his job. Then, together, we can figure out what my problem is and how I can best solve it. When it comes to *his* product, *he's* the expert. And that's the way I expect him to behave. When it comes to how I can best use his product, I'm the expert. I'll do all I can to work with him, and I expect him to do all he can to work with me. That seems perfectly reasonable."

This means that salesmen who do not measure up to professional standards are likely to get short shrift from the Q4 customer. Unless he sees fairly quick evidence that the salesman has the skill to solve problems and provide benefits, the Q4 may well become impatient and end the presentation. The Q4 is businesslike, purposeful, serious, a no-nonsense buyer.

We do not want to leave the impression, however, that he is a cold, humorless customer who's "all business." He can be, and usually is, friendly, engaging, and likable. He is willing to tell a joke or listen to one, indulge in small-talk, or compare notes on golf scores. *But only up to a point.* His main purpose during the sales presentation is businesslike: to find out "what benefit will I get out of all this?" and he keeps that purpose in the forefront at all times.

SECONDARY CUSTOMER STRATEGIES AND CUSTOMER MASKS

Customers, like salesmen, sometimes need to escape from pressures and frustrations. Customers, like salesmen, sometimes shift behavior, deliberately or unconsciously, to avoid anxiety and tension. So customers, too, employ secondary strategies and wear masks. The secondary strategies are likely to be the same as those used by their salesmen counterparts, while a variety of masks can be donned to suit the customers' purposes. Customers are most likely to don masks with salesmen they don't know or trust. Until they know where they stand with the salesman, they frequently adopt Q2 masks.

A Note on Customer Strategies

Sizable variations in style exist within each of the quadrants we have described. Not all Q1 customers, for example, are as suspicious and belligerent as the one we described. But all, to some degree, distrust salesmen, and all feel a need to protect themselves by offensive tactics. All, to some degree, give salesmen a rough time. And all, to some degree, enjoy the contention they stir up because it gives them an opportunity to assert their strength. So, while no two Q1 customers are exactly alike, there are strong and significant similarities between all of them. The same is true of customers in the other quadrants. Like salesmen, customers exhibit behavior that's a mixture of all four quadrants.

SUMMARY

The sales process cannot be understood until the behavior of *both* the salesman and the customer is understood. What really controls the outcome of the presentation is the meshing of the two behaviors. Customer behavior can be analyzed by using the Dimensional model.

The Q1 customer believes salesmen are untrustworthy and determined to sell him something he neither wants nor needs. To protect himself, he tries to control them by being tough and domineering. He tries to transform the sales presentation into a contest which he wins by either refusing to buy or by buying only after establishing his dominance over the salesman.

The Q2 customer believes salesmen are deviously intent upon selling him something he neither wants nor needs. In self-defense, he tries to avoid them or to minimize interaction with them. He is generally uncommunicative and withdrawn, revealing no more information than he must.

The Q3 customer believes that competitive products are often much alike and that it doesn't matter which one he buys, so he might as well buy from salesmen he likes. He sees his purchase as a way to help a friend. He is typically talkative, warm, and wasteful of time, avoiding disagreement and objections. If he thinks he is being exploited, however, he can be quite resistant.

The Q4 customer believes a purchase must benefit him (and his company), so he tries to buy from salesmen who produce a gain for him. Hardheaded and concerned with results, he is difficult to sell to, expecting salesmen to be knowledgeable, factual problem-solvers. He sees the presentation as a working partnership between himself and the salesman.

Customers, like salesmen, typically exhibit behavior that is a mixture of all four quadrants.

Dominance

Q1—The Dominant-Hostile Customer	*Q4—The Dominant-Warm Customer*
Salesmen cannot be trusted. They are determined to sell me something I don't want or need. To protect myself, I must control them by being tough and resistant. The best defense is a good offense.	I buy things because I expect them to benefit me. I buy from salesmen who prove they can help me get the benefit I need, and that they can produce a benefit that's bigger than their competitors'.

Hostility ————————————————————— Warmth

Q2—The Submissive-Hostile Customer	*Q3—The Submissive-Warm Customer*
Salesmen cannot be trusted. They are determined to sell me something I don't want or need. To defend myself, I try to avoid them. If I cannot avoid them, I stay as uninvolved with them as possible.	Many competitive products are pretty much alike. Since it doesn't really matter which one I buy, I might as well buy from a salesman I like.

Submission

FIGURE 2. The Dimensional model of customer behavior.

10

Salesman-Customer Interaction

IT TAKES TWO TO MAKE A SALE

The great English physician, William Harvey, had a thriving medical practice until he made one of the most momentous discoveries in the history of science, the discovery that blood circulates. After publishing his observations of the circulatory system, he acquired a reputation as a simpleton or even, some thought, a madman. As word spread that the once-respected doctor had become "crack-brained," his practice dwindled and his income shriveled. The moral of this sad (but true) story is that seeing things as they really are can sometimes be very costly and disrupting.

Happily, that's not true in selling. In fact, the reverse is true: in selling, the *failure* to see things as they really are can be (and frequently is) very costly and disrupting. Yet many salesmen and sales managers persist in this failure by talking and thinking in terms of "the" selling process. Whenever a salesman or sales manager talks about a "typical" sale or a "normal" sale or an "average" sale, he is thinking in terms as unrealistic as the idea that blood is motionless. And he is thinking in terms that can be very costly.

The notion of "the" selling process would be meaningful only if most salesmen were more or less alike and most customers were more or less alike most of the time. But, as our previous chapters have shown, they are not. For that reason, a sales presentation between, say, a Q1 salesman and a Q1 customer differs *in every significant interactional aspect* from a presentation between a Q3 salesman and a Q3 customer. To call one of these presentations "typical" or "normal" would be arbitrary and, even worse, misleading.

In fact, the notion of a selling process which is always, or nearly always, the same, should be scrapped. Like the notion that there is no circulatory system in human beings, it simply does not accord with what science knows. In its place should go the notion of *sales interactions,* the idea that the dynamics of selling vary as the behavioral strategies of the salesman and customer vary. Instead of "the" selling process, there are many selling processes. To be precise, there are (as the Dimensional model analyzes them) a minimum of *sixteen* basic selling processes (depending upon which of the four primary selling strategies interacts with which of the four primary buying strategies). And there are modifications of each of these sixteen selling processes, depending upon which secondary strategies and masks are used. The sixteen basic processes are summarized in the charts at the end of this chapter.

In this chapter, we describe the sixteen basic salesman–customer interactions. Our aim is not to make the subject of selling complex, but to make it *realistic.* The old notion of "the" all-inclusive selling process is not really simple, but simple-minded; it distorts and falsifies by ignoring certain fundamental aspects of what happens between salesmen and customers. Our purpose is to present a systematic picture of what *actually* happens, to replace make-believe with fact. We base our picture on two aspects of the interaction: relationship and results. Then we can talk meaningfully about how salesmen can *improve* their selling skills where it really matters: in the actual, workaday world.

THREE BASIC POINTS TO REMEMBER

The interactions described in this chapter (all of which are extreme caricatures) will make sense if the reader keeps three fundamental points in mind. Both Q2 and Q3 customers, because of their submissive traits, have strong needs to be led, guided, and directed by salesmen, but not in a way that takes advantage of their submissiveness. Submissive people tend to evoke disdain and even hostility in dominant people. Submissive people are usually sensitive about their submissiveness and very unwilling to have it taken advantage of.

We'll see these three principles illustrated time and again in this chapter.

How the Q1 Salesman Interacts with Customers

The Q1 salesman interacts in more or less the same way with all kinds of customers. What differs significantly is the way different kinds of customers *respond* to his overbearing tactics.

Q1 SALESMAN–Q1 CUSTOMER INTERACTION

Relationship. In their own hard-hitting competitive way, these two men get along quite well. They speak the same language; they recognize their strong similarities. Both enjoy verbal combat and one-upmanship; both are direct (almost painfully so), argumentative, and quick to take advantage of exposed weaknesses. Each regards the sales presentation as a test of strength, from which the winner can derive solid satisfaction because he has defeated a genuinely tough opponent. Usually, Q1–Q1 encounters conform (like boxing matches) to certain minimal "rules"; sometimes, though, the encounter gets out of hand, and degenerates from a prizefight to a brawl. Tempers flare, heated words are exchanged, and the relationship between the two men comes to a permanent end. Generally, however, a Q1 and a Q1 maintain their relationship over a period of calls because each respects (and sometimes even likes) the other. But, for all that, in a sales presentation they are exceedingly competitive.

Results. Q1–Q1 interactions lead to only average results, with approximately as many presentations ending in a stand-off as in a sale (a stand-off, of course, is a victory from the customer's point of view). In many instances, the Q1 salesman is strong enough to prevail over his rough-and-tumble customer, but in many the customer proves too strong. As a rule, the Q1 salesman feels somewhat less upset when he fails to make a sale to a Q1 customer than to any other type; while he detests losing, he is slightly comforted by the thought that he lost in a rugged fight in which he landed some bruising punches. "Win some, lose some," he says.

Q1 SALESMAN–Q2 CUSTOMER INTERACTION

Relationship. Dominant people usually respect (even when they don't like) other dominant people; this is obvious in the typical interaction between two Q1s. But they usually disdain submissive people; as a rule, the strong scorn the weak. This disdain is apparent in encounters between Q1 salesmen and Q2 customers. Once he has sized up the customer, the salesman treats him with disguised contempt, sometimes using blatantly manipulative tactics. The customer becomes a piece of clay to be kneaded and molded into whatever shape the salesman wishes. What often happens is that the customer, responding with both fear and resentment, begins to resist. He probably does not appear openly upset, but underneath he may be seething with indignation (the Q2, remember, *is* basically a hostile person who is unable to display his hostility as openly as the Q1). The salesman, unaware of his impact on the customer, thinks the sale will be a pushover, but the customer has other ideas. He may prove stubborn and unmanageable, refusing to talk or communicating only with grunts and nods. The whole relationship is characterized by smoldering animosity; the Q1 salesman considers the Q2 customer a weakling, and the Q2 customer considers the Q1 salesman a manipulator and an exploiter. Without realizing it, the Q1 salesman confirms all of the Q2 customer's fears and suspicions about salesmen.

Results.   Sales are usually below average, a fact the Q1 finds hard to understand. The customer seems ready to comply (offering few or no objections), but refuses to let the salesman close the sale. Seldom strong enough to utter a flat "no," he alibis and postpones instead. "I don't have the money" is one of his favorite put-offs. At the end, he can be as obstinate as the salesman is pushy.

This behavior is not hard to understand if we recall that the Q2 customer is often aware of and somewhat embarrassed by his own submissiveness. He especially resents those who not only recognize his weakness but try to exploit it. The Q1 salesman, who is everything the Q2 customer most fears, often makes the mistake of assuming that submissive people readily capitulate to strong people. On the contrary. Many submissive people (especially hostile ones) are fully able to protect themselves from manipulation and coercion. As Aesop's fables remind us time and again, shrewd lambs are not always helpless before hungry lions.

Q1 SALESMAN–Q3 CUSTOMER INTERACTION

Relationship.   The Q1 salesman has about as little respect for the Q3 customer as for the Q2. Both customers, in his opinion, are proof of Barnum's statement that "There's a sucker born every minute." But the Q3 customer usually likes the Q1 salesman, whom he characterizes as "a little bit too eager, but a nice guy underneath it all." (To the Q3, nearly everyone is a nice guy underneath it all.) Even more important, the Q3 customer, who has a strong need for guidance and direction, gets these from the Q1 salesman. What the Q3 customer is really saying by his behavior is: "Lead me and direct me, but without taking advantage of my submissiveness." The Q1 salesman does lead, but he also frequently exploits. Where the Q2 customer resents the Q1's bulldozing, the Q3 customer rationalizes it. ("He's probably under a lot of pressure to make sales.") While the Q2 customer usually responds to the salesman by freezing up, the Q3 usually responds with meandering chitchat. To the Q1 salesman, both responses are exasperating. He wants to make a quick sale, and this is extremely difficult with a Q3 customer.

Results.   Over the short haul, the Q1 salesman is more effective with Q3 customers than any others, getting sales results above the average. In the end, the Q3 is usually unable to resist the Q1's strength (although he can be very stubborn if he becomes convinced that the salesman is exploiting him), and he is seldom able to resist the Q3 masks that the Q1 wears so skillfully. But over the long haul, the Q1 salesman often fails to retain his Q3 customers, because he does such a poor job of delivering on promises and of follow-up, both of which are very important to the Q3 customer. To a Q3, follow-up is proof of the salesman's personal concern; if the salesman is not clearly interested in him, the Q3 is likely to seek out another salesman who is.

Once again, then, we find that submissive people do not like to be used; they want some sign from the salesman that he respects them and values them as people. But the fact is that the Q1 salesman does *not* respect and value Q3 customers any more than Q2. At its core, his behavior toward both men is condescending, perhaps even patronizing. Ultimately, both men are likely to rebel against this treatment. The difference is that the Q2 rebels early in the game by withdrawing, procrastinating, or refusing to buy at all; the Q3 rebels after buying, and after giving the salesman a chance to prove himself.

Q1 SALESMAN–Q4 CUSTOMER INTERACTION

Relationship.   The Q4 customer feels mixed admiration and wariness toward the Q1 salesman. He admires his direct, no-nonsense manner, but is wary of his overpowering approach. As a result, there is a degree of tension between the two men from the start. The salesman senses quite early that *this* customer is no pushover; the customer senses that the salesman can probably provide some benefit *if* he can be kept in line. Throughout the presentation, the Q1 salesman tries to gain the upper hand, but is steadily blocked by a customer who demands solutions, comparisons, and demonstration of benefits; the Q4 customer tries repeatedly to get straight information about what the product will do for him, but encounters a steady barrage of overstatements. Frustrated by the customer's refusal to be bowled over, the salesman presses all the harder, running the risk of seriously aggravating the customer and wearing out his welcome. As the presentation continues, the salesman's bafflement and perplexity increase while the customer's regard for the salesman diminishes. The Q1 sees the Q4 as stubborn and unreasonable; the Q4 sees the Q1 as superficial and domineering.

Results.   Over a period of time, Q1 salesmen obtain only average results with Q4 customers. A sufficiently persistent Q4 who refuses to be intimidated may succeed in getting the information he wants; if he does, he may buy even though he has mixed regard for the salesman. But Q4 customers seldom trust Q1 salesmen, and seldom have long-range relationships with them.

A PERSPECTIVE ON Q1 INTERACTIONS

The preceding vignettes should make it clear that the Q1 salesman behaves in essentially the same way with all kinds of customers; his primary strategy is invariably combative, overwhelming, opportunistic, and exploitative. But the various interactions differ considerably because of the way different kinds of customers respond to the Q1's rigid behavior. The Q1 customer, himself combative, overwhelming, opportunistic, and exploitative, zestfully accepts the salesman's challenge; he enjoys jousting. The Q2 customer, distrustful of salesmen to begin with, sees the Q1's behavior as confirmation of his distrust; he reacts uneasily and resentfully. The Q3 customer, eager to be liked, accepts the Q1 because he provides him with guidance and structure, both of which the Q3 needs; the Q3 bends over backwards not to be critical of the Q1's power tactics. And the Q4 customer is often frustrated because the Q1 refuses to deal with him straightforwardly, to encourage his involvement, or to point out what solutions and benefits he can expect from the product. Thus the Q1 salesman's inflexible behavior has a significantly different impact on different kinds of customers.

The Q1 pays a price, sometimes high, for his coercive behavior. Most customers, no matter what their strategy, don't like to be pushed, pressured, or browbeaten. Even the Q1 customer, who is exhilarated by combat with a Q1 salesman, reacts to this sort of treatment by becoming more aggressive himself. And the Q3 customer, who tries hard to excuse Q1 behavior, will not excuse it past a certain point. No one can deny that some people *do* buy because they're pressured or overwhelmed, but not nearly as many as the Q1 salesman likes to think.

The full impact of Q1 behavior is often not felt until *after* the sale. This accounts for much of the Q1 salesman's success or lack of it. Many customers don't resent his domineering tactics until they have had a chance to think about them, and this often happens after the salesman has departed with the *order*. Then, as the customer begins to recount the presentation to himself, he may realize, *for the first time,* that he has been taken advantage of, and he may resolve never to welcome the salesman back again. Resentment and indignation are often delayed reactions.

Many customers don't become fully aware of the Q1 salesman's lack of concern until long after the sale, when they need follow-up or service. As it becomes clear that there will be no, or little, follow-up, that the salesman does not really care whether the product is proving satisfactory, the customer may become disgruntled, complain, or even threaten to return the product.

None of this means that the Q1 salesman is destined to fail. He is, in fact, often quite successful, especially with passive Q3 customers. But he incurs a penalty, and a severe one: because he antagonizes so many customers, his customer attrition rate is high. Year after year, he must work hard to replenish lost customers who are now buying from a more concerned competitor. Even when successful, the Q1 is often on a sales treadmill, unable to relax without slipping backward.

How the Q2 Salesman Interacts with Customers

Like the Q1, the Q2 salesman behaves more or less the same way with all kinds of customers. But different kinds of customers *respond* differently.

Q2 SALESMAN–Q1 CUSTOMER INTERACTION

Relationship. Almost from the beginning of the presentation, the Q1 customer is scornful of the Q2's faltering and submissive manner, his timidity, and his obvious uneasiness. And the Q2 feels threatened by the customer's strong, arrogant tone. With almost no effort, the customer takes and keeps control. He repeatedly interrupts the salesman's rote presentation, and causes him to lose both his train of thought and what little composure he started with. For the salesman, the experience is painfully embarrassing. He feels put upon (but unable to retort), inadequate, and rattled by this customer who personifies all his fears about people. And, to make matters worse, he often reproaches himself for his inability to cope with the bullying and harassment. Filled with feelings of self-disdain and aware that he is unable to cope, he goes through the presentation mechanically, as long as the customer allows. If, as often happens, the customer stops him in the middle and flatly refuses to buy, the salesman caves in, with some relief, and leaves as quickly as he can. By ending his discomfort, the customer has been unintentionally helpful.

Results.   Sales are well below average. Except for the rare times when he stumbles across a customer with an urgent need for what he is selling, the Q2 rarely makes a sale to a Q1 customer.

Q2 SALESMAN—Q2 CUSTOMER INTERACTION

Relationship.   The entire presentation reeks of apathy. The salesman seems disinterested, almost bored, by what he is saying; his voice drones on monotonously; his motions are sluggish. He is obviously doing what he must do, not what he wants to do. The customer is usually indifferent. He listens quietly, says little, and seems preoccupied with other things. The interaction, if it can be called that, is so mechanical that both men seem to wish they were somewhere else. They are neither hostile nor warm, but impassive. Still and all, the Q2 salesman does have one advantage; he does not openly threaten the Q2 customer's security. He may bore the customer, but he does not reinforce his feelings of distrust; to the customer, this is significant.

Results.   Sales are average. If the customer's inventory is low, he will probably place an order with the Q2 salesman. The Q2 salesman's aloofness and lack of animation stand him in good stead, since involved, animated salesmen often frighten Q2 customers. However, whatever success the Q2 salesman has with Q2 customers is attributable to his good luck as an order-taker, not to his selling skills.

Q2 SALESMAN–Q3 CUSTOMER INTERACTION

Relationship.   This interaction can be compared to what happens between an ardent lover and the woman who spurns him. The Q3 customer, always searching for more friends, tries hard to break through the salesman's shell. The Q2 salesman ignores these attempts. He has a job to do, and he intends to do it with as little personal involvement or risk as possible. He does not want to be friends with the customer; he wants to do what he has to do and move on. In fact, the customer's warmth makes him uncomfortable. He has difficulty understanding the motivation behind it. The Q3 customer is as unwilling to be put off as the Q2 salesman is to be involved. He tries repeatedly to "warm up" the salesman. Eventually, he rationalizes his failure by attributing "terrific shyness" to the Q2. The Q2, of course, neither likes nor dislikes the customer; he is afraid of him. Convinced that friendly, outgoing people always have an ulterior motive, he is determined to protect himself from it. To the Q2 salesman, the Q3 customer is frustrating; he cannot cope with the steady stream of inconsequential small talk and interruptions, and the constant pressure to share his experiences and ideas. He tries, awkwardly and mechanically, to stick to the subject and bring the presentation to a reasonably prompt finish, a difficult thing to do with Q3 buyers.

Results.   Sales are average, but little credit goes to the salesman. Most of the orders are placed because the Q3 customer wants to be helpful, because he senses that the salesman is inept and pities him, or because he was about to place an order anyway. Most of these orders, however, are merely tokens; the bulk of the Q3's orders go to competitive salesmen. If the Q2 were warmer and more dynamic, he would unquestionably make bigger sales to the customer.

Q2 SALESMAN–Q4 CUSTOMER INTERACTION

Relationship.   In a curious reversal of roles, the customer does most of the probing and analyzing as he tries to learn *why* he should buy. The salesman doesn't volunteer this information, so the customer tries to dig it out. But the Q2's responses are inadequate; he rarely succeeds in talking about the customer and his problems in terms that are personally meaningful to the customer. His answers (in fact, his entire presentation) are vague and general; they rarely solve the customer's problem or tell him "what's in it for me." The Q2 salesman talks about product features, but fails to translate them into *reasons* for buying. Before the presentation is very old, both men are distressed. The Q4 customer, aware he is wasting his time, searches for ways to end the ordeal without being rude. The Q2 salesman, feeling more inept by the minute, also hopes the presentation ends quickly.

Results.   Sales are distinctly below average. Some sales may be made because the Q4 customer believes the Q2's product is worth buying in spite of the Q2's inadequate presentation. Thus, on occasion, the Q4 customer makes the sale to himself.

A PERSPECTIVE ON Q2 INTERACTIONS

The Q2's behavior is as rigid and unchanging as the Q1's. He is consistently withdrawn, tense, and humorless no matter what kind of customer he is dealing with. But the results differ depending upon the kind of customer. With Q1 and Q4 customers, the sales results are quite bad. The Q2 salesman simply cannot hold his own against dominant people; when he interacts with forceful, demanding customers (and *both* the Q1 and Q4 are forceful and demanding, although in different ways), he becomes even more defensive than usual, so that both the Q1 and Q4 customer lose regard for him. A man focusing all his energies on self-protection can hardly be expected to pay attention to the needs of someone else. It doesn't take long for either the Q1 or Q4 customer to realize that "I'm not going to get any sound solutions or benefits out of this guy."

Things are somewhat better with Q2 and Q3 customers, who are themselves submissive. While the Q2 salesman is suspicious of both of them, he feels less threatened by them. He relaxes somewhat, and is less concerned with keeping the customer at a distance. But, by and large, the Q2 salesman's limited order-taking success with Q2 and Q3 customers is basically due to *external* factors: the Q2 customer's preference for buying from a salesman who doesn't threaten him, and the Q3 customer's desire to be helpful.

It is no exaggeration to say that the Q2's ability to hang on, to continue to be a marginal producer year after year, is largely the result of factors over which he has very little control. No Q2 can hope to survive as a salesman for very long without a large measure of pure luck; he must be in the right places at the right times or have an exceptional product which really sells itself. On the basis of interactional skills alone, the classic Q2 could not, as this chapter has tried to show, be a salesman very long, at least not for one company. But most Q2's don't rely on interactional skills alone. They rely on the sympathy they evoke from customers, or on the quality of their product, or on the fact that any salesman who makes enough sales calls is sure to encounter a few customers who urgently need what he is selling. Consequently, Q2s usually meet their company's minimal standards. The Q2 salesman is often the *lucky* salesman, the salesman whose survival is due in significant measure to chance. Ironically, the Q2, the most security-conscious of all salesmen, relies on the riskiest of all sales tactics.

How the Q3 Salesman Interacts with Customers

In looking at the Q3 salesman, we will see, once again, a salesman whose behavior is rather inflexible, but who interacts differently with different kinds of customers because *their* behavior differs.

Q3 SALESMAN–Q1 CUSTOMER INTERACTION

Relationship. The customer feels an underlying disdain for the salesman. He considers the Q3 an unbusinesslike time-waster who lacks drive and practicalness (in the Q1's book, anyone who "squanders" time socializing is at least slightly impractical). The salesman, of course, likes the customer, but cannot understand why he seems in such a hurry ("This guy," he thinks, "ought to let up a little bit; it isn't healthy to push yourself as hard as he does"). From the start, the customer controls the presentation, and the Q3 salesman, not knowing what else to do, follows his lead. To keep things on track, the customer fires a series of terse questions at the salesman, who responds in his usual talkative, meandering way. This exasperates the Q1, who is convinced that the salesman is incapable of giving straight answers to straight questions. As the presentation progresses, the Q1 becomes increasingly edgy, irritated, and outspoken. Eventually, the salesman becomes flustered or upset by the pressure, and, to soothe the customer, redoubles his efforts to be sociable. This only further provokes the customer, who may, in turn, become openly antagonistic. The presentation becomes a vicious spiral, with the Q3 salesman trying harder and harder to socialize and the Q1 customer becoming more and more hostile.

Results. Results are usually well below average. The Q1 customer sees no good reason to buy from the Q3, and he usually ends the presentation as quickly as he can, since he is convinced that a jester masquerading as a salesman robbed him of valuable time.

Q3 SALESMAN–Q2 CUSTOMER INTERACTION

Relationship. The sales presentation usually becomes hopelessly bogged down in trifles. The Q3 salesman talks on and on about inconsequential matters while the Q2 customer fidgets and fumes underneath. The salesman's attempt to form a close relationship makes the customer uneasy. Unless the salesman finally forces himself to get down to business, the customer may express brief instances of open hostility, probably in the form of sarcasm. Usually, the Q3 is oblivious to these barbs. He persists in thinking that the customer is "a good guy who's probably under the weather," while the customer sees the salesman as a phony "pain-in-the-neck."

Results. Sales are average. The customer does not particularly like the salesman, but he seldom feels very strongly threatened by him either. To the Q2, the latter is very important. The Q3 may be a "wind bag," and a "pest" (the Q2 usually uses both words to describe him), but probably he's *safe*. This means the Q2 customer may relax a little, let down his guard, and buy if that seems the wise thing to do. As a rule, though, the Q3 salesman does not *sell* to the Q2; he functions as an order-taker.

Q3 SALESMAN–Q3 CUSTOMER INTERACTION

Relationship.   Of all sales interactions, this is the most blissful. It could almost be called a "love-in." Almost from the start, the presentation is a meeting of a two-man mutual-admiration society. The atmosphere is casual, sociable, and almost completely unbusinesslike. Conversation ranges widely, laughter is heard frequently, and geniality prevails. Most remarkable, the salesman makes practically no systematic effort to make a sale, and the customer makes practically no effort to extract information about the product or service.

Results.   Sales are well above average, although both men succeed, through a good part of the presentation, in not talking about (or even obliquely referring to) the subject. The fact that the salesman is there to make a sale is taken for granted; at the end, the natural and friendly thing to do seems to be to close the sale. In effect, the sale "just happens." Neither man considers this strange. "After all," they say, "that's what friends are for."

Q3 SALESMAN–Q4 CUSTOMER INTERACTION

Relationship.   The Q4 customer has mixed feelings about the Q3 salesman. He may like his warm manner, but he considers him un-businesslike and, therefore, hard to respect. He does not want to be curt, but he realizes rather early that he will have to rein in the salesman's galloping talkativeness. Usually, the Q4 customer takes the initiative by probing the salesman, and trying to make him stick to the subject. The salesman, unaware that the customer is doing his work for him, becomes slightly restive; he doesn't like such rigid control, and he is made very uncomfortable by the customer's demands for data, analysis, and solutions. But, at the same time, he does like and admire the Q4 customer, whose probing is much less abrasive than the Q1's. There is some tension during the presentation, but far less than when the Q3 salesman makes a presentation to a Q1 customer.

Results.   Sales are average. If the Q4 customer feels he has pried enough information from the salesman, and if he has satisfied himself that the product will produce a net gain for him, he will buy, even though he has received little help from the Q3 salesman. But if he cannot pry loose the information he needs, he will, kindly but firmly, turn the salesman away empty-handed.

At first, it might seem that *everyone* would respond to the Q3 salesman with warmth. As we've seen, however, this is definitely not the case. There is no assurance whatever (contrary to the Q3's optimistic view) that warmth will produce warmth. In the Q1 customer, it is almost sure to produce impatience and, sooner or later, antagonism and lack of respect; the Q3's behavior impresses the Q1 as impractical or aimless. Either way, it strikes him as "soft" behavior that fails to give him sound reasons to buy. In the Q2 customer, the Q3's warmth evokes mainly exasperation (and maybe suspicion). He wants to be allowed to keep his distance, and the Q3 won't let him. At the very least, the Q2 finds the salesman's pressure for acceptance slightly irritating; at most, it makes him subtly sarcastic. Although the Q2 customer usually admits that the Q3 salesman poses no threat, he is nevertheless partly repelled by him. In the Q4 customer, the Q3's warmth engenders some impatience, some wariness, and some defensiveness, and only minimal respect. The customer clearly recognizes that unless he quickly dams up the outpouring of irrelevancies, he may be swept away by the torrent.

Of all customers, then, only the Q3 responds to the Q3 in kind. With other customers, the Q3's smothering friendliness generates its opposite, or something close to it. This does *not* mean, obviously, that warmth usually produces hostile reactions; it means simply, that *unrestrained* warmth frequently produces resentment, hostility, or lack of respect in *selling* situations, especially with dominant customers. Few customers, including the basically hostile Q1 and Q2, are antagonized by moderated, tempered warmth. But the Q3 salesman seldom moderates his warmth. Most of the time, he is inappropriately warm. And this sets up barriers between him and many customers because it is not what they expect in a *business* setting. Ultimately, the Q3 salesman (remember that we are talking about the classic or typological Q3, who assumes countless variations in real life) conveys the impression that he lacks conviction, seriousness, or purpose. Equally bad, he seems to lack respect for the customer's time and energy. And all customers, of course, have a right to expect that the salesman to whom they give their time be serious and keep a businesslike goal in mind. The impression made by the Q3 is often, of course, not the impression he wants to make. But, as we have seen repeatedly, in selling, the impression, intentional or not, is what counts.

How the Q4 Salesman Interacts with Customers

The following descriptions will try to make clear the essential differences between Q4 selling behavior and other behavior. In each of our other salesmen, behavior remained essentially the same no matter what kind of customer was involved. The Q1, Q2, and Q3 salesman behaved with a rigid, inflexible sameness. The Q1 was preponderantly overcontrolling in each instance; the Q2 was largely mechanical; and the Q3 consistently sought acceptance through sociability. But with the Q4 we see a change from rigidity to *flexibility,* an ability to *adapt* behavior to suit the particular needs and expectations of particular customers, a willingness to shift, modify, or alter behavior. Let's illustrate.

Q4 SALESMAN–Q1 CUSTOMER INTERACTION

Relationship.   Both men are strong and assertive. The salesman likes the customer's skepticism and practicality, qualities he shares. The customer appreciates the salesman's forceful, businesslike approach; the Q4 conveys an impression of strength and confidence that appeals to the customer. So, for the most part, there is high mutual respect, although the Q4 salesman is no admirer of the Q1 customer's bulldozer tactics. Aware that the Q1 customer will resent not being permitted to assert himself, the salesman lets him do exactly that without turning control of the presentation over to him. This delicate tactic, in which the salesman gives the customer his head without letting him run wild, enables the Q4 salesman to direct the presentation without forcing the customer to lose face. The Q4 salesman makes no attempt to squelch the Q1 customer. He permits the customer to express strong emotions without trying to stifle them; he persistently tries to convert argument into dialogue. And, throughout, the Q4, by focusing on the customer's needs and how they relate to his product, presents hard, solid reasons for the Q1 to buy.

Results.   Sales are above average, not because the Q4 salesman has out-fought or out-foxed the Q1 customer, but because he has persuaded him that he will benefit by buying, and that he can do so with no loss of self-esteem. When a Q1 buys from a Q4, he doesn't feel he has lost a battle, but that he has gained a benefit. He feels committed to buying because he understands what he will get from his purchase.

Q4 SALESMAN–Q2 CUSTOMER INTERACTION

Relationship.   The Q4 salesman quickly recognizes that his main problem is to persuade the Q2 customer that he is reliable and non-threatening. So he starts out slowly in order to reassure the customer, to convince him that here, at least, is one salesman he can depend upon, who has *his* interests at heart. By methods that we will explain in detail in a later chapter, the Q4 salesman makes himself accepted by the Q2 customer as a helpful problem-solver. And, aware of the Q2's need for guidance, he behaves more assertively with the Q2 customer than he would with a Q1 or Q4 customer. The two men seldom if ever develop a very warm relationship, but they do develop a relationship grounded in respect and trust. The Q4 is the one salesman with whom the Q2 customer feels more or less at ease.

Results. Sales are above average. The Q2 customer buys willingly because he trusts the salesman and more or less understands why he should buy. Because the Q4 salesman forges a strong bond of confidence, the customer buys from him repeatedly. It is extremely difficult for competitors to dislodge the solidly entrenched Q4 salesman.

Q4 SALESMAN–Q3 CUSTOMER INTERACTION

Relationship. The two men establish positive rapport quickly, because the Q4 salesman is sensitive to the Q3's need for acceptance. The Q4 salesman may be somewhat impatient with the Q3's time-wasting, but he understands that the customer has a strong need to gain acceptance through socializing, and he responds to this need without being manipulative. Tactfully, he channels the customer's bubbling cordiality, and keeps it from getting out of hand. The Q4 is firm but friendly, so the customer submits to his guidance without resentment. It would be very difficult for the customer to resent the salesman, since the latter is obviously concerned about him; everything in the Q4's behavior indicates a desire to help and to benefit the customer. As with the Q2 customer, the Q4 salesman responds to the Q3's need for leadership and direction; once again, he is considerably more forceful than he would be with a Q1 or Q4 customer.

Results. Sales are well above average. The Q3 customer both trusts and respects the Q4 salesman (an almost irresistible combination) and willingly buys from him.

Q4 SALESMAN–Q4 CUSTOMER INTERACTION

Relationship. From the very beginning, the interaction is positive and businesslike. The presentation is marked by meaningful give-and-take, by constructive candor, and by a mutual desire to learn. The two men listen to one another open-mindedly and attentively. Instead of rivalry, there is partnership; both seem eager to work together, to cooperate, to contribute to one another's success.

Results. Sales are well above average.

A PERSPECTIVE ON Q4 INTERACTION

These brief vignettes (which will be supplemented in later chapters) should provide some insight into the Q4's flexibility. Let's analyze it in some detail.

The Q4 salesman recognizes that the Q1 customer needs to assert himself, to vent his feelings, and to prove that he's strong and competent, and he responds to his need in the presentation. He does not argue with the customer (this would be self-defeating), but he does give the customer plenty of opportunity to assert himself *without* using the salesman as a doormat. By his actions, the Q4 salesman says, in effect: "Look, very little can be gained by a struggle between us. I recognize your strength, and I respect it. I expect you to recognize and respect mine. I've got a job to do, and I intend to do it. That job is to demonstrate to you that my product will fill your needs and produce a net gain for you. You can't intimidate me, but you can gain a benefit for yourself by working with me." Thus, the Q4 tries to establish a relationship based on neither power nor submission, but on mutual understanding and commitment. He knows that if he appears submissive, he will earn the customer's contempt; if he appears overly dominant, he will evoke distrust from the customer and, even worse, active opposition. The only *workable* relationship, then, is one based on mutual understanding and commitment.

The Q4 salesman recognizes that the Q2 customer's major need is for firm guidance and reassurance. He knows the Q2 has stereotyped all salesmen as untrustworthy; his job, therefore, is to prove that *he* does not fit the stereotype. By what he says and how he says it, he establishes himself as a man of integrity, goodwill, and reliability. And, in a very firm but concerned way, he guides the Q2. Actually, submissive-hostile customers *want* to be guided toward sound buying decisions, but they fear guidance unless they trust the guide. It is this fear that the Q4 overcomes.

The Q4 salesman knows that his Q3 customers must be permitted to gain acceptance through sociability, but that the sociability must be kept within limits. He strives for balance between permissiveness and control; he is both amiable and businesslike. He recognizes the Q3's need for leadership, structure, and direction. As with the Q2, he is firm and decisive in a nonthreatening way. He provides guidance without fear.

With Q4 customers, the Q4 salesman spends less time meeting emotional needs, and quickly gets down to problem-solving. As with other kinds of customers, he is forceful, reassuring, and determined, but his main focus from the outset is to interact so that he can identify and fulfill the customer's product (or service) needs, as well as his personal needs.

Thus while always intent upon demonstrating that he can provide benefits and net gain for the customer, the Q4 salesman varies the *manner* in which he makes this point. His basic purpose always remains the same, to show how his product or service will benefit the customer while he and his company also benefit from the sale. But his *style* of approach to the customer varies. These changes in manner and style always depend upon the kind of customer he is trying to sell. This is what we mean by Q4 flexibility.

SUMMARY

The various interactions described in this chapter are summarized on the accompanying table. In the present summary, we want to stress the following points.

The Q1 salesman is combative, overwhelming, opportunistic, and exploitative, no matter what kind of customer he is interacting with. He pays a price for his behavior much of the time; most customers don't like to be browbeaten or bamboozled. As a result, his turnover of customers is high, and he must work hard to replace lost customers with new ones.

The Q2 salesman, like the Q1, interacts inflexibly with all kinds of customers. He is almost always unenthusiastic, aloof, tense, and humorless. He is more of an order-taker than a dynamic persuader. Most of his sales are based upon his being in the right place at the right time, or on his arousing sympathy in the buyer.

The Q3 salesman is also inflexible in interaction. His warmth and sociability often backfire, generating impatience, suspicion, or disdain in his customers. Only Q3 customers consistently respond to him in kind. Others see him as an unbusinesslike time-waster or a person they might like but don't much respect.

Only the Q4 is flexible in interaction, responding to the particular needs of particular customers. He recognizes the Q1 buyer's need to assert himself, the Q2 buyer's need for reassurance, the Q3 buyer's need for acceptance, and the Q4 buyer's need for sound solutions to problems. His basic purpose is always to demonstrate that he can provide benefit and net gain for the customer; to do this, he varies the style of his approach to each customer so that it opens lines of communication with the customer.

All of these interactions can most readily be understood in the light of three principles. Both Q2 and Q3 customers have strong needs for guidance, leadership, and direction by salesmen, but not at the cost of having their submissiveness exploited. Submissive people usually evoke disdain and even hostility in dominant people. Submissive people are usually sensitive about their submissiveness, and very unwilling to have it taken advantage of.

TABLE 4. Salesman–Customer Interaction

		Q1 customer (dominant-hostile)	Q2 customer (submissive-hostile)	Q3 customer (submissive-warm)	Q4 customer (dominant-warm)
Q1 salesman (dominant-hostile)	Sales relationship	Rapport readily established; businesslike; competitive; presentation is argumentative, a contest	Little rapport; salesman dominates and dictates; customer tensely withdraws	Rapport established easily; salesman dominates and dictates; customer, slightly uncomfortable, complies	Salesman struggles to dictate and dominate; customer struggles to gain information and understanding
	Regard	High mutual regard; each views other as formidable	Low mutual regard; salesman is disdainful, customer fearful	Mixed regard; salesman disdains customer's weakness; customer admires salesman	Mixed; salesman respects customer's businesslike approach; customer admires salesman's forcefulness but feels suspicious of him
	Sales result	Average	Below average; customer postpones commitment	Above average	Average
Q2 salesman (submissive-hostile)	Sales relationship	Little rapport; customer in control from outset; tries to get information, but salesman, intimidated, withdraws	Little rapport; both withdrawn; low interaction; not much said or done	Salesman aloof while customer tries to interact; inconsequential conversation; little business gets done	Customer tries to gain information and understanding; salesman remains aloof
	Regard	Low mutual regard	Neutral regard	Salesman neutral toward customer; customer positive toward salesman	Low mutual regard
	Sales result	Below average	Average; salesman primarily order-taker	Average; customer is eager to be nice helpful guy	Below average

145

TABLE 4 (Continued)

	Q1 customer (dominant–hostile)	Q2 customer (submissive–hostile)	Q3 customer (submissive–warm)	Q4 customer (dominant–warm)	
Q3 salesman (submissive–warm)	Customer peeved by salesman's meandering, unbusinesslike approach; dominates interview; salesman oblivious to customer's impatience	Salesman meanders; customer aloof and occasionally sarcastic; very unbusinesslike and unrestricted interview	Excellent rapport soon established; mutual admiration society; business secondary to personal relationship	Customer increasingly restive as salesman meanders and ignores business; customer tries to keep salesman on track	Sales relationship
	Customer disdainful; salesman has high regard for customer	Customer neutral; salesman has high regard for customer	High mutual regard	Salesman has high regard for customer; customer has mixed regard for salesman	Regard
	Below average	Average; salesman primarily order-taker	Above average	Average	Sales result
Q4 salesman (dominant–warm)	Businesslike climate; salesman flexible; aware of customer's needs for esteem and independence; customer responds by meeting questions realistically	Rapport established easily after slow start; salesman acts as a constructive, non-threatening guide to decision-making	Salesman controls customer's meandering but still responds to his social needs; guides customer gently but firmly	Excellent rapport; both men function as partners in problem-solving; atmosphere constructive and sales-oriented	Sales relationship
	High mutual regard	High mutual regard	High mutual regard	High mutual regard	Regard
	Above average	Above average	Above average	Above average	Sales result

11

Needs and Motivation

WHY PEOPLE BUY

Up to this point, we've been more concerned with the *what* of sales behavior than the *why*. Our early chapters have described behavior we can observe. They have not analyzed, to any significant extent, the underlying motivations of that behavior. The time has now come to explain in more detail *why* customers and salesmen behave as they do, to account for the differences in behavior in the different quadrants. So far, we've talked mainly about observable behavior. Now we're ready to look at the motives behind this behavior.

This chapter, then, deals with the underlying *causes* of sales and buying behavior, or, to use the word favored by behavioral scientists, with *motivation*.

NEEDS AND MOTIVATION

People are *motivated* by *needs,* some of which are physical and some psychological. People do what they do because they have needs to satisfy, and unless they satisfy them, they suffer or feel tension. To take two very simple examples: a hungry man who does not satisfy his need for food will suffer and eventually starve; a man who does not satisfy his need for affection is likely to experience the tension that comes from feeling unwanted, unloved, and unworthy.

These examples are self-evident but not very helpful. What's required is a *systematic* way of talking about and recognizing needs. Only then can we fully understand how customers and salesmen are motivated, and why they act, and interact, as they do. This chapter develops a systematic way to describe needs, then explains how needs motivate selling and buying behaviors, and finally explains how salesmen can use this knowledge to develop more effective sales strategies.

A SYSTEMATIC APPROACH TO NEEDS

Many behavioral scientists have investigated the impact of needs on human behavior, and all agree that needs can be categorized in a meaningful way. The analysis that follows is an adaptation and amplification of the work of Dr. Abraham Maslow, a psychologist who contributed very significantly to our understanding of how needs motivate people. His system is not the only one psychologists use to describe needs, but we believe it is the most practical and useful system for salesmen to master.

One way to understand human needs is to picture them as the layers of a pyramid, with the most basic needs (which must, as a general rule, be satisfied before the others are satisfied) at the bottom. Each higher layer then represents needs less important to staying alive but more important to living a satisfied and fulfilled life. Pictorially, the pyramid looks like the diagram on the following page.

Let's describe each level of needs.

The Biological Needs.   These are bodily needs that must be satisfied if the individual is to live and function: the need for food, oxygen, water, a livable range of outside temperature, and so on. Unless these needs are satisfied, there is virtually no possibility of satisfying any others. (There are rare exceptions to this statement. For example, a martyr may deliberately starve himself in order to fill another, higher need. But, for all practical purposes, our statement is sound.) We could list dozens of biological needs; the need for food, for instance, can be broken down into the need for protein, the need for calcium, and on and on. But the important thing, no matter how they are listed, is that the biological needs are basic, and must be satisfied before others. A desperately thirsty man cannot compose a symphony, a starving man cannot worry about whether his necktie is on straight, and a freezing man will not do very well in a sales training course. In discussing needs, the old adage, first

things first, applies. For most of us, of course, biological needs are satisfied without our thinking about them. A man in a comfortably heated, properly lit, well-ventilated office satisfies many biological needs without being aware of it. He is thus in a position to satisfy other, less basic needs.

The Security Needs.   Once biological needs are attended to, a person tries to satisfy security needs (for physical safety, familiar surroundings and people among whom he feels comfortable, some feeling that the world is essentially stable and predictable, protection from war, disease, crime, accidents, and so on). In filling these needs we help to insure that our biological needs will be met, and we feel "at home" in the world. All of us need some order, stability, and predictability in our lives. All of us need some system, some arrangement, some organization in the things we do. This very book, for example, is an attempt to bring system, order, and method into selling; without such attempts, the field would seem chaotic, and chaos threatens our sense of security. Much of what society does, from organizing police departments to developing sales training courses, is partly done to satisfy some aspect of the need for security.

The Social Needs.   People do not (except for hermits) live alone; they live with or among other people. Social needs vary in intensity from person to person, but all of us have needs that only other people can satisfy, and we do much of what we do to fill these needs. All of us need companionship, love, belonging, affection, and approval; all of us need to feel needed. Salesmen often satisfy their social needs, in part, by membership in sales organizations, lunches with customers, and in ordinary give-and-take during presentations. Salesmen, in fact, have a better opportunity than many people to fill their social needs on the job.

The Esteem Needs.   All of us need a good opinion of ourselves, and we base this opinion in part upon the way other people respond to us. After satisfying our biological, security, and social needs, we begin to concentrate on recognition, reputation, and status. Sometimes, of course, we satisfy our need for esteem not by the opinion of others but by our opinion of *ourselves*. A man may contribute to a charity publicly to impress other people, or privately to enhance his own image of himself. Either way, he satisfies his need for esteem. On the job, esteem needs are partly satisfied by promotions, awards, bonuses, status symbols, and titles. Many people who seek recognition or status are unable, for various reasons, to fill these needs; their behavior is self-defeating and their esteem needs are largely unfilled. A common example is the noisy braggart who tries to gain respect by impressing people with his importance; instead, he repels people, and therefore he feels impelled to become even more boastful, thus causing even greater rejection. Much of our behavior is motivated by our need for esteem, but the behavior does not always produce the intended result.

The Independence Needs.   All of us, to a greater or lesser extent, need to feel independent, to know we can stand alone, if necessary, and take care of ourselves, that we can cope with whatever life brings, that we are strong enough to assume responsibilities, and that we have some control over our destinies. This cluster of needs is one of the things that motivate us to learn. A salesman, for example, who masters his field, has good technical knowledge, solid interpersonal skills, understands human behavior and knows how to deal with it, is far more independent than a salesman without these qualities. The desire for competence, which leads to independence, underlies much training. Closely related is the desire for knowledge; we might even say that people have a need to *know*. Knowledge satisfies the need for independence by freeing people from superstition and error.

The Need for Self-Realization.   It might seem, on first thought, that a man who has satisfied all the needs we've described would lack nothing and want nothing, except to *retain* what he already has, to maintain the status quo. Nothing could be further from the truth. One need still remains. By its very nature it can never be completely satisfied, and it therefore continues, unceasingly, to motivate. This is the need for *self-realization*.

The self-realization needs are difficult to describe because they *vary* with every person; each of us realizes himself in highly distinct and individual ways. People realize themselves by writing poetry, managing Little League ball clubs, exploring remote areas of the world, gaining knowledge, doing a good job of work every day, fighting for their country, becoming president of a corporation, inventing, composing, getting elected to political office, striving after moral perfection, helping others, and on and on. People realize themselves in the business world, on the campus, in laboratories, in monasteries, on football fields, in forest ranger stations, at sea, in the air, ad infinitum. The meaning and the conditions of self-realization are as individualized, as personalized, as a man's name or face.

There is another elusive aspect of the need for self-realization. All other needs can be *fully* satisfied, at least for a time; a man can eat until he's stuffed, have all the friends he wants, make all the money he desires, have a strong, positive image of himself, and feel sufficiently independent. But he can never feel completely self-realized. A man's *self* is open-ended and perpetually unfinished. Often, in fact, the more a man grows, the more he feels he wants to continue growing; the more he develops, the more he feels incomplete. It is almost always the most brilliant scientist who is plagued by awareness of how much he does *not* know, the most successful salesman who most ardently seeks to establish more effective sales approaches.

So, at the summit of the pyramid we find a cluster of needs that each person defines differently, and that can never be completely satisfied. Not everyone feels these needs for self-realization; many people are far too busy filling lower needs to be concerned about personal growth. Survival, security, friends, esteem, and independence are all more basic. Only when these are more or less satisfied does a man, as a rule, have the energy or interest to concentrate on self-realization.

The Task Needs. On the left side of the pyramid of needs, running its entire length, is a category we call *task needs:*

Task needs are all the needs that must be filled so people can perform work. They include needs for paper clips, electronic data processing equipment, courses in baking pastries, and untold millions of other

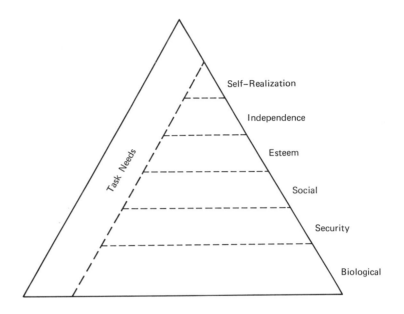

products and services. The task may be as simple as typing a letter, in which case the need can be satisfied by a typist, typewriter, paper, envelope, and a few other items, or as complex as putting together a conglomerate company, in which the services of dozens, perhaps hundreds, of different talents are needed (accountants, lawyers, secretaries, advisers, and so on) as well as thousands of things (from carbon paper to capital).

We've depicted the task needs in a special way, diagonally with a broken line separating them from the personal needs, for two reasons:

1.   The need to perform tasks can be present at *any* time, no matter what personal need a person may be trying to fill. This accounts for the vertical depiction. A hungry man eager to finish at the office so he can hurry home to dinner, is motivated by biological needs. But, he may be unable to finish his work quickly because he lacks a pencil or paper. He has, then, *both* unfilled biological needs and task needs. Or a young college graduate living with his parents may feel a strong need to be free of family constraints (independence need). To attain freedom, he may need a job and income, and, to get the job he wants, he may need an automobile (task need). Once again, the task need and the personal need exist side-by-side. Personal needs do *not* exclude task needs; rather, these needs coexist.

2. Instead of being entirely separate from personal needs, task needs are *frequently* interwoven with them. This accounts for the broken line on the pyramid. We could list many illustrations: the artist who cannot realize himself without canvas, paints, brushes, and the other materials of his craft; the foreman whose need for esteem can be filled by exceeding his monthly quota, but who cannot perform this task without specific equipment; the housewife whose social needs will be partially satisfied by giving a bridge party for some friends, who cannot give a bridge party without playing cards, a card table, and so on. A task need must often be filled in order that a related personal need can be filled. And our personal needs frequently influence what our task needs are. Task and personal needs constantly interact.

Some Important Points to Remember about Personal Needs

Personal needs overlap. In our diagram, the needs are distinctly separate from one another. Actually, however, it is sometimes difficult to tell if a man is motivated by a need for, say, esteem or independence. A man who feels independent usually feels more esteem than a man who does not; conversely a man with a good opinion of himself usually feels more independent, better able to stand on his own two feet, than one with weak esteem. Or, to take another example, the biological need for protection from the elements and the security need for safety from robbers are closely related; both are partly filled by living in a house. In selling, we frequently find that one product or service satisfies *more* than one personal need. A physician who buys an expensive, new piece of diagnostic equipment may *simultaneously* fill, in part, three personal needs: the need for self-realization (he will be able to publish the results of more meaningful research), for independence (he will no longer have to rely on reports from outside laboratories), and for esteem (his professional standing among other physicians may rise); at the same time, of course, he will fill a task need: rendering faster diagnoses. Generally, *one* personal need is the *fundamental* motivator of what we do, but *other* personal needs are frequently associated motivators.

The strength of each personal need varies with each person. Put another way, the "thickness" of each layer of the pyramid differs from person to person. If we were to draw a *separate* pyramid for every person, we'd find, for example, some people whose security needs are so intense that they could only be depicted by a disproportionately thick layer, or whose growth needs so overshadowed all others that the others could only be portrayed by comparatively narrow layers. The proverbial artist who's willing to live in an attic, eat crumbs, and wear rags in order to paint masterpieces has intense self-realization needs but very slight security needs. The miser who spends his days hoarding gold, completely unconcerned with the low opinion other people have of him, has very strong security needs, but very weak esteem needs. And the hermit, content to live in an attic from which he seldom emerges, preferring a solitary existence to the company of others, has very "thick" security needs (or perhaps independence needs) and very "thin" social needs.

The strength of needs not only varies from one person to another, but from one segment of society to another (or from one country to another). People living on welfare payments can be expected to be more aware of their security needs than people in middle-class suburbs (although this may not be true in certain cases; a middle-class suburbanite who is financially overextended and having trouble meeting his mortgage payments may be as motivated by security needs as a welfare recipient). College students may feel the need for independence more keenly than business executives. Adolescents have stronger sexual needs than their grandparents. In talking about needs, then, we must consider individual, social, and cultural differences.

In almost all cases a person is fundamentally motivated by his lowest unfilled personal need. A starving man is motivated to seek food, and little else. He has little or no concern for security (he may even take sizable personal risks to obtain food), little concern for social approval (he may grovel or beg in order to get something to eat), and little concern for esteem (he may steal, and thereby destroy his reputation, to get food). And he is certainly not concerned about independence or growth. However, a man whose biological and security needs are filled, and who has a circle of friends to fill his social needs, will be motivated to fill his need for esteem (which is probably already partly filled by the approval he gets from his friends). To enhance his esteem, he may buy a new home. The heavy mortgage he incurs will certainly not satisfy his need for independence, nor will it lead to self-realization (except indirectly, perhaps by forcing him to work harder on his job). The point is that he is not seeking satisfaction of his independence or self-realization needs; he is seeking satisfaction of his *lowest unfilled personal need,* and that is his need for esteem, a need that the new home satisfies in several ways (it wins him recognition as a man of means, it increases his status among his friends, it enables him to think of himself as a good provider for his family).

What this means for salesmen should be stressed: A salesman must demonstrate to a customer that his product or service will help to satisfy not only the customer's task needs but also the customer's *lowest unfilled personal need,* because both task and personal needs will motivate him to buy. Suppose that you're an automobile salesman making a presentation to a man and his wife. Their task need is for transportation to and from work. Early in the presentation, you learn that both prospects were recently in an accident caused by faulty brakes; the wife suffered a whiplash from which she just recovered, and the husband was badly shaken up. Both barely averted much more serious injury. The accident and the failure of their automobile to brake properly are very much on their minds. It would obviously be foolhardy for you to talk about the social status and the increased esteem this couple will gain when they buy one of your cars. These people are not, at this time, concerned about their social or esteem needs; they *are* concerned about their *security* needs, and it is at *this* level, the level of their lowest unfilled needs, that the benefits of your product should be discussed. The safety benefits of your car should be pointed out and described; special attention should be paid to the brake system. (After the security factors have been thoroughly presented, you may want to explain how other features of the car fill other needs. But the security factors should remain in the forefront.) Discussions of product features which are not related to personal needs are almost always a waste of time, because the customer does not see the *benefits* that these features can produce. The salesman must find out what motivates people and then *connect* the features of his product or service to that motivation. It is meaningless to talk about "advanced styling" or "sleek, racy lines" to an automobile buyer whose overriding concern at the moment is to find a car in which he can feel sure he is going to stay alive.

On the other hand, it is self-defeating to talk about product features at a personal need level that has already been filled. Several years ago, an automobile manufacturer decided to base an advertising campaign on *safety,* and, for a period of months, all the company's ads stressed safety features. The campaign failed and sales declined. At the same time, other manufacturers emphasized prestige, sociability, and esteem in their ads, and sales increased. Why?

The first manufacturer failed to consider the basic principle that *needs which are already satisfied have little power to motivate people.* We do the things we do, in general, to satisfy *unfilled* needs. At the time of the ad campaign in our example, the automobile buying public felt fairly certain that all cars were sufficiently safe; safety needs, in other words, were filled, and safety was not an urgent concern. Instead, car buyers were, by and large, concerned about higher *unfilled* needs: for status, recognition, social approval.

So there are two closely intertwined principles for salesmen to keep in mind:

- People are motivated by their *lowest unfilled personal needs.*
- Filled needs *no longer motivate.*

Quite obviously, then, a crucially important part of the salesman's job is to *discover the level at which his prospect's needs are unfilled.*

There are, on rather rare occasions, exceptions to our statement that men are motivated by their lowest unfilled personal needs. Men do, sometimes, ignore their lowest unfilled personal needs and strive, instead, to fill higher needs. This happens in instances of heroism. A man who rushes into a burning building to save a child obviously ignores security needs in favor of much higher needs (probably esteem or self-realization). There are other less dramatic examples. A man may willingly starve to produce an artistic masterpiece: once again, self-realization needs take precedence over lower needs. The explanation seems to be that in some people certain needs are so strong, so intense, that they overshadow all other needs: this is especially true of the self-realization needs. Men sometimes risk death (sacrifice of biological and security needs) to uphold an unpopular cause or bring help to the suffering. In these situations, only self-realization (as well as independence) seems to matter. Honor becomes more important than survival; integrity more significant than security. Nevertheless, for all *practical* purposes, these remain exceptions. In everyday life (about which the salesman is concerned) our earlier statement holds: men *are,* by and large, motivated by their *lowest unfilled personal needs.*

For the most part, personal needs can be filled in more than one way. A man dying of thirst, for example, can save his life in many ways: with water, milk, cactus juice, wine, and so on. Not all the ways, of course, are equally effective; his life might be saved by a couple of shots of bourbon, but with unpleasant side effects. Nevertheless, we can say that the means by which personal needs can be filled are usually broad rather than specific; a thirsting man needs liquid, rather than some particular kind of liquid.

This is obviously important in selling. A salesman must often show not only that his product will satisfy the customer's task and personal needs, but that it will do so *better* than some other method. A salesman of investment securities may learn that a prospect is worried about income for his retirement (security need); the salesman must demonstrate not only that stock investment will satisfy this need, but he may also have to demonstrate that stock investment will satisfy the need *better* than endowment life insurance, annuities, certificates of deposit, or an investment program managed by a competing company. A salesman of radio advertising time may have to prove to a prospect not only that radio commercials will satisfy his need for publicizing his product (task need), but also that radio commercials are superior to television time, newspaper or magazine ads, billboard space, matchbook covers, sky writing, and so forth.

What this means is that the successful salesman must be aware of the *unique* satisfactions provided by his product and be capable of proving these satisfactions to his prospect.

Suppose, for example, a salesman for a resort hotel wants to persuade a sales manager to hold his next sales meeting at his hotel. He knows, of course, that there are literally hundreds of hotels suitable for this purpose. So he tries to discover some of the prospect's *other* needs. If the sales manager has a very restricted budget, the salesman may be able to demonstrate that, when all costs are considered, the convention will cost less at his hotel. If the sales manager wants to impress his marketing director that he has good taste, the salesman may be able to show that his hotel has a nationwide reputation for elegance and high-style living. Whatever the situation, a salesman has a better chance to make a sale if he can present his product or service as a unique and distinctive satisfier of needs.

A man who thinks a particular set of needs is satisfied may suddenly find it is not. Put another way, dormant needs can be activated by events or people. Let's look at a couple of examples:

A wealthy man may take it for granted that his security needs are filled; in fact, he probably rarely thinks about them. Then, one day, the house next door to his burns to the ground, and the roof of his own home is partially destroyed in the blaze. Almost instantly, his security needs begin to dominate his thoughts; to satisfy these needs, he may call his insurance agent and increase the fire coverage on his house, he may buy a couple of fire-extinguishers for home use, or he may even move into a new glass-and-steel apartment building where he feels safer.

A man with numerous friends and a busy social life probably feels his social needs are satisfied. But, if a job promotion takes him to a new city where he knows few if any people, his social needs will suddenly be activated, and he'll probably spend considerable time and energy doing something he hasn't done for years: establishing a new circle of friends.

Some Q1 salesmen base their presentations on the fact that dormant needs can be activated. The life insurance salesman who opens an interview by asking a prospect, "What would your family do if you were hit by a truck today?", the radio announcer who threatens his listeners with loss of friends and status if they fail to use his brand of toothpaste, the automobile salesman who tells a prospect that "If I were you, I'd trade that car right away; it doesn't look safe to me," are all trying to bring submerged needs to the surface. The technique may work, but, unless it's used carefully and in the best interests of the customer, it may be dangerous for any salesman interested in *repeat* business. When the customer reflects upon his purchase, he may come to feel duped; he may resent an appeal made to his fear or his lack of security. And he may work off this resentment by refusing to buy from the salesman or company again.

A salesman can satisfy a customer's personal needs in two ways: by his method of presentation and by his product. As we'll soon see in detail, the very way in which a salesman communicates can do much to satisfy a customer's needs. A customer with unfilled needs for esteem and independence may find these partly satisfied by a salesman who lets him do most of the talking, who respects his knowledge and point of view, and who shows a desire *to learn* from the customer as well as inform him. A customer with unsatisfied social needs may find them partly satisfied by a salesman who takes the time to chat with him about nonbusiness matters, who doesn't seem eager to end the presentation and move on to his next call, and who seems genuinely interested in the customer as a *person*. A customer with unfilled security needs may find them partly satisfied by a salesman who is quiet and reassuring, not overbearing and threatening. All these are ways of satisfying personal needs by *method of presentation*.

Often, a presentation geared to a prospect's lowest unfilled personal need is the only kind of presentation that can get through to him successfully. Here's an example: Stan Irving, a pharmaceutical salesman, was detailing a brand-new, expensive, nontoxic antibiotic, for the first time. His first call was on Dr. Alcott, a remote, withdrawn Q2 with strong security needs. Stan, highly enthusiastic about the new product, began his presentation (after brief introductory remarks) by saying: "Dr. Alcott, I'd like to describe a brand-new, highly innovative product that, according to clinical studies, promises to be a major breakthrough in the diminution of ——." From this point on, Dr. Alcott became increasingly detached and disinterested until, a few minutes later, he glanced at his watch and, interrupting Stan in the middle of a sentence, said, "Sorry, Irving, but I've got to get over to the hospital. Maybe you can finish telling me about this product some other time."

Next, Stan went down the hall to the office of Dr. Whitman, a questioning, probing Q4 physician. Realizing that his presentation to Dr. Alcott had not gone well, Stan decided to try a different approach with Dr. Whitman. "Doctor," he said (after a brief exchange of greetings), "I'd like to tell you about a product that reduces to zero allergic effects which can cause serious complications in your patients." The doctor immediately responded with, "Maybe some other time. Today's an awfully busy day, and I really can't spare the time unless you've got something new and exciting to tell me." At that, Stan immediately changed his tack and hastily assured the doctor that he did, indeed, have something new to describe, meanwhile reproaching himself for nearly "messing up" the interview.

It's plain that, in both cases, the salesman failed to meet unfilled needs by his method of presentation. In talking to submissive-hostile Dr. Alcott, he stressed the product's *newness*, its *innovative* qualities, and its *breakthrough* impact, all of which were certain to create barriers in anyone whose chief concern is with *security*. Q2s, as a rule, shun products that threaten to disrupt or change established patterns; they avoid anything that might undermine the stability and certainty that are so important to them. Newness, innovations, and breakthroughs are the very things that Q2s do *not* want. (This is not to say that Q2 physicians never try anything new; of course they do. But the best way to introduce them to something new is to stress its *conservative* or *nonthreatening* features first.)

On the other hand, in talking to dominant-warm Dr. Whitman, Stan stressed *safety* and *security* factors which were unlikely to elicit enthusiasm from a Q4 because allergic reactions to drugs are not, as a percentage of total drug use, all that common. (This is not to say that a Q4 physician would not be interested in safety; he would, of course. But his primary interest would be in the positive effects of the drug.) A Q4 physician would respond most to a presentation that stressed the ways in which the drug represented an *advance* or *improvement* over existing drugs; he would be mainly interested in its *novel* or *original* features.

In effect, then, the salesman got his approaches mixed. The first approach, stressing newness and innovation, should have been made to the second (Q4) physician, and the second approach, stressing security and caution, should have been made to the first (Q2) physician. *Method* of presentation can go a long way toward filling customer needs.

At the same time, many needs can be satisfied by the *product* (or service) itself. Task needs, of course, are satisfied *only* by a product or service; a man who needs a hammer to complete a task needs a hammer; he may ultimately be satisfied by something else (any hard, heavy object that can serve as a hammer) but he cannot hope to have his need satisfied by a salesman's method of presentation. Biological needs are satisfied *only* by products, or by things found in nature (sunlight, air, and so on); like task needs, they cannot be satisfied by a salesman's method of presentation. But other needs can frequently be satisfied both ways. A clothing salesman selling a suit to a man with strong esteem needs will not only treat him with honest respect, but will stress those qualities that will enhance the man's esteem (for example, the suit has been tailored by one of America's leading designers, it features the same kind of jacket worn by some well-known people, it makes the wearer look dignified).

Now, this is not manipulative if it's done with the customer's interest in mind. Manipulation is control of other people by crafty, unfair, or insidious means for one's own advantage. We are *not* recommending that. We *are* recommending *communication,* not manipulation. An elementary fact of human behavior is that it's easier to *get through* to people and achieve a meeting of minds when you talk to them on the level of *their* needs, *their* aspirations, and *their* interests. A man with strong esteem needs who goes into a clothing store to buy a suit is *interested* in how the suit looks on him; he *wants* to know who designed the suit and the names of other people who are wearing the same style. A salesman who talks to him on the level of his needs and interests is only talking to him on a level that the customer finds meaningful and significant. Since the customer does not have compelling security needs, and since he is not interested in how long the suit will last, it would be foolish for the salesman to dwell upon the quality of the fabric or the way the buttons are stitched. This kind of presentation would fail to tell the customer what *he* wants to know.

Communication (we are talking now about *real* communication resulting in mutual understanding, not mere verbal exchange) can best take place on the level of people's interests and concerns, and people's interests and concerns are largely determined by their needs. A clothing salesman who discovers a need for esteem in a customer and then conscientiously describes how a given suit can fill that need, is a salesman who communicates; a clothing salesman who discovers the same need and then tries to fill it with a suit that is obviously not right for the customer (perhaps in hopes of making a higher commission than he would on a suit that clearly looks better), is a salesman who manipulates. Communication is forthright and sincere; manipulation is sly and crafty.

Every salesman should have a threefold obligation: to his customer, to his company, and to himself. A sale, as the Q4 salesman insists, should benefit all three. If only the salesman gains from the transaction, he has been either manipulative or inept. Manipulation, it must be remembered, is always done for one's *own* advantage. Where there is genuine concern for his customer and his own company as well, where the sale is based on *mutual* understanding and *mutual* commitment, there can be no manipulation.

NEEDS, MOTIVATION AND BEHAVIORAL STRATEGIES

It is usually not very difficult to uncover a customer's task needs. But *how* does a salesman uncover and identify a customer's *personal* needs?

The answer, quite simply, is by *observation of the customer's behavior* and through *successful communication*. Communication is the subject of later chapters; here we will only say that people, frequently unwittingly, reveal a great deal about their motives and their needs by the way they act and the things they say. If a customer has a lavish office, with expensive furniture and fine prints on the walls, and if he's smartly dressed and smokes expensive cigars, it's obvious that his biological and security needs have been filled, and it's likely (this is a clue the salesman must follow up) that he has strong social needs (probably for acceptance by others) and strong esteem needs (for status and recognition). No salesman should jump to this conclusion as final, but no salesman should fail to test the assumption, either. All of this will be considered in detail in later chapters.

Right now, the important thing is that needs can usually be *inferred* from behavior. Selling, in fact, is a process in which the salesman infers the customer's needs and then demonstrates how the features of his product fill those needs so as to produce a benefit to the customer. Stated in a simple formula, this definition can easily be remembered as:

Customer Needs + Product Features = Benefit to Customer

To see how this formula works out in practice, let's examine the needs and motivations underlying each customer strategy. In doing this, it might help to have a picture of the pyramid of personal needs clearly in mind.

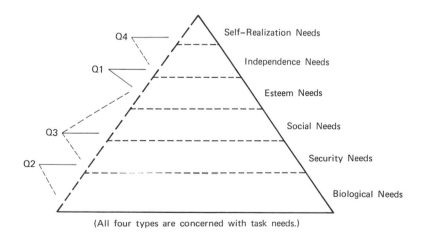

(All four types are concerned with task needs.)

The Q1 Customer's Needs

The dominant-hostile (Q1) customer is basically motivated by the need for *esteem* and the need for *independence*.

The need for esteem, for recognition and reputation, underlies much of his behavior. He rationalizes his forceful, domineering behavior by saying that he acts that way to protect himself from the wiles of salesmen. He insists that salesmen are not to be trusted, that they are determined to sell him something he neither wants nor needs, and that only by defiant and aggressive behavior can he defend himself. In truth, however, the Q1 behaves this way largely because of his *own* needs for esteem and independence. Only by maintaining the upper hand in his encounters with salesmen, only by controlling situations so that *he* comes out on top, can he maintain an image of himself as strong and worthy of respect. Only by proving that he doesn't need the salesman's advice or help, that he will buy only when he is ready, can he maintain his self-image as an independent person who doesn't have to lean on other people.

In spite of the Q1's repeated assertions that aggressive behavior is forced on him by salesmen, the fact is that he is motivated largely by his own internal needs. But there are exceptions to this generalization. For example, a purchasing agent may act in a Q1 manner because his boss has threatened to fire him unless he becomes tougher and stronger in his buying practices; his need for security, exemplified by his fear of losing his job, is the fundamental motivator. In a situation like this, an observant salesman, through careful communication techniques, can frequently discover the *real* need; he may notice, for instance, that the purchasing agent, although wearing a Q1 mask, seems ill at ease, and, through careful probing, he may discover why. Then, too, a customer may behave like a Q1 because past experience has taught him to be tough with a particular salesman or group of salesmen. Thus a buyer who is not ordinarily a Q1 may don a Q1 mask when confronting a widget salesman because, *in the past,* he has found widget salesmen to be sly, manipulative, overbearing, and so forth.

In general, however, a Q1 customer usually seeks to satisfy a need for esteem (by feeling strong, superior, masterful, and in control of salesmen) or a need for independence (by demonstrating that he can get along fine without salesmen, that he is self-sufficient, and that he cannot be fooled).

HOW THE Q1 CUSTOMER EXPRESSES
HIS ESTEEM AND INDEPENDENCE NEEDS

Customers express their personal needs both verbally and nonverbally. By thoughtfully listening to his customers and observing them carefully, a salesman can often detect their motivating personal needs.

The Q1 customer typically expresses his *esteem* needs in the following ways: he makes a bid for respect and admiration; he makes it plain that he wants to be thought of as a powerful, intelligent, competent person; he seeks recognition for his achievements; and he is eager not to lose face. His conversation is largely filled with references to himself, his ideas, and his accomplishments; his tone is self-congratulatory, self-approving, perhaps boastful. He is very skillful at bringing the discussion around to himself, so that he becomes the focus of whatever is being talked about. His entire manner is one in which he tries hard to elicit approval and praise.

The Q1 customer typically expresses his *independence* needs by trying to control the presentation, by making independent decisions without seeking the advice or opinion of the salesman, and by making it plain that he does not want (and does not need) to be told what to do. His behavior conveys the message: "Don't tell me what *you* think. *I* know better." Frequently, if he does accept an idea or suggestion from the salesman, he will rephrase it and then present it *back* to the salesman as if it were *his,* the customer's, original idea.

ESTABLISHING BENEFITS WITH Q1 CUSTOMERS

In selling to a Q1, it is important to satisfy his needs for esteem and independence. A couple of examples will make this clear:

An insurance salesman, calling on a prospect, found himself struggling from the outset to establish himself as the prospect's equal. He encountered a barrage of statements like "I know everything I need to know about insurance; I used to sell the stuff myself," and "You guys have got it easy these days, with all those printed sales aids; I used to do all my selling without any help from anybody or anything." Instead of pausing to analyze these remarks, the salesman charged ahead and began talking about his company's new income-protection plan. At the end of the presentation, during which the prospect was cold and unhelpful, the prospect said, "You've just wasted your time; I've got all the income-protection I need," and ended the interview.

What the prospect really needed, of course, was some indication from the salesman that the latter recognized the prospect's expertise, and that he saw the prospect as a man who knew a considerable amount about insurance. The prospect's boastful remarks really expressed a need for esteem and independence, but the salesman failed to pick up the clues.

Compare that case with this one:

An account executive in an advertising agency heard through the grapevine that a local company was about to change agencies. The account executive, who had many years of experience in his field, called on the marketing director of the company to investigate the possibility of making a formal presentation to the company. At the start of the interview the marketing director was gruff and unfriendly. Through careful probing, the account executive learned that the marketing director had been visited by a series of advertising agency representatives, all of whom had treated him as someone who knew less about advertising than they did. "I don't need anybody to tell me anything about the ad business," objected the marketing director, "and I'm getting sick and tired of being told how to run my business." Realizing that the marketing director's esteem had been wounded, the account executive made sure that he treated him with the respect his position and experience entitled him to. Instead of trying to impress the marketing director, he drew him out, encouraged him to participate, and let the latter impress *him*. Instead of telling the marketing director what to do, he let him do much of the talking. By responding to the prospect's personal needs, the account executive added the firm to his roster of clients where other men offering exactly the same services had failed.

The Q2 Customer's Needs

The submissive-hostile (Q2) customer is largely motivated by *security* needs, and, to a lesser extent, by *biological* needs. The Q2, especially the extreme Q2, feels uncomfortable and apprehensive much of the time. His fears are diffuse, not concentrated; he is frightened by the world in general, rather than some specific part of it. He tries to withdraw or remain aloof from a world where he feels threatened, intimidated, ill at ease. He may fear being badly treated by other people, losing his job, not being understood or appreciated, not being able to maintain his family. He feels both physically and emotionally insecure.

Unhappily, there is seldom any way for the Q2 to find the security he craves, except temporarily. Even when alone, when he has shut out the world and withdrawn into himself, he feels inadequate; his shortcomings and failures only deepen his feeling of insecurity. The constant effort to assure himself that he is not as inadequate as he feels accounts for his unending deprecation of others; he tries to assure himself that he *is* a strong, masterful person who is not appreciated. Under this veneer of pretense and rationalization, however, he feels weak, ineffective, and inept, and readily submits to guidance and control by others. Assailed by doubts about his own strength, feeling a strong need for security and certainty in an unfriendly and menacing world, he is ready to succumb to the leadership of stronger people *if* he can do so without damaging his already frail and bruised self-image. He craves security, and he resents having his weaknesses exploited.

The salesman trying to sell a Q2 customer must fill his needs for security *without* exploiting his submissiveness; he must allay fears, set doubts to rest, and provide reassurance. Only then can he get the Q2 to give up his unresponsive silence (which is the Q2's way of screening out threats and protecting himself) and to get *involved* in the sale. The salesman must remember that the Q2 really wants to be guided and led; he has a strong need for direction that can be relied upon.

HOW THE Q2 CUSTOMER EXPRESSES HIS SECURITY NEEDS

Typically, the Q2 customer expresses his strong security needs by the following behavior: he is cautious, unenthusiastic about any suggested changes in his present way of doing things, slow to act or make decisions, unwilling to share or provide information, and unwilling to reveal his opinions or feelings. He talks less than other customers, and then mainly about unimportant or impersonal matters. He rarely commits himself in very positive terms; he hedges many of his statements, always trying to leave himself an exit by which he can back out of a remark. At the same time, he is quite rigid, holding tight to whatever ideas he does have. His whole attitude seems to say: "Why don't we just leave well enough alone?"

ESTABLISHING BENEFITS WITH Q2 CUSTOMERS

The Q2 customer has none of the Q1's desire to stand out from the crowd and attract attention. He prefers to be submerged in the crowd; he feels safest when not noticed, not singled out. This is important to any salesman who wants to fill the Q2's security needs. Let's look at an example:

A clothing salesman, unaware of the different needs of different customers, was so enthusiastic about a new line of brightly colored plaid suits that he decided to show them to every prospect who came into the store. One customer made it very plain, at the start of the presentation, that he wanted a traditional dark grey suit; the salesman, however, insisted on showing him a noisy plaid, and suggested a loud shirt and tie to match. The customer became visibly upset and threatened to leave and shop at some other store. Only then did the salesman show him a conservative grey suit. If the salesman had probed the customer's original statement and taken time to chat with him about his clothing preferences, he would have discovered that the customer was manifesting Q2 behavior in regard to his dress; he did not want attention-getting clothes, he did not want to attract stares, and he wanted a suit that would be indistinguishable from most other suits. The Q2's quest for security is frequently expressed in the clothes he wears.

Q2 customers are often put off by salesmen with hearty, enthusiastic styles of speaking; they prefer the reassuring manner of the restrained, soft-spoken salesman. They are almost always distressed by the openly aggressive manner of the Q1 salesman. Constantly on guard against what they regard as threatening behavior, Q2s are exceedingly sensitive to the *style* of a salesman's presentation: his choice of words, his inflections and intonations, his entire manner of presenting himself.

Many of us take for granted that our security needs will be satisfied, so we do not think much about them. But these needs can be temporarily activated and brought to the surface; when this happens, we may behave like Q2s although our customary buying behavior is in some other quadrant.

An insurance salesman called on a prospect whose typical behavior was Q3: relaxed, outgoing, and sociable. After a pleasant and rambling conversation on a variety of topics, the agent began to discuss the prospect's need for additional personal property insurance coverage. "Remember," he said, "you haven't increased your coverage in fifteen years, and you own a lot more personal property now than you did then." "That's true," responded the prospect, "but I don't see why I need more coverage. There's never been a burglary in this neighborhood. This house couldn't be safer. Why bother to increase my coverage?" "Because," said the agent, "you're never as safe as you think. Another one of my policy holders lives in a neighborhood like this. Safe, secure, never burglarized. About six months ago, his place was broken into, and he was robbed of more than $5000 worth of personal property. The police told him it was the first time in more than thirty years that a burglary had taken place on his street." At that, a troubled look clouded the prospect's face, and he immediately agreed to increase his coverage.

The Q3 Customer's Needs

Basically, the Q3 customer is motivated by *social* needs. *Security* needs and *esteem* needs are lesser but important elements in his behavior.

We have already spoken of the Q3's deep needs for acceptance, affection, warmth, approval, and companionship. Closely allied to these needs are equally deep needs to smooth over conflict, confrontation, tension, hostility, disagreement, or unpleasantness of any kind. The Q3 engages in an unending effort to enjoy warm, affectionate experiences and *evade* harsh, disagreeable ones.

Security and esteem needs are frequently tied to his strong social needs. When the Q3 gets friendship and affection, he feels secure and safe; at the same time, he sees himself as worthwhile, a "nice guy" who is approved by others. As long as people like him, enjoy being with him, and respond to him good-naturedly, he maintains a positive self-image. But, when he encounters animosity things change abruptly. His security crumbles, and is replaced by anxiety, perhaps even fear. He starts to feel apprehensive, worried, tense. Afflicted by self-doubt and unwilling to blame others for the animosity, (which would, in his eyes, be a hostile and unfriendly thing to do), he is likely to blame himself. "There must be something wrong with me," he thinks. So unsettling is this feeling that he goes to great lengths to avoid it; he spends much of his life pursuing happy moments while fleeing from unhappy ones.

The Q3's social, security, and esteem needs are so compelling that he needs constant *proof* that people think well of him, constant affirmation of his likability. He spends unreasonable amounts of time in seemingly idle chatter with salesmen, to confirm his popularity to himself. From the Q3's point of view, this apparently aimless talk serves an important purpose: it reinforces his image of himself as someone who is accepted, a "nice guy," the only image he can live with comfortably.

In his own way, the Q3 customer is as insecure and fearful as the Q2. But, because he is much warmer, he relieves his insecurity in a different way. From the salesman's viewpoint, the Q3 customer is pleasanter to deal with than the Q2, but not necessarily easier.

HOW THE Q3 CUSTOMER EXPRESSES
HIS SOCIAL, ESTEEM, AND SECURITY NEEDS

Typically, the Q3 customer expresses his motivating needs by the following types of behavior.

Social and Security Needs. The Q3 customer goes out of his way to please. He is usually very submissive, dodging any hint of disagreement or argument. He gives in easily on both major and minor points. He frequently uses phrases like "You're absolutely right," "I agree 100%," "You took the words right out of my mouth," "You can say that again" and "Truer words were never spoken." If he does venture any slight disagreement, he hedges it with so many qualifying remarks that the disagreement is likely to be completely lost.

Esteem needs. Where the Q1 customer wants to be esteemed as a powerful, intelligent, and competent person, the Q3 customer wants to be esteemed as a "nice guy." To get this esteem, he tries to come across as pleasant, cooperative, sympathetic, understanding, good-natured, responsive, helpful, appreciative, and encouraging. Where the Q1 tries to gain esteem by patting himself on the back, the Q3 tries to gain esteem by being pleasant, by refusing to push himself forward, by making the salesman "feel good."

ESTABLISHING BENEFITS WITH Q3 CUSTOMERS

Q3 customers generally admire strong, assertive people, which explains why Q1 salesmen, so different from Q3s in so many important ways, obtain better than average results in selling to them. Because they are submissive, Q3 customers have strong needs for being guided. Their behavior is really a plea for direction, for leadership that will help them to make decisions. They want strong guidance, but without being taken. A Q3 can easily be hurt by a salesman who manipulates and domineers, especially if the salesman exploits his submissiveness; when this happens, the customer may withdraw, baffled and hurt. The Q3 wants the direction *without* the exploitation.

A sheet-steel salesman made a first call on a purchasing agent, who proved to be unusually outgoing and amiable. At the outset, the P.A. made the point that "I like to get to know the people I buy from. After all, if you're going to do business with a man, you want to think of him as a friend." The salesman, intent upon getting an order and moving on, ignored this statement, and immediately launched into a description of the features of his steel sheets. The P.A., unwilling to be pushed into a product discussion so quickly, tried to divert the salesman. At one point, he mentioned golf; at another, he commented on a new automobile he had purchased; at still another point, he referred to an old friend who used to be a salesman for another steel company. To every one of these attempts to establish a congenial atmosphere, the salesman responded brusquely. After a while, although the salesman was too insensitive and unobservant to realize it, the customer, stung by the constant rebuffs, began to withdraw, and finally ended the interview by telling the salesman that "I think we'll stick with our present supplier."

As the example makes clear, the salesman was too inflexible to respond to the customer's social needs; his behavior was inappropriate to the situation. Although he thought the customer's remarks were irrelevant, the *customer* considered them highly relevant. Q3s cannot be expected to respond with affable smiles to any kind of treatment. Most of them can be goaded into assertive, even forceful, behavior, and any salesman who does the goading does so at his peril.

To establish benefits with a Q3 customer, then, the salesman must establish himself as a person receptive to the Q3's social needs. Only then will the customer be motivated to listen to product features and benefits.

When discussing benefits with a Q3, the salesman should stress those product features that will win approval or perhaps affection for the customer. This may not always be possible, but it *is* possible more often than might be thought. A Q3 office manager may be receptive to a salesman's assertion that by buying a copying machine to lessen the workload in the office, the office manager can win the gratitude of the people who work there. Or a Q3 father might be especially receptive to an automobile salesman's claim that, by buying a station wagon, he'll be more popular than ever with his family.

It is important, of course, not to oversimplify the Q3 customer. Not all his purchases are motivated by social, security, and esteem needs. A Q3 is certainly unlikely to buy a copying machine merely to make himself popular with the office force; he must first have a *task* need for the machine. And he is even less likely to buy a machine with a bad reputation, or an overpriced machine, merely to win affection; he will almost surely explore quality and price carefully. We are merely saying that in buying any product or service, the Q3 attaches great importance to his social, security, and esteem needs, and that any salesman should be aware of this fact. In meeting these needs, the salesman increases the probability of capturing the mind of the customer.

The Q4 Customer's Needs

The Q4 customer is largely motivated by a need for *self-realization* and, secondarily, for *independence*. We said earlier that the self-realization needs are hardest of all to understand; in many ways, the Q4 customer is the hardest of all customers to understand. So let's look at him in some detail.

One important way in which the Q4 differs from other customers is that he is willing, and sometimes eager, to *take risks*. He does so not for thrills or excitement, but because he cannot grow without taking chances, trying new approaches, experimenting, innovating, and, if necessary, failing. This does not mean he is foolhardy or headstrong, only that he is willing to hazard a certain amount of security in an effort to develop and grow. This willingness to venture, to explore new avenues, to search and probe, to be innovative and distinctive, leads to self-realization. So it is usually the Q4 who most readily tries new products, avidly listens to new ideas, and tries new ways of doing things. It is the Q4 buyer who is receptive to the *breakthrough,* the advanced product or service that will bring him new efficiency, or bigger profits, or whatever it is he considers important to his own development.

But the Q4 customer is much more than an innovator; he is an *objective* person who understands himself and others better than the Q1, Q2, or Q3 customer does. More realistic about his own strengths and weaknesses, and more aware of other people's, he does a better job of evaluating his own motivations, and other people's. Less closely bound by lower needs, less immersed in the daily struggle to find security or make friends or bolster his self-image, he is *freer* to stand back and look at himself and the world around him. His perspective is less distorted by fears and anxieties, his point of view less colored by his own apprehensions and worries.

His greater objectivity makes him more *realistic about people,* a fact reflected in his view of salesmen. To the Q1, Q2, or Q3 customer, all salesmen are perceived narrowly; the Q1 and Q2 think of salesmen as sly, untrustworthy, dangerous; the Q3 thinks of them as pleasant, warm, friendly. But the Q4 takes a broader view. He knows that salesmen differ from one another as much as other people do, so it is unrealistic to generalize about them. He prefers to take them one-by-one, forming his opinions on first-hand knowledge. Unless his experience proves to the contrary, he treats all salesmen as problem-solving businessmen. The Q4 customer's actions are not restricted by preconceived stereotypes about salesmen; he treats each salesman individually.

But his objectivity extends beyond his attitudes toward salesmen; it influences his interaction with salesmen. The Q4 customer tries to keep his emotions from interfering with his practical judgment in the sales interview. Less concerned than the Q1 customer about proving his strength, less concerned than the Q2 about protecting himself, less concerned than the Q3 about gaining acceptance, the Q4 customer is freer to concentrate on factual analysis of his needs and the product's features. This is not to say he is free of emotion. But, far more than the Q1, Q2, or Q3 customer, he *understands* his feelings and keeps them from intruding upon his decisions.

Another way to say this is that the Q4 can take self-criticism. He has enough inner security, enough self-assurance, to question and doubt himself, and to listen to questions and doubts expressed by others. A salesman can be considerably more candid and more direct with a Q4 customer than with any other kind, since the Q4 does not consider candor an attack that must either be repelled or escaped.

Unlike the Q1 customer, the Q4 does not need to reinforce his mastery and control; unlike the Q2, he doesn't have to worry about constant assaults upon his security; and unlike the Q3, he doesn't have to prove repeatedly that he has qualities people like. So he can afford to be more searching, more analytic, more open, more responsive to new ideas, more amenable to change. All these qualities, of course, lead to self-realization.

Closely related to the way he sees himself is the Q4 customer's basic *optimism*. The Q1, Q2, and Q3 customers see the world as essentially threatening; the Q1 overcomes the threat by striking first, by landing the first blow, by refusing to let others get the upper hand; the Q2 avoids the threat by withdrawing; the Q3 pretends the threat doesn't exist, that his own worst fears are unfounded, that people really are friendly and warm (but he never succeeds in *thoroughly* persuading himself, and always lives on the edge of fear). The Q4 customer is much more positive. He thinks in terms of opportunity, not threat; when he confronts other people, he feels challenged, not menaced. He knows his growth requires openness to experience, willingness to meet others at least half way, and receptivity to new ideas.

Because growth is so important to him, the Q4 customer enjoys grappling with problems; he is exhilarated by overcoming difficulties. This cannot be said of other customers, who try, one way or another, to avoid problems. Superficially, the Q1 customer seems to enjoy wrestling with problems; underneath, he is afraid they will overwhelm him. So he tries to overwhelm them first. The Q2, of course, retreats from problems, and the Q3 works hard to keep them from arising in the first place. But the Q4 customer actually *likes* problem solving. In resolving what appears irresolvable, by striving against heavy odds, by overcoming obstacles, he becomes conscious of growth. He especially likes salesmen who, like himself, enjoy tackling tough problems and delving beneath the surface of things to search for *real* answers to hard questions. When he meets such a salesman, he treats him as a working partner.

With his concern for development, his willingness to innovate, his objectivity, his acceptance of criticism, his basically optimistic view, his openness and receptivity, and his zest in confronting and solving problems, it is no wonder the Q4 customer is able to balance his concern for himself with a concern for the salesmen with whom he deals. Unlike the Q1, Q2, and Q3 customers, who are enmeshed in their own interests and problems, the Q4 directs his energies outward as well as inward; he is aware of the significance of other people as well as of himself. He is free to think of salesmen as colleagues, not enemies or buddies. He regards sales presentations not as pitched battles or holding operations, but as opportunities for problem-solving and for growth from which everyone can benefit.

Typically, the Q4 customer expresses his independence needs by the following behavior: by getting involved in the presentation, offering his ideas and opinions, venting his feelings openly, and, in general, participating as a full partner in the sales process. This contrasts with the Q1's bid for independence, which is based on an "I know best" attitude. The Q4 says, by his behavior, "Let's use our joint resources to solve my problem." He is not interested in making the presentation a one-man show in which he alone is on stage while the salesman applauds from the wings.

ESTABLISHING BENEFITS WITH Q4 CUSTOMERS

Because self-realization is defined differently by different people, the salesman who wants to sell a Q4 customer cannot afford to tie himself down to preconceptions. He must remain as open, as willing to probe, and as receptive to new ideas as the customer; only by searching out the customer's views, and by patiently analyzing the information he gets from the customer, can the salesman determine *how* the customer defines self-realization. A few examples should clarify this point:

A Q4 physician might interpret self-realization in terms of *better care of patients* and the *acquisition of new knowledge*. A salesman for a medical equipment company, trying to sell a new item of diagnostic equipment, would probably find that its greatest appeal to the physician was that it enabled him to do a more accurate job of diagnosis, thus contributing to better patient care, and that it freed him from a certain amount of time-consuming detail work, giving him extra time to keep up with professional journals and attend medical seminars.

Compare this physician's attitude with that of a Q1, Q2, or Q3 physician. The Q1 might buy the new equipment partly to enhance his feelings of mastery and his prestige among his colleagues; his basic concern would be with esteem. The Q2 might be attracted to the equipment because it would give him more time to be by himself, away from patients and nurses. The Q3 would perhaps buy the equipment to gain more free time, some of which could be used to fill social needs. But the Q4 would be motivated by growth needs which he would define *in his own way*. (Once again, we point out that these would not be the *only* reasons the physicians might buy the machine; a real task need would also have to be present.)

A young man might interpret self-realization in terms of *expressing his individuality*. An automobile salesman would probably find that the young man would be most interested in a car rarely seen on the road, a model with special equipment and relatively unique features.

A fairly wealthy woman might interpret self-realization in terms of *assisting underprivileged children*. A saleswoman in a department store might find it fruitless to try to sell a fur-trimmed coat to the woman because the latter would consider it inappropriate to wear to the day-care center at which she spends much of her time, and because she feels the money would be better spent helping the youngsters to whom she is devoted.

A purchasing agent might interpret self-realization in terms of *outstanding performance on the job,* which he defines as buying the best quality at the best price. A salesman would probably find that the purchasing agent demands plenty of data to back up claims, that he insists on detailed cost analyses, and that he is relatively uninfluenced by emotional factors.

These examples could be extended, but the point is no doubt clear by now: all Q4 customers are largely motivated by self-realization needs, but these needs are satisfied in a host of *different* and highly *personal* ways. The salesman must discover, through careful probing and analysis, *how* a particular Q4's needs for self-realization can be fulfilled.

It must be stressed, once again, that the Q4 is not an emotional robot. Quite the contrary. While *basically* motivated by self-realization needs, he still has other needs to which he responds. A Q4 customer may buy a necktie for no other reason than that he wants to impress his fiancee (esteem need), he may buy a station wagon to make his wife and children happy when he really prefers a hard-top (social need), he may buy a new set of brake drums because he's having trouble stopping his car (security need). To base *every* buying decision on self-realization needs would be less than human.

However, we *can* say that the Q4 customer faces up to his emotions more willingly than other customers; he is more analytic, more objective, more candid about himself. He acknowledges what other customers try to hide; he admits what they try to rationalize. In a phrase, the Q4 is less emotional about his emotions. He is more willing to listen to and be persuaded by reasonable, factual discussion.

It must not be thought that, because he is less entangled in a web of emotions, the Q4 customer is easy to sell. If anything, he may be the toughest of all customers. Only a salesman who is perceptive, analytic, thoughtful, and a master of communication skills can do a consistently good job of selling the Q4 customer. Working successfully with a Q4 requires a thorough-going knowledge of the customer, based upon patient probing, careful observation, and attentive listening; it requires detailed knowledge of the product, and the ability to *relate* product features to the customer's needs; and it requires objectivity and the ability to see things as they are, unobscured by a fog of emotions. Selling the Q4 consistently requires Q4 salesmanship.

The Needs of Salesmen

So far, we've talked mainly about customer needs. By now, however, it is probably clear that salesmen are *similarly* motivated.

THE Q1 SALESMAN'S NEEDS

Like the Q1 customer, the Q1 salesman is motivated largely by strong *esteem* and *independence* needs. This accounts for his forceful, hard-driving manner, his intense desire to make sales, and his willingness to bend facts or distort information to make sales. When he fails to close a sale, his self-image is diminished and he is assailed by doubts about his competence. A man with a deep need *not* to fail, he needs an unending series of sales to relieve his fears about himself. Each sale is considered proof of his own worth. Only by adding sale to sale can he respect himself; only by making each sales presentation a struggle that he wins, can he feel strong and independent.

THE Q2 SALESMAN'S NEEDS

The Q2, like his customer counterpart, is motivated essentially by *security* needs. Basically insecure and oppressed by anxiety, he is especially concerned about protection; his aloof, withdrawn manner is a defensive device. He fears rebuffs and snubs, so he maintains a distance between himself and his customers. His remoteness is a kind of armor to keep him from getting hurt emotionally.

THE Q3 SALESMAN'S NEEDS

The Q3 is motivated basically by *social* and, to a lesser extent, *security* and *esteem* needs. His primary need is for affection and acceptance by others. In this light, his outgoing, socializing manner is easy to understand. His behavior is an attempt to draw warmth from others, to establish himself as pleasant and likeable. This need is so compelling that he would rather lose a sale than a friend.

THE Q4 SALESMAN'S NEEDS

The Q4 is concerned with *self-realization* and *independence*. He sees his job as a way to attain both. He wants job enrichment and responsibility. He wants to be a valued counselor to his customers. He believes personal growth and development can be realized only if he conducts himself as a professional problem-solver, and that without growth and development, his independence will diminish. Independence, after all, is enjoyed only by those who can *control* situations; those at the mercy of situations have very little autonomy. The Q1 salesman enjoys less autonomy than the Q4; he controls only those situations in which the customer is willing to submit to his coercion, but he has little or no control over strong-minded customers with a will of their own. The Q2 is almost completely at the mercy of his customers; he makes sales only when *they* are ready to buy, or because *they* feel sorry for him. The Q3 is a hostage to his own need for affection; he cannot control situations in which conflict or problems are dominant. Only the Q4 salesman is flexible and adaptable enough to control all kinds of situations involving all kinds of customers. While he sometimes depends on people and situations that he cannot manage, he enjoys far greater independence than either the Q1, the Q2, or the Q3 salesman.

SUMMARY

People are motivated by task and personal needs. This chapter has analyzed needs by adapting and amplifying the work of psychologist Dr. Abraham Maslow. Needs can be pictured as the layers of a pyramid with the most basic needs, the biological ones, at the bottom. Each succeeding layer represents needs less important to staying alive but more important to living a fulfilled life. From the bottom, the needs are: biological, security, social, esteem, independence, and self-realization. A seventh category of needs, task needs, can also be depicted. Task needs are all the needs that must be filled so people can perform tasks. These can be present at any time, no matter what personal need a person may be trying to satisfy. Task needs are frequently interwoven with personal needs.

In thinking about personal needs, eight points are especially worth remembering: (*1*) personal needs overlap, (*2*) the strength of each personal need varies with each person, (3) in almost all cases, a person is fundamentally motivated by his lowest unfilled personal need, (4) personal needs which are already satisfied have little power to motivate people, (5) there are, on rare occasions, exceptions to the statement that men are motivated by their lowest unfilled personal needs, (6) for the most part, personal needs can be filled in more than one way, (7) a man who thinks a particular set of personal needs is satisfied may suddenly find it is not, and (8) a salesman can satisfy a customer's personal needs in two ways: by his method of presentation and by his product.

A salesman can uncover and identify a customer's task and personal needs by observing his behavior and communicating successfully with him. Selling is a process in which the salesman infers the customer's needs and then demonstrates how the features of his product fill those needs so as to produce a benefit to the customer. This can be expressed in the following formula:

Customer Needs + Product Features = Benefit to Customer

Q1 customers are basically motivated by needs for esteem and independence; Q2s by security and, to a lesser extent, biological needs; Q3s by social, security, and esteem needs; and Q4s by self-realization and independence needs.

12

Communication
Strategies

TO PERSUADE OR NOT TO PERSUADE . . .

In the past few years, the behavioral sciences have inaugurated a quiet but profound revolution in the way we think about *communication,* a revolution that promises to make a significant impact on salesmen and sales managers.

When most of us were in school, we were taught two things about communication: Communication is basically a matter of *words,* so the person who uses words well will communicate well, and anyone who uses words the right way can communicate almost anything to anyone. Or, put another way, communication is mainly *verbal,* and communication is something someone does *to* someone else. The behavioral sciences disagree on both points.

Thanks to the efforts of numerous researchers, we now know that communication is basically a matter of *behavior* (and words are only a part, and certainly not always the most important part, of behavior), and communication is a process that occurs *between* people, so that we can only communicate *with,* never to. Or, put another way, communication is *behavioral,* and communication is *interactional.* This is a deep-seated and fundamental change in our thinking.

THE NEW VIEW OF COMMUNICATION

Let's examine both ideas briefly:

1. Communication is behavioral. This means literally what it says. People communicate with their total behavior, not merely with words. A customer can *tell* a salesman that he's interested in what the salesman is saying, but that is not the message that will get through to the salesman if the customer persistently yawns, fidgets, and stares absentmindedly into space. A salesman can *insist* to his sales manager that he is deliriously happy with the territory reassignment he just received, but the manager will get a different message if the salesman's face wears a scowl and his eyes have a hostile look. It is no exaggeration to say that *everything* we do communicates, and our total behavior frequently delivers a message contrary to, or at least different from, our words.

2. Communication is interactional. Real communication (that is, communication that leads to mutual comprehension and mutual understanding) is always the result of the active participation of *two* (or more) people. Getting through to others requires listening as well as talking, it requires give-and-take, it requires reciprocal action. A man can talk for hours, fluently and articulately, and yet fail miserably to get his message across. Communication requires that the listener understand what is in the mind of the speaker, and *that* requires an active, engaged listener. Unless the listener is fully involved, what the speaker does is a monologue; it is *not* communication. (It is worth noting that *communication* derives from a Latin word meaning *common*. Unless an idea is shared in common by both speaker and listener, there is no communication.)

The practical implication of these two behavioral science findings is quite significant. Communication, we now know, is far more complex than we once thought. Using words correctly is hard enough, but being aware of the impact of one's *total behavior* (every gesture, every expression, every intonation) is immensely more difficult. And keeping *oneself* intelligently involved in communication is tough enough, but getting and keeping the *other* person intelligently involved is immeasurably tougher. Yet both are essential if one is to *get through to* customers.

Verbal skills alone will not do the job. Equally important, salesmen must *listen* attentively and analytically, observe reactions, and actively probe for understanding of what the customer is really saying. And they must communicate *skeptically*. The skeptical salesman never takes anything for granted; he never *assumes* he is getting through; he never flatters himself that his customer *really* understands simply because the customer *says* he understands. The glib nod of assent, the quick "I understand," the instant "Okay," are often—very often—cover-ups for doubt and bewilderment.

Management theorist Peter Drucker has made the point that, contrary to our most deeply held beliefs, speakers do not and *cannot* communicate. They can only make sounds. These sounds become communication—that is, they *get a message across*—only if the listener permits them to do so. Thus, says Drucker, the fact is that the *listener* communicates, not the speaker. Drucker's view, which may sound extreme, is really not extreme at all. He is merely saying that words are little more than noises unless they are uttered in a way that persuades the listener to *let* them get through to him, which is another way of saying that communication is a result *not* of verbalization but of *interaction*.

Drucker's point is that much so-called communication is really noise-making, sounds falling on ears that are, for all practical purposes, deaf. And, ironically, some salesmen who consider themselves excellent communicators (because they are constantly being praised for their silver-tongued use of words) do consistently poor jobs of *getting through,* while others, less eloquent and less loquacious, really *do* communicate. Fluency is only one part of a very complex two-way process.

Small wonder, then, that salesmen and sales managers are so often frustrated and confused in their attempts to get through. Small wonder that all of us so frequently encounter misunderstandings, confusion, and complications. And small wonder that the effort to communicate sometimes leaves us fatigued. Communicating is tough and exhausting business.

COMMUNICATION STRATEGIES

Each basic selling strategy and each basic buying strategy manifests itself in a distinctive *communication* strategy.

Following are descriptions of the strategies used by the four basic types of salesmen and customers. Once again, we are drawing extreme pictures, deliberately exaggerated; very few, if any, salesmen or customers fit them perfectly. But most salesmen and most customers use communications strategies more or less like the following.

Salesmen's Communication Strategies

THE DOMINANT-HOSTILE SALESMAN (Q1): ONE-WAY COMMUNICATION

His communications strategy is inflexible, strongly assertive, and resistant to new ideas. The salesman verbally bludgeons the prospect, hoping his forcefulness will persuade or coerce the latter to buy. Convinced he has little to learn from the prospect, he listens unwillingly and undiscerningly, and prefers to do most of the talking himself. As a listener, he pays close attention only to those points that support his own point of view. His manner conveys lack of regard for the prospect as a significant person who has something worthwhile to impart. The Q1 salesman is sure he already knows what the customer wants (or *should* want), so he has nothing to learn. He considers communication a *one-way* process, *from* salesman *to* prospect. The only response he wants from the prospect is the words, "I'll buy." Only this response satisfies his needs for esteem and independence.

THE SUBMISSIVE-HOSTILE SALESMAN (Q2): NO-WAY COMMUNICATION

His communications strategy is aloof, unresponsive, mechanical, and disinterested. Convinced that careful listening and persuasive talking are both pointless, he makes listless, rote presentations lacking animation and zest. He presumes the customer knows his own needs, and will buy whenever he's ready to buy, so the Q2 salesman feels he can do little to influence the customer.

The communication climate is fatalistic, characterized by a belief that whatever will be will be, and that nothing of importance can be communicated by either party. We might almost say that the Q2 considers communication a *no-way* process, with nothing of significance passing in either direction. This style of communication protects him from exposure to a supposedly hostile world, and thus satisfies his need for security.

THE SUBMISSIVE-WARM SALESMAN (Q3): PARTIAL COMMUNICATION

His communications strategy is relaxed, sociable, and highly informal. Eager to look at the bright side of things and avoid issues that might generate tension or disagreement, the Q3 salesman inhibits communication, although this might not be apparent. Anything that threatens to disrupt his happy view of the world is played down, rationalized, or brushed aside. This results in *partial* communication, in which pleasant ideas and information are permitted to pass while unpleasant ideas and information are not. In the process, his needs for warmth and affection are satisfied even though the sale might not be advanced.

THE DOMINANT-WARM SALESMAN (Q4): TWO-WAY COMMUNICATION

His communications strategy is open and receptive, and stimulates a candid exchange of ideas. The Q4 salesman is alert to any clues the prospect provides, sensitive to his personal needs as well as his task needs, and willing to listen as well as talk. He seeks understanding, whether favorable or unfavorable, about the prospect's needs, so that he can demonstrate how his product will satisfy those needs. To gain this understanding, he uses a whole gamut of communications skills. He tries to facilitate insight, comprehension, and knowledge of benefits. He realizes that professional salesmanship depends upon real *two-way* communication. And only professional salesmanship satisfies his need for self-realization and independence.

Customers' Communication Strategies

THE DOMINANT-HOSTILE CUSTOMER (Q1): ONE-WAY COMMUNICATION

His communications strategy is distrustful, argumentative, and unreceptive. The Q1 customer, whose mind is closed at the outset, is concerned only with self-defense and self-assertion, not with learning from the salesman. Because he thinks of the sales presentation as a duel, he is an unwilling and suspicious listener and a belligerent talker, intent upon beating down the salesman before the salesman has a chance to beat him down. By winning this duel, he proves, in his own eyes, that he is the stronger of the two men, and he thereby satisfies his needs for independence and esteem.

THE SUBMISSIVE-HOSTILE CUSTOMER (Q2): NO-WAY COMMUNICATION

His communications strategy is aloof, unresponsive, cautious. Feeling threatened and insecure, he hopes that the salesman will get discouraged and go away. So he is secretive and glum, fearful that anything he says might be used against him. He has no wish to communicate, but wants only to be left alone. Only when alone does he feel fairly secure.

THE SUBMISSIVE-WARM CUSTOMER (Q3): PARTIAL COMMUNICATION

His communications strategy is hearty, affable, easygoing. More interested in sociability and good relationships than in learning, he shows little inclination to stick to business. He is easy to talk to, but hard to hold to a businesslike line of thought. Talk about business does not fill his personal need for warmth and acceptance to the same degree that small talk does.

THE DOMINANT-WARM CUSTOMER (Q4): TWO-WAY COMMUNICATION

His communications strategy is penetrating, frank, eager to learn. Realizing that the salesman can help him if he is given sufficient information, the Q4 customer willingly shares data and ideas. He regards the sales interview as a cooperative venture which can succeed only if there is reciprocal candor. He expects honest, forthright salesmanship, and responds in kind. He is an analytic man who places high value on analytic salesmen. He wants salesmen to back up their claims with provable facts and workable solutions to problems, and to demonstrate clearly the benefits he will get if he buys their product.

Five Steps to the Sale

Q4 sales communication is not only two-way communication; it is also *well-organized* communication. Q4 presentations do not follow a pat formula, but they do, as a rule, follow five logical steps: (*1*) precall preparation, (*2*) opening, (*3*) exploration of needs, (*4*) demonstration of benefits, and (*5*) close. Let's examine each step briefly.

1. *Precall preparation.*

There is a mistaken notion among many salesmen that sales communication begins the instant salesman and customer start talking face-to-face. Many times, of course, this *is* what happens. The Q1 salesman, for example, seldom begins the communications process until he's looking the customer in the eye; he thinks of communication as a *personal* encounter. The Q2 sees no point in preparation *before* the call. And the Q3, relying on friendliness, sees no need for preparation, since friendliness can only be exercised man-to-man. Only the Q4 understands the first principle of effective sales communication: that *communication is easier if it is based upon data gathered before the interview.* The communication process should begin *before* customer and salesman set eyes on one another.

At this point, many salesmen will no doubt object that this is impossible. After all, furniture salesmen, automobile salesmen, direct-call salesmen—in fact, practically *all* retail salesmen—as well as salesmen making cold-calls, know nothing about their customers until the call begins. But this objection falls apart under analysis. Much precall preparation has to do with the salesman *himself*—his attitudes, expectations, knowledge of his own product and his competitors'. A significant amount of advance preparation is *always* possible. Even an analysis of *past* sales presentations—with emphasis on how to correct the errors—is preparation for the *next* presentation. As every highly successful retail salesman knows, the fact is that there's *plenty* to do between presentations. For *all* salesmen, sales communication is a full-time job.

Surprisingly few salesmen understand this. To them, communication is equated with *talking:* this means it is something that happens in the customer's presence. They fail to understand that effective communication can only take place in a receptive climate, and an important part of the salesman's job is to prepare the climate so that it *is* receptive. This process begins *before* the sales interview. Countless sales have been lost because the salesman didn't do the preliminary work needed to establish a hospitable climate.

The Q4 salesman is committed to intensive pre-call preparation. Usually, this preparation is in four phases: a review of *facts* about himself, his company, his customer and his competitors; a review of *attitudes* about the same topics; a tentative identification of customer needs; and planning of a flexible opening. For some salesmen, especially those in direct-to-consumer selling, this preparation will be less complete than for others, but *all* salesmen can do much of it.

If he can, the Q4 salesman anticipates the customer's behavior based on what he knows from former experiences (will he be initially hostile, withdrawn, sociable, or businesslike?), and he tries to foresee the customer's responses to his ideas. He reviews what he knows about the customer's personal needs, and takes them into account in planning his approach. As far as he can, the Q4 salesman tries to eliminate the unexpected, the surprising, the disconcerting elements of the interview, and to *gain an understanding of the call before he even shakes the customer's hand.*

Now, nobody claims that pre-call preparation will eliminate all communication barriers. But preparation helps *diminish* the barriers in two ways: it makes the salesman's behavior more *thoughtful* and less mechanical, and it enables him to anticipate some of the barriers that the customer is likely to set up, and to have strategies available for dealing with them. A quarterback who's seen movies of himself in action, and who has good scouting reports on the opposition, is a better quarterback than he would otherwise be because he understands his own weaknesses and the opposition's strengths, and can therefore do something about both of them. The analogy obviously applies to selling.

Many salesmen rationalize their failure to prepare carefully for each call by saying that preparation inhibits their flexibility. They prefer to "take things as they come" and "play it by ear." They're kidding themselves. Preparation *increases* flexibility by lessening the amount of learning that the salesman must do on the spot. The unprepared salesman has to gather all his data during the interview: he is often so busy trying to find out what's going on that he unwittingly over-controls the customer or he relinquishes control of the interview to the customer. The unprepared salesman, by his need to catch up, *reduces* his freedom to adapt.

The prepared salesman is able to expend his energies on adapting his behavior to suit the situation.

2. *Opening.*

A good opening should do three things: tell the customer *why* the call is being made; explain why *he* should take part in the interview; and establish a *receptive* climate for what is to follow.

The Q4, who understands that *total* customer involvement is essential before real communication can take place, opens in a manner that is *planned* to achieve customer involvement at the outset. Very early in the interview he sizes up the customer as either Q1 (hostile and defiant), Q2 (quiet and withdrawn), Q3 (meandering and friendly), or Q4 (open and involved), and adjusts his own communications accordingly.

Whatever his assessment of the customer, the Q4 salesman devises a suitable strategy for dealing with him. He listens for evidence of negative attitudes (hostility, fear, boredom, and so on) which are essentially *emotional,* and for evidence of negative beliefs (doubts that the product will work, doubts that it fits the customer's needs, etc.) which are essentially related to *facts.* Then, like a golfer selecting the right club for a shot, he selects the communications technique or techniques best suited to coping with the negativism. He may, for instance, give the customer an opportunity to vent hostile emotions, realizing that hostility diminishes in intensity if it is brought into the open. Or he may try to get at the reason underlying the hostility by drawing out the customer through skillful use of neutral phrases ("I see," "Hm-hm"), pauses, questions, and reflective statements in which he encourages the customer to talk by mirroring the customer's feelings back to him.

Many salesmen fail to establish a receptive communications climate at the outset of the interview because they don't understand what a receptive communication climate is. In the *receptive* climate, ideas and information move back and forth freely and purposefully. While neither the salesman nor the customer impedes the flow, neither indulges in an unending stream of irrelevancies. Instead, each man communicates in a *self-disciplined* way, contributing information that's pertinent to the subject. These contributions are candid and open; information is neither withheld nor obscured.

In an *unreceptive* climate, either the salesman or the customer *or both* set up barriers to communication. These barriers take many forms, like retreating into silence, or hopping from objection to objection, or talking about irrelevancies, or not paying attention, or remaining uninvolved, or acting defensively. These barriers serve one of two purposes: they are either *protective* devices that help a man protect his self-image or ward off what he perceives as a threat or to spare himself embarrassment, or they are *emotional* releases that enable a person to work off tensions, worry, or exuberance that he's having trouble containing.

How long does the Q4 salesman's opening last? As long as necessary to do the three things he set out to do: state the purpose of his call, get the customer involved, and establish receptivity. Only then is he ready to move on to the second step in the presentation.

3. *Exploration of needs.*

Only after establishing a receptive climate does the Q4 salesman proceed to collect data about the customer's task and personal needs. Throughout this portion of the interview, the salesman's behavior is marked by a sincere desire to learn, and a willingness to listen respectfully. Many Q4 salesmen do remarkably little talking during this second step, letting the customer do most of the talking in response to probes.

Once the Q4 salesman thinks he has the information he needs, he compares it with his starting assumptions, makes whatever revisions in those assumptions are called for, and then *tests* his modified assumptions and his understanding of the customer's needs. This is one more instance of his systematic approach to communications. Instead of taking it for granted that he has all the right answers, he summarizes his assumptions and his understanding and gets confirmation or denial from the customer. He refuses to charge ahead until he's sure of his ground.

In essence, then, before the Q4 salesman begins to discuss the features and advantages of his product, he establishes a climate that will be receptive to what he has to say and he collects data about the customer's needs. Only then does he try to demonstrate benefits.

4. *Demonstration of Benefits.*

Only *after* eliminating or diminishing communication barriers and determining the customer's needs does the Q4 salesman begin to demonstrate benefits and net gain. The stage is now set to discuss the ways in which the salesman's product will satisfy the customer's needs. Obstacles to communication have, for the most part, been eliminated, the air has largely been cleared of emotional obstructions, and significant facts have been agreed upon by salesman and customer. Receptivity to new ideas should now be at its peak. From now on, the Q4 works to establish the connection between needs, product features, and benefits, to achieve customer commitment, and to close.

The Q4 salesman now correlates the customer's needs with the features of his product, demonstrating that the customer will benefit from the product. He proceeds deliberately and carefully, making sure the customer really understands the benefits he will get from the product. This is in contrast to the Q1's technique, which is to coerce the customer into accepting correlations that he may not really believe exist. The Q4 strives for *conviction;* the Q1 is satisfied with mere *acquiescence.*

Customers display different kinds of communications behavior during the benefit-establishing step in a presentation. Q1 customers try not to admit any correlation between needs and product features; to do so, they feel, would be a sign that they are weakening or giving in to the salesman. So the salesman, who may have expended considerable time and effort in eliminating emotional barriers to communication, must now begin again, patiently and thoroughly, to knock down a new set of barriers through skillful probing. Or, in dealing with a Q2, the salesman may find that the customer's fears have once again become dominant and forced him into withdrawal; once again, methodical drawing out must be used. And, as a rule, the salesman will discover that the Q3 customer is unwilling or unable to stick to the subject. So the salesman must once again cope with irrelevancies and rationalizations.

   5.   *Closing.*

The only close the Q4 salesman is willing to settle for is one in which the customer firmly commits himself to one of two kinds of action: a purchase, or an agreement to discuss a purchase again at a specified future date. So the Q4 close might better be labeled the *movement toward commitment.*

At the same time, the Q4 tries to close on a note of high receptivity, so that he is welcome back on future sales calls. Thus, his close is *both* a conclusion to the present call and a warm-up for future calls.

The five Q4 steps to the sale can be summarized as follows:

1.   Precall preparation
     a.   Review of facts about self, company, customer, and competitors
     b.   Review of attitudes about same topics
     c.   Tentative identification of customer needs
     d.   Planning of a flexible opening

2.   Opening
     a.   Statement of purpose
     b.   Statement of tentative benefit to customer
     c.   Establishment of climate for testing-out tentative benefit

3.   Exploration of Needs
     a.   Gathering of data about customer's personal needs
     b.   Gathering of data about customer's task needs

    c. Comparison of new information with initial assumptions

    d. Revision of initial assumptions if necessary

4. Demonstration of benefits and net gain

    a. Establishing benefits through linking needs with product features and advantages

    b. Testing-out of benefits

5. Close

    a. Agreement on action

    b. Establishment of climate for further sales calls

How the Q4 Salesman Demonstrates Net Gain

The primary purpose of Q4 communication is to link product *features* (or service features) and *advantages* to customer *needs* so as to establish *benefits* and *net gain*. For the Q4 salesman, the fourth step to the sale is the crucial one. Our last chapter dealt at length with customer needs. Now it's important to talk at some length about features, advantages, benefits, and net gain. In doing so, we'll get a much clearer picture of the differences between Q4 communication and Q1, Q2, and Q3 communication.

Let us begin by making a point that's basic, but not always obvious: customers frequently do not know, or are unsure of, what their needs are. One of the primary functions of Q4 communication is to help customers discover their own needs, to bring these needs to the surface and to crystallize them so that both customer and salesman can agree on what the needs really are. The Q4 salesman never assumes that a prospect is fully aware of his own needs. He assumes that the prospect may be unaware, uncertain, confused, or simply wrong about his needs. (How many life insurance buyers, for example, know, *without any help from a salesman,* whether they need any insurance at all, or, if they do, whether they need term insurance, industrial life insurance, ordinary life insurance, endowment insurance, an annuity, or one of several dozen specialized policies? How many buyers of luggage know, *without any help from a salesman,* whether, given the amount of traveling they do, they need leather, plastic, cloth-covered luggage, or luggage with rigid covering or soft covering? Similar questions could be asked about the buyers of almost any product or service.)

To evolve and crystallize customer needs, the Q4 salesman probes, questions, listens, investigates, and inquires. He lets the customer talk, he encourages involvement, he follows up promising clues, and he investigates disagreements in a never-ending search for further understanding. Of all selling strategies, *only* the Q4 brings customer needs into the open in a systematic way. Only *after* he and the customer understand what these needs are does the Q4 salesman attempt to demonstrate how his product or service will fill the needs.

The fact that a certain product or service *will* satisfy a customer's needs is something the *salesman* must help the customer to understand. The Q4 salesman demonstrates that his product or service will *do something* for the customer that he needs done, that it will provide solutions, satisfaction, or fulfillment.

What the product or service will do to satisfy the customer's needs is the *benefit*. But the Q4 salesman does not stop at the benefit. He goes on to demonstrate that the amount of need satisfaction the benefit will bring to the customer is *greater* than he is now getting. This is the *net gain*.

This last point is critical. It is not good enough merely to establish benefits. That is, it is not good enough merely to show the customer what the product or service will do for him. The Q4 salesman goes one step further and shows that the benefit will in some way make the customer *better off*. He demonstrates that a need will be satisfied that is not being satisfied now, or that a need that is being satisfied now will be satisfied better. He shows that the product or service will not only *do something* for the customer; it will do something that is *not now* being done. This is what's meant by *net gain*. The ultimate aim of the Q4 salesman is to demonstrate that he can produce *benefits leading to net gain*. Unless he does, he has not really given the customer a reason to buy.

Unfortunately, many salesmen seldom get to this point in a presentation. They don't establish benefits leading to net gain because they're not really clear about what benefits *are*. Instead of selling benefits, they sell *features* or *advantages,* neither of which give a customer a reason to buy. Let's examine this point further by distinguishing features, advantages, and benefits.

Features.   A feature is a *property* or *attribute* of a product or service. It is a characteristic or trait that's actually *part* of the product or service. Thus, a product's features are comparable to a *man's* features. If you were asked, for example, to describe a man's features, you might mention his "Roman nose," or his "square, rugged chin," or his "bushy eyebrows." All of these are parts of the man himself, properties or attributes that make him what he is. Similarly, an automobile's features might be described as power windows, or air-conditioning, or four-wheel drive. A shirt's features might be pure nylon, two-inch spread collar, or double-button barrel cuffs. And a typewriter's features might be proportional spacing, partial carriage return, or cartridge ribbon. Features tell something about the product or service *itself*.

Advantages. An *advantage* is what a feature *does*. It describes the *purpose* or *function* of a feature. For example, an electric knife with a turnable handle (feature) slices meat either horizontally or vertically while the hand remains in the same position (advantage). Drip-dry (feature) trousers can be washed without losing their crease (advantage). Portable (feature) TV can be carried from place to place (advantage). Lifetime lubrication (feature) keeps a product properly oiled for its entire period of use (advantage). Teflon (feature) pans keep food from sticking (advantage). Pop-up (feature) toasters toast bread to desired crispness without being watched (advantage). And so forth. If *features* describe the product itself, *advantages* describe what the features *do*.

Benefits. A *benefit* is the value or worth that the user derives from a product or service. It tells the customer "what's in it for me." While a feature describes the product itself, and an advantage tells what the feature does, a *benefit* relates all of this to the *user*. Unless features and advantages have been related to the *user* and his *needs,* no benefit has been shown. This correlation, this connecting of features and advantages to the user's needs, is the *critical link* that many salesmen fail to make. They stop short of this point. Because they do, they are unable to take the next step and demonstrate net gain, thereby giving the customer a *reason* to buy.

Let's examine this idea. Customers want to know "What's in it for me?" They do *not* get the answer to this question from an explanation of features and advantages. The fact that a frying pan is made of Teflon (feature) will *not* tell the customer "what's in it for me." The fact that Teflon keeps food from sticking (advantage) will *not* tell the customer "what's in it for me." The fact that food tastes or looks better when it doesn't stick *does* answer the customer's question. So does the fact that cooking becomes more convenient because nonstick frying pans don't have to be tended as carefully. So does the fact that nonstick frying pans save time and energy because they're easier to wash. All of these are *benefits* because all of them link the feature and the advantage to the customer's *needs*. Better taste, greater convenience, and saving of time and energy represent values that help satisfy the customer's needs. A Teflon frying pan may help to satisfy a housewife's biological needs (conserving her energy), her social needs (helping her make an impression on her family as an excellent cook), and possibly even her independence needs (giving her free time that would otherwise be spent scraping and washing scorched pans). *These* are the things that have meaning and *relevance* to customers.

Put another way, customers really want to hear about *themselves* in a presentation. As long as a salesman talks about features or advantages, he's talking about the product, *not* about the customer.

Let's look at a few more examples of features, advantages, and benefits to make sure that the distinction between them is completely clear.

TABLE 5. Examples of Features, Advantages, and Benefits

Product	Feature (describes the product)	Advantage (explains what the feature does)	Benefit (explains what the customer gets out of the feature)
Luggage	Steel ribbing	Keeps sides of luggage from being crushed	Saves money by lasting longer than other luggage Looks handsomer, because luggage keeps shape Protects property inside luggage
Lawn mower	Automatic shut-off blade	Blade stops turning as soon as mower hits rock or other object	Safer, because foreign objects will not hurtle through air and strike someone More convenient because a youngster can operate it safely Easier and less costly to maintain, because blade needs less sharpening
Carpeting	Special nonsoil finish	Keeps dirt from becoming imbedded in fibers	Lasts longer because there is no friction against fibers from dirt granules More convenient because spots can be removed with water Less expensive, because professional carpet cleaning is seldom needed

By now it is obvious that a single feature frequently has a single advantage but *numerous* benefits. Many salesmen, however, confuse advantages with benefits, and thereby seriously, perhaps disastrously, weaken their presentation. Suppose a luggage salesman, mistaking an advantage for a benefit, tells a customer that a steel-ribbed two suiter cannot be crushed. If he stops at that point, he leaves the *customer* to figure out the benefits for *himself*. But the customer may not make this connection for himself. Why should he? He may have other and more important things on his mind. Instead of buying the luggage, he may walk away wondering "So what?" This, in fact, is the typical response to a description of advantages as long as customers don't understand the link between features, advantages, and their own *needs*.

Net Gain. It should be clearly understood, however, that a salesman does not necessarily give a customer sufficient reason to buy merely by demonstrating *benefits*. He must also demonstrate *net gain,* which we define as the *benefit the customer does not now have and cannot get elsewhere.*

Let's suppose, to take a far-fetched but useful example, that an automobile salesman tells a customer that a new-model car has a Super-Thrust engine (feature) that can attain speeds up to 100 miles an hour in less than 15 seconds (advantage) and that will make it possible for the customer to decrease driving time (benefit). The customer will probably reason that buying the car to get this benefit will *not* make him *better off,* even though he has a need to save time. After all, he is only permitted to drive 30 miles an hour in the city and 70 on the highway, and these speeds are easily attainable in his *present* car. By buying a car that accelerates to 100 miles an hour in 15 seconds, he will in no way be better off than he is *right now;* the benefit does not lead to a *net gain*. There may be *other* benefits that would give the customer a *reason* to buy, but not this one. For example, the salesman might have pointed out that acceleration to 100 miles an hour in 15 seconds is exclusive to the car he is selling, and would enable the customer to pass other cars on the highway more quickly and safely than in his present car. In this way, he could have established *net gain* by establishing a benefit that the customer does *not now* have and cannot get elsewhere.

Let's take another, and somewhat less extreme, example. Suppose a carpeting salesman is trying to sell a woman carpeting with special nonsoil finish. Let's imagine that he does an excellent job of explaining the advantage (keeps dirt from becoming imbedded in fibers) and the benefits (lasts longer, is more convenient, and less expensive). All these benefits may meet some of the customer's existing needs, and yet she may not buy because her *present* antique Persian rug satisfies her personal needs for esteem and social approval, and these are stronger than her task needs for economy and convenience.

Once again, then, we see that benefits do *not* always produce *net gain*. Unless they do, it is unlikely the sale can be closed. In this example, the salesman might have demonstrated that nonsoil carpeting stays new-looking for years, and is bound to win the admiration of friends as a result. If the customer was thus persuaded that the new carpeting would satisfy her needs for esteem and social approval *better* than her Persian rug, she might buy it. But it would be unrealistic to expect her to buy unless some *net gain* was first established.

Net Gain and the Basic Selling Strategies

NET GAIN AND Q1 COMMUNICATION

The Q1 salesman uses features, advantages, benefits, and net gain as devices for controlling and overwhelming the customer. Like the general who believes in crushing the enemy by sheer force, he uses all the ammunition he can muster to wear down or wipe out the opposition. To the Q1, features, advantages, benefits, and net gain are ammunition to use unrelentingly until the customer, beaten down, surrenders.

The Q1 makes strong use of benefit statements, but these do not always reflect real benefits. He is a master at promising distorted benefits that are unrelated to features and advantages. Some of his stated benefits are exaggerations, or even deliberate misstatements. A benefit is not real unless it is related to an actual feature or advantage. This correlation is something the Q1 often fails to make. He prefers to promise lavish, impressive-sounding, but unsubstantiated and frequently unprovable benefits.

Similarly, he seldom takes the time to establish net gain. Instead, he showers benefits upon the customer, assuming that some of them, at least, will have some impact. If he does establish net gain, he usually does so in a purposely exaggerated way. Once again, his unwillingness to explore customer needs makes it very difficult to demonstrate net gain, since net gain is inseparable from needs.

The Q1 salesman is not interested in the relationship between features, advantages, benefits, and net gain. He is like a basketball player who doesn't care about the intricacies of the game (passing, ball handling, defense, and so forth) but wants only to get his hands on the ball and shoot. "Throw enough balls at the basket," he says, "and you're bound to score some points. And scoring points is all that matters." For the

Q1, this might be paraphrased: "Throw enough features, advantages, distorted benefits and exaggerated net gains at the customer, and you're bound to make some sales. And making sales is all that matters."

NET GAIN AND Q2 COMMUNICATION

The Q2 salesman seldom discusses benefits or net gain. He concentrates on features and advantages, frequently reciting these in a rote, mechanical manner. The Q2 has no desire to rock the boat or call attention to himself; one way he protects himself is by learning the product information his company gives him. He may be able to spell out details about features and advantages, but his recital is lackluster. Even worse, his basic assumption that people cannot be persuaded to buy prevents him from exploring customer needs and linking them to the advantages and features. In his view, this link-up is pointless, a meaningless waste of time that cannot influence the customer. If the link-up is to be made at all, the customer must do it for himself.

In this regard, the contrast between the Q1 and Q2 is stark. Where the Q1 salesman tries to pulverize the customer with a barrage of benefits, the Q2 holds back, scarcely using his most powerful weapons. As a result, customers often fail to buy from him because they don't understand *why* they should. Their most fundamental question, "What's in it for me?", is never answered.

NET GAIN AND Q3 COMMUNICATION

The Q3 salesman believes it is more important to sell himself than his product or service. If he sells himself successfully, he reasons, the sale of his product or service is bound to follow. Since features, advantages, benefits, and net gain don't relate to him personally, he does not use them effectively.

The Q3 often believes his product is exceptional, but he feels no need to know much about it. Content with the belief that what he sells is unsurpassed, he's not really interested in the details. As a result, he usually does an overgeneralized and vague job of explaining features, advantages, benefits, and net gain. He meanders from topic to topic, rarely getting around to a thorough discussion of necessary details. None of this bothers him, since, as he sees it, he is selling *himself*. Features, advantages, benefits, net gain are all secondary to the personal aspects of the presentation. What really counts is establishing a friendly relationship with the customer, not some tedious explanation of details about the product. From his point of view, the real net gain to the customer is the warmth he enjoys during the presentation itself.

Only the Q4 salesman systematically correlates features and advantages with customer needs to establish benefits resulting in net gain. By solving problems, he gives the customer reasons to buy. This is the hallmark of Q4 selling. It leads to the mutual commitment toward which all Q4 selling is directed. The details of *how* the Q4 salesman carries this process forward is the burden of later chapters.

A Perspective on the Basic Communication Strategies

In the end, any one of the four types of salesmen may close a sale. But the closes are based on widely different kinds of communication, or lack of it. Only in the case of the Q4 salesman can we say that real two-way communication precedes the close. The Q4 makes sure his customer understands what the product will do for him; the customer buys because he has been persuaded that it will be to his advantage to buy.

In Q1 selling, the sale is often closed because the customer caves in. He may feel overwhelmed, tired of listening, or intimidated, and capitulate to the salesman even though he does not fully understand why he should buy and is not fully committed to buying. (This is, of course, not true of all Q1 sales, but it is true of a large number.) The Q1, on the other hand, cares little about data; his basic goal is to wear the customer down, erode his resistance through sheer dominance, and impel him to give in. He doesn't really care if the customer understands how his needs correlate with the product features. Because the Q1 doesn't value learning *from* the customer, but wants only to make certain points clear *to* the customer, we have described his communication as *one-way*.

Similarly, there is no real communication in a Q2 sale. When a Q2 closes a sale he does so because the customer feels sorry for him or because he happened to call when the customer was ready to place an order anyway. His closes are based on luck or sympathy, rarely on understanding or commitment. The customer often has not thought through the relationship between his needs and the product (unless he has used the product before, and is merely reordering), and the salesman seldom really understands the customer's needs. If the customer does clearly understand why he should buy the product and if he does feel committed to his purchase, it is because he has arrived at his *own* understanding and commitment, with little help from the salesman. So it can be said, correctly, that Q2 selling is characterized by *no-way* communication.

In a Q3 presentation, there is ample communication, but little that offers solutions to problems or pragmatic reasons to buy. At the end of a Q3 sales interview, both salesman and customer may understand a great deal about one another's golf game, families, hobbies, and so forth, but neither will understand much about the correlation between needs and product. The close, if there is one, is based mainly on intimacy or on the customer's attaining understanding and commitment on his own. The Q3 willingly exchanges pleasantries, but is less eager to probe, analyze, and uncover customer needs. And he is downright anxious to smooth over unpleasantness of any kind. This is *partial* communication, in which an effort is made to see the world as the salesman wants to see it, not as it really is.

Only the Q4 communicates in a *two-way manner*. The criteria by which he decides when to close a sale are *understanding* and *commitment*. If he and the customer are aware of the customer's needs and understand how the features and advantages of the product correlate with those needs, the time has come to close. The whole purpose of the presentation, in his view, is to develop this understanding as far as possible to obtain a commitment to action by the customer. This requires *two-way* communication, in which he constantly checks his understanding to determine its validity and revises it whenever necessary.

Conclusion: Communication is Behavior

So, the old and still common notion that a man who is a "good talker" is sure to be a good salesman is wrong. Eloquence and mastery of language do not, by themselves, create understanding and commitment; where there is no understanding and commitment, there is no real communication. Communication is considerably more than talking. It is, in fact, inseparable from a man's *total* behavior. The effectiveness with which a salesman communicates depends upon his verbal skills, his listening skills, his observational skills, his attitude toward his customer, his attitude toward his product, his attitude toward selling, the way he sees himself, his ability to think, his ability to organize data, his ability to ask questions, his ability to probe, his ability to stick to the subject, his patience, his fears, his anxieties, his need for approval—in short, communication depends upon a whole host of behavioral traits. Any salesman who wants to become a better communicator should therefore understand five points.

1. Not only what a man *says,* but everything he *does,* communicates *something* to others. A scowl, a laugh, a grimace all say as much or perhaps more than words. A customer who persistently drums his fingers on his desk and darts his gaze distractedly in many directions, says, "I'm impatient," as persuasively as any words can.

2. The effectiveness of communication is determined by the *interaction* between the two people who are supposed to be communicating. The old idea that communication is a one-sided activity in which only the salesman's actions count is transparently false. Communication is a *process* that involves two or more people. Any explanation of sales communication that fails to consider the *total relationship* between salesman and customer is merely an oversimplification of what is, in fact, a very complex interaction.

3. A specific communication situation can be understood only if the *behavior* of both the salesman and the customer is understood. Communication is quite different between a Q1 salesman and a Q3 customer than between a Q2 salesman and a Q2 customer, but neither is understandable without knowledge of the behavioral strategies involved.

4. The most effective communicators are therefore not merely articulate talkers who know how to say things clearly and forcefully. *They are students of human behavior.*

5. Salesmen can, to a large degree, *learn* to be effective communicators. Such learning must be based upon awareness of the communication impact of the salesman's total behavior, understanding of his communication strategy, ability to analyze the interactions between his communication strategy and those of his customers, and knowledge of and *practice in* communication skills. *All* these factors must be present before communication can be significantly improved.

Too many salesmen damage their chances for success by believing worn-out notions that destroy their effectiveness as communicators. They accept at face-value such provably false statements as "A good talker can sell anything" or "A good product sells itself" or "Sell benefits and you'll close lots of sales." What will a "good talker" achieve if he's talking to a man who has tuned him out and is thinking only about leaving the office and going fishing? How can a "good product" be sold if the customer doesn't understand what it will do for him? What good will "selling benefits" do if the benefits are presented to a man who's hostile or distrustful?

By understanding that all behavior communicates, a salesman can save himself from many self-defeating errors like these.

SUMMARY

Contrary to the traditional view that communication is mainly verbal and something that one person does to another, behavioral science has shown that communication is behavioral and interactional. Speakers can communicate only if the listener permits them to do so; words are mere noises until the listener lets them get through to him.

Each basic selling strategy manifests itself in a distinctive communication strategy. The Q1 salesman's communication strategy is inflexible, strongly assertive, and resistant to new ideas; the Q2, cold, unresponsive, and disinterested; the Q3, relaxed, sociable, and highly informal; and the Q4, open, receptive, probing, and conducive to candid exchange of ideas.

Similarly, each basic buying strategy manifests itself in a distinctive communication strategy. The Q1 customer's communication strategy is distrustful, argumentative, and unreceptive; the Q2's, aloof, wary and unresponsive; the Q3's, hearty, affable, and easygoing; and the Q4's, perceptive, frank, eager to learn.

A Q4 sales presentation typically follows four steps: opening, exploration of needs, demonstration of benefits and net gain, and close.

The purpose of Q4 communication is to link the customer's personal and task needs with product features and advantages to establish benefits and net gain. A feature is a property or attribute of a product or service. An advantage is what a feature does. A benefit is the value or worth that the user derives from a product or service. Net gain is any benefit the user derives over and above the benefits he is presently enjoying.

Q1 salesmen use features, advantages, benefits, and net gain to overwhelm the customer; benefits and net gain are often exaggerated or not correlated with customer needs. Q2 salesmen generally do not discuss benefits or net gain. Q3 salesmen focus on selling themselves rather than their product; features, advantages, benefits, and net gain are all secondary. Only the Q4 correlates features and advantages with customer needs to establish benefits resulting in net gain.

Q1 communication is basically one-way; Q2, no-way; Q3, partial; and Q4, two-way.

A salesman who wants to become a better communicator should understand five points: not only what a man says, but everything he does, communicates; the effectiveness of communication is determined by the interaction between customer and salesman; a specific communication situation can be understood only if the behavior of both the salesman and the customer is understood; effective communicators are students of human behavior; salesmen can, to a large degree, learn to be effective communicators.

TABLE 6. Communications Strategies of Salesmen and Customers

	Q1	Q2	Q3	Q4
Salesmen	One-way: inflexible, strongly assertive, resistant to new ideas; poor listener; tries to dominate discussion; feels he can learn little from customer; wants to force his ideas on customer by sheer power	No-way: cold, unresponsive, disinterested; convinced persuasion is impossible; presentations listless and rote; goes through motions, but does not really try to influence customer	Partial: relaxed, sociable, informal; plays down, rationalizes, or brushes aside any negative facts or ideas; only positive data is allowed to pass without hindrance; more concerned with gaining acceptance than with transmitting ideas	Two-way: open, receptive, encouraging; good listening and probing; seeks full understanding of both positive and negative data: demonstrates respect for customer's ideas
Customers	Distrustful, argumentative, unreceptive; concerned with self-assertion, not with learning from salesmen; unwilling listener; belligerent talker; makes flat assertions; often expresses strong negative emotions	Aloof, wary, unresponsive, secretive; assumes anything he says might be used against him; has no wish to communicate anything	Hearty, affable, easygoing, encouraging; easy to talk to, but hard to hold to a businesslike line of thought; prefers small talk to discussion of product; tries to please and gain acceptance; agreeable, assents readily, talks more about positive than negative	Penetrating, frank, eager to learn; willingly shares data and ideas; strives for mutual candor; analyzes salesman's claims carefully; very businesslike

13

The Techniques of Q4 Communication

HOW TO GAIN COMMITMENT

We have described the various communication strategies; now it's time to discuss the communication techniques that make the Q4 strategy the most successful of all. In this chapter, we describe *methods* by which Q4 salesmen generate customer commitment based on proven net gain.

Throughout this chapter, we talk about *communication*, not manipulation. We will describe *how* salesman and customer achieve *mutual* understanding, and the commitment that flows from such understanding. We will *not* talk about ways of imposing the salesman's ideas on the customer, although Q1 salesmen frequently try to do exactly that by using some of the techniques we'll describe. Properly used, the techniques are the essence of *Q4* communication, which is based on *reciprocal* understanding.

Once again, the behavioral sciences can help us. Let's begin by looking at some pertinent research findings.

FACTORS AFFECTING EASE OF PERSUASION

The ease with which ideas get accepted depends upon several factors:

1. Readiness to change
2. Emotional investment in the present way of doing things
3. How widely accepted the idea is
4. Trust in person communicating the idea

1. *Readiness to change*

It is easier to get someone to accept a new idea if he is *ready* to change anyway, just as it's easier to topple a tree that's partly sawed through. It probably won't be difficult to persuade a customer to double his previous order if he's been thinking that a larger order *might* be a good way to prevent inventory problems. And it probably won't be very difficult to sell a station wagon to the owner of a two-seat sports car if he's been thinking that a station wagon would better accommodate his growing family. But persuading a customer to double his previous order if he's been thinking of cutting expenses by *reducing* his next order, or selling a station wagon to a bachelor who feels a small sports car enhances his image as a man-about-town is much tougher. Readiness, *susceptibility in advance*, makes a lot of difference.

2. *Emotional investment in the present way of doing things*

Acceptance of new ideas becomes more difficult as *emotional* investment in the present way of doing things increases. It would probably be so difficult for a real estate agent to sell a new house to a homeowner who takes great pride in the garden he's developed over many years, that he might not even try. And it would probably be equally tough to sell a Scandinavian modern chair to a woman who's spent many years acquiring rare pieces of Victorian furniture for her home. When emotional investment is extremely high, persuasion is extremely difficult.

3. *How widely accepted the idea may be*

Generally speaking, the more widely held an idea is, the more easily people can be persuaded to accept it. The idea of inoculation, once vigorously resisted, is now commonplace; doctors, who once spent much time persuading people to get smallpox vaccinations, no longer do. New methods are typically resisted. There are exceptions to this principle, of course. Some people take pride in welcoming the new and adventurous. But, in general, people resist giving up cherished old notions for new ones.

4. *Trust in person communicating the idea*

People more readily accept new ideas from people they know and trust. If a man's closest friend tells him Brand X is excellent, the man will probably accept that judgment with little or no hesitation. But if the same man hears a TV announcer tell him that Brand X is excellent, he may be dubious or downright disbelieving. There is a close correlation between willingness to accept new ideas and how well a person knows or thinks of the *source* of those ideas. *Every* salesman, at least on a first call, has to establish his believability and his trustworthiness; he must overcome the suspicion (held by *many* customers, not merely Q1s and Q2s) that salesmen can be slightly devious and interested only in their own welfare. Unless he establishes his dependability, he has little hope of persuading any customer of anything.

How, then, does the Q4 salesman persuade people to accept new ideas? How does he overcome resistance by customers who have no readiness to buy? How does he introduce new ideas to customers who prize old ones and may fear the new? How does he establish his believability with customers who are skeptical of *all* salesmen? To answer these questions, we must first understand what happens when two people communicate.

THE COMMUNICATIONS CYCLE

Getting ideas across to another person requires a six-phase cycle:

1. Exposition (by speaker)
2. Integration (by listener)
3. Response (by listener)
4. Integration of response (by speaker)
5. Reaction to feedback (by speaker)
6. Agreement or disagreement (by listener)

This cycle may at first seem complex, but an understanding of the cycle is essential to effective sales (and sales management) communication. We'll review each phase briefly before examining it in detail.

Exposition

Active communication begins when one person (the speaker) *expounds* an idea to another (the listener). He may describe, explain, bawl out, accuse, joke, plead, order, instruct, request, demand, or do any of dozens of other things. But he must expound *some kind of information*—factual, emotional, or a combination—to another person.

Integration

The information expounded by the speaker must next be integrated by the listener. It must be absorbed, organized, arranged, considered, judged, and evaluated. In every case, the listener *does something* to the information he receives.

Response

After the listener integrates the information with both his personal needs (emotional integration) and his thinking processes (intellectual integration), he responds to it. He may express interest, excitement, boredom, amusement, consternation, doubt, agreement, disagreement, indignation, or any of dozens of other reactions. He may ask a question, make a statement, yawn, smile, remain silent, nod his head, cough embarrassedly, or punch the speaker in the nose. But, *in some way,* verbally or nonverbally, he always *responds.*

Integration of Response

When the listener responds, he and the speaker reverse roles. The listener becomes, for the time being, the speaker, and the speaker becomes, for the time being, the listener. As such, the original speaker now integrates what *he* hears (the response from the original listener). The original speaker now processes what he hears, and accepts, rejects, ignores, or modifies it.

Reaction to Feedback

The original speaker now resumes his original role. After integrating the listener's response (or feedback), he determines whether or not he's getting through to the listener, and then (if he's getting through) reacts with further ideas (exposition), or (if he's not getting through) reacts by probing to find out why he's not getting through. Put another way, the listener's response, when fed back to the speaker, enables the speaker to evaluate what he has communicated, to determine whether or not the listener has understood, and do something about it.

Agreement or Disagreement

Obviously, the listener either agrees or disagrees with the speaker's reaction. If the listener agrees, the speaker can now introduce an additional idea (exposition) and the cycle begins again. If, however, the listener disagrees, the speaker goes back a step, and begins probing for the factors underlying the disagreement.

This process is portrayed in the following diagram, which depicts the continuing interaction between speaker and listener:

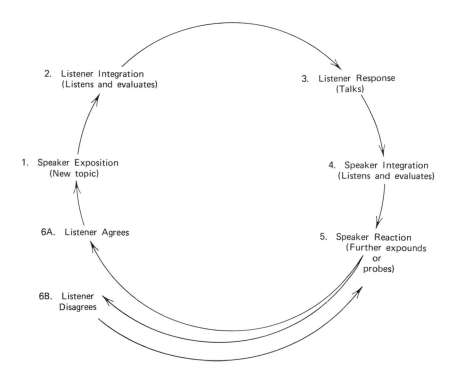

With this cycle in mind, let's describe its six phases in detail. Our description is based upon many years of behavioral science research; it represents a scientific approach to communication that any salesman or sales manager can, with understanding and practice, profitably substitute for costly trial and error. In what follows, we will talk about *salesman* rather than speaker and *customer* rather than listener. The reader should remember, however, that the principles apply to *any* speaker and *any* listener.

WHAT THE Q4 SALESMAN DOES IN EACH PHASE OF THE COMMUNICATION CYCLE

Exposition

When initially expounding, a salesman must accomplish three major tasks: establish receptivity, get and hold attention, and make himself clearly understood. Let's look at each in turn.

ESTABLISHING RECEPTIVITY

Any salesman who is honest with himself knows that many customers are not especially enthusiastic about talking to him. They are often apathetic, distracted, uninterested—in a word, unreceptive. Receptivity—the willingness to listen attentively and with an open mind—is a condition the *salesman* must establish. There are exceptions, but, in general, in the opening of a sales presentation, the salesman should state the purpose and tentative benefit of his call and achieve customer participation.

Statement of purpose and tentative customer benefit(s). In most successful sales presentations, the customer *learns* something, and learning occurs best when the subject *means something* to the learner, when it's related to his needs. That's why a good initial statement of purpose and benefits is so important.

Such a statement, *if properly worded,* can do much to establish receptivity. While we could discuss purpose separately from benefits, the two are so closely related in practice that we should consider them together. A statement of purpose by itself is likely to evoke a "So what?" response. The customer cannot be expected to be receptive unless the presentation has some meaning for *him*, and the presentation takes on such meaning only when potential *benefits* have been stated. Thus, a statement of *purpose* ("I'd like to explain a new method of copying letters") is not likely to have much impact unless it's joined to a statement of potential *benefit* ("This new method has cut copying costs by 10–12% for those companies now using it, and there's a good chance it can do the same for you"). A purpose–benefit statement gives the customer a *reason* to listen to the salesman. Without a reason, he is almost sure to remain unreceptive.

Achieving customer participation. People learn best when they are personally *involved* in what they're learning. The best way to involve a customer is to get him to *participate* in the presentation. The customer must be *urged* and *encouraged* to talk. From the outset, the presentation should be a *two-way* exchange of ideas, attitudes, and information. Through *probing* (discussed at length in our next chapter) the customer can be drawn into the exchange. Unless he feels he is a significant part of the presentation with a real stake in the outcome, his receptivity will remain low.

GETTING AND HOLDING ATTENTION

High receptivity will not remain high automatically. Unless the salesman works to hold the customer's attention at every step, the tug of the customer's other thoughts and interests will prove irresistible. Attention can be kept at a high level in three ways (in addition, of course, to the *primary* way of appealing to the customer's needs): through use of novelty and contrast, appeal to several senses, and movement and change.

Novelty and contrast. As the makers of television commercials long ago discovered, novelty grips the attention. Salesmen can seldom, if ever, indulge in the kind of novel (and sometimes bizarre) presentation techniques seen on television, but they can do a great deal to make their presentations less drab. Novel ideas obviously differ with the salesman and the product: some salesmen use portable sound-slide projectors during portions of their presentations, some have unique ways of demonstrating the qualities of various materials (like tightly knotting a necktie, then unknotting it and laying it down flat to prove it's wrinkle-proof, or pouring water on trousers to demonstrate that the crease really is permanent), and some use clever sales aids prepared by their company. Novelty cannot be introduced into every presentation but, where it can, it should be used carefully as an attention-getter.

Appeal to several senses. As a general rule, people learn more rapidly as more of their senses are engaged. A salesman will communicate more effectively if he engages not only the customer's ear, but, where possible, his eye and touch. *Telling* a customer about a new fabric gives him a limited idea of what it's like; telling him and *showing* him a swatch gives him a much fuller idea; telling him, showing him, and letting him *feel* the fabric gives him still fuller understanding. Many salesmen mistakenly think of themselves exclusively as *talkers*, and disdain the use of visual aids and samples or consider them secondary to the spoken presentation.

Actually, visual aids, samples, and demonstrations are a fundamental part of communicating. Anyone who doubts this should compare the great difficulty perfume manufacturers have in describing their products in printed ads, and the ease with which the same product is presented (and frequently sold) by the saleslady behind the perfume counter who lets the customer *smell* the perfume.

Movement and change. Movement and change help rivet attention. It's easier to maintain a customer's interest if he is required to watch something move (perhaps the salesman himself, who may noticeably shift position from time to time, or perhaps samples or visual aids which are shifted from point to point), or listen to changes in the pitch and volume of the salesman's voice. *Any* presentation can, if the salesman is sufficiently ingenious, include at least a little movement or change. Insurance salesmen know one way to enliven a presentation is to use pencil and paper to work out arithmetic computations *in front of* the customer, even though the computations could easily have been done *before* the presentation; besides getting the customer personally involved, this technique insures that he will see some movement and change (and that his eye will be engaged as well as his ear) and thus pay more attention to the salesman.

To sum up: attention is slippery and elusive, hard to get hold of, and easy to lose. The salesman constantly competes for the customer's attention with the customer's own thoughts. The salesman who fails to use novelty, contrast, movement, change, and an appeal to multiple senses makes his job all the tougher for himself.

MAKING HIMSELF CLEARLY UNDERSTOOD

We come now to the very heart of the communication process. Even though the customer may be receptive, and paying close attention, he may still not *understand* the salesman. In countless presentations, the way in which the product will satisfy the customer's need is never completely clear; the benefits the customer will obtain are not fully appreciated because they're not thoroughly understood; and the net gain to the customer is not firmly implanted in his mind. In place of concise, point-by-point understanding of what he will get out of the purchase, the customer has only a vague, disorganized, and superficial feeling that *in some way* things may be better for him if he buys the product. No wonder so many presentations end not in closes but in put-offs, alibis, and endless procrastination.

There are two reasons for this frequent lack of understanding. One, as we've already stressed, is that *communication is never easy.* The second, closely related, is that many salesmen fail to use the *techniques* by which meaning can be clearly conveyed.

There are at least four basic principles that the salesman should know and *use* if he is to make his meaning clear to customers: words have emotional impact, spaced ideas are easier to learn than bunched ideas, repetition aids learning, and highly specific concrete words and ideas communicate better than abstract or highly general words.

Words have emotional impact. Many sales are lost, or at least made much more difficult, because the salesman uses words with negative emotional impact. Literally thousands of English words have five or six synonyms apiece; these words mean approximately the same in a *dictionary* sense. But they often have very different meanings in an *emotional* sense. Most men, for example, like to think of themselves, in one way or another, as *average*, yet most men seldom, if ever, think of themselves as *mediocre*. Yet, both words mean essentially the same as far as the dictionary is concerned. Saleswomen eagerly tell customers that they look *slender* in a dress, or perhaps *slim*, but never *skinny*, yet the three words have virtually identical dictionary meanings. Owners of second-hand stores refer to their merchandise as *reconditioned*, which obviously means second-hand.

We could go on listing examples for pages, but the point is no doubt clear: the emotional impact of words is as important to the salesman as their basic dictionary meaning. If a customer hears key words that strike him as bad or distasteful or unpleasant, he may become upset or indignant, or screen them out. But he is *not* likely to use them to grasp the salesman's meaning.

This is *not* a manipulative Q1 approach. By being aware of the emotional value of words, and choosing words with a positive impact, the salesman does *not* mislead the customer; he merely communicates with him on the level of the customer's *needs*. The ideas suggested by harsh, rough, or severe words often threaten our needs for security or esteem. This threat may trigger fear, discomfort, or anxiety, all of which distract us from the underlying meaning of the words. Basic meaning can be conveyed more easily by carefully chosen words.

Spaced ideas are easier to learn than bunched ideas. There are some exceptions to this principle but, in general, ideas are easier to learn when time elapses between the presentation of each idea than when the ideas are all grouped together and hurled at the listener without any time between each. When ideas are spaced out, the listener has time to mull them over and master them, one by one. Learning is thus made easier.

Real spacing of ideas is rare in sales communication. Typically, a salesman is so eager to tell his story that he pours it out in a torrent of words. One idea flows into another, and the customer gets no time to consider one idea before going on to the next. What the salesman thinks is an impressive array of facts and ideas is little more than a confusing mish-mash to the customer.

Sometimes, of course, spacing is impractical. The pharmaceutical sales-man forced by circumstances to "detail" a drug to a physician in 90 sec-onds as the physician walks down a hospital corridor, may not be able to space his ideas. Similarly, the announcer of a half-minute radio com-mercial cannot do any serious spacing. Too many half-minute com-mercials, crammed with information, are extremely difficult to remember, even if listened to carefully. When time is severely limited and spacing is difficult, it is probably best to keep the presentation as *simple* as possible. It would be far better, surely, for a physician to understand one or two key elements of information about a detailed drug than fail to under-stand any of ten or twelve elements.

Whenever practical, ideas, information, features, and benefits (anything important for the customer to understand) should be spaced out. The in-formation should be presented in appropriately small amounts, with pauses and probes between. The salesman should test the customer's understanding of each key idea before going on to the next. Whenever possible, he should make sure the customer is keeping up with him before he proceeds. Without allowing time for customer feedback, the salesman has no way of knowing if he is getting through.

Repetition aids learning. Advertisers mastered this principle long ago. This is one reason TV commercials are almost always repeated dozens, perhaps hundreds, of times, and why the product name is repeated so often during commercials. The mere repetition of a message helps to get it across.

This is not to say that salesmen should repeat every idea again and again. But *key* ideas, especially *new* ones, should be repeated. The pre-sentation need not sound as if it's being made in an echo-chamber; the phrasing of the ideas can vary. But the ideas themselves should be re-peated. One way to repeat ideas without monotony is by *examples*. An example is nothing more than a repetition of an idea reduced to a spe-cific case. Another way to avoid tedious repetition is to use synonyms for key words, rather than repeat the same word over and over again. Still another technique is to *enlarge* upon the basic idea each time it's re-peated by adding a bit more information each time.

Salesmen should, of course, scrupulously avoid exasperating customers by repeating ideas merely to fill a pause in the presentation, or by repeating obvious ideas or ideas the customer has clearly mastered. Repetition should emphasize *significant* points that might otherwise be ignored or distorted.

Specific or concrete words and ideas communicate better than abstract or general words. If you were to tell a neighbor that an animal in your house had just given birth to a litter, and that you wanted to sell one of the litter to him, you wouldn't get very far. Words like *animal* and *litter* are abstractions; they don't evoke clear images in the listener's mind. Your neighbor wouldn't know if he was being asked to buy a dog, cat, or cheetah. If you told the same neighbor your *dog* had given birth to a litter, you might make some headway, but it's unlikely you'd arouse great enthusiasm. But, if you told him your black and white Dalmatian dog had just given birth to six pups, and that you wanted to sell him one with a large black spot surrounding its left eye, you would be far more likely to create a mental image. Only the last statement gives the listener a clear mental image of what he's being asked to buy.

Abstractions do not communicate very much to anybody. *Specific, concrete* words and phrases do. Phrases like "costs less," "saves you money," and "is more efficient" don't tell the customer enough. He needs to know *how much* less the product costs, *how much* money it will save, and *exactly how* it is more efficient. In general, specific *numbers* communicate better than adjectives like "more," "less," "high," "low," "expensive," and "inexpensive." There's nothing wrong with these, but they're not sufficient by themselves. (Because they are specific, numerical statements give the customer something definite to grasp. As such, they sometimes help to reduce customer anxiety.)

Similarly, words that help the customer *visualize* are better: "red Fiat two-seater with white convertible top" is better than "foreign sports car," "will enable you to eliminate all carbon paper and smudged fingers" is better than "will improve your office procedures," and "cannot be consumed by fire" is better than "safe." (People have a tendency to visualize anyway, but the chances of incorrect visualization increase as language becomes more abstract. If you say "chair," the listener may imagine an overstuffed livingroom chair with a floral pattern while you mean a wrought-iron chair with a wicker seat.)

These principles of exposition boil down to this: A salesman who wants to communicate effectively must do much more than mere random talking. He must first of all remember that he is *teaching;* he is trying to modify or change old ideas. To do this, he must know something about *how* people learn. He must present his material in an organized way, and he must use proven techniques to establish receptivity, to get and hold attention, and to make himself clearly understood. Even if he does all these things, he will not necessarily get through to the customer; as we shall see in a minute, he will still come up against a number of barriers when the customer begins to integrate the information. But, by using the principles we've mentioned so far, he'll find his job immeasurably less difficult than otherwise. And that's saying a great deal.

Integration

Here the communication process becomes complicated. The information received from the salesman is almost always *changed* in some way by the customer; the change may be slight (for example, a point the salesman wanted to emphasize strongly may be somewhat de-emphasized by the customer) or it may be a transformation (for example, a statement the salesman intended as a compliment may be interpreted by the customer as an insult). But, always, *something* happens to the information as it's processed by the customer. It may be added to, subtracted from, twisted, turned upside-down, or completely ignored, but it almost never emerges from the integration process exactly as it went in. In this section, we'll talk about four general processes of integration: establishment of personal meaningfulness, testing of familiarity, consonance, and reinforcement.

ESTABLISHMENT OF PERSONAL MEANINGFULNESS

Everyone defines *meaningfulness* differently. The announcement of a new synthetic bristle that can be shaped to a sharp point will be personally meaningful to an artist, but probably not to a stockholder; news of a debenture issue will be personally meaningful to the stockbroker, but probably not to the artist. The artist will probably listen attentively to a salesman talking about brushes with the new bristle, and the stockbroker will listen just as attentively to the debenture announcement. This kind of selectivity goes on all the time, although not always consciously. We selectively tune in to information that has *personal* meaning for us, and pay attention to it. If we can relate information to our task or personal needs, especially those that are our strongest motivators, we consider it meaningful.

Meaningfulness, however, is not always easy to establish. Many times, we fail to see that information has personal meaning for us. Thus, the salesman must make sure the customer understands *how* the presentation relates to him. He uses an opening purpose–benefit statement to tell the customer "what's in it for me." An encyclopedia salesman who tells a devoted father that "I'd like to explain how this new edition will help your child get better grades at school and improve his chances of getting into college," *has* established meaningfulness by showing that the encyclopedia is *relevant* to the customer's needs.

TESTING OF FAMILIARITY

One thing the customer does with the information he gets is compare it with what he already knows to determine whether it's *familiar*. If it is, it's easier to understand and assimilate. This point is especially important.

The *degree* of the customer's familiarity with the information has much to do with the kind of presentation the salesman must make. Imagine a salesman of electronic data processing equipment describing a computer to a businessman whose company has always done manual accounting and never used EDP; the salesman obviously has to explain many things that would scarcely need mentioning to a customer who has used computers for years. In fact, establishing *familiarity* where none exists may be so big a task that several sales calls may be required to do the job. Now imagine the same salesman calling on a businessman who knows a great deal about computers, but is using a competitive brand. The content of the presentation, the information that's imparted, will obviously differ considerably. Yet it may actually prove easier to make a sale to the first customer than to the second.

Why? Because once familiarity is established, it may be easier to establish benefits in the first case (where net gain will probably be quite large) than in the second (where net gain may be quite small). The more difficult it is to establish familiarity, the easier it may be to make the sale, although there are instances when this is not true. One factor working against this possibility is that people tend to stick with the familiar; the better we know things, the more comfortable we feel with them, while new things may seem unsettling or even threatening.

So there are three questions the salesman must ask himself:

1. How will the customer's familiarity or lack of familiarity with my product affect the content of my presentation? How much explanation does the customer need to understand what I'm talking about? (You can't sell a camel to an Arab and an Eskimo with the same presentation.)

2. Can I use the customer's lack of familiarity to establish a dramatic net gain? (A Volkswagen owner who buys a Cadillac will realize more impressive net gain than a Buick owner who buys a Cadillac.)

3. Will the customer's lack of familiarity create any negative attitudes

toward my product and, if so, how can I overcome them? (It's almost always harder to sell air travel to a man who's never been in an airplane and is fearful of flying than to a man who's logged hundreds of thousands of air miles.)

CONSONANCE

We all need to make the things we know, believe, and feel *fit together*. We want our attitudes, beliefs, and knowledge to agree; in the language of behavioral science, we want *consonance* (fitting together), not *dissonance* (failure to fit together). When dissonance exists, when things don't agree or mesh or form a sensible pattern, we feel uncomfortable, bothered, and insecure. To overcome our uneasiness and discomfort, we usually adjust one of the nonfitting elements until it fits.

A couple of examples may make this clearer: A man with positive feelings about smoking ("I enjoy a good smoke. It relaxes me. I feel less tense when I'm smoking a cigarette") may hear something that creates conflicting feelings ("Smoking is bad for you. Tars cause cancer in mice. There's evidence they cause cancer in humans"). This conflict, or dissonance, caused by information which doesn't mesh with an existing attitude, makes the smoker uncomfortable; until the new information and the old attitude can be made to agree, he may feel restless, edgy, worried. To eliminate these feelings, he may do one of several things: stop smoking, tell himself there's no conclusive evidence linking smoking and cancer so it's silly to be bothered, or persuade himself that it's more important to take care of an immediate problem, like eliminating tension by smoking, than to worry about a long-range possibility, like developing disease by smoking. Thus, the smoker may change his habits to fit the evidence, or he may *change the evidence* to fit his habits. People do not always seek the truth, but they *do* always seek relief from the discomfort that arises when knowledge and attitudes do not agree.

Another example is an advertising manager who takes great pride in his company's current advertising campaign (full-color pages in national magazines) but is told by a salesman for a TV station that this campaign is wasteful, and that more results per dollar could be obtained from television advertising. The salesman backs up his argument with an impressive array of statistics gathered by an independent research agency. This information sets up considerable discomfort in the ad manager, who has received many compliments about the magazine ads, who likes to see his company's name in prestigious national publications, and who has staked his professional reputation on the success of the ads, but who *also* is a man of conscience who believes in getting the most for his company's dollar. These conflicting feelings must be resolved if his uneasiness is to be overcome. To make the various elements fit together, he may cancel the remainder of his magazine ad schedule and buy TV time instead, tell himself that the salesman's statistics are unreliable because they were gathered by a sloppy research technique, persuade himself that the many compliments he's received on the ads represent an intangible "extra" that is of great importance to his company and should not be cast aside for an untried approach, or tell himself that his original intuition, which led him to buy magazine space instead of television time, is worth more than all the statistics in the world, and that he is being paid to make the decisions based on his best professional judgment, not on the basis of a lot of numbers. Whatever his final decision, he may change his mind or he may manipulate the outside evidence to make a change of mind unnecessary.

Some of the *adjustments* a customer may make to eliminate dissonance are exaggeration, leveling, and screening out.

Exaggeration. He may increase the importance of information by intensifying it. A purchasing agent who feels insecure in his job, and who craves reassurance, may describe his present inventory-control system to a salesman, who may respond with, "That's not a bad way to do it." The purchasing agent may hear this as "That's an excellent way to do it," and thereby make the information fit his need.

Leveling. This is exaggeration in reverse. A purchasing agent using an inventory-control system set up by his predecessor, of whom he feels jealous, may be eager to install a new system for which he can take full credit. When describing the present system to a salesman, the salesman may respond with "That's a good approach, really," but the purchasing agent may hear this as "That's not bad, but . . . ."

Screening out. If information is sufficiently threatening, the listener may not record it in his memory, but wipe it out, like chalk marks from a blackboard. A purchasing agent who describes his inventory-control system to a salesman may be told that, "I know another P.A. who installed a system just like that one. It created such a mess, and the records got so fouled up, that they fired the poor guy." If the purchasing agent is insecure and worried about his job, he may not remember, a few hours later, even having heard the remark. (Conversely, of course, he may be unable to get it out of his mind and, as a result, be ridden by anxiety.)

REINFORCEMENT

People learn more readily when they are supported and rewarded by others. Psychologists call this support and reward *reinforcement*. Reinforcement is often verbal, consisting of praise, encouragement, or agreement ("Good!" "Keep on, you're doing fine." "That's right; go on!"). But it may be nonverbal (a heartening smile, a hand on the shoulder, or an encouraging nod of the head). Customers are invariably alert to signs of support or lack of support from salesmen. If a customer feels he is being reinforced, he will more easily integrate information from the salesman.

The salesman reinforces the customer by showing, by words and manner, that he is *interested* in the customer, that he wants to help him crystallize his needs and express himself. The Q4 salesman reinforces the customer by *listening* as well as talking. A sympathetic and interested salesman makes the customer feel he is being supported and encouraged. A salesman who monopolizes the presentation, insists on doing most of the talking, listens impatiently or cuts short the customer, yawns and indicates boredom, *deprives* the customer of support and fails to reinforce his efforts to learn.

In effect, then, reinforcement fills customers' personal needs (for social approval, esteem, and independence) and people learn best when their needs are being met. The salesman who recognizes and meets these needs gives the customer the *support* so vital to learning.

Reinforcement can be looked at as a way to provide *personal benefits* to the customer (as distinct from *product* benefits). When a customer's personal need is filled, he derives a personal benefit, just as he derives a product benefit when his task needs are filled. Often, when a customer must choose between competing products that are similar in quality and identical in price, he is likely to buy from the salesman who provides both product benefits and personal benefits. Thus, the salesman who provides reinforcement may well be the salesman with the competitive edge.

When interacting with a customer the Q4 salesman repeatedly asks himself: "Am I, by words or actions, *lending support* to the customer or *depriving him of support?* Am I meeting the *customer's* needs or using him to meet my *own* needs? Are my actions and words really directed *outward* to the customer or *inward* to myself? Am I applying personal *benefits* to the customer by my presentation?" These questions go to the very heart of the communication process.

By now, it is clear that the customer is never passive in the communication process; he is never an empty receptacle into which ideas can be poured at will. He constantly *does something* with the information he receives: he integrates it with what he already knows, tests it against the rules of logic, against his own thinking and feelings, and against his own experience; he determines (consciously or unconsciously) whether it fits his needs, whether it has meaning for him, and he accepts it, rejects it, or changes it. Thus, when information, attitudes, or ideas are imparted by a salesman to a customer, *the salesman momentarily loses control of what happens to the information, attitudes, or ideas.* The next step is up to the *customer.* No matter what the salesman wishes, the customer is free to do whatever he likes with the information: ignore it, believe it, agree with it, distort it, twist it out of recognition. If the salesman has done a good job of establishing receptivity, getting and holding attention, and making himself clear, the chances that the customer will ignore the information or grossly distort it are lessened. But it is still the *customer,* not the salesman, who decides what is done with the information. For a brief time, control of the communication process has passed from salesman to customer. If the salesman is to communicate persuasively, *he must be alert to the customer's responses* and *know how to react to them* to elicit further responses from the customer that are *favorable.* The customer's responses are clues that tell the salesman *what to do next* in order to get further responses that will help him to reach a commitment. Let's look at these customer responses in some detail.

Response

Once the customer integrates information, he can respond in one of three ways: direct acceptance, direct rejection, or indirect rejection. All but the first present serious problems for the salesman; for that reason, we will talk briefly about direct acceptance, and at greater length about the others.

DIRECT ACCEPTANCE

This can be expressed in many ways: by outright agreement ("You're right," "Absolutely"), encouragement ("Keep going," "Tell me more"), positive sounds or statements ("Uh-huh" "Good"), signs (a nod, a smile, even a wink), or questions. Acceptance is easy to recognize, but hard to interpret. Some customers indicate agreement not because they agree, but because they are Q3s who don't want to hurt the salesman's feelings or arouse conflict. Others agree not with what the salesman said, but with what they *think* he said. And still others agree in a mechanical Q2 way because they have not been listening attentively, like husbands who grunt assent to whatever their wives say, oblivious of what they're assenting to because they're really concentrating on the sports page.

Customer agreement should never, therefore, be taken at face value.

Instead, it should be weighed in the light of two questions: Does the customer *really* agree? Does he agree with what I *really* mean, or with a *misinterpretation* of what I mean?

DIRECT REJECTION

There are at least three ways a customer indicates directly that he either disagrees with the salesman, or that he is not firmly convinced. These are stated disagreements or negative flat assertions, venting, and belligerent questioning.

Stated disagreement or negative flat assertions. These are the most direct methods, especially characteristic of Q1 customers. The customer candidly responds to the salesman by saying something like "I don't agree," or "That's all wrong, if you ask me," or "That's not the way I see it." These are negative *flat assertions;* they indicate that the customer's mind is made up (it can be changed, but that's a task for the salesman) and, more important, that he is *not* receptive to new ideas. This is important: a customer who makes a flat assertion ("I like the model I'm using now, and I'm not going to buy another brand," "The car I'm driving now is perfect for me; I'm not interested in a new one,") is *not* amenable to talk about features or benefits. And he is *not* receptive to logic, arguments, or statistical data. He is in a period of *low receptivity* to new ideas. It is useless to talk to him about new ideas (in fact, such talk may only aggravate or antagonize him) *until his low receptivity is changed to high receptivity.* We'll discuss how the salesman can do this later in the chapter.

Venting. Venting, "blowing off steam," is often characteristic of Q1 customers. Customers who need to vent should be permitted to do so. Allowing a customer to vent his emotions does not imply that the salesman agrees with him; it merely implies that he understands the customer's need to "pop off." Venting tells the salesman something about what's bothering the customer, and helps the customer get rid of some of his negative emotions so low receptivity can turn into high. Negative emotions are heavy barriers to communication. Strong feelings like fear and anger often cause customers to behave irrationally, to interpret what they hear in very personal and illogical terms. Customers who suppress strong negative feelings, who aren't allowed to get rid of them, are likely to base their decisions on emotion rather than fact. Thus the Q4 salesman encourages venting; it helps to clear the way for logic, facts, and objectivity. Like a penicillin shot for a sick man, venting may not be fun, but it improves the situation.

This point cannot be overstressed. A customer who harbors strong, pent-up feelings is likely to be so concerned with those feelings that he cannot easily concentrate on what the salesman is saying. The customer who vents these strong emotions can view things with greater *perspective;* less wrapped up in himself, he can make more detached judgments. In addition, he feels better. He is more relaxed, and easier to talk to. For all these reasons, it is important to give tense customers an opportunity to vent.

Unfortunately, many salesmen have a strong aversion to emotional outbursts, tirades, sarcasm, tongue-lashings, rebukes, scoldings, reprimands, or any form of venting by their customers. Yet this may be the *only* way to get to a point in the presentation at which the customer will *listen,* calmly and attentively. The customer will be unable to focus on what the salesman says until after he discharges his anxiety, fear, anger, or whatever negative feelings are preoccupying him.

This is only one side of the coin however. A customer may be so preoccupied with *positive* or *pleasant* thoughts that he cannot give undivided attention to the salesman. This frame of mind is described in phrases like "bursting with good news" or "overcome with joy." These customers, too, must be permitted to *vent.* Nothing will be gained, for example, and much may be lost, by refusing to listen to a customer who wants to describe at some length the baby daughter his wife gave birth to yesterday. As with negative feelings, customers with strong positive emotions must vent them *before* serious communicating can take place.

Belligerent questioning. Not all questioning indicates direct rejection. Some may, on the contrary, indicate tentative acceptance or receptivity ("Can I arrange to buy on 90-day terms?" "How quickly could you deliver?" "Do you carry them in stock locally?") But snide questions ("Do you call *that* a bargain?" "Do you really expect me to go along with a deal like *that*?") or questions that are flat assertions in disguise ("You don't really think I'm stupid enough to buy one of those, do you?" "Do you expect me to stop buying from my brother-in-law after all these years?") are forms of direct rejection. They let a customer vent sarcasm or pique or exasperation while they enable him to say "no" in fairly clear terms. None of these is really a *serious* question, a request for information. Questions that indicate rejection are *not* requests for answers; they are *rhetorical* questions, questions that *imply their own answers* and do *not,* therefore, need an answer from anyone else. Salesmen often fall into the trap of responding to these questions by arguing, and soon find themselves in a win–lose contest that they are sure to lose.

Questions that indicate direct rejection, then, also indicate low receptivity. Like flat assertions, these questions must be probed, not argued with. Answers should be provided later; exploration must come first.

INDIRECT REJECTION

What the customer hears from the salesman may create *anxieties* by threatening one of his basic needs, perhaps for security or esteem. As a result of something the salesman says, the customer may begin to doubt the wisdom of the way he's doing things, he may begin to fear for his job, he may be beset by anxiety because he knows that he *should* buy, but is afraid to admit there is a better product than the one he's now using. The salesman is trying to *change* the customer's behavior, to get him to do something *differently,* and, for many people, change is threatening and unwelcome.

Let's look at an example: A man whose father was wiped out financially by a bank failure in a major economic recession grew up believing that banks are unreliable. He refuses to use banking services, and keeps a sizable amount of cash and his important personal papers at home. One day, when talking to his insurance agent, he takes a number of insurance policies out of a metal box. As he does so, the insurance salesman spots several other important documents, including stock certificates. The insurance agent immediately says: "You know, you really ought to keep those things in a safe-deposit box. You never know when something might happen to them. Just last week, one of my clients who lives a few blocks from here was robbed. The poor guy lost silverware, jewelry, everything. As your insurance adviser, I'd suggest you get that stuff out of the house before it's too late." This information, when compared to the injunctions the customer learned from his father, is likely to create real anxiety.

The various techniques of indirect rejection help the individual to overcome, or at least reduce, anxiety; they help him defend himself against what he experiences as conflict or threat. The customer using indirect rejection is usually quite unaware of the fact. Without knowing it, he sets up barriers to communication.

Internal anxiety may be handled in one of the three ways we detailed earlier: exaggeration, leveling or screening out. Indirect rejection is manifested by procrastination, rationalization, silence, meandering, objection hopping, boredom, or confusion. All of these may indicate that the listener is unable or unwilling to reject the speaker's idea directly.

Procrastination. By procrastinating, a customer postpones or delays a head-on encounter with what the salesman is saying. Procrastination takes many forms. Some of the more common ones are: trying to change the subject, excusing oneself momentarily ("Pardon me, but I've got to check something I gave to my secretary this morning; I'll be back in a minute"), requesting an extension of time ("Give me a few weeks to think about it"), or insisting that a further response must be delayed ("We really ought to talk about this when my partner is here, and he won't get back to town until next week"). Procrastination is the customer's way of saying that "I never do today what I can put off until tomorrow." It means he is not genuinely committed to what the salesman is selling.

Rationalization. Rationalization is alibi making, the invention of reasons to explain a decision whose real reasons the customer prefers not to admit. A customer's real reason for rejecting a salesman's ideas may be that he distrusts the salesman; his rationalization may be "I'm too busy to talk any more today; come back later this year, when things have slowed down a little." Only by probing can a salesman determine whether a response is genuine or a rationalization. Rationalizations usually *sound* reasonable; on the surface, they seem factual. To find out if they really are, the salesman must get below the surface.

Indirect rejection, then, tells the salesman that he has said or done something to set up barriers to communication. Obviously, the next step is to find out *why*.

Silence. Silence may imply several things: that the listener agrees with what has been said, but hasn't bothered to say so; that he does *not* understand or agree, but is unwilling to say so; that he is unsure of his own feelings; that he hasn't paid attention and doesn't know whether to agree or not. A customer may be silent because what is being said has no personal meaning for him, because he is afraid to sound stupid, because he is thinking about something else, because he doesn't want to hurt the salesman's feelings, or because he is afraid. The salesman must *interpret* the silence. He can never assume that silence implies agreement or disagreement. He must find out for himself through probing.

Meandering. The customer who wanders off the subject, drags in irrelevant topics, and refuses to stick to business may be saying, "I'm bored," or "This discussion means nothing to me, so let's talk about something that does," or "I have a need to be sociable." In any event, meandering indicates that the salesman is probably not addressing himself to the customer's task or personal needs. It cannot be effectively dealt with until its reasons are uncovered.

Objection hopping. The customer may insist on jumping from one objection to another, setting up a new hurdle each time the salesman leaps the previous one. Usually, objection hopping indicates that the customer, for some reason, is unwilling to voice his *real* objection. For example, he may not have the money to buy, but is embarrassed to admit it. He may then use a series of other objections as a smoke screen to hide his real objection. Once again, probing is called for.

Boredom. Boredom usually signifies indifference. Yawns, distracted glances, toying with papers on one's desk, idle stares, gestures of impatience, all indicate that the customer may be finding the presentation meaningless, tedious, dull. A salesman confronted with these responses must find out *why* the customer is bored before he can eliminate them.

Confusion. The salesman cannot be sure whether the confused customer accepts or rejects. He is obviously indicating that he does not know how to proceed with the presentation. Many times, confusion is *implied* rather than stated; a customer may *think* he understands, but something he says may reveal that he is perplexed, mistaken, or vague. He may ask a question that the salesman has already answered. Or, embarrassed or afraid to admit he has not understood, he may lapse into silence. The salesman who waits for a customer to say "I don't get it," may wait a long time.

We can summarize this discussion of *response by customer* by pointing out, again, that the customer's response is often *not* what the salesman intended. To repeat: the customer is not an empty receptacle into which ideas can be poured. His mind is already filled with an immeasurable number of ideas, any of which may affect his response to a *new* idea. His response is not only shaped by what he hears, but by his *personal needs* and his *thought processes,* his emotions and his intellect. Response is the result of the interaction of all these elements.

Integration of Response

At this phase in the cycle, salesman and customer exchange communication roles. The customer becomes, for the time being, the speaker, and the salesman becomes, for the time being, the listener. As listener, the salesman integrates the response he gets from the customer, using the same techniques of integration described earlier in this chapter. In integrating, the salesman can distort or change what *he* hears just as the customer can. Thus, an entirely new set of obstacles to clear communication may be erected, this time *by the salesman* rather than the customer.

Reaction to Feedback

By paying careful attention to the customer's responses, the salesman can answer a number of important questions: Am I getting through? Does he understand? Does he agree? What should I do next? The responses from the customer are *feedback,* information that tells him how he's doing.

Unless the customer responds with clear-cut acceptance, his response may puzzle or confuse the salesman. For example, a customer who seems to be listening carefully but says nothing may be implying one of several things: that he agrees, that he disagrees, that he is confused, that he is not paying attention, or that he is hard of hearing. How is the salesman to know? A customer who responds by telling an irrelevant joke may be saying, "I agree, so let's move on to another and more entertaining topic," or "I disagree, but I don't want to embarrass you by saying so," or "I'm bored; let's liven up the discussion." How can the salesman be sure?

This brings us to two basic rules of sales communication. They are that customer responses should seldom be accepted at face value, and the best technique for getting to the customer's *real* feelings is *probing*.

CUSTOMER RESPONSES SHOULD SELDOM BE ACCEPTED AT FACE VALUE

Sometimes customers mean exactly what they say, but sometimes they don't. It is often difficult for the salesman to tell. The customer who says, with conviction, "Your price is too high," may really be saying, "I don't have the money, but I'm ashamed to say so." The customer who seems vexed with a salesman may really be vexed with his own wife, who just bought an expensive and unneeded fur coat. The customer who nods in eager agreement may be a pleasant chap who does not want to hurt the salesman's feelings by telling him that he doesn't really understand the presentation. The antidote for this problem is *analytic* communication that never accepts anything at face value.

THE BEST TECHNIQUE FOR GETTING TO THE CUSTOMER'S REAL FEELINGS IS PROBING

Probing is not a single technique but a whole cluster of techniques, all of which enable the salesman to do exactly what the surgeon does when he probes: to get beneath the surface, to explore, to search and examine in a careful, systematic way. Because probing skills are vital to analytic communication, we'll devote all of our next chapter to them.

Agreement or Disagreement

In this final phase of the communication cycle, the customer can agree or disagree with the salesman's reaction to what he has said. If he agrees, the salesman can move on to phase 1 of the cycle (exposition) all over again, and introduce a new or enlarged idea. However, if the customer disagrees, the salesman must probe until he discovers the reason for the disagreement. Then he must work to establish agreement. Until he establishes agreement or effectively manages the customer's resistance, it is useless to proceed with the exposition of a new idea or ideas.

SUMMARY

Persuasive communication is seldom easy. It's difficult to replace old ideas with new ones; nevertheless people often do accept new ideas if the ideas are related to satisfying their needs. Four of the principal factors affecting the ease of persuasion are the listener's readiness to change, his emotional investment in the present way of doing things, how widely accepted the idea is, and how much trust the listener reposes in the person communicating the idea.

Getting ideas across to another person requires a six-phase cycle consisting of exposition by the speaker, integration by the listener, response by the listener, integration of response by the speaker, reaction to feedback by the speaker, and agreement or disagreement by the listener.

In the first phase, exposition, the salesman must establish receptivity, get and hold the customer's attention, and make himself clearly understood. To establish receptivity, he should state the purpose and tentative benefit of his call, and achieve customer participation. To get and hold attention, he should use novelty and contrast, appeal to several senses, and use movement and change. To make himself clearly understood, he should select words with positive emotional impact, space his ideas rather than bunch them, repeat key ideas, and use concrete words in preference to abstract ones.

In the integration phase the customer decides whether the ideas he has heard are personally meaningful, tests them for familiarity, tries to establish consonance between the new idea and his old ideas, and seeks reinforcement from the salesman. In establishing consonance, he may exaggerate, level, or screen out the new idea. In any event, during this phase the salesman loses control, temporarily, of what happens to the information he has imparted.

In the third phase, response, the customer may accept the idea or reject it directly or indirectly. Direct acceptance should never be taken at face value, but probed. Direct rejection can be evidenced by stated disagreement or negative flat assertions, by venting, or by belligerent questioning. Indirect rejection may be manifested in numerous ways: by anxiety, procrastination, rationalization, silence, meandering, objection hopping, boredom, or confusion.

In the fourth phase, integration of response, the salesman and customer exchange communication roles; the customer becomes the speaker and the salesman becomes the listener. The salesman integrates the response he gets from the customer by the same techniques the customer used.

In the next phase, reaction to feedback, the salesman should recall that customer responses should seldom be accepted at face value, and that the best technique for getting to the customer's real feelings is probing. Genuine mutual understanding is essential before the salesman can profitably move on to a new or enlarged topic.

In the final phase, the customer either agrees or disagrees with the salesman's reaction. If he agrees, the salesman can begin the cycle again by introducing an additional idea. But if the customer disagrees, the salesman must probe to uncover the reason for the disagreement. Until the disagreement has been eliminated, there is little point in expounding additional ideas.

TABLE 7. Basic Principles of Sales Exposition

Major tasks	How to do them
Establish receptivity	State the purpose of your call and a tentative benefit to the customer
	Get the customer to participate through probing
Get and hold attention	Use novelty and contrast
	Appeal to several senses
	Use movement and change
Make yourself clearly understood	Be aware of the emotional impact of the words you use
	Space your ideas, don't bunch
	Repeat key ideas
	Use concrete words and ideas instead of abstract ones

TABLE 8. How Customers Integrate Ideas and Information

Four processes of integration	How they are accomplished
Establishment of personal effectiveness	Customer tunes-in to those ideas and data that are relevant to his interests; tunes-out others
Testing of familiarity	Customer compares what he is hearing to what he already knows
Establishment of consonance (fit)	Exaggeration, customer increases importance of information by intensifying it Leveling, customer reduces importance of information by de-emphasizing it Screening out, customer wipes out information from his memory
Reinforcement	Customer notes any signs (verbal or non-verbal) of support and encouragement from salesman

TABLE 9. How Customers Respond After Integrating Ideas and Information

Three kinds of response	How they are accomplished
Direct acceptance	Outright agreement Encouragement Signs
Direct rejection	Stated disagreements or negative flat assertions Venting Belligerent questioning
Indirect rejection	Procrastination Rationalization Silence Meandering Objection-hopping Boredom Confusion

14

Probing

THE SALESMAN'S INDISPENSABLE TOOL

Probing is a technique (actually a group of techniques) designed to help the customer uncover or clarify information or vent emotions. It is the key technique by which the Q4 salesman reacts to feedback from customers. Probing is so important, and so neglected, that we are devoting an entire chapter to it. Probing skills are probably the most ignored of all communication techniques; they are also the most useful, valuable and capable of producing results.

Effective probing is seldom or ineptly done by Q1, Q2, and Q3 salesmen. Probing when done effectively allows a salesman to get at the truth, to bring the whole story to the surface, to uncover the customer's reactions, ideas, feelings, needs, and desires, whatever they may be. And, as we well know by now, the Q1, Q2, and Q3 salesman, each for his own reasons, does not uncover the whole story. Only the Q4, who bases his success upon understanding, probes thoroughly and tenaciously.

PROBING: A MULTIPURPOSE TOOL

Probing is important because it helps to achieve many of the communications goals described in the previous chapter. It is a multipurpose tool that (1) gets the customer to participate in the presentation, (2) elicits information about the customer's thoughts, and feelings, (3) reinforces the customer's learning, (4) draws out the silent or unresponsive customer, (5) helps to control meandering, (6) makes the presentation more meaningful to the customer by enabling him to inject *his* ideas, (7) converts low receptivity to high receptivity, and (8) requires the salesman to listen attentively.

Getting the customer to participate. By its very nature, a probe gets the customer involved. Its whole purpose is to create a response. Probes elicit, they extract, they evoke; they always bring something forth from the customer. The typical probe is quite brief; its structure forces the salesman to shut up and let the customer talk. Therefore, probes are ideal for establishing the interaction without which there is no communication; they are the perfect remedy for salesmen who confuse selling with speechmaking.

Eliciting information about the customer's thoughts and feelings. A probe is a technique for getting information that the customer has not volunteered. Probes can be used to draw forth an immense variety of information relating to either ideas, attitudes, or emotions. They help the salesman to learn what he could not learn in any other way.

Reinforcing the customer's learning. Probes provide the support and encouragement so important to learning new ideas. Every probe implies that the salesman is *interested* in the customer; it says, in effect, "I want to hear more, I want to learn from you." Furthermore, every probe implies that the salesman *respects* the customer. It says, in effect, "Your opinion counts." Interest and respect are two of the basic elements of reinforcement.

Drawing out the silent customer. Few things frustrate salesmen more than a tight-lipped customer who does little more than grunt and nod, if even that. Salesmen typically respond to this kind of customer by talking harder and faster; they try desperately to fill the silence with the sound of their own voices. This often drives the customer further into speechlessness; in fact, it makes it difficult for him to say anything even if he wants to. Probes help overcome this problem.

Controlling meandering. Probes lend structure to a presentation. They give it focus and direction. Not even the most talkative Q3 buyer can roam aimlessly from topic to topic when he is confronted at every turn by purposeful probes which force him to get back to the main subject. Probes are a highly effective *control* device; they restrain freewheeling customers as nothing else can.

Making the presentation meaningful to the customer. If we are interested in anything, it is our own words; if we especially like any sound, it is the sound of our own voices. Probing helps make the presentation meaningful, relevant, and appealing to the customer by enabling him to voice his *own* ideas, sentiments, and concerns. It lets him relate the presentation to his *own* needs. It transforms the presentation from an impersonal to a personal experience.

Converting low receptivity to high receptivity. Our previous chapter defined low receptivity as being closed to new ideas; a customer in a state of low receptivity is likely to make flat, dogmatic assertions which indicate that his mind is made up and he is not interested in changing it. Obviously, any customer in this frame of mind must be converted to high receptivity, a willingness to consider new ideas and question old ones, before a sale can be made.

Many salesmen handle low receptivity ineffectively. The Q1 disputes flat assertions, often driving the customer into a more stubborn (and argumentative) posture. The Q2 ignores flat assertions ("You can't change people's minds, so why try?"), leaving the customer as resistant as ever. And the Q3 treats them lightly or minimizes them, but does nothing to change them.

The effective way to handle flat assertions and thereby heighten receptivity is to probe them. When drawn out through probes, customers often clarify their thinking and moderate their previously unyielding positions; they examine their logic and qualify their remarks, and, in doing so, become more receptive to other ideas; they become less certain, more doubtful, more inquiring. Low receptivity shifts to high.

Requiring the salesman to listen attentively. The salesman who probes *must* listen attentively, because probes are usually serial, one following another until the salesman has the information he wants. But no salesman can probe intelligently unless he understands *what* has preceded each probe. A probe not only leads to a response, it is itself a *reaction* to a response. The value of any probe thus depends upon the attention and understanding with which the salesman heard the previous response. Probing without listening can only lead to zany dialogue, like the old Abbott and Costello "Who's on first, what's on second" routine. These exchanges are always funny (or pathetic), but never profitable. They are "dialogues of the deaf" in which each person talks *at* the other but neither really hears nor understands.

Our reason, then, for devoting so much space to probing is that sound probing accomplishes so much. Many sales presentations are dull monologues, boring recitations, or tiresome lectures; comparatively few are two-way exchanges of information. What can convert the former into the latter is *probing*, the hallmark of Q4 salesmanship.

A FUNCTIONAL APPROACH TO PROBING

No matter what purpose it is used for, probing serves three functions in the communications process: (*1*) it *starts* information flowing, (2) it *keeps* information flowing until the salesman learns what he needs to know, and (*3*) it helps the salesman *check* his understanding of the information, and gain a specific commitment to action.

Starting the flow of information. Probes test the customer's willingness to communicate and they prompt him to start talking. The salesman cannot be sure the customer is willing to communicate unless he probes to find out. Even if the customer is ready and willing to exchange information, the salesman must start the exchange. Probes are indispensable for both purposes.

Much of the information that customers give is not given spontaneously. As we have seen many times, Q1, Q2, and Q3 customers often withhold data that the salesman needs before he can demonstrate real benefits and net gain. Probing is an important tool for uncovering these data.

Keeping the flow of information going. Most customers don't *continue* talking meaningfully and understandably until they have said everything the salesman needs to know. Many talk briefly and then stop before they finish the subject, or they wander off the topic, or they talk confusingly. In each instance, the salesman must probe to keep the flow of information constant, relevant, and clear. Otherwise, he is likely to lose vital information or jump to premature conclusions.

Checking understanding and gaining a commitment to action. No matter how clear the information *seems,* the salesman should probe to *check* his understanding. Otherwise, he may misinterpret what is on the customer's mind. Imagine a customer who responds to everything the salesman says with "Great." What is he really saying? Almost everything customers utter is subject to multiple interpretations. Unless the salesman probes to check his interpretation, it may lead him wildly astray. Once he has determined by probing that he and the customer understand and agree with one another, the salesman can present a solution or try to get a commitment to action, either by closing the sale or arranging a date for a further discussion. Understanding must precede commitment and specific action, and understanding is best checked by probing.

Probably the most convenient way to describe the various probes is to group each under one of these three major functions. That's the approach we'll use in this chapter.

Types of Probe

Let's talk now about specific probes and how they start flow, keep flow going and check understanding. Here's the outline we'll follow:

1. *Probes that start the flow of information*

   OPEN-END QUESTIONS: Questions phrased so as to elicit a wide-ranging response from the customer on broad topics

2. *Probes that keep the flow of information going*

   PAUSES: Silences that permit the customer to integrate what he's heard and to formulate a response

   REFLECTIVE STATEMENTS: Statements that mirror the customer's feelings without implying that the salesman agrees

   NEUTRAL QUESTIONS AND PHRASES: Phrases and questions that elicit a broad response on a narrow topic, not as open as open-end questions, nor as closed as closed-end questions

   BRIEF ASSERTIONS OF INTEREST: Short statements that encourage the customer to continue talking

3. *Probes that check for understanding*

   LEADING QUESTIONS: Questions that imply or suggest their own answer

   SUMMARY STATEMENTS: Statements that summarize factual information received from the customer

   CLOSED-END QUESTIONS: Questions phrased so as to elicit a very narrow answer to a very specific question

As we'll see, a given probe can actually function in more than one way. The outline above does not mean that each probe has only one function, but that each has one *major* function.

STARTING THE FLOW OF INFORMATION

Open-end questions. Open-end questions are used to produce large amounts of information about broad, general subjects. They typically begin with "what," "why," "how do," or "tell me." Any question that can be answered "yes" or "no" is, by definition, *not* an open-end question.

A man who asks "What do you think of the current political situation?" may get a very short, uninformative reply ("It's okay") or a very long, detailed one that lasts several hours (or even longer). A salesman who asks an open-end question like "How do you feel about our delivery service?" may receive a terse response ("It's fine") or a lengthy recitation of complaints with examples and details. Once a salesman asks an open-end question, he has little or no control over the length of the reply, but he usually increases the likelihood that he will get a considerable amount of information. Open-end questions encourage the customer to provide large amounts of data by asking or stimulating him to speak on a *general topic* rather than a *specific fact*. "Do you like the color of this car?" is *not* an open-end question; it limits the customer to information about a single fact and tends to limit him to a "yes" or "no" response. "What do you think of this model?" *is* an open-end question; it enables the customer to talk about the entire subject of the automobile. Obviously, the salesman who wants large chunks of general information should not ask questions that can be answered yes or no. Instead, he should ask questions that begin "What do you think," "What's your opinion," "How do you feel about," "Tell me about your reactions," and so forth.

Salesmen often ask open-end questions and then, without realizing it, immediately convert them to "yes" or "no" questions. Here's an example: "What experience have you had with our delivery service? It's lived up to my promises, hasn't it?" The first question is open-end; the second question, designed to get a favorable "yes" answer, is closed-end. This technique, which is quite common, defeats the purpose of the original open-end question, which was to obtain a sizable amount of information. Open-end questions cannot be used successfully unless the salesman is willing to incur the risk of an unfavorable answer as well as a favorable one. If he insists on guaranteeing a favorable answer by asking a closed-end question immediately after the open-end, he might as well not bother to ask the open-end question at all.

Open-end questions are useful both for establishing the customer's *willingness* to communicate, and for getting him to begin communicating. A question like "How does your present investment program measure up to your expectations?" will, when answered, tell a great deal about the customer's *readiness* to respond, and, if successful, it will start a *flow* of information.

In addition to giving the customer a chance to provide information, open-end questions also get the customer *involved* in the presentation, and make it *meaningful* to him. The opportunity to answer "yes" or "no" does little to make a customer feel that he is a significant part of what's happening. But the opportunity to tell a salesman what he knows, thinks, feels, or believes makes the customer feel like a participant instead of a spectator.

Of course, not all customers respond to open-end questions the same way. When asked "What do you think of this car?", the Q3 is likely to launch into a lengthy response loaded with personal remarks; in response to the same question, the Q2 is likely to answer "It's okay," and say nothing more. There's no assurance that a single open-end question will start information flowing. If it doesn't, a second or third question may be needed. For example, an automobile salesman who received a terse "It's okay" reply from a Q2 customer might follow with "What do you like about it?" or, even better, "How does it stack up against your present car?" Where one open-end question is not sufficient to prime the pump, several will usually do the job.

PROBES THAT KEEP THE FLOW OF INFORMATION GOING

Pauses. Because most salesmen equate selling with talking, they feel uncomfortable when neither they nor the customer are speaking. Many salesmen cannot tolerate more than a second or two of silence; the absence of any human voice makes them fidgety and embarrassed.

Brief, strategically spaced pauses, in which both salesman and customer think their own thoughts for a few seconds, achieve three things:

1. They enable the customer to mull over and evaluate what he has heard. This is particularly important when a significant point has been made, or when complicated information has been explained. Customers need *time* and *quiet* in which to *absorb* ideas and *think* about them. Such pauses, for obvious reasons, are frequently called *pregnant pauses*.

2. Pauses enable the customer to formulate a *response* to what he has heard. Customers are not, after all, machines that spew out responses on demand. They need time in which to phrase their thoughts. Customers sometimes impress salesmen as being dull-witted and unresponsive, when actually they have had no opportunity to express their own thoughts satisfactorily; the fault is the salesman's, not theirs.

3. Pauses relax the pace of the presentation, and give the customer the feeling that he is *not* being pressured or coerced. A rapid-fire presentation in which words are shot forth at a machine-gun tempo, or a tediously wordy presentation in which there is never a break in the stream of speech, often overwhelms the customer with a feeling of helplessness or powerlessness. It may make him antagonistic or withdrawn.

In addition to what it does for the customer, the pause is also useful to the *salesman*. It enables him to collect his thoughts, evaluate the presentation, and plan *his* next step. It is no exaggeration to say that most salesmen talk too much. For that reason, they are often their own worst enemies.

Pauses, it should be added, are especially useful in dealing with uncommunicative Q2 customers. Like the salesman, the Q2 customer will probably feel uneasy and awkward when periods of silence occur. If the salesman sits quietly and waits, he will frequently find that it is the *customer* who fills the silence. This technique requires considerable self-discipline, but it's usually worth the effort. It is, in fact, frequently indispensable to keeping the flow of information going.

Reflective statements. These indicate understanding of (but not necessarily agreement with) a customer's emotions and point of view; they reflect, or mirror, his feelings. They're especially useful for coping with negative emotions like anger, indignation, and irritation, and for handling complaints. They permit the customer to "let off steam." They are also useful for allowing positive emotions (elation, enthusiasm) to be vented.

Reflective statements ("I can see you're angry about this") imply that the salesman *understands,* that he has no wish to argue or disagree with the customer, and that he *respects* the customer's feelings without implying agreement. They make it plain that while the salesman does not necessarily agree with the customer's position, he does understand it. Reflective statements show the customer that the salesman is an alert and sensitive listener who comprehends even though he may not share the customer's emotions. There is no surer way to defuse an explosive customer than to demonstrate respect. At one time or another, all of us have had the wind taken out of our sails when, expecting an argument, we find calm understanding instead. Here's an illustration:

CUSTOMER: "Let me tell you, I'm plenty annoyed at the terrible service your company's been giving me. I had to call for delivery half-a-dozen times before my last order was shipped. That's ridiculous. Time is money, and I don't have either to waste on unnecessary phone calls."

SALESMAN: "You were really upset, weren't you?"

CUSTOMER: "I sure was! And I'm glad to see you understand the problem. Let's talk about how I can get some decent service from you people."

By the end of this example, it's obvious the customer has vented most of his hostility, and is ready to do business. The salesman's reflective statement implied understanding and respect, and defused a potentially explosive situation.

The result would have been far different, and far less favorable, if the salesman had argued, or ignored or minimized the problem. Anger frequently evaporates in the face of understanding. The flow of information can then be resumed without impediment.

Reflective statements, then, are very useful for converting low receptivity to high, so that real problem-solving can take place. A customer with a gripe is seldom open to new ideas; his vexation must be discharged before his receptivity can be raised. The antagonistic flat assertions which are a sure sign of low receptivity can often be countered and overcome by skillful use of reflective statements.

Salesmen should bear in mind two points about flat, emotionally charged assertions:

1. Many customers do not literally mean what their flat assertions say. Speech is often more emphatic and picturesque than the meanings that underlie it. Extravagant exaggeration is an ailment that afflicts all of us. The salesman must determine *how much* of what a customer says is fact, and how much is overstatement.

2. Customers will sometimes talk *themselves* out of extreme positions if given the opportunity. The mistake many salesmen make is to accept every customer statement at face value, and to respond to it immediately instead of letting the customer amplify and perhaps modify it. Reflective statements permit the customer to do exactly that, by giving him an opportunity to examine and evaluate his own logic.

Neutral questions and phrases. These ask the customer to provide broad information upon a particular topic. They are more focused than open-end questions, and therefore give the customer less freedom of response than open-end questions. But they still enable him to respond at length, rather than by a simple yes or no. Thus, neutral phrases and questions can be thought of as lying midway between open-end and closed-end questions.

Here are a few examples: "What capital-goods expenditures do you expect to make in the next fiscal year?" "How does this process differ from the one you use in your Akron plant?" "Tell me more about why you're so pessimistic about your quarterly profit picture."

Nearly all customers, even the open and responsive Q4, volunteer less information on certain topics than the salesman needs. This is not necessarily because they are deliberately withholding information (although, of course, they may be), but because they do not know how much information the salesman needs. Neutral questions and phrases tell the customer that the salesman needs more information on a given point, and thus they facilitate the flow of data. Here's an example:

CUSTOMER: "Fred, I'd like nothing better than to buy that new-model copier. It looks like a great piece of equipment. But I'm scared to . . . really scared. The way things are going around here, I just don't want to lay out any extra money. Our profit picture . . . to be perfectly blunt about it . . . looks lousy."

SALESMAN: "Dave, can you tell me a little more about that, please? Why are profits down when your sales are up?"

CUSTOMER: "Costs. That's the answer in a nutshell. Our costs are way out of line. And we're going to have to retrench around here . . . or I'm going to have some very important people, starting with the president of the company, breathing down my neck."

SALESMAN: "Can you get a little more specific, Fred? Where do the costs seem out of line?"

CUSTOMER: "Two areas, mainly. Sales costs and administrative costs. We're already working on the sales costs. We're reexamining our entire commission structure. In fact, we expect to announce a new schedule of commissions in a few weeks. But the administrative costs are still driving me crazy. The expenses in running this office are sky-high. It's got me stymied. I can't seem to pin down the problem."

SALESMAN: "Well, Dave, I think I can provide a piece of the answer. Let me show you how this new copier can actually reduce copying costs in less than a year. In fact, I may be able to demonstrate that your savings will be greater than the extra cost of the machine."

Here, neutral questions were used to get answers to specific questions on clearly-defined subjects. Each question provided some direction for the customer without suggesting an answer to him. Within the confines of the questions, the customer had ample freedom to provide whatever answers he wanted. If the salesman had not asked these questions, he would never have learned anything useful beyond the fact that "our profit picture looks lousy."

Brief assertions of interest. Generally, people need only a little *encouragement* to share their thoughts with someone else; they need some signal that the other person is interested in and is following what they say. *Brief assertions* provide this signal.

Statements like "I see," "I understand," "Of course," "Keep going," "That's interesting," tell the customer that he's getting through. Ordinarily, when a customer responds to a brief assertion, he adds to what he's already said, so the assertion brings out *more* information. It establishes receptivity, and most of us *like* to talk to receptive people. Thus, brief assertions are useful for getting customer participation and maintaining positive rapport.

A word of caution: brief assertions like those above should not be used unless they're true. A salesman who uses phrases mechanically will sooner or later come across as insincere and manipulative. The customer is bound to realize that in spite of his brief assertions the salesman is *not* interested, or does *not* understand. When this happens, the delicate bond of trust on which all communication is based breaks. Correctly used, however, brief assertions do much to keep information flowing.

CHECKING FOR UNDERSTANDING AND GETTING COMMITMENT TO ACTION

Leading questions. In a sense, all questions are leading, because all questions *direct* and *guide* the customer's thinking to some extent. The salesman who asks "How does that coat feel on you?" leads the customer to talk about the *coat,* rather than baseball or the weather. But those questions we call leading questions do more than that. They imply, at least usually, what the *answer* will be. They do this by suggesting the answer. "You want to buy from a company that provides first-class service after installation, don't you?", "I'd say that it's smart to buy the best product at the lowest cost, wouldn't you?", "It's worth a few pennies more to get a product that's completely dependable, isn't it?" are examples. Leading questions are manipulative if they're used to entrap the customer, but they're valuable and sound if they're used to get the customer to commit himself to an idea that he's clearly in favor of anyway.

Leading questions help to check understanding by determining whether or not the assumption the salesman has built into the question is correct. If a salesman asks "It's worth a few pennies more to get a product that's completely dependable, isn't it?" and gets a "Yes, but I don't see why I should consider your product completely dependable" answer, he knows he hasn't proven his case, so he must go back to the point in the presentation where he discussed quality, and probe the customer's understanding of the discussion. On the other hand, if the customer simply answers "Yes," the salesman knows that he's willing to pay a somewhat high price for the product in question.

A note of caution: leading questions should be used sparingly. When fired at a customer in rapid succession, they give the presentation a Q1 third-degree quality that many customers rightfully resent. Customers want to take part in presentations, but they don't want to feel that they're being grilled.

Summary statements. These are brief restatements, in *different* words, by the salesman of information he's received from the customer (as contrasted to reflective statements, which are brief restatements of the customer's *feelings*). By rephrasing and repeating his thinking back to the customer in brief, summary form, the salesman can check his own understanding of what the customer has said. The customer can then respond by agreeing with the summary statement, which means the salesman is on the right track, or by disagreeing and explaining why the salesman is wrong. Either way, the salesman learns something important, and obtains customer participation in the process. Sometimes, the customer both agrees and adds further information. Here's an example:

CUSTOMER: "I'm not really sure this is the right time to install a new system. We've had a lot of expenses around here lately, and third quarter profits were down a little. We've been trying to tighten up our budget and reduce costs."

SALESMAN: "I see. At present, you think this is not the right time to install because of budget restrictions."

CUSTOMER: "Well, not exactly. It's not a question of whether we should install a new system, really, but of showing a better profit in the fourth quarter."

SALESMAN: "You feel that buying this system will increase costs and lead to reduced profits."

CUSTOMER: "Not really. In fact, I like the system, and I think it would probably save money for us in the long run, but I don't want to incur the expense of buying and installing it now."

SALESMAN: "Your position, then, is that you've got to tighten up your budget and reduce costs because expenses have been rising and profits are slightly down. You think the new system should be installed, and that it will probably save money over the long haul, but that this is not the time to buy it, because, if you do, it may hurt your fourth-quarter profits."

CUSTOMER: "Yes, that's exactly right."

SALESMAN: "Let me show you, then, how you can install this system immediately and not pay a cent for it for ninety days, so your fourth-quarter profits won't be affected in the least."

As this example demonstrates, the briefly rephrased summary of the customer's thinking is invaluable for keeping a presentation on track, and for making sure that the salesman doesn't ride off on a long and costly detour. The final, overall summary statement made sure that the two men clearly understood the problem, thus paving the way for a workable solution.

Summary statements are obviously very similar to reflective statements; the difference is that summary statements are used mainly to recap factual information, while reflective statements mirror the customer's moods and emotions. Like reflective statements, summary statements can be used to keep the flow of information going as well as to check understanding.

Closed-end questions. These are the most rigidly structured of all probes, because they permit a very narrow answer to a very specific question: "Does that coat fit comfortably?" "Shall we ship all of these at once, or in two lots?" "Do you want 90-day billing?" Generally, closed-end questions can be answered with a single word (yes, no, maybe) or a short phrase. They are ideal for checking understanding and, equally important, for getting the customer to make the final commitment to action ("We seem to be in complete agreement. Shall I go ahead and write up the order?").

CONCLUSIONS

We can summarize this discussion of probing by reiterating the following points:

1. The salesman is not powerless before the customer's responses. An upset or withdrawn or silent or sullen customer is certainly not easy to deal with, but he can be dealt with if the salesman knows how. A salesman who answers every argument with another argument, who tells the customer instead of listening to him, who fears a few seconds of silence, only succeeds in making the upset customer more upset, the sullen one more sullen, and the withdrawn one more withdrawn. The great value of probing is that it enables the salesman to *learn more,* to create a better climate for the exchange of ideas, and to create *optimal conditions for achieving understanding and commitment.*

Which brings us back to a very basic point: a salesman must consider himself *both* a teacher and a *learner.* In fact, his effectiveness as a teacher depends, in large part, upon his skill as a learner. Unless he can uncover *real* client needs, discover real customer feelings, and obtain *basic* customer data, he is unlikely to make a sale with even the most eloquent presentation. Probing is immensely valuable because it is both a teaching device and a learning device.

2. One reason so many salesmen have difficulty probing is that they feel *they* should do most of the talking. The typical probe is very short— the customer does most of the verbalizing, and that, of course, is the whole idea. Unless a salesman accepts the premise that he sometimes gains more by listening than talking, he cannot deal with the broad range of responses he gets from customers.

3. Most salesmen use closed-end and leading questions, but ignore other types of probes, especially pauses, reflective statements, and summary statements. A Q1 salesman, for example, may avoid open-end questions because he fears losing control of the presentation. By restricting

himself largely to leading and closed-end questions and brief assertions, he deprives himself of valuable communication techniques, much like a carpenter who uses only one blade in his saw, no matter what kind of wood he cuts. Closed-end and leading questions and brief assertions are useful, but they will not do the *whole* job of probing. A salesman who uses *all* kinds of probes, and uses them skillfully, can usually handle open hostility, deal with silent customers, and bring meandering customers back to the subject. He need not fear losing control more than momentarily.

4. Probing leads to involvement by customers. The significance of this has already been discussed at length.

SUMMARY

Probing is a multipurpose communication tool that achieves at least eight goals:

1. It gets the customer to participate in the presentation.
2. It elicits information about the customer's thoughts and feelings.
3. It reinforces the customer's learning.
4. It draws out the silent or unresponsive customer.
5. It helps control meandering.
6. It makes the presentation more meaningful to the customer by enabling him to inject *his* ideas.
7. It converts low receptivity to high.
8. It requires the salesman to listen attentively.

Probing serves three functions in the communication process: It starts information flowing, keeps information flowing until the salesman learns what he needs to know, and helps the salesman check his understanding of the information and gain a commitment to action.

Most probes can function in more than one way, but each usually has one major function. Open-end questions (questions phrased so as to elicit a wide-ranging response from the customer on a broad topic) are especially useful for starting the flow of information.

To keep the flow of information going, the following probes are very useful: pauses (silences that permit the customer to integrate what he's heard and to formulate a response), reflective statements (statements that mirror the customer's feelings without implying that the salesman agrees), neutral questions and phrases (questions and phrases that elicit a broad response on a narrow topic), and brief assertions of interest (short statements that encourage the customer to continue talking).

The following probes are especially useful for checking understanding and gaining a commitment to action: leading questions (questions that imply or suggest their own answer), summary statements (statements that summarize factual information received from the customer), and closed-end questions (questions phrased so as to elicit a very narrow answer to a very specific question).

TABLE 10. Probing

Function	Type of Probe	Characteristics
Starting the flow of information	Open-end questions	Draw out wide-ranging response on broad topic Usually begin with what, why, how do, tell me Get customer involved in presentation by allowing him to tell the salesman what he knows or thinks
Keeping the flow of information going	Pauses	Silences that permit customer to integrate what he's heard and respond to it Relax pace of the presentation so customer doesn't feel pressured Enable salesman to collect his thoughts and plan next step Excellent for dealing with uncommunicative customers
	Reflective statements	Mirror customer's feelings without implying salesman agrees Help cope with negative emotions Allow positive emotions to vent Help convert low receptivity to high
	Neutral questions and phrases	Draw out broad response on narrow topic More focused than open-end questions, less narrow than closed-end Tell customer what further data salesman needs
	Brief assertions of interest	Short statements that encourage customer to continue talking Help establish and maintain positive rapport Usually produce additional information
Checking understanding	Leading questions	Imply their own answer Excellent for getting customer to commit self Help salesman check understanding by telling him whether the assumption he has built into the question is correct
	Summary statements	Summarize factual data received from customer Similar to reflective statements, except summary statements recap facts while reflective statements mirror feelings
	Closed-end questions	Draw out narrow answer to specific question Excellent for getting final ("yes") commitment from customer

240

15

How the Q4
Salesman Sells
PROFESSIONALISM IN ACTION

This chapter, we hope, will provide the payoff for all the reading you've done up to this point. We are now ready to tie everything together—the Dimensional model, motivation, and communication—and show *how* the Q4 salesman uses flexible sales techniques to persuade Q1, Q2, Q3, and Q4 customers. In this way, we hope to demonstrate to the reader what he can gain if he puts these techniques and principles to use in his daily work.

Throughout, we urge the reader to pay special attention to the Q4 salesman's *flexibility,* to note that his strategy for selling each type of customer differs, and that he adapts himself, in each case, to both the task and personal needs of the customer he is facing. The Q4 doesn't interact with customers as stereotypes, but as specific people in specific situations. He is always flexible and always responsive to what he actually experiences. But he is flexible without being manipulative. His aim is always threefold: to produce net gain for his customer, his company, and himself.

THE Q4 STRATEGY FOR SELLING Q1 CUSTOMERS

DON'T ARGUE WITH THE Q1 CUSTOMER

The Q1's belligerence sometimes provokes salesmen to argue. When confronted by an antagonistic and overbearing customer, some salesmen respond with behavior that consciously or unconsciously indicates: "I'll show him he can't push me around," or "I'm not going to let him get away with that," or "Wait until I show him how wrong he is." Nothing could be more self-defeating. When the Q1 customer encounters strong opposition, he usually becomes all the more determined to win the argument, since the fulfillment of his esteem and independence needs depends on beating his opponent. Salesmen must avoid transforming the sales interview into a win–lose struggle; in such a struggle a Q1 customer is usually a formidable foe.

This doesn't mean a salesman can never win an argument with a Q1 customer. He can, of course, but he is likely to win the fight only to lose the sale. When bested in an argument, Q1 customers may try to get even or withdraw; either way, they may refuse to buy. The Q4 salesman never forgets that, in the end, the *customer* always has the power to buy or not to buy.

ALLOW THE Q1 CUSTOMER TO VENT HIS STRONG NEGATIVE EMOTIONS

Initially hostile behavior by the Q1 customer is often his way to establish his position with the salesman and assert his independence and esteem needs. Rather than try to keep these negative emotions submerged, the salesman should let them surface, so he can explore and deal with them. This is best done by heavy use of reflective statements, which defuse the situation and, at the same time, prevent the salesman from arguing with the customer. Negative emotions that are not vented are a severe obstacle to communication and to closing the sale; suppressed emotions distract the customer, because he is more concerned with his inner feelings than with anything the salesman has to say. Once these emotions are brought into the open, they can be dealt with and frequently dispelled. Q1 customers are the most likely of all customers to express strong negative emotions explosively. Q2 and Q3 customers bottle up these emotions (although the Q2 often vents them as sarcasm or pouting) while the Q4 expresses them candidly but constructively. The strongest open expression of negative emotions usually comes from Q1 customers.

RECOGNIZE THE Q1 CUSTOMER'S PERSONAL NEEDS FOR INDEPENDENCE AND ESTEEM

The Q1 customer's domineering manner is his way of saying to the salesman (and himself): "Look, I don't need you to tell me how to run my business. I'm tough, capable, and self-reliant." The Q4 salesman understands this. Instead of casting the Q1 customer in the role of a loud-mouthed villain, he sees him as a human being with certain clear-cut personal *needs.* He recognizes one of the basic rules of successful human interaction: it is far more productive to try to *understand* people than to blame them. In understanding the Q1's needs for independence and esteem, he can come to grips with the customer by satisfying those needs. By his words and manner, the Q4 salesman acknowledges the customer's strength. This acknowledgment is what the customer really wants; it confirms his image of himself.

Conversely, the Q4 salesman never deliberately plays down the Q1's strength and power, and he never deliberately puts him into a situation where the customer might lose esteem. There is no surer way to alienate a Q1 customer than to fail to show respect for his toughness.

PROBE THE Q1 CUSTOMER'S FLAT ASSERTIONS

Q1 customers frequently make flat assertions, terse, dogmatic statements that brook no argument ("The product's no good," "Your delivery is lousy," "The price is too high."). These flat assertions signify that the customer's receptivity to other ideas is low, that his mind is shut, and that he is not optimally responsive to logic, argument, reasoning, pleading, or analysis. Before the salesman can change the customer's mind through presentation of facts, he must transform low receptivity to high, and this must be done by *probing.*

A flat assertion is much more than a strong statement of opinion: it is an indication that the customer considers the matter closed. A customer who asserts something flatly really says, "I don't think the matter merits further discussion; as far as I'm concerned, there's nothing more to talk about."

The salesman's job is to re-open the discussion. Through probing, he can get the customer himself to talk more about the subject. Here's an example:

CUSTOMER: "Look, it's ridiculous to pursue this matter. Your price is too high . . . absolutely too high. Nobody in his right mind would ever pay a unit price like that. Your price per unit is way out of line."

SALESMAN: "Well, I certainly understand your feelings. It *is* ridiculous to pay a price that's too high. And you feel that our unit price is far higher than it should be."

CUSTOMER: "You said it! Why . . . you people have the highest price in the industry. You're far higher than anyone else."

SALESMAN: "You believe that our price is highest in the industry."

CUSTOMER: "Of course it is. You know that as well as I do. You're higher than Amalgamated, you're higher than Consolidated, and you're higher than Conglomerate."

SALESMAN: "I see. You believe we're higher than any of our three competitors. How long ago did you get a price list from them?"

CUSTOMER: "Fairly recently. The Amalgamated rep was here just three or four months ago, and he showed me their latest price sheet. Why, they must be 10% lower than you guys, across the board. And the Consolidated man came in about the same time. I don't exactly remember his prices, but I know they were lower than yours. And of course I know what Conglomerate's price is, because I've been buying from them for the past year or so. We've had a few problems with them from time to time, but we've never had to pay them a price like the one you're asking.

SALESMAN: "You've had problems with your present supplier, but never pricing problems, is that right?"

CUSTOMER: "Right. Never any pricing problems."

SALESMAN: "I wonder if you'd describe some of the other problems."

CUSTOMER: "Sure. They're no secret. Conglomerate has been late on delivery a few times. After all, nobody is perfect. Of course, late deliveries do foul up our production schedule, but I guess that's unavoidable sometimes."

SALESMAN: "Does that lead to any other problems?"

CUSTOMER: "Sure. Any time you reshuffle a production schedule you create problems. You may antagonize a few customers by being late on delivery yourself. Or you may have to pay overtime to get back on schedule. Or you may have to pay the changeover costs for shifting to production of another item. One way or another, changing production schedules costs money."

SALESMAN: "Then let me show you some information about our delivery system that could help you to avoid down-time costs. Our local warehousing system and computerized inventory control may be just what you need to control those costs."

CUSTOMER: "Listen, I wasn't born yesterday. I know what you're going to do. You're going to try to show me that I may end up saving money by buying from you even though your unit price is higher. I'm pretty skeptical. But okay . . . go ahead and show me."

Nobody claims, of course, that this kind of probing will automatically lead to a sale. But it will heighten receptivity. In our example, the customer began by saying that "It's ridiculous to pursue the matter." But, because the salesman insisted on probing (instead of arguing or capitulating), the customer himself pursued the matter. As he continued to talk, he fed bits of new information to the salesman, which the salesman was able to use to his own advantage. By the end of the example, the customer was saying "go ahead and show me," which was an enormous stride forward from his earlier "It's ridiculous to pursue the matter."

This is not to say that probing always transforms low receptivity to high. Some Q1s are so resistant that they refuse to respond to even the most skillful probing. But if probing doesn't do the job, nothing else will. And unless low receptivity *is* changed to high, the salesman is wasting his time by presenting logic and benefits.

SHOW THE Q1 CUSTOMER YOU ARE LISTENING

Q1 customers are poor listeners, but they are extremely eager to be listened to. To a Q1, a *listening* salesman is a respectful salesman who recognizes that he has something valuable to say; a listening salesman thereby confirms the Q1 customer's self-image. Any salesman who wants to antagonize a Q1 customer can do so easily by refusing to listen, by listening half-heartedly or impatiently, or (the surest way of all) by listening rudely and interrupting him before he is finished talking.

One way the Q4 salesman demonstrates to the Q1 customer that he has listened to him thoughtfully and that he respects his thinking is by summing up the customer's arguments and presenting them back to him. Summary statements are virtually indispensable in communicating with a Q1. There is probably no better way to show a man that you take him *seriously*, that you *value* his ideas, and that you are giving *full weight* to his thinking. At the same time, however, it's important to try to get *him* to sum up *your* point-of-view. This maintains equilibrium between customer and salesman, demonstrates to the customer that your ideas deserve consideration as much as *his*, makes it plain that your position is equal, *not* subordinate, to his. Of course, *all* probes, not only summary statements, indicate to the customer that the salesman is giving weight to his ideas.

BE FACTUAL AND READY TO GIVE DETAILS TO THE Q1 CUSTOMER

Q1 customers pride themselves on being logical, cost-conscious, rational, and hard-headed. Paradoxically, while they frequently make exaggerated and unsupportable statements, they insist that salesmen make statements that can be verified. The Q1 customer is generally suspicious of any unsupported claim (probably because he knows, from his own experience, how easy such claims are to make). He enters every presentation with a strong bias against the salesman, whom he probably regards with suspicion or worse. He is skeptical, distrustful, and constantly on guard against being cheated or defrauded.

The best way to disarm the wary Q1 customer is to make factual statements and then back them up with details and proof. Glowing but vague descriptions usually aggravate him; they prove to him that his worst suspicions are grounded in reality, that the salesman really is manipulative. The best proof of a salesman's claims is, of course, demonstrated proof. The Q1 believes what he *sees*; he is more readily persuaded by a factual, visual demonstration than by an elegant but overgeneralized description. For the Q1 customer, actions are far louder than words. Sometimes, he even considers sales aids an elaborate form of bamboozlement, contrived by the salesman's company to hoodwink him. But he is usually impressed by visible demonstrations. Whenever possible, such demonstrations should be part of the presentation.

BE FIRM WITH THE Q1 CUSTOMER

The Q1 needs an adversary against whom he can prove himself and thus enhance his esteem. But not just any adversary will do; he prefers one he can respect. There is, after all, small satisfaction in contending with someone who gives in easily. Many salesmen make the serious tactical error of capitulating at the first signs of hostility from a Q1. What they should do, instead, is stand their ground, remain neutral (by reflecting and summarizing) *but firm*, and remember that strong, dominant people almost invariably disdain submissive, passive people. Once a Q1 understands that the salesman is as determined and firm as he is, he will often give him his grudging but sincere respect; once this happens, he is likely to begin interacting with the salesman on a much more productive level. Give-and-take with someone he genuinely respects will satisfy the Q1's need for esteem far better than routing a salesman who retreats at the first sign of opposition. A Q4 salesman *can* successfully disagree with a Q1 customer *if* it is clear to the customer that the salesman's opinion is grounded in logic and facts, and that it has been arrived at *after* probing.

An important psychological principle is involved here. In the vast majority of cases, submissive people arouse contempt or dislike or lack of respect in dominant people (this is one reason Q2 and Q3 salesmen get generally bad results with Q1 and Q4 customers). Submissive salesmen make dominant customers feel scornful or simply uncomfortable. The Q1 customer, in particular, is unlikely to buy from anyone he doesn't respect. Any salesman who wants to sell a Q1 had better come across as strong and firm, but not argumentative.

MAKE THE Q1 CUSTOMER FACE THE FACTS ABOUT HIMSELF

As a last resort, if the Q1 customer remains, in spite of the salesman's best efforts, overbearing and immovable, the salesman should try to make him confront the facts about himself. As calmly and candidly as he can, he might say something like this: "Mr. Strong, I've tried to the best of my ability to exchange views with you in a way that will produce good results for both of us. I hope you feel I've listened to you carefully, I've given you every opportunity to make yourself heard, I've explored all of your ideas. But you don't seem willing to do the same with me. I really believe I can produce a genuine benefit for you if you'll listen to what I have to say. Can you tell me *why* I'm not getting through?" Naturally, this must be said firmly but without any hint of hostility or argument.

This kind of openness will produce one of two results. It may startle the Q1 into an awareness of just how trying his behavior has been, and stimulate a change in his behavior. Or it may bring the presentation to an abrupt end. If the latter, nothing has been lost. But, many times, the Q1 customer will pause and reflect on whether his behavior is really in his own best interest. Very few customers, even Q1s, feel comfortable with the knowledge that they are coming across as argumentative, overbearing, and hostile; many Q1 customers will halt such behavior after it has been called to their attention. In fact, the customer may respect the salesman's candor and firmness. In any event, putting the cards on the table in this way is justified when all else fails.

A Perspective on Selling Q1 Customers

Any salesman who wants to succeed consistently with Q1 customers must master a difficult and delicate balancing act. On the one hand, he must remain firm and decisive *without* himself becoming overbearing or domineering; on the other hand, he must show respect and esteem for the customer *without* becoming submissive and letting himself be steam-rollered. He must make his point without arguing, and defend it without seeming to have a chip on his shoulder. He must be factual without overwhelming the customer with logic. He must constantly guard against falling into a win–lose trap. Never, under any circumstances, must he give the customer an excuse for quarreling with or clobbering him.

Furthermore, the salesman must remember that the Q1 has strong needs for independence and esteem. As soon as the salesman makes the easy mistake of believing that the Q1 is simply ornery, he has sealed his fate; believing this, he will almost surely lower his chances of making the sale. The key to selling Q1 customers is the realization that beneath their trying behavior are very ordinary, and very understandable, human needs.

No one denies that the Q1 customer can be very annoying, that he delights in baiting and badgering salesmen, or that making a sale to him sometimes requires vast patience and forbearance. No one claims that making a sale to a Q1 is easy; it seldom is. But the salesman who, like the Q4, can discipline himself to probe instead of argue, allow negative emotions to vent, listen attentively, stand his ground firmly yet respectfully, be precise and factual, and withstand verbal abuse, can make such sales *more often than not.*

THE Q4 STRATEGY FOR SELLING Q2 CUSTOMERS

BEHAVE REASSURINGLY TOWARD THE Q2 CUSTOMER

Recognize his needs for security. The Q2 is an insecure man, who finds most encounters with other people uncomfortable or unsettling. He is a low risk-taker who needs reassurance and bolstering, the knowledge that things are not going to change too drastically or too quickly. The salesman who comes across as trustworthy and reliable, as someone who is not a threat and who may actually be a support, will sometimes find the Q2's icy exterior melting to reveal a person who, if not warm and outgoing, at least responds to discussion and exchanges ideas. The salesman's first job is to chip away the ice; this can only be done by a salesman who instills confidence and assurance.

What the Q2 customer is really saying by his behavior is this: "Salesmen frighten me. Their forcefulness, their drive, their aggressiveness, all make me very uneasy. When I meet a salesman, I feel overmatched and weak; my only defense against his persuasive skills is withdrawal." To sell a Q2, then, the salesman must provide reassurance. He must get across the idea that "I'm one salesman you can trust. I have no intention of taking advantage of you, manipulating you, or exploiting you. I am here for only one reason: to arrange a sale that will be of benefit to *both* of us. I respect you far too much to do anything else."

This message must be conveyed not only by what the salesman says, but by his entire manner. He must come across as a solid, dependable person. If he does, he is likely to find the Q2 developing into one of his most loyal and long-range customers.

AVOID MOVING IN TOO FAST ON THE Q2 CUSTOMER; ESTABLISH TRUST

The Q2 customer is afraid of being overwhelmed, of being maneuvered into buying before he has thought things through. Any salesman who moves too quickly (speaks fast, bunches his ideas instead of spacing them, asks one closed-end question after another, tries for a quick close) is sure to confirm the Q2's worst suspicions. He will come across as pushy, unconcerned, overeager, not to be trusted. A deliberate, low-key approach will often achieve far better results.

Unhappily, it is difficult to take a deliberate approach to a Q2 customer because he is usually so quiet and withdrawn that he often provokes salesmen to a frenzy of words. Not knowing how to deal with him, they begin to talk at a fast, staccato pace. With every rapid-fire sentence, they dig the hole in which they're standing a little deeper.

It is important to understand that the Q2 customer is likely to distrust *any* salesman who moves in too fast, including salesmen who are too friendly, too open, at the very outset. The salesman must establish trust before even his warm behavior will be accepted by the Q2. Otherwise, the Q2 customer is likely to wonder suspiciously: "What is this guy up to?"

GET THE CUSTOMER INVOLVED THROUGH PROBING

Many salesmen are easily frustrated by Q2 customers; they become rattled by the latter's silent and uncommunicative behavior. Talking to an extreme Q2 can be unsettling. But the salesman who becomes flustered only aggravates an already difficult situation; usually, his frustration causes him to press, which, in turn, causes the customer to feel even more threatened and to withdraw all the further, or perhaps to respond with brief bursts of sarcasm. Patient probing with open-ended questions of the customer's attitudes and feelings will help him relax slightly and finally to participate; frantic pressure tactics, on the other hand, only reinforce his belief that the salesman is out to take advantage of him, and must therefore be resisted.

Q2s are self-controlled people who prefer to keep their thoughts to themselves; they fear that by exposing their ideas they become more vulnerable to manipulation. Cautious probing helps overcome Q2 secretiveness. All probes, of course, require two people, one to probe and one to respond. Probes are ideal for drawing aloof customers into conversation. Once the customer is involved, some of his fear will probably dissolve. He will relax somewhat as he realizes that the salesman really is interested in him, and really wants to hear from him. It is very difficult to sell Q2 customers without first breaking the silence barrier; probing does this.

MAKE HEAVY USE OF PROBING PAUSES WITH Q2 CUSTOMERS; AVOID TALKING TOO MUCH

In selling to Q2 customers, silence is almost literally golden. Many Q2 customers fear the salesman's *wordiness*. And for good reason. Words *are* many times used to manipulate and control people; Q1 salesmen, in particular, *do* sometimes use words to exploit. So the Q2 customer is likely to shrug off even true statements if they are presented too rapidly. Therefore, judiciously spaced pauses, in which the salesman shuts up and stays shut up for a brief period, can be very productive for three reasons: they reassure the Q2 customer by offering him relief from the barrage of words he has been expecting and fearing; they give him time to mull over what the salesman has said; and they give him a chance to speak. Let's examine each reason briefly.

The Q2 has a stereotyped image of the salesman. He expects him to be a smooth-talking trickster who conjures illusions and deception by verbal agility. He is likely to be favorably impressed by any salesman who, restrained and moderate in his use of words, fails to fit this stereotype. Pauses are one way of saying "I am *not* the slick, glib, crafty salesman you expect me to be."

The Q2 likes to have time in which to ponder the salesman's words. A torrent of words only confirms his suspicion that the salesman wants to sweep him off his feet by not giving him a chance to think. Pauses have the opposite effect; they persuade him that the salesman is willing to give him time in which to weigh the message. Pauses are evidence that the salesman has no intention of drowning him in a sea of words.

Q2 customers are not always speechless by choice. Frequently, a Q2 would like to say something but doesn't get the opportunity. Too submissive to break into the salesman's monologue, he clams up and retreats into silence. But the silence is not always of his making; it is often forced on him by an insensitive salesman. Pauses encourage the Q2 to speak; they give him the opening he is unable to make for himself. As such, they are indispensable to getting him involved.

AVOID EXPLOITING THE Q2'S SUBMISSIVENESS

As a general rule, a salesman who tries to take advantage of a Q2 customer's submissiveness once is unlikely to get a second chance to do so. Once a Q2, who is sensitive about his passiveness anyway, realizes he has been taken, he is sure to become provoked, resentful, even vindictive. He may avenge himself by refusing to see the salesman again, or by seeing him again and then, after using up a great deal of his time, steadfastly refusing to buy. It is a gross mistake to think that submissive people are submissive all the time. When provoked by unfair or manipulative treatment, they can be surprisingly tough. Any salesman who entraps a Q2 customer does so at his peril.

GUIDE THE Q2 CUSTOMER GENTLY BUT FIRMLY

The dilemma of the Q2 customer is that, as a submissive person, he *wants* guidance from other people, but, as a hostile person, he *distrusts* others and therefore fears their guidance. Aware of this, the Q4 salesman provides guidance that is firm but nonthreatening, that comes across as helpful. He does this in all the ways we've described: by behaving reassuringly, by moving at a deliberate pace, by getting the customer involved, by using a variety of probes, by refusing to bombard the customer with words, and by not exploiting his submissiveness. Or, to sum up in a phrase, by establishing trust. Once trust is established, the Q2 customer accepts guidance willingly, even eagerly.

MAKE THE Q2 CUSTOMER AWARE HE'S RESISTING

When all is said and done, the Q2 customer may still be withdrawn and uninvolved. Bringing his passive resistance into the open can sometimes turn a very bad situation around. It's important to remember that his sullen behavior is not something he deliberately plans as each salesman walks through the front door; it is a *habitual* way of acting. Because this behavior *is* habitual, the Q2 frequently offers strong resistance to salesmen without realizing it. By making him aware he is being resistant, the salesman can sometimes get him to take part in the presentation without making him feel threatened.

When more subtle means fail, a brief statement followed by a direct question often changes the entire mood of the presentation: "I notice that you're not responding to my remarks. I wonder if you'd tell me why?" It's extremely important, of course, that statements and questions like these *not* imply antagonism or impatience. They should be spoken in an interested, matter-of-fact tone. The very directness and candor of these statements and questions frequently open up communications with the Q2 and assure him of the salesman's interest.

With Q2 customers, candor is itself reassuring, because candor is the very thing the Q2 does not expect from the salesman. He expects manipulation and deception. When, instead, he gets openness and honesty, he is sure to be pleasantly surprised. By making the customer aware that he's resisting, and by doing it in plain, unvarnished language, the salesman really says, "I'm honest and trustworthy. I'm putting all my cards on the table. Won't you do the same?" This may be the only medicine that will work in this situation.

A Perspective on Selling Q2 Customers

To the Q2 customer, all salesmen are descendants of the sideshow barker and the hawker of quack medicines; part charlatan, part confidence man, and part swindler. Any salesman who wants to make sales consistently to Q2s must overcome this image by coming across as a trustworthy problem-solver with real concern for the customer. Once he succeeds in shattering the Q2's stereotyped image of the typical salesman and replaces it with a realistic Q4 self-portrait, he is very likely to develop an unusually loyal and steadfast customer.

The significant thing about the Q2 is that he is probably going to buy something from *someone*. He may be withdrawn, but he is certainly not withdrawn from the market place. Like everyone else, Q2s spend their money on everything from accordions to zithers. The only question is whom they will buy from. In the overwhelming majority of cases, the answer is salesmen who engender trust, confidence, and reliability. Once the Q2 finds such a salesman, he is very likely to stick with him.

As with Q1 customers, selling Q2s requires delicate balancing. The salesman must guide without overwhelming, and behave gently without seeming weak. He must come across as an expert, but not monopolize the presentation. He must probe without seeming to pry, and he must, at times, prod without pushing. None of this is easy; all of it is essential.

THE Q4 STRATEGY FOR SELLING Q3 CUSTOMERS

RECOGNIZE THE Q3 CUSTOMER'S SOCIAL, ESTEEM, AND SECURITY NEEDS

Some salesmen shortsightedly assume it is unbusinesslike, or a waste of time, to let the Q3 customer make friendly small talk. Actually, it is essential to do so. The customer's social needs may seem irrelevant to the salesman, but they're very meaningful to the customer. Until the Q3 feels he has established a bond with the salesman based upon mutual friendship and esteem, he will not be ready to discuss less personal matters. In fact, if he cannot satisfy himself that such a bond exists, he may be so unsure of, and uneasy about, the relationship between himself and the salesman that he will think about little else. A man preoccupied with his impact upon people has little time or energy left over for other matters. Only when his social needs have been met will he listen, openly and without tension, to the salesman's presentation.

The Q4 salesman recognizes that, for the Q3 customer, the presentation is not simply a sales presentation. It is an opportunity to test his likableness, a chance to satisfy himself, once again, that he is deserving of warmth and approval. It is a way of satisfying not only his social needs, but his esteem and security needs. These needs are continuously felt by the Q3, and they must be satisfied anew each time he interacts with a salesman. Any salesman who denies the Q3 this opportunity erects enormous barriers between himself and the sale.

UNCOVER THE Q3 CUSTOMER'S UNSPOKEN OBJECTIONS AND RATIONALIZATIONS

Because he *is* eager to please, gain acceptance, and avoid conflict, the Q3 customer seldom offers substantive objections. Instead, he very readily says "yes" to most of what the salesman says, even though he may have a number of doubts or objections in mind. Salesmen often mistake this Q3 agreeableness for commitment, when actually it is only an unwillingness to say anything that might upset or disconcert the salesman. But, even though the objections are unvoiced, they may be strong enough to keep the customer from buying. Or he may buy and cancel the order after the salesman leaves. Many times, a Q3 customer tries to let a salesman down easy by telling him "I can't make a decision until I check with my partner" or "I'd sure like to buy but I just don't have the money." All of this behavior covers up the fact that the customer has not really been persuaded but is unwilling to say so. Thus it's very important that the Q3's overeager agreement be probed *without* making him uncomfortable or ill at ease. In particular, any statement that sounds as if it might be an alibi, an evasion, or a rationalization should be examined carefully. All these statements can be recognized by two characteristics: they are always phrased in impersonal terms that in no way imply criticism of the salesman, and they are always used as explanations for *not* buying.

The Q3 never intentionally says anything to hurt a salesman's feelings, but he frequently refuses to buy something that doesn't seem in his best interest. To justify his refusal, he gives plausible reasons but not the *real* reasons. He tries to let the salesman down easy, to maintain his own image as a nice, likable guy.

ALLOW THE Q3 CUSTOMER TO DO SOME MEANDERING WITHOUT LOSING DIRECTION

Irksome though it may be to the salesman, the Q3 customer must be permitted to indulge in a certain amount of random talking. This talking may strike the salesman as an utter waste of time, but it is important to the customer. However, this vagrant chitchat must not be permitted to get out of hand; some Q3s talk in such roundabout ways that, unless the salesman makes some effort to guide, both salesman and customer may end up in a no-exit maze.

There is a real danger here, and any salesman had better be aware of it. If he refuses to permit any meandering, he is sure to create tensions that distract the customer from the business at hand; a Q3 who is not allowed to stray from the topic from time to time becomes exceedingly restive and difficult to communicate with. But a Q3 who is allowed to meander at will is sure to get lost sooner or later, and the salesman with him. There is, of course, no rule to determine how much meandering is enough. This is for the salesman to decide separately in each case. Obviously, the less meandering the better; but it is self-defeating to try to keep a Q3 customer from meandering at all. The salesman may consider the chitchat irrelevant; to the customer, it is not irrelevant at all. Because it helps him cement good personal relationships, chitchat is very meaningful to the Q3.

Skillful probing is the only way to restrain a roving customer. When the Q3 has roamed as long as the salesman judges proper, he must be brought back to the main topic by carefully structured questions that get and keep him on the subject. Without probing, Q3s usually prove unmanageable.

PROBE THE Q3 CUSTOMER'S READY ASSENTS

Even direct statements of agreement or understanding by the Q3 should be probed. The Q3 customer often says "I see" when he is confused,

"I agree" when he objects, and "Right" when he thinks the salesman is wrong. He frequently says "Great" or "Terrific" to disguise a lack of enthusiasm (and he says it with remarkable conviction), he praises products he dislikes, and (worst trap of all!) he holds out hope where there is no hope ("Drop by the next time you're in the neighborhood; I'm sure I'll be in a position to buy by then"). Only probing can protect the salesman from this lulling cheerfulness. Selling a Q3 requires constant vigilance and constant skepticism.

AVOID EXPLOITING THE Q3 CUSTOMER'S SUBMISSIVENESS

Submissive Q3s dislike being taken advantage of as much as Q2s. They generally disdain their own submissiveness, and resent having it used as a weapon against them. Sometimes a very docile Q3 will agree to buy because he cannot bring himself to say no; if, however, he feels he has been manipulated or pushed too hard by the salesman, he will, in all probability, not buy from him again. Other Q3s can be pushed only to a point; if they feel exploited, they may finally summon the determination to end the interview without buying, or, shifting to a Q1 secondary strategy, they may lash out briefly at the salesman. In our society, passive qualities like submissiveness and passivity are seldom regarded as virtues, so submissive people are often sensitive about their readiness to give in to others, and especially resentful when others take advantage of this quality.

A good general rule to remember is this: any behavior which indicates that the salesman regards the customer as a pushover, a sucker, a chump, a dupe, an easy mark, a fool, or a gull is likely to backfire. Also, Q3 masks put on by the salesman are likely to backfire. Put another way, submissive customers want *respect* as much as dominant ones, and they usually reward the salesman who demonstrates respect with their repeat business.

AVOID DROWNING THE Q3 CUSTOMER WITH FACTUAL DETAILS

Q3 customers are usually bored by specifics, and the salesman who floods them with large amounts of detailed data will only lose their attention. The Q3 wants to know that the product is acceptable, but he is not especially interested in having detailed factual proof. He mainly wants to know whether the *salesman* is pleasant and reliable. If he is, then the Q3 assumes he is also trustworthy, and that his claims for his product (if not obviously wild and unbelievable) are valid. Q3s sometimes find it hard to believe that an amiable, outgoing salesman could recommend anything but a good, dependable product.

This does not mean that details and facts have no place in a presentation to a Q3 customer. It means only that details and facts should be basic and pertinent. Overemphasis on minute and highly complex details should be avoided, as should heavy use of statistics and graphs. Q3s feel most comfortable with fairly broad data which provide general reassurance.

GUIDE THE Q3 CUSTOMER FIRMLY BUT WITHOUT MANIPULATION

The Q4 salesman avoids exploiting the Q3 customer's submissiveness. But, when all is said and done, the customer cannot be permitted to focus on his social and approval needs interminably; sooner or later, the salesman must discuss his *product* and what it will do for the customer. This means he must guide, lead, and direct the presentation. The Q3 will respond to this direction as long as his needs for acceptance are met. In fact he is eager to cooperate with the salesman, since he feels this is one way to gain the latter's approval. So the salesman must be assertive without being coercive, curt, exploitative, unfriendly, or manipulative; he must guide the presentation to a conclusion without arousing discomfort, worry, or insecurity. A firm and organized approach which allows the Q3 a limited amount of room for expressing his social needs through digressions and irrelevancies yet always brings him back to the main subject is the ideal. If *no* scope is provided for digressions, the customer is likely to think the salesman lacks concern; if no direction or structure is provided, the presentation may drag on without ever coming to a successful conclusion.

A Perspective on Selling Q3 Customers

There is a serious danger of underestimating the Q3 customer. Outgoing, good-natured people are often (usually unjustifiably) considered slightly naive, and it is only a short step from naivete to gullibility. Unfortunately, a large number of salesmen assume that any Q3 customer *is* gullible, easily led, and prepared to accept almost any claim uncritically. Believing this, they sell *down* to the customer; their manner verges on condescension.

So it is important to understand that a man with strong social, security, and esteem needs is *not* on that account unsophisticated or naive. Q3 customers can be as discriminating as any others. They can be critical, analytic, discerning, and prudent. What distinguishes them from other customers is a willingness to trust salesmen who impress them as warm, friendly people without requiring supporting proof, and an unwillingness to be candid with salesmen they consider unreliable or untrustworthy. The fact that the Q3 tries to avoid any display of unpleasantness does not mean he will accept any kind of treatment. As much as any other customer, he wants respect from salesmen.

The risk lies in patronizing the Q3, in treating him like a lovable clown who is not to be taken seriously. In the long run, this attitude can only raise major barriers to persuading and selling the submissive-warm customer.

THE Q4 STRATEGY FOR SELLING Q4 CUSTOMERS

KNOW YOUR FACTS WITH THE Q4 CUSTOMER

The Q4 customer respects competence and ability, and he looks for these qualities in salesmen. He bases his buying decisions largely on analysis of data, on logic, and on comparisons. So salesmen calling on Q4s must be thoroughly knowledgeable; they must know their own products, their competition's products, the prospect's needs, and how all of these mesh together. Their opinions must be based on *hard information;* their assertions must be supported by proof. (At the same time, when a salesman doesn't know something that is pertinent, the Q4 customer expects him to admit it.) The Q4 expects professionalism, and he equates it with *expertness.*

It is not, however, necessary to drown the Q4 customer in an ocean of details. In fact, long recitations of fact do not, by themselves, impress him. What does impress him is the ability to couple facts with his task needs, to see connections and consequences, and to solve his problems. Q4 customers respect *associative* knowledge, the ability to see how things relate and fit together. Or, to use the terms we have used before, Q4 customers are not especially interested in a recitation of features or advantages as such; they are interested in having features and advantages tied to their needs so as to produce benefits and net gain. The Q4 will be dissatisfied with any discussion of features and advantages that does not lead to a statement of benefits and net gain. At the same time, he will be equally dissatisfied by any discussion of benefits and net gain that is not based on thorough knowledge of features and advantages.

BE ORGANIZED YET FLEXIBLE WITH Q4 CUSTOMERS

The Q4 is job-oriented. He likes to get to the nub of things in a straightforward, businesslike way. This is not to say he's curt; on the contrary, Q4 customers are often affable people willing to engage in appropriate pleasantries. But they have little patience with disorganized, rambling presentations; they consider haphazard salesmanship a waste of their time, and they resent being taken advantage of by salesmen who have expended neither time nor energy to get themselves organized. The Q4 regards organized presentations, which are logical, clear, and concise, as proof of professionalism, and he listens to these willingly, even eagerly. This does *not* mean the salesman should make a mechanical presentation; the presentation should be lively but not meandering, animated but not irrelevant. It should demonstrate that the salesman respects the customer's schedule, and is determined not to waste time.

One point must be stressed. What we call an organized presentation is not a "canned" presentation, even though canned presentations may be very well organized. A canned presentation is usually a mechanical device, limiting the salesman to the role of vocal robot. What we mean by an organized presentation is one that is orderly, moving from point to point systematically and coherently, but still leaving the salesman all the room he needs to adapt, to shift, to adjust his argument as the situation requires. An organized presentation provides an opportunity for real dialogue. The presentation should follow a pattern, but the pattern should be a guideline, not a blueprint.

KNOW YOUR COMPETITION AND USE YOUR KNOWLEDGE
WITH THE Q4 CUSTOMER

The Q4 customer wants *net gain* from every purchase. We defined net gain as the benefit that a buyer receives over and above any benefits he is now getting, as the *something extra* that justifies his purchase. Obviously, any customer seeking net gain wants the greatest possible net gain; he wants to be sure his purchase will bring him a benefit beyond what he is presently getting, and also that it will bring him benefits beyond those obtainable from a competitive product or company. In other words, he wants *optimum* net gain.

A salesman cannot prove optimum net gain without knowing almost as much about his competition as he knows about his own product. The Q4 customer expects salesmen to have such knowledge. He constantly compares, contrasts, and collates; he matches competing items to make sure his decision is not merely a good one, but the *best* one. And he considers it the salesman's job to help him in this process. If a salesman doesn't have solid knowledge of the competition, the Q4 customer is likely to seek out the competitor to get answers to his questions.

QUANTIFY FOR THE Q4 CUSTOMER WHENEVER POSSIBLE

Q4 customers are not motivated much by vague claims. They base their decisions not on poetic assertions but on precise data; they want to know *exactly* what they're buying. The surest way for a salesman to satisfy this demand is by quantifying his statements whenever possible. This doesn't mean he should abandon English for the language of mathematics; it means words should be supplemented and supported by numbers. If a Q4 buyer hears that a car has a smaller turning ratio, he wants to know how much smaller. If he is told that a grinding machine will operate longer than any comparable product without sharpening, he wants to know how much longer. If he's assured that a life insurance policy will save money, he wants to know how much.

By quantifying, the salesman does three things: He makes it plain that his claims are not imaginary but fact. He enhances his image as an expert. He enables the customer to make meaningful comparisons. (It is impossible to choose intelligently between two "low cost" hospitalization plans, but it is easy to choose between a premium of $25 each quarter and a premium of $32 each quarter.)

Even when not quantifying, the Q4 salesman tries to present his ideas with precision. Instead of saying, "This model comes in a wide variety of colors," and letting it go at that, he shows samples of the colors. Instead of saying, "This pattern is based on the work of a famous European designer," and stopping there, he names the designer. And so forth. Whenever possible, he pinpoints, explains, illustrates, and clarifies; whenever he can be, he is definite, explicit, and factual.

CONTINUALLY CHECK YOUR UNDERSTANDING OF THE Q4
CUSTOMER THROUGH USE OF SUMMARY STATEMENTS

Q4 customers like to do business with salesmen who take pains to make sure they understand the customer. More than anything else, the Q4 buyer wants to know that the salesman comprehends *his* needs, not some vague, generalized needs, but his specific needs. He wants the presentation to be based on his real needs, not his needs as the salesman has preconceived them. The frequent use of summary statements, in which his thinking is summed up and restated, makes a strong impression on the Q4 customer, and, of course, helps the salesman to clarify his own thinking.

DON'T RAZZLE-DAZZLE THE Q4 CUSTOMER BY USING
LAVISH BENEFITS OR LOGIC

Because the Q4 makes a point of becoming *actively* engaged in the sales presentation, because he *participates* with the salesman, there is no need to crush him with benefits or logic. The salesman should be clear, emphatic, and pointed, but not overwhelming. Clear, definite statements, without bombast or exaggeration, go a long way with the Q4. Verbal overkill will, if anything, only alienate him.

The Q4 customer's attitude can be summarized this way: "I'm a competent, attentive, perceptive guy. I need the salesman's help in arriving at sound buying decisions, but I don't need to be hit over the head. Any salesman who tries to razzle-dazzle me must have very little respect for my judgment or my intelligence."

RECOGNIZE THE Q4 CUSTOMER'S NEEDS FOR SELF-REALIZATION AND INDEPENDENCE

The Q4 customer satisfies his need for independence, in part, by making up his own mind. He dislikes coercive salesmen largely because they try to restrict his freedom of judgment. The Q4 highly values joint problem-solving, and he participates in such problem-solving willingly. But, at the same time, he has a strong need to feel that he's playing a key role in shaping the decisions that affect him. He sees the customer–salesman relationship as a full partnership, with each man contributing whatever resources he can bring to bear. This doesn't mean that the Q4 customer resents attempts to persuade him; he appreciates the fact that the salesman's job is to persuade. But he wants to make the final decision to buy because he *has* been persuaded, not because he's been bulldozed. Put another way, he wants the final buying decision to be his, not imposed by someone else. He wants to buy because he understands what the product will do for him and because he's committed to it. All of this is very closely tied to his need for independence.

Furthermore, the Q4 customer is open to any idea that promises to further his self-realization. Sales presentations which focus on security, esteem, and sociability do not impress him, and probably bore him. For the Q4 buyer, these are satisfied needs which no longer motivate. No wonder he can be one of the most difficult of all customers to sell.

It is comparatively easy to appeal to a man's needs for security, esteem, and sociability. But self-realization is a much more elusive idea, hard to get hold of and hard to handle. To do a thoroughly successful job of selling a Q4, the salesman must learn in depth what the customer means by self-realization. Because the concept is so highly individualized, and because it is the prime motivator of Q4s, the salesman who wants to sell to a Q4 needs more insight into the Q4 customer than into any other. Achieving this insight is hard, even grueling work, requiring command of the entire battery of communications skills.

EMPHASIZE INNOVATIVE ASPECTS OF THE PRODUCT TO THE Q4 CUSTOMER

The Q4 customer is attracted to the new, the creative, the innovative; he likes to explore untried, and hopefully better, ways of solving problems. He sees a clear connection between inventiveness and self-realization, between originality and self-development. So the salesman should emphasize new product features that are genuinely distinctive or unique or pioneering. The Q4 derives deep satisfaction from being in the forefront, from doing things first and taking risks; he looks with favor on any product that helps him to do so.

A Perspective on Selling Q4 Customers

Q4 customers are especially challenging because they are especially complex. Seeking to realize themselves through self-realization and independence, they like doing business with salesmen who can help them find more of each. They eagerly buy products that help them live fuller and more autonomous lives. But the trouble with all this, from the salesman's point of view, is that it is so abstract, so impersonal. And that's precisely the point we are trying to make: it is the salesman's job to transform the abstract concepts of self-realization and independence into *personal* concepts. He must make the abstract *concrete*. He must relate these vague ideas individually to each individual Q4 customer. Only when he knows something about how a *specific* Q4 buyer interprets self-realization is he really ready to produce net gain for that buyer.

The only way to bring the concept of self-realization to life is to engage the customer in real dialogue, and real dialogue, as opposed to reciprocal noise-making, depends upon Q4 exposition, Q4 listening, and Q4 probing. Only through dialogue can a salesman really comprehend what is needed to produce net gain for a complex Q4 buyer. For the Q4 customer, net gain means: this product can make a greater contribution to your self-realization and your independence (as well as a greater contribution to your company) than any comparable or competitive product. This cannot be proven until the salesman knows what the customer *means* by self-realization and independence (and what the needs of the customer's company are). And that cannot be learned without dialogue.

But that's not all. *Dialogue* challenges and involves the Q4 customer; the very fact of *taking part* in the presentation in a *significant* way gives him a certain measure of self-realization. Q4 customers like being an integral part of things. So it's doubly important for salesmen to engage them in dialogue.

Is selling a Q4 customer worth the effort? It is if the salesman wants repeating, long-range business. Once a Q4 buyer finds a Q4 salesman, he usually develops a sustained, long-lasting relationship with him. Q4 customers regard Q4 salesmen as they do other professionals, and they no more flit from salesman to salesman than they do from lawyer to lawyer.

SUMMARY

The Q4 salesman uses the following flexible strategies for selling each type of customer: For Q1 customers: (*1*) don't argue, (*2*) allow the customer to vent his strong negative emotions, (*3*) recognize his needs for independence and esteem, (*4*) probe flat assertions, (*5*) show you're listening, (*6*) be factual and ready to give details, (*7*) be firm, and (*8*) make the customer face the facts about himself.

For Q2 customers: (*1*) behave reassuringly, (*2*) avoid moving in too fast, (*3*) get the customer involved through probing, (*4*) make heavy use of probing pauses and don't talk too much, (*5*) avoid exploiting his submissiveness, (*6*) guide him gently but firmly, and (*7*) make him aware he's resisting.

For Q3 customers: (*1*) recognize his social, esteem, and security needs, (*2*) uncover unspoken objections and rationalizations, (*3*) allow some meandering without losing direction, (*4*) probe ready assents, (*5*) avoid exploiting his submissiveness, (*6*) avoid drowning him with factual details, and (*7*) guide him without manipulation.

With the Q4 customer: (*1*) know your facts, (*2*) be organized yet flexible, (*3*) know your competition, (*4*) quantify whenever possible, (*5*) continually check your understanding through use of summary statements, (*6*) don't razzle-dazzle by using lavish lists of benefits or too many arguments, (*7*) recognize the customer's needs for self-realization and independence, and (*8*) emphasize the innovative aspects of the product.

TABLE 11. Q4 Sales Strategies

With Q1 customers	With Q2 customers	With Q3 customers	With Q4 customers
Don't argue	Act reassuringly toward customer	Recognize customer's social, esteem, and security needs	Know your facts
Allow customer to vent strong negative emotions	Avoid moving in too fast; establish trust	Uncover customer's unspoken objections and rationalizations	Be organized, yet flexible
Recognize customer's personal needs for independence and esteem	Get customer involved through probing	Allow customer some meandering without losing direction	Know your competition and use this knowledge
Probe customer's flat assertions	Make heavy use of probing pauses; don't talk too much	Probe his ready assents	Quantify whenever possible
Show customer you're listening		Avoid exploiting his submissiveness	Continually check your understanding of customer through summary statements
Be factual and ready to give details	Don't exploit customer's submissiveness	Don't drown him with factual details	Don't razzle-dazzle with lavish benefits or logic
Be firm	Guide customer gently but firmly	Guide customer firmly but without manipulation	Recognize customer's needs for self-realization and independence
As last resort, make customer face the facts about himself	As last resort, make customer aware he's resisting		Emphasize innovative aspects of your product

263

16

Sales Management Strategies

THE DIMENSIONS OF MANAGERIAL SUCCESS

By now, the reader may have forgotten that this book is about sales management as well as selling. Although most of our earlier chapters have largely applied to sales managers as well as salesmen, in this chapter we'll shift our focus directly to managers. As the reader probably figured out for himself long ago, sales managers' behavior can be described by the Dimensional model. On the following page are the basic beliefs that underlie the four basic types of sales management behavior.

Let's look closely now at each managerial type. We'll begin by taking a look at the manager through his salesmen's eyes; then we'll examine his motivation; and, finally, we'll look at the way he interacts with his men.

THE QUADRANT 1 SALES MANAGER

Don Carlyle is a first-line sales manager for Technoplastics, a company that manufactures plastic containers and packaging. At 36, he has been

*Q1.   The Dominant-Hostile
Sales Manager*

His basic managerial belief: Nothing matters as much as getting the job done, no matter how. Salesmen are generally lazy, apathetic, and uncooperative, so the only way to get the job done is to control them very rigidly. The hard-nosed manager is the one who gets results.

*Q4.   The Dominant-Warm
Sales Manager*

His basic belief: High-producing managers are those whose salesmen are committed to their company's goals because they understand how their own needs and objectives square with those goals. To achieve this understanding and commitment, a manager must allow his men to participate and feel involved with the organization.

HOSTILITY ——————————————————————— WARMTH

*Q2.   The Submissive-Hostile
Sales Manager*

His basic managerial belief: Getting by is what counts. Salesmen and sales are both secondary to personal survival in the harsh, unfriendly world of business. The smart manager looks after himself and produces enough results to get by.

*Q3.   The Submissive-Warm
Sales Manager*

His basic managerial belief: Managers who emphasize sociability, harmony, and togetherness get their salesmen to produce. Salesmen will cooperate with you and do good work if you go out of your way to gain their approval. Lavish plenty of friendliness on them and create a supportive, happy climate.

SUBMISSION

FIGURE 3.   The Dimensional model of sales management behavior.

in his present job for two years; before that, he spent four years as a salesman for the same company. His district comprises four states, and he supervises eight salesmen, all of whom call on manufacturers and food processors. He is considered a good manager by top marketing management; his district consistently ranks in the top 20% of the company in sales volume. Let's see what a couple of his salesmen think of Carlyle.

SALESMAN A: "He's a real driver. The guy never stops pushing. Sometimes I think he missed his real calling; he should have been a drill sergeant. He never lets up on you, not for a minute. But I will say this for him: he knows what he wants, and he knows how to get it. He's all business . . . He can be pretty aggravating at times, though. I wish he'd loosen up and relax a little, but I don't think he ever will. People like Carlyle just don't seem happy unless they're giving orders and barking commands. I've got a pretty good sales record myself, so he doesn't give me too hard a time. In fact, he's gone to bat for me a few times to get me some raises. But some of the men in this office are scared to death of the guy. In a way, I understand how they feel. When it comes to bawling out, Carlyle is one of the best shouters I've ever known, and . . . believe me . . . I've known quite a few."

SALESMAN B: "You really want my opinion of Don Carlyle? Okay, you asked for it. I think he's cold and insensitive. He's sarcastic, short-tempered, and he makes completely unreasonable demands. All he thinks about is sales, not people . . . . Of course, there's no denying that he gets results. This office produces a lot of sales. But, if you ask me, the price is high. Half the guys in this district are nervous wrecks. Morale is low, and nobody has the nerve to tell Carlyle the truth. If I could find another sales job with a salary guarantee as good as this one, I think I'd leave Technoplastics tomorrow. Life's too short to spend it all working for a guy like Carlyle."

What motivates the Q1 sales manager?

The dominant-hostile sales manager, like all Q1 people, is mainly motivated by *esteem* and *independence* needs.

He sees personal power as the best way to gratify these needs. To the Q1, power deserves esteem; it deserves to be looked up to and respected. But he cares little for subtle, understated power; to him, power means outright domination and control of others.

When the Q1 sales manager insists that his salesmen are undependable, lazy, and uncooperative and that they must be rigidly controlled, he really tells more about himself than about them. The fact is that he can maintain a self-image as a person who is strong and worthy of respect only as long as he maintains tight, domineering control over others. By controlling others and pushing hard to achieve, he avoids feelings of failure. As he sees it, domination signifies strength, and strength deserves esteem, whereas submission (unless used as a tactic to further his own advancement) signifies weakness, and weakness evokes little or no esteem.

This is one reason the Q1 sales manager lacks regard for his salesmen. If *all* men were equally strong, all would deserve equal esteem, and esteem would lose significance. Esteem is only meaningful when it is accorded to a *few* men; thus, the Q1 must separate himself from the men he supervises. He does this by assuming they are weak and ineffectual (unless they prove otherwise), while he demonstrates strength, forcefulness, and effectiveness. His esteem is based on the contrast (usually largely imaginary) between himself and his salesmen. If he were to acknowledge that they have considerable potential, he would demolish the difference between himself and them, and destroy the foundation on which his self-image is built.

The Q1 sales manager wants power for another reason: it makes him feel *independent*. To the Q1, freedom belongs to those who control others; to be controlled is to be unfree. Obviously, very few Q1s feel totally independent, since virtually all are controlled by someone. But the desire to be completely independent is one reason the Q1 seeks more and more power. Because independence increases as control over others increases, he is not satisfied with his present power; he always wants more. His need for independence also affects his attitude toward salesmen. Freedom, he believes, is more than controlling others; it is standing out from the mass, being distinctive. Q1 managers dislike being, or being considered, "one of the herd," since no member of a herd has any significant individuality or autonomy. The Q1 sees his salesmen as a herd, largely lethargic, inept, and undependable. That is why they are subordinate to him; to be a subordinate is to lack the qualities that enable one to move out of the mass. The Q1 never applies this analysis to himself, of course. As he sees it, one ceases to be a subordinate when one becomes a sales manager.

Once again, we caution that this is an extreme description of Q1 motivation. Many Q1s have neither an unsatisfiable lust for power nor an unsatisfiable craving for independence; their needs for esteem and independence are not as strong as we've described. But *all* Q1 sales managers are motivated essentially by these two needs. All distinguish between their own capabilities and those of their salesmen, and few are satisfied for long at mediocre levels of achievement. The Q1 is typically restless, questing, discontented.

How the Q1 Sales Manager Interacts with His Salesmen

When coaching salesmen, the Q1 sales manager is harsh or even destructive. He does little probing to find out why a salesman acts the way he does, but is quick to blame, carp, denounce, and demean. Not surprisingly, he gets results largely through fear or, at best, grudging cooperation. (Some Q1 sales managers do evoke genuine loyalty from their men by trading "protection" for "performance." In effect, they strike a kind of bargain: "Work like crazy and produce results, and I'll see what can be done about getting you a bigger expense account.") He suppresses conflict, or tries to resolve it by issuing firm edicts which he expects others to obey unquestioningly, instead of exploring the underlying tensions and trying to resolve them.

Because he sees himself as the pivot of the sales organization, the Q1 manager does little to encourage independent thinking or creativity. He sets arbitrary goals, and then drives his salesmen hard to attain them.

Distrustful of others, and unwilling to share responsibility, he overorganizes in the belief that a tight structure will keep his men in line. Often, however, this overdirection leads to low morale and high turnover, since it deprives the men of opportunities for personal fulfillment on the job. Q1s are autocratic; they feel secure only when they're in complete control of situations and people.

Nevertheless, the Q1 sales manager does get generally good short-run results. Over a longer period, he often runs into trouble. He fails to obtain the commitment that's essential to long-run results. His salesmen feel that the challenge and enrichment have been drained from their jobs, and this feeling ultimately has bad effects on their productivity. Morale plunges, and turnover becomes an increasingly severe problem. Meanwhile, the Q1 contends that "The only way to get these guys to sell is to push them hard, and never let up." He's fond of phrases like "We run a tight ship around here," and "Nobody gets away with anything in this office."

One aspect of Q1 behavior seems paradoxical. As a sales manager, he maintains a double standard of right and wrong, good and bad. He demands unswerving obedience to company policies and procedures, yet he himself will subvert or ignore them if he thinks it will do him some good. He insists that his salesmen go through official channels, yet frequently makes his own channels if it will serve his purpose. He scrutinizes his men's expense reports to make sure no money is misspent, yet sometimes spends large amounts on self-enhancing projects. He sternly enforces his own way of doing things, yet sometimes, if he thinks he can get away with it, ignores *his* boss's way of doing things. He is certain his salesmen are lazy, sloppy, and ineffective, yet is equally sure *he* is hardworking, dynamic, and effective. He suppresses conflict among his salesmen with a heavy hand, yet is in frequent conflict with people at the home office, especially those who are not in the sales department. He considers it of first importance that his men listen to him carefully and even eagerly, yet he listens to them only superficially, frequently cutting them off in midsentence. He seldom gives credit for creativity to his salesmen, yet is not above appropriating a creative idea from them and boasting of it as his own. On the surface, Q1 behavior seems thoroughly contradictory.

Of course, it is not contradictory at all. It is consistent. Throughout, the Q1 sales manager acts like a man who believes there is a real difference between himself and the people who report to him. They are lethargic; he is energetic. They are weak; he is strong. They need control; he is a born controller. They are unreliable; he is a paragon of dependability. And so forth. Given this set of beliefs, it makes sense for him to apply different standards to himself and his subordinates.

A Perspective on the Q1 Sales Manager

We all measure ourselves by certain kinds of achievements; we all form an opinion of ourselves that is based, in part, upon whether or not we attain what is important to us. The dominant-hostile sales manager measures himself by the sales achievements of the men he supervises; his opinion of himself is good as long as his salesmen attain high sales records. There is nothing noteworthy about any of this.

What *is* noteworthy is the fact that the Q1's self-image depends upon the efforts of people he distrusts. If we can imagine the feelings of a symphony conductor whose life is wrapped up in the production of great music, but who is forced to lead an orchestra made up, as he sees it, of musical bumblers, we can better appreciate the dilemma of the Q1 sales manager. Whether his salesmen are bumblers or not is entirely beside the point; he *believes* they are, and this means his self-image, which depends upon them, is constantly under threat. If his salesmen are given any significant degree of autonomy, they are, in his opinion, sure to mess things up, and sales are sure to plummet. To keep this from happening, to insure that they produce the kind of sales record he can take pride in, he controls them as closely and tightly as he can. And, just as our proud maestro would surely rave and rant at his bungling musicians from time to time, the Q1 sales manager frequently makes life unpleasant for his salesmen.

It is easy to judge the Q1 a tyrant who deserves no sympathy. But it is a good deal more realistic (and psychologically acceptable) to see him as a man in a really tight bind. The things he wants, self-respect and esteem, are things many of us want. But the Q1 sales manager is convinced that he cannot get them unless he is domineering and tough. Even his desire for power is easy to appreciate; many men, after all, want some kind of power. But the Q1 fears that power will elude him unless he is consistently hard-driving and domineering. If he relaxes his grip on his men, then, he feels sure, his most cherished goals will prove unachievable. From the Q1's point of view, he has *no choice* but to be what he *is*.

It is worth noting that Q1 sales managers don't treat every salesman identically. The *degree* of control they exercise varies somewhat depending on the salesman. In our hypothetical interviews, Salesman A made the point that Don Carlyle didn't give him "too hard a time" because "I've got a pretty good sales record." But Salesman B, who was pleased with his salary guarantee but was presumably not making much commission, indicated that he was a "nervous wreck." This is typical. High-producing salesmen with consistently good records are given somewhat more freedom by Q1 sales managers; low-producing men are harried, baited, bullied, and pressured. It is the marginal or poor salesman whose life is made most miserable by the Q1 sales manager, although life is seldom a paradise even for high producers. (The exception to this is the "star" salesman whose record is so outstanding that even the Q1 sales manager respects him and fears losing him. Such salesmen are often given kid-glove treatment by Q1s, who rarely risk offending the goose who lays the golden egg.)

THE QUADRANT 2 SALES MANAGER

Jeff Ruskin is a 43-year-old sales manager for Scribbler Products, an old, well-established manufacturer of stationary items. He supervises six salesmen in a large metropolitan area, where he has been manager for nearly thirteen years. Before becoming manager, he was chief sales correspondent in Scribbler's home office, and, before that, he was a salesman for Scribbler in a middle-size western city. He has worked for Scribbler ever since leaving college. Ruskin is considered a fair sales manager by home office executives; his office usually makes its quota, or goes slightly above or below. In twelve years, his record has never deviated more than one or two percentage points from his assigned sales objective. Let's see what a couple of Ruskin's salesmen think about him.

SALESMAN A: "Jeff's okay. He leaves me alone, and very seldom gives me any trouble. I've worked for the man for four years, and I've never had a serious run-in with him. He gets a little nervous sometimes, but, by and large, he's easy to live with . . . . He's a funny guy in some ways. Keeps pretty much to himself. I don't think anyone in the office knows him very well. He's not very talkative. But I guess the home office is well pleased with him. After all, he's been around a long time."

SALESMAN B: "To be perfectly frank, I think I could do better with some other manager. I came to Scribbler about a year ago, and I haven't learned anything from Ruskin. I'm not attacking him personally . . . but I just don't think he *manages*. He doesn't seem to exert leadership. He's gone into the field with me a few times, but he's never taught me anything I couldn't have picked up on my own. He never tells you anything worth knowing, and lots of times it's impossible to find out what he thinks. My wife and I are both disappointed in my progress with the company. I should be making more money. I'm not saying the fault is entirely Ruskin's, but I do feel I'd be earning more if I worked for a go-getter."

What motivates the Q2 sales manager?

The submissive-hostile sales manager is largely motivated by *security* needs. The Q2, especially the extreme Q2, is fearful, uncomfortable, and apprehensive much of the time. His fears are diffuse, not concentrated; he is frightened by things in general, rather than some specific thing. So he tries to withdraw or remain aloof from the threat. He may fear being badly treated by others, losing his job, or not being understood or appreciated. He feels uncertain and emotionally insecure.

There is no such thing, of course, as absolute security. To be alive is to experience doubt, ambiguity, and unpredictability. But whereas other sales managers can tolerate uncertainty, the Q2 finds it difficult. Skeptical of his ability to control situations, he feels defenseless in an ever-changing world. While many sales managers feel their strength is a match for whatever happens, the Q2 is as unsure of his own strength as he is of the world outside. So he approaches life in a cautious, conservative way.

The Q2 sales manager does not naively assume he can find security by minimizing interaction with his salesmen, but he does believe he can cut down the opportunities for trouble that way. Because he thinks the worst threats come from people, not circumstances, he generally avoids people when he can.

But it is not necessarily true that he avoids everyone. When the Q2 is convinced, from experience, that a salesman can be steadfastly relied upon, he often interacts with that salesman in a fairly open manner. But until a man has proven he is trustworthy, the Q2 tries to keep a safe distance.

The Q2 sales manager, it should be emphasized, is not an organizational hermit. He is simply a man who feels most comfortable alone or with a few proven people.

How the Q2 Sales Manager Interacts with His Salesmen

Q2 sales management is sometimes called "on-the-job-retirement." The Q2 is a passive manager who fears that direct activity on his part will rock the boat, so he leaves his salesmen alone as long as they sell enough to get by. Not unexpectedly, he frequently produces mediocre results. He coaches his salesmen mechanically and superficially, with no serious attempt to analyze their problems or help them improve their effectiveness. He attains little commitment from his men, who are usually put off by his apathy, lack of leadership, and unwillingness to involve them. He withdraws from conflict or avoids it instead of resolving it, hopeful that if he ignores a bad situation long enough, it will go away.

Since his prime aim is to preserve the status quo, virtually no creativity emerges from the men who work for him. The Q2 sales manager is satisfied with getting by, so his men sell enough to keep their jobs, but seldom more. As a planner, he does what the company expects of him, but his efforts lack dynamism and a sense of purpose.

The Q2 can be described as uninspired, mechanical, and apathetic, and the same words apply to the results he obtains. He tries to remain neutral and uninvolved, keeping his ideas, feelings, and opinions to himself. He insists that "Whatever you do isn't going to make any difference; you can't really do anything to increase sales." A defeatist with little confidence in himself or others, his main concern is to make sure he gets by, and to do this he plays it safe. "Cover your backside" is his motto.

For the most part, the Q2 sales manager leads by following. He provides little direction and guidance; he has few "take charge" qualities. Most leaders think in terms of *progress, change,* and *growth;* he thinks in terms of *stability, endurance,* and *sameness.* Seldom satisfied with things as they are, he never forgets that change could make things worse. The status quo may not be much, but at least it's familiar.

More than this, he neither derives challenge from managing salesmen, nor relishes the give-and-take that should be a basic part of the sales manager's job. Unlike the Q1, he does not enjoy power. He is a contradictory figure; a manager who barely manages, a leader who often leads by following.

A Perspective on the Q2 Sales Manager.

Most companies with Q2 sales managers are frustrated and baffled by them. In many ways, the Q2's performance is unassailable. He staunchly supports any and every company policy; he transmits management directives punctually and accurately; he rarely deviates from company rules or procedures; he is a model budgeter who spends money very carefully; his paperwork usually meets expectations; and, most important of all, he usually makes his sales quota. It is possible, of course, but never easy, to fire such a man.

Yet top management is seldom really satisfied with the Q2 sales manager, not because of what he does wrong (he seldom does anything that's downright wrong) but because of what he fails to do at all. He fails to assume managerial initiative, preferring to act as a transmitter of ideas from people higher in the power structure; he fails to develop his men; he fails to tackle problems, preferring to let them fester; he fails to make hard decisions; he fails to motivate and inspire; he fails to stimulate creativity or commitment; and, worst of all, he fails to exceed his assigned sales objectives. He is, at best, a marginal manager.

We can easily understand, then, Salesman B's disgruntled opinion of Jeff Ruskin. Any salesman who wants to grow will get little help from a Q2 manager, and would, without doubt, be better off working for someone more dynamic. There can be very little growth in an atmosphere dedicated to maintaining the status quo.

The Q2 sales manager isn't interested in growth. He wants a well-ordered, predictable, manageable existence, basically free of worry and anxiety. He wants to take as few risks as possible. He wants assured survival without constant striving and competition. As much as anything, he wants to be let alone, unbothered and unburdened. He seeks not total resignation, withdrawal, or detachment, but a situation in which he can do his job without fear of others or without being forceful and dynamic. There is nothing strange or unusual about this; the Q2 is, after all, *not* forceful and dynamic, and he is naturally ill at ease in situations where these characteristics are prized.

THE QUADRANT 3 SALES MANAGER

Daniel Arnold is sales manager for Browning Agency, a large brokerage specializing in the sale of fire and casualty insurance. He's 40, and he has been in his job five years; before that, he spent ten years as a salesman for several local insurance agencies. During his years as a salesman, in which he was moderately successful, he became well acquainted with a very large number of people. When Browning's old sales manager retired, it seemed only natural to hire Arnold for the job because, as one Browning executive put it, "He knows everybody in town." Let's listen to a couple of Arnold's salesmen describe him.

SALESMAN A: "Dan's a prince of a guy. He's more than a boss, really . . . he's a friend. He's never too busy to talk to you, to ask about your family, to listen to your problems. He's the only sales manager I've ever worked for who can always pick me up when I'm down. And Dan's a practical man, too. He knows that you can't make much money if you sit in the office all day filling out forms. So he almost never pesters us about paperwork. He's really a very understanding person."

SALESMAN B: "I like Dan. I really do. In fact, I don't know anyone who doesn't. But I've got to admit that sometimes I wish he weren't so doggoned friendly . . . that he seemed more concerned about sales, more businesslike. Dan Arnold can waste more time talking about nothing than any man I've ever met. And, you know, in this business, time is money. That's one reason I don't come into the office any more often than necessary. Once I get there, Dan is sure to begin bending my ear about something. I'd rather be out making sales calls. But . . . as I said before . . . he really is a wonderful person. Exasperating, but wonderful."

What motivates the Q3 sales manager?

Basically, the Q3 sales manager is motivated by *social* needs and, to a lesser extent, by *security* and *esteem* needs. The Q3 has deep needs for acceptance, belonging, warmth, approval, and companionship. He also has deep needs to smooth over conflict, confrontation, tension, hostility, or unpleasantness of any kind. He seeks out positive experiences and evades or glosses over harsh ones.

Security and esteem needs are frequently tied to strong social needs.

When the Q3 sales manager receives friendship and acceptance, he feels secure, and he sees himself as a worthwhile person, a "nice guy" who elicits approval from others. As long as his salesmen like him, enjoy his company, and respond to him good-naturedly, he maintains a positive self-image. When he encounters animosity, or gets involved in a situation that's harsh or unpleasant, things change abruptly. His security evaporates. An uneasy feeling, perhaps even fear, comes over him. He feels apprehensive and anxious; he begins to worry that he may not elicit approval from others, that he may even arouse dislike. His self-image, fragile at best, begins to crumble. So disquieting is this experience that he goes to great lengths to avoid it; he spends much of his life pursuing happy moments and fleeing from unhappy ones.

The Q3's social, security, and esteem needs are so compelling that he is not satisfied merely to know that people like him. He needs constant affirmation of the fact. To fulfill this need, he often spends unreasonable amounts of time in seemingly idle chatter with his salesmen. From his point of view, there is nothing idle about it at all. This apparently aimless talk serves an important purpose: it reinforces his self-image as a "nice guy," a guy who belongs, the only image he can live with comfortably.

In his own way, the Q3 sales manager is as insecure and fearful as the Q2. But, because he is much warmer, he handles his insecurity differently.

How the Q3 Sales Manager Interacts with His Salesmen

The Q3 directs his salesmen by indirection; he tries to cement strong social relationships with them, assuming that, as friends, they won't let him down. He believes men work hard and well for someone they like, and nearly all his men like him (although some regard him as a congenial pushover). He does an ineffective job of coaching his salesmen, because he minimizes and glosses over problems instead of facing up to them. He handles conflict in the same way, by dodging the underlying problem and minimizing, rather than coping with, the disagreement. He attains a high measure of social loyalty from his men, but not always a high measure of respect. He seldom stimulates creativity; new ideas mean change, and change means tension, which he prefers to avoid. In setting sales goals, he does a balancing act in which he tries to keep everybody happy, which means getting enough sales from his men to satisfy the company without creating pressures on the men themselves.

He is a loose, disorganized planner with an aversion to systems; to the Q3 sales manager friendship counts, not organization. He places great emphasis on human relations, as exemplified by his "Treat 'em right and they'll work their hearts out for you" attitude. He's fond of reminding his salesmen that "We're all one great big happy family," and he spends much of his time, when in the office, chatting sociably with any salesmen who happen to be around.

The Q3 thinks of his salesmen as *equals*. He insists that "We're all the same around here. I'm just one of the boys." And that's the way he behaves. He refuses to "boss" his men. For him, "boss" means "push" and he believes nothing can be accomplished by pushing. People do good work because they like the person they're working for; friendship and goodwill are the only effective motivators. He is convinced that people who are pushed resist, so that domineering management is self-defeating. (Nevertheless, he is unhesitatingly loyal to his own manager, no matter what his own manager's behavior may be.)

The Q3 sales manager tries hard to make everyone happy. But, the world being what it is, unpleasantness sometimes intrudes. His superior may, for instance, ask the Q3 to pass down an instruction that is certain to cause dissatisfaction. When this happens, the Q3 tempers the instruction to make it less disturbing. Then he transmits the smoothed-over version with a plea for cooperation, appealing to his men to prove their devotion to himself and the company. A master at putting things in their best possible light, he often finds silver linings in the darkest clouds.

At the base of his attitude is a kind of optimistic equation in which goodwill on one side of a relationship equals goodwill on the other; treat people well, he says, and they will treat you well. Nothing could be further from the bleak attitude of the Q1 and Q2 sales managers.

A Perspective on the Q3 Sales Manager

The Q3 sales manager is *people-oriented*. He wants, quite literally, to be everyone's friend. Status, rank, position, and hierarchy make him uncomfortable; they are obstacles to friendship. He has difficulty understanding competition, rivalry, or other arrangements that divide people instead of unite them. He believes nice guys do win ball games, and, when they don't, that they have more fun playing than anyone else.

Unable to tolerate hostility in himself or others, the Q3 expends much energy to protect himself from coldness, anger, resentment, and aggression. His definition of hostility is very broad; it includes not only open aggression, but even firmness, dominance and assertiveness. He tries to control any leanings he may feel toward dominance by being constantly agreeable, friendly, and conventional. Any assertiveness is masked, hidden not only from others but from himself.

It is wrong to think of Q3 sales managers as being unconcerned about their jobs. They want to do well, to help their companies, and to "come through" for their superiors. But they are convinced that the only way to do this (or at least the only way they feel comfortable with) is through warm concern for their men. To the Q3 sales manager, happy, satisfied salesmen are inseparable from good sales results. If backed into a corner, he will admit that some sales managers get good results in other ways, but he will insist that, *in the long run*, his way is best. "Sooner or later," he says, "any sales manager who puts results ahead of people is going to have real trouble."

As might be expected, the Q3 sales manager is pleasant to have around. Other people think of him as extroverted, jolly, friendly, sympathetic, encouraging, and positive-minded. He is basically optimistic and communicates his optimism to others. Nevertheless, not all salesmen are happy working for a Q3. Some, like Salesman B in our illustration, feel he is too unbusinesslike. "He's too nice for his own good" is the way they sum it up. Thus the Q3 sales manager sometimes pays a price for his popularity by being more liked than respected; to some of his men, he is a "pushover," a "nice guy but something of a chump." He is almost always unaware of these verdicts. He sees himself as both liked and approved, although, in fact, the affection usually outweighs the approval. The affection is not gained effortlessly, but he doesn't really care. Important things are worth working for, and nothing is more important to the submissive-warm sales manager than being liked and popular.

THE QUADRANT 4 SALES MANAGER

Warren Coleridge is sales manager for Chromatic Graphics Company, a large printer specializing in fine color printing. At 38, he supervises twelve salesmen who cover the eastern half of a large southern state. He has been in the printing business for 15 years, starting as an estimator and then going on the road as a salesman. He became Chromatic's sales manager four years ago. In that time, the company has experienced four annual increases in sales, and each increase has been well above the industry's average. It is generally believed that Coleridge will be promoted to a vice-presidency in another year or two. Here are evaluations of him by two of his salesmen:

SALESMAN A: "You bet I've got high regard for Warren Coleridge. I hate to admit it, but when he took over as sales manager, I was floundering . . . badly. My wife and I had even talked about my going into some other kind of work. Then Warren came along and began to teach me how to sell. Until then, I hadn't realized how many things I was doing wrong. Let me tell you, he worked many hours with me, and he refused to give up. In six months' time, he had me well above quota, and I've been there ever since. If it weren't for Warren, I wouldn't be with this company today. That man knows what he's doing."

SALESMAN B: "Coleridge is the first sales manager I've ever worked with that I was able to get along with . . . and I've been in selling for nine years. I say this even though he's one of the toughest managers I've ever worked for. I'm a little bit of a loner . . . and I don't take instructions very well. In fact, one of my old bosses once called me a rebel. So I've had plenty of run-ins with various sales managers. But, with Coleridge, it's been different. He's tough-minded but also open-minded . . . and he doesn't try to make me do things his way. I've had more real freedom . . . and higher sales . . . under Coleridge than any other boss I've worked for. And the funny thing is, I'm less of a maverick than I used to be. As a matter of fact, for the first time in my life, I've actually been cooperating with some of the other guys in the office. The strangest part of it all is that Coleridge is really a very hard-nosed, demanding guy . . . but, for some reason, I don't resent his demands. I don't know how he does it, but he deserves a lot of credit."

What motivates the Q4 sales manager?

The Q4 sales manager is motivated by a need for *self-realization,* a need that's largely filled by his work. In managing, he uses his talents to the fullest; he tests and proves himself. He likes to achieve, to attain goals, master situations, and influence events. He wants to succeed. All this is consistent with the dominant strain in his behavior. At the same time, his warmth generates an equally strong regard for people, and respect for their needs, ideas, and goals.

Because he needs to achieve, he is persistent; whether he's training a salesman who's slow to learn or trying to make a sales quota that seems impossible, he does not give up easily. Usually, obstacles only increase his determination. Few things gratify him more than getting a hard job done. Frustrations along the way only increase his eagerness to "get on with it."

The Q4 sales manager has definite goals. He knows where he is going, and when and how he expects to get there. He is not so ambitious that he leaps before he looks, but he does not procrastinate, either. He moves forward in a deliberate, orderly way. He considers money important; it helps him buy the things he wants, and it is a good measure of achievement. High earnings mean he is a successful manager; low earnings usually mean he is not. But, in most cases, *personal development,* not just money, is the prime motivator of the Q4.

Although realistic, the Q4's level of aspiration is very high. He constantly stretches, constantly forces himself to put out extra effort. Sometimes this effort pays off in unexpected achievements, sometimes not.

He sees his salesmen as contributors to his growth who can, at the same time, enhance their own growth. So he emphasizes *mutuality* and interaction. He does not ask, "How can I use other people?" but "How can we contribute to one another?" Sensitive to the needs and goals of his men, he is able to link these needs and goals to the needs and goals of the organization. In this way, he generates commitment to organizational objectives. Because growth means change, he especially values creative salesmen and innovative situations. Not surprisingly, he finds sales management exciting, and his commitment to his job is usually stronger than other managers'.

How the Q4 Sales Manager Interacts with His Salesmen

Because of his basic respect and regard for his men, and his firm belief that they want their jobs to have some significance, the Q4 sales manager relies heavily on team and participative management. He involves his salesmen in decision-making about matters which affect their jobs. In coaching, for example, he renders analytic, open feedback so that the salesman can join him in identifying strengths and problem areas. He prefers self-discovery to cramming his own point-of-view down the salesman's throat. He handles conflict in a similar way, trying to let the salesmen join him in resolving the problem; conflict, in fact, is treated as contributing to learning, creativity and innovation. He encourages creative thinking, and is quick to reward it.

The Q4 sales manager attains high commitment from his men, because they know they have a significant personal stake in improved performance. None of this means that he abdicates his position of leadership or tries to evade responsibility for making decisions. This is an extremely important point. It is easy, and *wrong,* to see the Q4 sales manager as weak and indecisive because he involves his men in basic tasks like problem-solving, goal-setting, and decision-making. Far from being weak and indecisive, he is firm and forceful.

He knows that in the last analysis *he* must decide; he must lead, not moderate. But he knows his decisions will be better, and will generate greater commitment from his men, if he seeks out and considers their ideas and opinions. Far from renouncing responsibility, he makes intelligent use of the full resources of the organization, so his decisions are not made in a vacuum.

The Q4's behavior is powered by a view of people that is widely supported by behavioral scientists: the view that most men, to a greater or lesser extent, seek growth, challenge, and the opportunity to be creative in their work. This need for personal development can easily be stifled unless the work-environment stimulates it. The Q4 sales manager sees himself as the stimulating agent, the catalyst of development, who recognizes that his company's growth is inseparable from his own growth, which in turn is inseparable from his salesmen's growth.

The Q4 sales manager is optimistic about his salesmen. He believes they have stores of untapped, perhaps unrecognized, potential that he can bring to the surface. He firmly believes that his men are inherently valuable. At the same time, he is realistic about the contribution each man is capable of making; he evaluates his men on a one-by-one basis, never generalizing about them. Then he tries to maximize their *use* of their potential, whatever it may be. This calls for a flexible, individualized approach to each man.

At the core of Q4 sales management is the concept of *teamwork*. His job, as the Q4 sees it, is to utilize his salesmen's resources and knowledge to the fullest in making decisions and solving problems. He believes he can best achieve his goals by welding his men and himself into a genuine team on which everyone is expected to make continuous contributions. He always remains firmly in control of the team; he is always its leader, never just "one of the boys."

The Q4 sales manager believes that salesmen perform best when they're *committed* to their company's goals, and that commitment comes from *personal involvement* in setting goals. If a man takes part in decisions about his job, he feels a personal stake in successfully implementing those decisions. Men may resent decisions imposed from outside, but they are committed to decisions in which they have been *involved,* even when they do not agree with those decisions. So the Q4 tries to involve his salesmen because involvement leads to commitment and commitment leads to increased sales.

The Q4 sales manager relates to his own superior with respect mixed with a strong desire for involvement. He respects his boss's leadership, and at the same time wants his own talents utilized by his superior. He is ambitious, but hopes to succeed through performance, not politics.

This does not mean that he tries to assume more responsibility than he is entitled to. All he asks is that when his ideas will be useful, he be asked to participate in the managerial process. If, then, a decision is made that's contrary to his own best judgment, he supports it willingly, knowing he was consulted and his views were considered. His loyalty is not unquestioning, however; he reserves the right to question, probe, and criticize if justified. He speaks his mind, maintains full communication with his boss, and transmits all kinds of feedback, both positive and negative.

One Q4 hallmark is his high commitment to his work. No matter what kind of superior he works for, he feels strongly responsible about his own role. He refuses to take advantage of bosses weaker than he; he tries to do his job to the best of his capacity, even when that is not easy. He knows self-realization is never easy or cheap.

Of the four basic types of sales managers, only the Q4 practices team participative management, in which salesmen are involved in goal-setting, decision-making, and problem-solving in matters that concern them and their jobs. The Q1 is too disdainful of his salesmen to involve them; he does not permit people he considers unreliable to make decisions. The Q2 is too fearful of his men; genuine involvement cannot take place where there is distrust and insecurity. The Q3 goes overboard for *social* participation rather than active problem-solving; he searches for popular solutions, not necessarily sound ones. But the Q4 respects *both* the process of participation and the people who participate. He believes his salesmen have resources, information, creativity, and common sense to offer, if only he can bring these qualities to the fore.

A CLOSER LOOK AT TEAM AND PARTICIPATIVE MANAGEMENT

Because understanding the concept of team and participative management is so vital to understanding how the Q4 sales manager gets results, let's take a closer look at it in this section.

Nobody, obviously, can pursue contradictory goals at the same time. If a company's demands on a salesman conflict with his own priorities, something has to give. The salesman may pursue his own goals while ignoring or sabotaging the company's; he may pursue the company's goals halfheartedly and haphazardly, not caring very much about results; he may pursue his goals outside the company; or, feeling trapped and frustrated, he may quit and go to work somewhere else.

There will always be some difference between the salesman's goals and the organization's as long as the organization *imposes* its goals on the salesman. This is the reason for *participative* management, for letting the salesman take part in decision-making and goal setting which affect *his* job. Even when the manager makes a decision *contrary* to the salesman's thinking, the salesman is more likely to support it if he was *involved* in the process leading up to the decision. Participative management is not a wooly-minded concept. It is not a gimmick. It's a tough-minded approach based on the simple fact that *commitment* and *results* flow from *involvement,* from playing a personal role in structuring our own lives.

The participative approach not only generates commitment; it helps satisfy the salesman's needs for independence and self-realization. A person who takes part in decisions that affect his job is literally more independent than one who only implements decisions made by others. Independence is more than the ability to move around without constant scrutiny by the boss. It's also the ability to shape, or help shape, the way one does his job. In exercising this ability, the salesman contributes to his own growth.

A Perspective on the Q4 Sales Manager

The reader may think we have made the Q4 sales manager sound too good to be true. If so, the fault is with our description, not with the Q4. Actually, he is a very solid, down-to-earth human being. He sometimes forgets the value of two-way communication, and loses his temper instead of probing patiently; he sometimes caves in to pressures and makes decisions without consulting or even informing his men; he sometimes seeks advice from his salesmen and then promptly ignores it; he sometimes handles conflict curtly, failing to resolve the underlying problem; he is sometimes overcontrolling, bad-humored, hostile to new ideas. He is, in short, decidedly real. But he does *try* to practice sales management much as we've described it.

A second caution is in order: The Q4 sales manager's emphasis on teamwork does not mean he hires only well-adjusted Q3 or Q4 salesmen who get along with one another, nor that he values social skills more than other skills. A team is not a social club, nor is it necessarily a group of close friends. The Q4 sales manager willingly hires Q1 salesmen (Salesman B, who was hired by Warren Coleridge, is a good example) *if* they can do the job, *if* they can contribute to their own growth and that of the team, and *if* they can help achieve the organization's goals. The ability to contribute to the sales team does *not* depend on sociability; in fact, some very outgoing salesmen may make only minimal contributions. We can go even further and say that the Q4 sales manager deliberately seeks abrasive, hard-nosed, candid salesmen. They are an invaluable source of new ideas, the yeast in the team loaf. Nothing in this chapter means that the Q1 salesman has no place in the Q4 sales management environment. *As long as he is willing and able to work toward organizational goals,* he is valued and welcomed.

One other vital point: the reader must not get the idea that the Q4 sales manager, because he practices team and participative management, is soft, bland, or feeble. He is every bit as hard-driving, as assertive, and as determined as the Q1 sales manager, *but in a different way.* He is firm, resolute, and decisive *without* forgetting or overlooking the needs of his men. He is unswervingly goal-directed *without* showing any lack of concern for the people who must help him achieve his goals. He is tough, strong, and job-minded *without* being autocratic, dogmatic, or out of touch with his men. In a phrase, the dominant-warm sales manager is exactly that: dominant *and* warm.

MANAGERIAL MOTIVATION

Before discussing the interactions between sales managers and salesmen, let's look at the pyramid of needs again and see, at a glance, where the basic motivation of each managerial type lies:

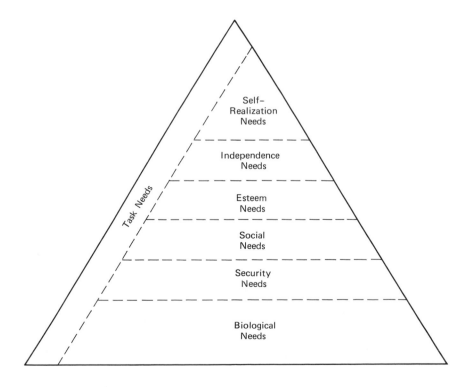

The reader will find it useful to keep the pyramid in mind as he reads the following sections.

Interactions Between Sales Managers and Salesmen

Interactions between any sales management strategy and any salesman's strategy is governed largely by the same principles that govern salesman–customer interaction. The sales manager who has some insight into his own needs and motivations as well as those of his salesmen is therefore better able to adapt his behavior to attain better management results.

One of the sales manager's key jobs is to provide his salesmen with coaching and training that give them more insight into their behavior and its impact on customers. Without this awareness, there is little hope of improvement or progressive change. Coaching and training can be much more effective if the manager himself understands the needs that motivate his men. A sales manager who understands the role that needs play in motivating people, and who is sensitive to the needs of the men he supervises, can *respond* to those needs intelligently and helpfully. He can bolster the self-image of a Q1 who craves attention and applause; he can provide a supportive, nonthreatening climate in which a withdrawn Q2 can begin to experiment with new and more effective sales approaches; and he can help the Q3 find warmth and sociability. Then, as these needs are satisfied, he can help them move to higher levels of motivation, where greater growth and development can occur. More than this, the sales manager can help each of these salesmen to understand his own behavior better. Many salesmen are simply not realistically aware of how other people see them, of their effect upon others. Because they don't understand their behavior, they have great difficulty improving it. Here is a challenging and enormously promising area in which the sales manager, armed with a knowledge of needs, can be very helpful.

The guidelines we have set forth for dealing with various customer types apply to various salesmen types, too. The sales manager cannot deal successfully with a Q3 salesman in the same way that he deals with a Q1. Each salesman has his own needs, and, to a large extent, these dictate the kind of strategy and communications that the sales manager should use in trying to get through to him. Salesman–customer and salesman–sales manager interaction share many similarities.

In evaluating ideas, sales managers will find it useful to ask, "How does this idea help fill the needs of my salesmen?" This is not, of course, the only test to which ideas should be submitted, but it is a meaningful one. Compensation plans, sales contests, quota systems, new forms and reports, new procedures, alignment of territories, and many other ideas and programs can be usefully evaluated by how well they satisfy the needs of the salesmen who will be involved. By weighing ideas against needs, the sales manager can often improve his original thinking, and take action to make his ideas more acceptable and more workable.

The sales manager who neglects the needs of the people with whom he interacts, who overlooks or disregards them, does so at his peril.

Let's look now at how each sales manager typically interacts with his salesmen.

THE Q1 SALES MANAGER

The Q1 is invariably aware of power relationships. He seldom forgets that he has far-ranging control over the destinies of his salesmen. He maintains tight control, regularly reminding them, sometimes subtly and sometimes not so subtly, that he is a man to be feared. He realizes, however, that it becomes increasingly difficult to motivate through fear alone, and he is sensitive enough to know that raw power sometimes leads to rebellion, hostility, or indifference, all of which he prefers to avoid.

So we often find the Q1 sales manager is *both* autocratic and protective; he expects unquestioning obedience from his men, and, in return, he looks out for their interests. Many Q1s fight hard to get more money or privileges for their salesmen. In fact, the Q1 frequently *enjoys* the sense of power that comes from conferring favors.

So, while some Q1 sales managers come close to being considered dictators by their salesmen, others are considered unrelenting but protective taskmasters to be feared but also relied upon. Some are detested or at least strongly disliked, while others are looked upon with a mixture of awe and admiration.

Of course, the Q1 sales manager's behavior toward any specific salesman is partly conditioned by the salesman's behavior toward him. With ambitious, aggressive Q1 salesmen, he is suspicious and cagey, realistically assuming that "I know you'll stab me in the back the minute you get the chance." While he grudgingly admires the forceful salesman who reflects his own traits, he nevertheless moves quickly to neutralize him if he becomes a threat to his own safety. With a withdrawn, apathetic Q2 salesman, the Q1 sales manager is usually disdainful. Few things arouse his scorn as much as weakness, and he is not above treating the weak salesman as a puppet (if he doesn't fire him and replace him with a more productive man). With easygoing, amiable Q3 salesmen the Q1 sales manager sometimes lets up and is less aggressive, since they are compliant enough to follow orders without coercion. Or, unable to resist the opportunity, he may unashamedly exploit the Q3 in numerous ways. With businesslike Q4 salesmen, the Q1 sales manager makes sure they don't challenge his authority. Within limits, he lets them function in their own way as long as they don't get "out of line." If they do, he quickly slaps them back into place, a tactic that is likely, sooner or later, to alienate the salesman sufficiently to cause him to transfer or get another job.

In brief, the Q1 sales manager lets his men operate in their own way as long as they adhere to his leadership, give him complete loyalty and support, and do nothing to undermine his authority. Put another way, he demands that they implement *his* plan for achieving power in the organization; they must subjugate their initiatives and follow his. In return, they get to keep their jobs, or if lucky, they get strong support and protection.

THE Q2 SALES MANAGER

The Q2's relationship to his salesmen is characterized by caution and prudence. He knows they can easily get out of line and create trouble, so he watches them carefully. His idea of proper behavior by salesmen is the way *he* behaves toward *his* boss. As he sees it, his job is to transmit instructions from his superior to his salesmen, and their job is to follow through without question. When he has no instructions to transmit, his salesmen are free to mark time, as long as they stick to the company's rules and don't create problems. He is a pipeline through which orders flow from the man who originates them to the men who implement them. He considers himself a transmitter, not an originator, and he makes it plain that the orders are not *his*. This way, he cannot be blamed if the orders are unpopular.

With negative leadership like this, there is often much wasted time and motion among the salesmen who work for a Q2. Firm direction leading to growth and increased sales is almost always lacking. Not surprisingly, ambitious salesmen with strong growth needs are oppressed by this climate.

The Q2 sales manager has serious problems with forceful Q1 salesmen, who are difficult to control and who try to circumvent him. He considers them troublemakers, but cannot deal with them on his own. His best solution is to point out to them that they are not really circumventing *him,* but his *boss,* and that they may be headed for real trouble unless they stop stirring things up. Whenever the Q2 sales manager needs the strength of authority, he borrows it from his superior; he has no desire to assert himself in his own right.

The Q2 sales manager gets along well with Q2 salesmen. They do what he tells them, or at least they do enough to get by, and they remain inconspicuous. With affable Q3 salesmen, the Q2 sales manager feels uncomfortable. They make demands upon him that he is unable to fulfill; they constantly ask for support and acceptance, which would require him to become involved. He considers them bothersome pests, and he tries to keep them at a distance; the last thing he wants is close contact with them. With Q4 salesmen, the Q2 sales manager is even more uncomfortable. They are hardest of all to manage—they bombard him with suggestions, they innovate, and, most bothersome of all, they expect him to *follow through*. They like change and variation, the things that most upset the Q2. He responds to them in the only way he knows—by putting them off.

None of this is surprising. The Q2 sales manager is security-oriented. Since salesmen can deprive him of security by creating trouble for him, he avoids or minimizes interaction. At his most extreme, he lapses into management by default, in which no one really seems to be running things.

THE Q3 SALES MANAGER

The Q3 is typically less aware of power relationships than are other sales managers. He treats everyone as an equal and a friend. In the real world, of course, power relationships are inescapable, but he tries to ignore them and, instead, interacts on a friend-to-friend basis.

In dealing with stubborn Q1 salesmen, the Q3 sales manager appeases and compromises. He humors them and promises them favors in return for their cooperation, as he would "overgrown kids" who have to be continuously bribed to stay in line. He reminds them that a great future can be theirs if only they stop getting "all worked up." Because he is so permissive and so eager for peace and goodwill, he sometimes puts himself in a situation where his Q1 salesmen end up controlling *him*. A Q3 sales manager who gets into this bind finds himself constantly reacting to his salesmen's initiatives; they call the tune while he dances.

The Q3 sales manager gets along quite well with Q2 salesmen. Puzzled by their withdrawn behavior, he often rationalizes it as shyness. Obviously, he gets along superbly with Q3 salesmen, although he wastes a good deal of time talking with them about matters that have nothing to do with business. He has his greatest problems with Q4 salesmen. As realists, they are skeptical of much that he says, and continuously bring up major issues which may cause some conflict and tension before they can be resolved. Q4 salesmen, by insisting on going to the root of problems, on facing up to disagreement, and on being candid, often create a great deal of tension and frustration for the let's-split-it-down-the-middle Q3 sales manager. In the end, the Q3 usually gets along with his Q4 salesmen by constantly patching up compromises, or by letting them do as they please and praying for the best, or by moving back and forth between the two approaches. He never really controls them.

Q3 sales management is blindly optimistic management that assumes achievement inevitably follows good fellowship; achievement is valued, but sociability is seen as the key to achievement.

THE Q4 SALES MANAGER

The Q4's growth-orientation is not solely self-centered; he wants to foster growth in his men as well. He tries to stimulate their self-realization and his. Far from fearing ambitious salesmen as threats, he sees them as *vital* to his development and his company's success. He assumes that his own progress hinges on his salesmen's progress; if he helps them succeed, he is sure to succeed himself. So he tries to enhance their growth while making certain that current results are not neglected in favor of future results.

This means the Q4 sales manager tries to do two difficult jobs at the same time. On the one hand, he tries to help each of his salesmen fill his lowest unfilled need, whatever it may be; he tries to work with each man on the level at which that man is motivated. He does not interact with a security-oriented Q2 salesman in the same way that he interacts with an esteem-oriented Q1. On the other hand, he tries to help each of his men to move *up* the pyramid of needs, to become more motivated by needs for independence and self-realization. Being a practical man, he focuses on immediate needs as a short-range goal, and makes newer and higher needs a long-range goal. He is too hard-headed and realistic to think that any man's motivation can be redirected quickly or easily. Yet, to whatever extent he can, he tries, over the long run, to move his men toward the independence and self-realization levels of the pyramid.

Over the short range, his managerial strategy is flexible, varying with the salesman. He tries to satisfy his Q1 salesmen's strong needs for independence and esteem by involving them intimately in problem-solving and goal-setting, and by giving them plenty of recognition and acclaim. But he is careful to impress them with *his* strength, knowing they will exploit any apparent weaknesses. He never lets them forget who's boss. He tries to draw his Q2 salesmen into decision-making but does not always succeed. When he doesn't, he exerts forceful leadership so they do not lapse into apathy. He provides them with plenty of structure and guidance, realizing that structure makes them feel more secure. With Q3 salesmen, he stresses sales goals while recognizing that their social needs must also be met. He tries to organize their haphazard work habits. Realizing that their submissiveness indicates a need for guidance, he gives them more than the ordinary amount of direction. His own outlook, of course, meshes best with that of his Q4 salesmen. Their needs for self-realization and independence make them strong team members; they relish involvement and challenge. He especially values the open attitude and give-and-take which leads to their growth and his.

Thus the Q4 sales manager tries to foster his salesmen's climb up the pyramid of needs by treating them as individuals with differing present needs, and helping them meet those needs in a *productive* way. For example, he helps the Q1 salesman grow by involvement, thus satisfying the Q1's needs for esteem and independence. But the Q1 salesman is not permitted to ride roughshod over other men, nor manipulate them, nor is he given a chance to elbow aside his manager in a power play. His aggressiveness is channeled into *selling* by a tough, shrewd manager who will not let him use his aggressiveness in destructive ways. The Q4 sales manager helps his men to fill their needs constructively. And, as these needs are filled, he patiently and diligently tries to awaken in them other and higher needs.

SECONDARY MANAGERIAL STRATEGIES AND MANAGERIAL MASKS

So far, we've talked as if sales managers always manifest one and only one strategy. In actual fact, of course, they don't. Like everyone else, sales managers may, when sufficiently frustrated or pressed, shift automatically into a secondary strategy or deliberately don a mask. Let's look briefly at the most typical secondary and mask strategies. While a manager can shift to any quadrant, the shifts described below are the most likely.

Secondary Strategies Typically Used with Salesmen

A sales manager can move to any quadrant of behavior when he shifts to a secondary strategy, but the shifts described below are those most likely to occur.

THE Q1 SALES MANAGER

When thwarted by a salesman (who may act unwisely, fail to cooperate, or create problems in some other way), the Q1 sales manager usually intensifies his primary behavior. He becomes more controlling, more sarcastic, more dictatorial. But, if his frustration continues, he sometimes slips (unwittingly, of course) into Q2 behavior, saying, in effect, "I give up. You just can't depend on anybody." As always, *he* is right, the *salesman* is wrong.

THE Q2 SALES MANAGER

While generally finding it difficult to assert himself, the Q2 sales manager, if pushed hard enough, automatically shifts to a brief Q1 secondary strategy with his salesmen, the only people against whom he dares show hostility for any considerable length of time. He usually does this when something happens that may put him in a bad light with *his* boss. When the shift occurs, he becomes domineering and unreasonable, making it plain to one and all that "I'm the boss, and I want it done my way." He is unable to sustain this forceful behavior, however, and, if the frustration mounts, he reverts to his usual Q2 strategy, becoming even more aloof than usual and declaring that "I wash my hands of the whole mess." And, having washed his hands, he often refuses to get involved, preferring to sit in his office and sulk.

THE Q3 SALES MANAGER

When frustrated by his salesmen, the Q3 sales manager, in exasperation, usually lashes out briefly in a Q1 manner, reminding his men that "I'm the boss and I want it done my way." But he is never a comfortable Q1, not even momentarily. Unless his autocratic approach brings very fast results, he makes a more comfortable automatic shift to Q2 behavior, which is easier to maintain, and withdraws with a "Forget it; it's not worth getting worked up about" attitude.

THE Q4 SALES MANAGER

The Q4 sales manager has considerable patience with his salesmen, but, like anyone, he can become so annoyed or irritated by their failure that he bursts forth with Q1 behavior. When this happens, a stubborn assertiveness comes to the surface, and he takes a "Do what I say, whether you like it or not" approach. This is the very opposite of his standard behavior, and it is quite unconscious. If this secondary strategy fails, as it can, he automatically lapses into a Q2 strategy. "You can't count on anybody," he tells himself. This withdrawal is generally short-lived, and his underlying commitment to confronting problems usually surfaces quickly.

Mask Strategies Typically Used with Salesmen

Any manager can assume any mask, although in actuality Q3 and Q1 masks are donned most often.

THE Q1 SALES MANAGER

The Q1 sales manager often impresses his salesmen as so overwhelming and tough that they may become antagonistic or apathetic. If the Q1 sees this happening, he may try honey instead of vinegar, manifesting an insincere but frequently persuasive concern for his men. He soothes them and restores morale to the point where effective functioning can take place. This is the reason his salesmen sometimes say: "My boss is a funny guy. He's usually tough as nails. But sometimes, for no good reason, he can be the friendliest guy in the world." Unknown to the salesmen, there *is* a good reason for this shift from aggression to peace-making. Over a period of time, these shifts may come to be perceived as manipulative and insincere. (With his *own* boss, the Q1 sales manager usually adopts a Q2 or Q3 mask.)

THE Q2 SALES MANAGER

Sometimes the Q2 sales manager discerns that his aloofness and neutrality create problems among his men, and that sterner measures are needed to get them back into line. If so, he may respond by putting on a Q1 mask, and pretending to be a decisive leader. This facade usually crumbles rapidly, and he withdraws into his shell once again. He lacks the confidence to act the role of leader for a long period.

THE Q3 SALES MANAGER

To many of his salesmen, the Q3 sales manager is a pushover, and they take advantage of him. Sensitive to any charges that he's "soft," he resents this exploitation, and may try to overcome it by donning a Q1 mask. He may, for a few days and at some discomfort to himself, play the part of autocrat, finally reverting to more congenial behavior. Not unexpectedly, those salesmen who exploited him before go back to exploiting him again.

THE Q4 SALES MANAGER

Like the Q4 salesman, the Q4 sales manager does not don a mask until he experiences frustration that exceeds his frustration-tolerance level, which is considerably higher than other sales managers'. So he is less likely to experience unmanageable frustration or pressure. Up to his frustration-tolerance level, his behavior is flexible and adaptive, but he does not wear masks. His *primary* strategy is one in which he *naturally* shifts his behavior to fit circumstances. Beyond his frustration-tolerance level, however, the Q4 sales manager may shift automatically to Q1 or Q2 secondary behavior; at these times, when he is functioning in a secondary quadrant, he is likely to don managerial masks. The mask he usually selects is a Q3, or a more intense Q2.

SUMMARY

The Q1 sales manager believes that nothing counts as much as getting the job done, and that salesmen are as a rule lazy, apathetic, and un-cooperative, so they must be controlled very rigidly if the job is going to get done. The Q2 sales manager's main concern is with getting by; he believes the important thing is to keep a low profile and look out for himself, making sure that he produces enough results to survive. The Q3 sales manager believes salesmen will work hard and effectively for a manager who goes out of his way to be friendly and supportive. The Q4 sales manager believes high sales production depends upon salesmen who understand how their own goals mesh with the company's goals, and who are therefore committed to the company's goals.

The Q1 sales manager is basically motivated by esteem and independence needs. By domineering and overcontrolling his men, he enhances both his esteem and independence. He is tough, hard-driving, autocratic, demanding, and often unreasonable. He is convinced that his salesmen's traits are widely different from his own, and that he dare not give them any real autonomy.

The Q2 sales manager is basically motivated by security needs. His main concern is to preserve what he already has. Because he fears that involvement with his salesmen might disrupt the status quo, he tries to keep it to a minimum. He provides little leadership, serving primarily as a transmitter of orders from above.

The Q3 sales manager is motivated basically by social, and to a lesser extent, security and esteem needs. Eager to be liked and accepted, he believes that by being pleasant to his salesmen he can stimulate them to work effectively. He is a compromiser who detests conflict of any kind, and who focuses most of his efforts on establishing a warm social climate.

The Q4 sales manager is motivated basically by self-realization and independence needs. He is a tough, goal-directed manager who combines assertiveness and ambition with concern for his salesmen. He practices team and participative management in which all his salesmen are genuinely involved in problem-solving, goal-setting, and decision-making in matters that affect their jobs. He and his men function as a team, not as freewheelers.

In team and participative management, the salesman's participation must be a matter of personal engagement, it must be linked to goals, and the goals must have personal meaning. The participative approach is valuable because, by establishing links between the salesman's goals and the company's goals, it generates commitment.

Each of the basic sales management strategies is modified somewhat by the strategy of the salesman with whom the sales manager interacts. In all such interactions, however, the Q1 sales manager is aware of power relationships, the Q2 sales manager is wary and cautious, the Q3 sales manager wants primarily to gain acceptance and is not especially concerned about power relationships, and the Q4 sales manager tries to foster growth in his men as well as himself.

When frustrated or under pressure, any sales manager may shift to an unplanned secondary strategy or consciously don a managerial mask.

TABLE 12. Sales Management Strategies

	Q1	Q2	Q3	Q4
Developing plans	Unwilling to involve others; plans alone, convinced he knows best; considers planning a basic managerial prerogative not to be shared with salesmen	Prefers to let top management make plans while he concentrates on transmitting them; sticks to nuts-and-bolts planning where risk is low	Finds planning tedious; prefers to work things out on a situation-to-situation basis in close personal interaction with others; believes plans are really unnecessary where there is goodwill	Rational, methodical planner; enlists help wherever it might be useful; tries to involve salesmen who should be involved; does both short and long-range planning to avoid "crisis management"
Setting goals	Makes no effort to involve others in goal setting; goals announced like edicts	Acts as pipeline for goals developed by top management; sets few goals of his own, beyond survival	Establishes goals everyone can reach without frustration; goals fail to stimulate; as a result, those salesmen who seek growth are often frustrated, although the goals were intended to prevent frustration	Strives for commitment to goals by involving salesmen; refuses to exercise power arbitrarily; uses goal-setting as key motivation
Recruitment and selection	Looks for salesmen he can control; wants men who will make him "look good" and also be manageable; smug about his ability to judge people; makes snap judgments; spurns outside help in selecting or relies heavily on "quickie" tests	Looks for salesmen who will not rock the boat, and who will do good enough job to insure his survival; ineffective interviewer with little insight into people; leans heavily on his boss's thinking in making selections	Ineffective recruiter; fails to differentiate between people; likes nearly everybody, rationalizes failures, and sometimes hires inept salesmen; suffers real anguish if he must later fire them	Seeks salesmen with capacity to grow and interact effectively; does thorough job of hiring; uses outside sources, avoids snap judgments, and is aware that good hiring is highly complex and demanding

TABLE 12 (Continued)

	Q1	Q2	Q3	Q4
Delegating	Seldom delegates real responsibility; draws sharp line between those who make decisions (managers) and those who implement them (salesmen); never shares power willingly; gives orders and expects them to be followed	Is frightened by the idea of vesting authority in someone else; usually delegates very little responsibility, although sometimes he delegates to give himself chance to blame someone if things go wrong	Frequently delegates, but with little system or logic; delegation is highly personal, based on belief that salesman will carry out his responsibility because of the warm bond between him and the boss	Practices real delegation; eager to assign responsibility as key way to get salesmen involved; retains ultimate responsibility but is able to entrust operational decision making without anxiety
Structuring	Insists salesmen adhere to company structure; infuriated by people who operate outside channels; considers this evidence of disloyalty, especially if someone goes over his head; however, frequently goes out of channels himself	Considers company structure a protective device; likes anything that establishes roles and eliminates ambiguity; sticks closely to organization chart and hopes his salesmen do the same	Less concerned about structure than about good human relationships; seldom gets worked up over protocol; encourages informal groupings and relaxed interaction between different levels of hierarchy	Respects company structure, and expects adherence to it, but not blindly; encourages critique of existing systems and suggestions for improvement; always ready to listen to better ideas, but expects present structure to be used meanwhile
Teamwork	Considers teamwork a crutch for the weak; teamwork requires dependability, and he regards his salesmen as undependable; very ineffective team worker	Sees no real value in teamwork; the less interaction he has with his salesmen the better he likes it; teamwork is seen as risky; prefers to operate as loner	Likes idea of teamwork, but fails to build effective team; poor coordinator who does not confront issues; his sales team lacks drive and system, although its meetings are affable	Sees himself and his salesmen as a team; no one on team is viewed as independent of others; collaboration in pursuit of common goals is stressed; synergism (concept that when people interact effectively, they accomplish more as a group than the total sum of their efforts as individuals) is emphasized

TABLE 12 (Continued)

	Q1	Q2	Q3	Q4
Policies and procedures	Takes dual point-of-view; insists salesmen adhere strictly to established policies and procedures; a strict disciplinarian; but readily breaks rules himself; violating policies gives him sense of independence	Sticks to the rules like a leech; well-defined guidelines make him feel secure; so rigid that he is sometimes inflexible; when things go wrong, he often alibis that he "was only following rules"	Readily accepts policies and procedures as an extension of his superiors' authority; considers an attack on the company's regulations as an attack on his superiors; however, he winks his eye at infractions, preferring to avoid conflict over them	Respects the need for firm policies and procedures, and follows them faithfully; but he is not uncritical; judges rules by their practical results, and fights hard to change them if needed
Budgeting	Uses budgets as tools in his bid for power; if superiors are budget-conscious, so is he; otherwise, spends large amounts on self-enhancing projects; watches his salesmen's spending carefully, and insists on frugality	Cautious, conservative budgeter; more concerned with staying within fiscal guidelines than in making bold effort to maximize profits; model of prudence and frugality	Somewhat careless; not a money-oriented man; sometimes impractical about money matters; devotes little thought to budgets; takes attitude that "life is too short to worry about things like money"	Creates high level of cost-consciousness, salesmen know how their actions affect the company financially; spending is purposeful; extravagance and stinginess avoided
Output	Attains high sales over short run, and average sales over long haul; in general his coercive tactics do stimulate his men to work hard; but he fails to produce selfless enthusiasm and commitment; and he sometimes generates resentment and sabotage	Gets only adequate sales; his cautiousness infects his men, who seldom stretch themselves; he fails to provide stimulus to go beyond the average; his belief that people cannot be motivated becomes self-fulfilling prophecy	Attains fair or mediocre sales, seldom excellent; does not generate high efficiency; his men lack a sense of urgency; atmosphere is too casual for really high output	Gets consistently high sales; his men are committed and willing to stretch themselves

TABLE 12 (Continued)

	Q1	Q2	Q3	Q4
Performance standards	Rigidly insists things be done his way; intolerant of other approaches; convinced salesman will "mess things up" unless they follow his lead; wants them to follow mechanical instructions, not to show initiative	Stickler for procedures; spells out standards in detail and gives written copies to everyone; seldom deviates from them; these standards are tangible signs of stability that help fill his need for security	Sets very permissive standards; when salesman fails to meet them, manager tries to alibi for him; sometimes incurs personal risk by covering for his man; insists "people are human, they do the best they can"	Sets standards that stress growth; standards provide room for different approaches to getting job done, as long as approach contributes to both the individual and the company; avoids rigid, constricting standards
Evaluating	Uses evaluations to keep his men in line; evaluation based on two questions: Did salesman do things my way? Does he work without backtalk? Carping and fault-finding, with low tolerance for mistakes, which he views as an affront to his authority	Superficially evaluates salesmen as "good workers" who do not rock the boat, and "troublemakers" who refuse to be submissive; thus his own security is the real standard by which he evaluates	Very tolerant; seldom confronts a salesman with his faults; glosses over mistakes; spends time extolling salesman's strengths; as a result, his men seldom get useful feedback; get distorted self-image instead	Evaluations are candid and balanced, stressing both strengths and weaknesses; compares performance to clearly stated goals; is never arbitrary; salesman is involved as full participant
Correcting	Very authoritarian; insists that salesmen start doing things right; unwilling to explore reasons for error; harsh, punitive, frequently unreasonable	Seldom corrects in a helpful way; ignores mistakes unless they disrupt usual routine; then he admonishes salesman by explaining that his (the manager's) boss wants the error corrected; tries to avoid personal involvement	Forbearing and indulgent; accentuates the positive, minimizes the negative; makes things seem better than they really are	Views correction as teaching not punishment; instructs instead of censures; helps salesman set realistic improvement goals; counsels regularly with him on his progress

TABLE 12 (Continued)

	Q1	Q2	Q3	Q4
Making decisions	Makes decisions alone, expects them to be followed without question; before deciding, he weighs impact of decision on his own fortunes; considers decision good if it will advance him; decision-making is highly political	Dislikes making decisions; adept at putting them off; prefers to avoid taking responsibility for consequences of decisions; procrastinates; when he must decide, plays it safe and chooses course with least risk	Strives for popular decisions that will not demoralize men; believes unpopular decision is always a bad decision; in deciding, he puts human considerations ahead of profit and output	Makes full use of salesmen when decision calls for it; he knows that people tend to resist decisions made by fiat; sees decision-making as inseparable from generating commitment
Motivating	Considers salesmen as motivated only by economic and security needs; tries to motivate by threats to security; believes men work in response to fear but rarely for other reasons; considers self one of few self-motivated people	Doesn't really believe in motivation; insists people are what they are, and that they cannot be much improved; claims he is powerless to stimulate change; this becomes a rationalization for inaction	Considers motivation natural result of cementing good relationships and making salesmen happy; insists that a friendly manager doesn't have to motivate his men because they're _naturally_ motivated	Considers motivation a natural outcome of participation and joint goal setting; sees his role as that of activating motivation through involvement, and then directing it toward achievement of salesmen's and company's goals
Conflict and disagreement	Suppresses conflict quickly, before it causes trouble; imposes own decisions on those who disagree; makes no effort to explore conflict; in many of his men, suppressed conflict continues to smolder, erupting from time to time	Apathetic climate usually discourages conflict; when disagreement does erupt, he ignores it in hope it will go away; either lets conflict fester, or, in uncharacteristic burst of initiative, tries to squelch it	Deplores conflict; tries hard to smooth it over; instead of probing reasons, he appeases the disagreeing parties; seldom if ever resolves problems; frequently compromises without getting to root of disagreement	Welcomes conflict, as long as it relates to job; considers it a catalyst of new ideas; brings disagreement into open where it can be explored and resolved; dislikes constant serenity, fearing that it will lead to complacency or apathy

TABLE 12 (Continued)

	Q1	Q2	Q3	Q4
Communication	One-way communication; ideas flow toward salesman but not in other direction; not really interested in what salesmen think; spends much time letting them know what he wants; poor listener; prefers monologues to dialogues	No-way communication; little flow of ideas in either direction; communicates ideas from above, but very little of his own thinking	Partial communication, in which all negatives are screened out or distorted; communicates only what will make his men happy	Two-way communication; leads to real dialogue with salesmen; seeks full information and genuine understanding; good listener and talker; insists on candor from both himself and men
Creativity and innovation	Discourages creativity as disruptive force; sees innovation as threat to his prerogatives; sometimes appropriates salesman's new ideas as his own; may unwittingly stimulate anti-organizational creativity; but in general squelches creativity	Stifles new ideas; fresh thinking disrupts the status quo, and is not welcome; innovative people become discouraged in this climate; manager tries to avoid anything that betokens change	Open to new ideas, which he listens to avidly; yet seldom acts upon them; likes to encourage everybody, but fails to discriminate between ideas; underneath, he really fears innovation because it might disrupt placid status quo	Highly values new ideas because they lead to growth; sees creativity as byproduct of teamwork; considers it his job to stimulate and nurture new ideas; places high premium on dissent
Commitment	Generates low commitment, frequently mingled with high resentment; does not help his men align their needs with the company's, except in a negative sense; his men do their jobs because they feel compelled but not committed	Generates little commitment, since he seldom involves salesmen in meaningful decisions or problems; he doesn't really want commitment; he wants a docile work force that will help him stay out of trouble	Generates high morale but low commitment; his salesmen do enough not to let him down, but rarely put forth intense effort; his failure to encourage meaningful involvement keeps commitment low	Attains high commitment, largely through participative management; does not consider participation a panacea, but knows that it achieves far more than coercion or affability

17

Coaching and Counseling Salesmen

THE KEY TO GREATER SALES

One of the first-line sales manager's most critical jobs, perhaps the most critical, is the development of his salesmen. This is often called coaching and counseling. Coaching and counseling can be defined as sales manager–salesman communication leading to maximum results for the company and maximum development for the salesman. Coaching and counseling are the means by which the sales manager motivates his salesmen to produce better results and helps them develop. To do the most effective coaching and counseling, the sales manager must have a thorough understanding of motivation and salesmen's needs, and a thorough mastery of communication skills. These have been discussed in detail in earlier chapters.

In this chapter, we examine the four basic types of coaching and counseling. We look first at the assumptions each sales manager makes about coaching and counseling, his objectives in coaching and counseling, and the general skills he uses in the coaching and counseling interview. (More specific skills, especially in communication, are described in earlier chapters.)

300

ASSUMPTIONS, OBJECTIVES, AND SKILLS

Q1 SALES MANAGER'S ASSUMPTIONS

"Salesmen are lazy. They will improve their selling skills only if they're pushed and threatened. I can make them sell better by threatening their security needs. In coaching and counseling, I appeal to, or threaten, my salesmen's economic self-interest, so that they become motivated either through greed or fear. I tell the salesman where and how he needs to improve, and make sure he is sufficiently fearful and apprehensive to follow through."

Q1 SALES MANAGER'S OBJECTIVES

"I have two objectives in the coaching and counseling interview: (1) to tell the salesman what he's doing right and wrong, with emphasis on the wrong, and (2) to put him on notice that he'd better improve or suffer the consequences. I use the interview as an instrument of *control*."

Q1 SALES MANAGER'S SKILLS

"The most important skills in the interview are dominance and strength. I dominate the session from start to finish, keeping the salesman passive and submissive. I communicate *strength* both by word and manner; I let the salesman know that I have the power to make things easy or difficult for him, depending upon whether or not he takes my warnings seriously. Finally, I make it clear that I will follow up on my threats, if necessary."

Q2 SALES MANAGER'S ASSUMPTIONS

"Salesmen learn only if they want to and if they're ready to. I can do little or nothing to help my salesmen improve. If salesmen learn at all, they do so on their own. As a training device, coaching and counseling are useless, although they're sometimes useful for chastising salesmen when things go wrong. As long as my men meet minimal expectations, I don't bother with these interviews at all unless top management wants me to."

Q2 SALES MANAGER'S OBJECTIVES

"At best, I have two objectives in the interview: (1) to censure my salesmen when they mess things up so badly that *I* might get into trouble, and (2) to insure my survival. I let my salesmen know I'm aware of the problems they've created so that, hopefully, they don't create any more."

Q2 SALES MANAGER'S SKILLS

"To coach and counsel effectively, a sales manager must keep his distance from his salesman and be good at blaming him for things that go wrong. If I can fix blame and make a fuss when things get messed up, my men may be more careful in the future."

Q3 SALES MANAGER'S ASSUMPTIONS

"Salesmen need plenty of praise and encouragement from someone they like. This helps them do a better job. Coaching and counseling enable me to bolster their morale and prove that I'm a sympathetic, likable person. That's all it takes to get them to improve."

Q3 SALES MANAGER'S OBJECTIVES

"I try to focus on the salesman's strengths, in order to achieve two objectives: (1) to keep him happy, and (2) to motivate him to do even better in the future. There's no point in stressing problems or negatives; this only demoralizes salesmen. If mistakes have been made, the best thing is to overlook them and hope for better luck next time."

Q3 SALES MANAGER'S SKILLS

"For effective coaching and counseling, a sales manager needs a boundless supply of optimism and goodwill, ability to smooth out problems, sociability, and plenty of warmth and acceptance. By giving of *myself* in the interview, I will be amply rewarded by my subordinates."

Q4 SALES MANAGER'S ASSUMPTIONS

"Salesmen enjoy their work and are motivated to grow when they take an active part in identifying personal improvement areas and setting improvement goals. In coaching and counseling, I can stimulate my salesmen's development by giving them the opportunity to set personal improvement objectives based upon their own needs aligned with the company's goals."

Q4 SALES MANAGER'S OBJECTIVES

"I have five interview objectives: (1) to make my salesmen aware of their strengths, so their effective behavior is reinforced, (2) to help them understand what improvement they need and how they can bring it about, (3) to help them see the relationship between their own needs, the improvement areas, and the company's needs, (4) to demonstrate that their needs and the company's can be satisfied by improved performance, and (5) to help them set priorities and develop a plan of action for achieving their improvement goals."

Q4 SALES MANAGER'S SKILLS

"The skills I find most useful in the interview are communication, problem-solving, decision-making, and goal-setting skills. I try to make the interview a genuine dialogue."

In effect, the Q4 is the only sales manager who does meaningful coaching or counseling. The Q1 *bribes* and *preaches,* using appeals to economic self-interest and fear; the Q2 *undermanages* and *overreacts,* since he does little or nothing until trouble occurs, and then responds with tirades and tantrums; the Q3 *soothes* and *cheers on,* hoping to make the salesman feel good and to increase his own popularity. But all three sales managers call their activities coaching and counseling, so we'll do the same. In this chapter we describe how each of them, as well as the Q4, coaches and counsels.

We will consider eight phases of the coaching and counseling interview: (1) initial interaction, (2) communication, (3) direction, (4) climate, (5) handling of disagreements and emotions, (6) final resolution, (7) goal setting, and (8) outcome. To make the contrasts between each manager clear, we discuss each phase as it's handled by each sales manager before we move on to the next.

INITIAL INTERACTION

Many impressions are formed right at the beginning of any interview. Since the salesman is likely to feel some apprehension at the start, he is usually especially alert to early clues about his sales manager's mood and intention. He evaluates the situation and adjusts his own behavior to fit it. A gruff, unfriendly greeting by the manager may make the salesman even more apprehensive; a warm, encouraging greeting may relax him. What happens *initially,* during the first few minutes of the interview, sets the tone and strongly influences everything that follows.

Q1 SALES MANAGER'S INITIAL INTERACTION

The Q1 sales manager tries to seize total control of the interview right away. He makes it plain, by words or implication, that he knows more about the salesman's strengths and weaknesses than the salesman does, and that the latter should therefore listen carefully. He emphasizes faults, weaknesses, and mistakes; the salesman is on the defensive from the beginning. The sales manager, like a colonial schoolmaster telling a young boy that he's about to administer a whipping for the boy's own good, makes it clear that he knows what's best for the salesman, and that if the salesman is smart he'll do as he's told for his own good. The Q1 does not try to find out what the salesman feels or thinks. The only questions he asks are about the salesman's shortcomings on the job. The climate is "third-degree," and the salesman quickly gets the idea that, unless his work improves, he's in trouble.

Q2 SALES MANAGER'S INITIAL INTERACTION

The typical Q2 sales manager sees little reason to coach or counsel unless a salesman does something seriously wrong, in which case he censures him in a half-desperate attempt to prevent a repetition of the mistake. But, in many companies managers are required to coach and counsel periodically, whether anything is seriously wrong or not. The Q2 handles these enforced interviews mechanically, going through the motions but little else. He opens the interview aimlessly, showing little interest and some aversion to the entire procedure. He seems unsure of himself; his voice carries little authority or conviction. He conducts the interview because he must, not because he sees value in it. The salesman usually responds apathetically, since he realizes that the interview obviously has no significance. Or he may seize control of the interview and try to use it for his own purposes.

Q3 SALES MANAGER'S INITIAL INTERACTION

Q3 coaching and counseling begins like a social visit. The sales manager starts with small talk, making almost no mention of performance except, perhaps, for a generalization like "Great job you're doing, Joe." But he never clearly states that the job Joe is doing is the *subject* of the interview. The interview seems to have no subject at all. The opening is so relaxed and unfocused that the salesman has no clear idea what's going to happen next. Eager to seem friendly and encouraging, the Q3 lets the salesman inject almost any topic into the interview. The whole approach is loose and unstructured.

Q4 SALES MANAGER'S INITIAL INTERACTION

In a Q4 opening, the salesman is told what the interview is about and what he can expect to get out of it. He clearly understands that the interview will be a joint venture in which he is expected to participate. The Q4 sales manager makes it plain he has not prejudged the salesman; he does have definite ideas about the latter's performance, but they are subject to discussion and change. The manager avoids making judgments; he prefers to catalyze learning. His role is nòt, as he sees it, to condemn, but to help grow. Sensitive to the salesman's feelings and ideas but also businesslike, his warmth is not smothering like the Q3's. He is objective, candid, openminded, and eager to *help*. Instead of beginning with a stern lecture, he begins with a thorough discussion of both weaknesses and strengths. He conveys *respect* for the salesman, who is treated as a man the manager can learn from as well as teach.

To summarize: In their *initial interaction,* the Q1 is domineering and accusatory, the Q2 apathetic and purposeless (except when he has reason to "chew out" the salesman), the Q3 ingratiating and meandering, and the Q4 result-oriented and helpful.

COMMUNICATION

Now let's explore how each sales manager communicates in the coaching and counseling interview. Our standard is two-way interactional communication throughout the interview. As we will see, a two-way interchange of ideas based upon listening and probing as well as verbal skills, is relatively rare.

Q1 SALES MANAGER'S COMMUNICATION

Q1 coaching and counseling is a one-man show. It may be a lecture or a sermon; invariably, the sales manager does most of the talking, and the salesman presumably listens (although he may tune out the manager and think his own thoughts instead). The manager may adopt any of several roles—all-knowing expert, all-powerful father, harsh judge—but whichever he assumes, he makes it plain that he knows considerably more than the salesman.

He often treats the salesman as an erring child or conscienceless criminal, not as someone on his own level of understanding. The Q1 sales manager listens very little, and then impatiently. He bunches his ideas and tosses them like hand grenades, one after the other, at the salesman. If the latter tries to defend himself, the manager argues rather than probes. Virtually the only probes he uses are closed-end probes and leading questions; he wants answers that will confirm his own conclusions, rather than clarify or provide new information. If the salesman brings up a grievance or a problem, the subject is quickly suppressed or denied. Throughout, the manager is harshly candid about those topics he wants to be candid about; he is evasive when it suits his purposes. The salesman is treated like a defendant in a topsy-turvy court, where he is presumed guilty until proven innocent, but where, because of the procedures, innocence is impossible to prove.

Q2 SALES MANAGER'S COMMUNICATION

Very little meaningful information is exchanged in an interview with a Q2 sales manager. The Q2 deals with symptoms and superficialities; he does not want to discover the reasons for the salesman's behavior. Probing might create problems for the sales manager, who wants to get through the prescribed chore as easily as possible. Probing may unearth issues that are better left buried, so he confines himself to inconsequential questions. Like his talking, his listening is mechanical. If he hears something that may arouse tension, he ignores it or minimizes it. Like a general with a whole arsenal of weapons that he refuses to use, the Q2 sales manager ignores virtually the entire battery of communication techniques. And, like the general, he wins nothing from the experience. Because so little significant communication takes place, the interview is dull, boring, and viewed as a waste of time by both men.

Q3 SALES MANAGER'S COMMUNICATION

The notable thing about Q3 coaching and counseling is that the sales manager uses a fairly complete variety of communication techniques, but for very narrow purposes. When he probes, he probes in pleasant, nonthreatening areas; when he listens, he listens for happy or at least harmless ideas. As the old song put it, he accentuates the positive and eliminates the negative. His seemingly aimless wandering from topic to topic has a definite aim: to impress his salesman as a likable person and to avoid unpleasantness. The idea of using the interview to confront problems head-on is completely unacceptable to him. In fact, it is virtually meaningless, since he hardly recognizes the existence of any problems. If he does, he is convinced that, like a hurtful cut, the problems will disappear if he only applies enough salve. And that is what Q3 communication is: verbal salve, an ointment designed to soothe aches and make them go away.

Q4 SALES MANAGER'S COMMUNICATION

In coaching and counseling, the Q4 moves logically from point to point instead of wandering haphazardly from topic to topic. His initial assumptions are treated as such, not as data carved in stone; they are tested and, if necessary, replaced. The salesman is encouraged to talk by the sales manager's obvious willingness to listen interestedly, and by probes. The Q4 manager makes his most significant points when receptivity is high. Instead of hurling his ideas like missiles designed to wipe out opposition, he spaces them and gets reactions before proceeding. He faces issues squarely, no matter how unpleasant or difficult. He is candid, and encourages his salesmen to be candid. His communication is balanced, focusing on strengths and weaknesses, pluses and minuses. He wants his salesman to finish the interview with greater self-awareness than he had at the start. In a phrase, the Q4 is distinguished from other sales managers because he wants to know what his *salesman* thinks. Other managers prefer not to know; real insight into their men's thoughts might prove burdensome or unsettling. But the Q4 *wants* to know, and he works hard to find out by *involving* his salesmen. The whole process is a joint process, in which the salesman uncovers ideas for himself and draws his own valid conclusions about what improvements are needed. The manager guides the learning process, but he never forces this thinking upon the salesman.

The Q4 realizes that few salesmen grow as long as the boss tells them what to do; significant growth comes through self-discovery. The Q4 considers himself a stimulator of self-discovery. The Q1 sales manager, who squelches discovery by imposing his own ideas, stimulates dependence, not growth; like a botanist cultivating dwarf trees, he inhibits development. Both the Q2 and Q3 sales managers fail to develop a climate for self-discovery by salesmen, since this requires probing into areas that may produce disagreement, tension, or argument. There are never any guarantees, as the Q4 sales manager well knows, that self-discovery will be placid, smooth, or easy.

DIRECTION OF INTERVIEW

The sales manager should guide the coaching and counseling interview toward a specific goal. We call this the *direction*. Direction should characterize the interview from start to finish. Some interviews, however, drift like rudderless boats. Let's see why.

Q1 SALES MANAGER'S DIRECTION

The Q1 sales manager knows where he's going: toward greater personal power. His goal is to produce capable but subservient salesmen whom he can use to further his personal goals. If a salesman is unwilling to be used, he must be coerced. So the Q1 directs the interview rigidly. He does a good job of direction; unless pitted against an unusually agile Q4 salesman, he moves toward his goal surely and swiftly. A managerial bull-dozer, he sweeps aside or knocks down anything in his way as he moves down his self-appointed path.

Q2 SALES MANAGER'S DIRECTION

The Q2 sales manager has no clear goal. He knows what he wants to avoid, but not what he wants to achieve. He makes a number of irrelevant or inconsequential points, and usually ends on an ambiguous note. The interview has no point or direction, except when the salesman, seeing an opportunity, seizes control and gives it a direction of his own choosing.

Q3 SALES MANAGER'S DIRECTION

If a goal is something in the future, then the Q3 sales manager has no interview goal. He simply wants to *maintain* what he has: goodwill and acceptance. As we use the term, a goal is something *different* from what the manager now has. It requires dynamic, striving management; the Q3 specializes in static, soothing management. The Q3's coaching and coun-seling is directionless; instead of moving *toward* a goal, he moves *around* the existing situation, seeking more of the same, not something different.

Q4 SALES MANAGER'S DIRECTION

The Q4 sales manager uses the interview to develop a salesman who wants to become a better salesman. He moves forward as decisively as the Q1. But the Q4's job is tougher, since he wants his salesman to collaborate in moving *with* him. The Q1 drags his salesman, who may resist, until both reach the goal. The Q4's method requires greater skill. He brings the salesman to the goal *without* coercion or manipulation. And he shares responsibility for setting direction with the salesman. That he succeeds is testimony to his communications ability.

On the surface, the Q1's direction may appear firmer than the Q4's. The Q1 moves relentlessly toward his objective; the Q4, because he wants to involve his salesman, may sometimes seem sidetracked and delayed. To the uncritical observer, his use of probes and willingness to listen may seem like hesitation and indecision. They are, however, the only ways to attain significant and lasting understanding and commitment.

CLIMATE

Climate is the general mood or temper of the entire interview. The differences in climate generated by the different sales managers are as broad as the differences in climate between the polar zones, the temperate zones, and the tropics.

Q1 SALES MANAGER'S CLIMATE

The Q1 climate is tense, antagonistic, and distrustful. There is sometimes an electric, almost crackling, quality in the air, as if a storm is about to erupt. If it does, voices rise and strong emotions are vented. Or the climate may be heavy with apprehension as the salesman tenses himself for a tongue-lashing or a dose of sarcasm. Sometimes, the salesman shows no outward sign of resentment, and the climate becomes almost painfully oppressive. At its best, the climate is decidedly uncomfortable, with the salesman squirming as the manager recites his faults, weaknesses, and shortcomings.

Q2 SALES MANAGER'S CLIMATE

The Q2 climate is lifeless, awkward, and somewhat uncomfortable. The interview is so purposeless, so low-keyed, that the salesman wonders why his time is being wasted. He may become fidgety or bored. The interaction lacks zest or spontaneity.

Q3 SALES MANAGER'S CLIMATE

The Q3 sales manager's warmth stimulates either acceptance or exasperation. In a Q3 sales manager's interview with a Q3 salesman, the climate is unbusinesslike, overly relaxed, unhurried, and pleasant. In interviews between a Q3 sales manager and a Q1, Q2, or Q4 salesman, the climate is a bit strained, although the manager is often not aware of it. Q1 and Q4 salesmen especially may become impatient with the manager's meandering and indecisiveness; the Q2 salesman may become peeved by his insistence on sociability. The climate varies from easygoing fellowship to pique to outright tension.

Q4 SALES MANAGER'S CLIMATE

The Q4 sales manager generates a trustful, analytic, candid, and challenging climate. The salesman talks openly because he has no fear that whatever he says may be used against him. While feelings are forthrightly expressed, the atmosphere is not strained. Problems are discussed in situational and interactional terms, not as personal failings or character flaws; personal weaknesses are discussed without blame. Mistakes are considered opportunities for learning, not for punishment. Strengths are discussed as openly as weaknesses. The critique is grounded in respect. The Q4 sales manager emphasizes growth, not fear.

HANDLING OF DISAGREEMENT AND EMOTIONS

Unless a salesman is intimidated or unusually self-effacing, a certain amount of disagreement is inevitable from time to time in the coaching and counseling interview. After all, the subject being discussed is the salesman's performance, a subject about which many salesmen are sensitive or defensive. While the interview should focus on strengths as well as problems, there are often some matters about which the sales manager and the salesman are bound to disagree. Facing up to disagreement is neither easy nor pleasant for many people, so the interview may fail to come to grips with major issues. Each sales manager, as we shall see, handles disagreement and emotions differently.

Q1 SALES MANAGER'S HANDLING OF DISAGREEMENT

The Q1 sales manager tries to suppress disagreement with pat answers that brook no argument. The salesman must be "convinced" he is wrong. The Q1 manager fears that willingness to discuss a disputed point will seem like weakness on his part. Emotion is also choked off; the salesman is told that fear or anger is foolish and counterproductive, and must be squelched. Or he is warned that his disagreement is dangerously close to insubordination, and that insubordination cannot be tolerated. This does not always work, however. Some salesmen respond with increased fear or anger; if the manager cannot handle these responses, he may cut off the interview. The Q1 manager's unwillingness to see emotions displayed never applies to himself; he often indulges in bursts of temper. In a sense, it is inaccurate to say that he *handles* disagreement and emotion; actually, he tries to wipe them out. But, like insects fleeing an exterminator, disagreement and emotion often disappear underground to continue a hidden existence. Underground emotions are often the most dangerous; they fester and grow, and sometimes cause real trouble.

Q2 SALES MANAGER'S HANDLING OF DISAGREEMENT

The Q2 sales manager operates on the reassuring but dangerous premise that if he ignores the unpleasant or puts it off, it will go away. He refuses to face up to disagreement and emotion. He tells himself that disagreement and anger are sources of tension and problems that he is better off not acknowledging or that they are signs of stubbornness that do not merit his time or attention. Thus he feels free to ignore such unpleasantness, and he does.

Q3 SALES MANAGER'S HANDLING OF DISAGREEMENT

The Q3 handles disagreement casually, by appeasing it, or by compromise. If a salesman voices disagreement, the Q3 urges him to look at the bright side, and then talks glowingly about that "bright side" until the dark side seems to fade. Or, if he cannot perform this feat, he may "fail" to hear the grievance, or treat it so casually it begins to seem unimportant. He tries to soothe the troubled salesman with syrupy words, cliches, extravagant promises, anything that will pacify him.

Watching a classic Q3 sales manager in action is like watching an anxious mother tell a child in pain, "There, there, it doesn't really hurt." Sometimes, when verbal pampering fails to work, the Q3 strikes a bargain with the salesman. A strong believer in "splitting things down the middle," he is quick to make concessions so that everybody comes out happy. Usually, these concessions do not solve the problem, but they do bury it for a while. They may convert disagreement into agreement, but seldom into commitment. And where there is no commitment there is rarely any excellence.

Q4 SALES MANAGER'S HANDLING OF DISAGREEMENT

The Q4 treats disagreement and emotion openly and seriously. He knows they are real and urgent to the salesman. They must therefore be faced up to, probed, and understood. He does not feel threatened by disagreement. He considers it instructive; it tells him things he should know but may not; it is vital to growth. He tries to resolve it by marshalling facts and exploring alternatives, not by quashing it. He seeks root causes, not superficial symptoms. Nor does he treat emotions lightly. Instead of implying that they are shameful or unsuitable, he accepts them as clues to his salesman's thinking. He probes emotions thoroughly, allows them to vent, and responds to them at a level that has meaning for both him and the salesman. He uses open-end probes that encourage the salesman to express himself fully.

The Q4 sales manager is *unafraid* of disagreement and emotion. Other managers, including the Q1, fear disagreement and emotion as either threatening, unpleasant, or unimportant. They want to make the problem go away; the Q4 wants to *resolve* it.

FINAL RESOLUTION

Resolution is the discovery of an answer to a problem. It is relatively rare in coaching and counseling interviews. The purpose of these interviews is supposed to be to find ways to motivate salesmen to pursue excellence: surprisingly few sales managers do this. What they call resolution is often a burial of a problem rather than an answer. Because the problem is buried before it is dead, it often, to the manager's dismay, comes back to haunt him.

Q1 SALES MANAGER'S FINAL RESOLUTION

The Q1 sales manager forces acceptance of *his* answer. The acceptance is often halfhearted and resentful. The salesman rightly feels that he has been exploited. In retribution, he may sabotage the solution by working against it or by inaction. At the very least, he probably has serious reservations about the manager's answer. Even if the final answer is brilliant in every way, it is still not *his* answer, he has not played any part in shaping it, and he does not see how it relates to *his* needs, if it does. Coupled with resentment is lack of commitment; the salesman has been *told* what he is doing wrong, but he is not necessarily committed to the idea. He may instead believe that the boss is wrong, that the evaluation has been unfair, or that no consideration has been given to extenuating circumstances. Commitment cannot be imposed on salesmen.

Q2 SALES MANAGER'S FINAL RESOLUTION

The Q2 sales manager, having no good reason to conduct the interview in the first place, ends it on a vague note. The salesman frequently walks away with no clear notion why the meeting was held; even worse, he may feel it was a waste of time. In all likelihood, needed decisions were deferred, and the salesman gained little insight into himself. To someone who wants to know how he's doing in his job, this is frustrating and unsatisfying.

Q3 SALES MANAGER'S FINAL RESOLUTION

The Q3 sales manager, like a writer of children's stories, is master of the happy ending. In resolving the interview, he avoids disagreeable solutions and compromises problems. Neither manager nor salesman has any apparent reason to feel disgruntled at the results. From the manager's point of view, the interview is a complete success because it bolsters his popularity. But the salesman is likely to be hurt because he gets a distorted view of himself; he may leave the session feeling good but, unknowingly, hindered in his development.

Q4 SALES MANAGER'S FINAL RESOLUTION

The Q4 sales manager makes sure he and the salesman jointly discover the best way for the salesman to improve his performance. At the same time, through candid interplay, the manager learns something about himself and his own performance. The interview leads to *mutual* development. The resolution is joint, not imposed by the stronger upon the weaker. The manager makes sure both he and his salesman understand the solution. He often does this by asking the salesman to summarize his understanding. Agreement is reached on *action* to be completed by the next interview. The salesman gets a clear idea of where he is now, where he is supposed to be by the next coaching and counseling session, and how he is going to achieve his objectives. The resolution is specific, practical, and agreed upon.

This does not mean that the two men necessarily agree on everything. The sales manager seeks as much agreement as possible without coercion. but he does not try to eliminate all dissent. He realizes that men can disagree on certain points and still work together effectively if they respect one another and agree on basic goals. In the end, of course, if the remaining areas of disagreement cannot be reconciled, the manager's approach must and does prevail. But he tries to shrink the areas of disagreement to the smallest possible size before making his views prevail. Imposing his ideas by his superior strength is a last resort. But even when the Q4 sales manager does impose his resolution, the salesman is likely to feel committed to the manager's solution even though he does not agree with it, because he, the salesman, has been listened to and understood.

GOAL SETTING AND PLAN OF ACTION

To improve, salesmen need more than awareness of their strengths and shortcomings. They need clearly defined goals, priorities, and a plan for reaching them, otherwise coaching and counseling are somewhat futile. Let's see what each sales manager does about setting his salesmen on the track leading out of the woods.

Q1 SALES MANAGER'S GOAL SETTING

The Q1 sets arbitrary goals and makes it plain he expects them to be met. He is likely to consider all the goals top-priority, thus putting them beyond the salesman's ability to achieve. He may set out a plan of action which merely describes the way *he* would do the job if he were in the salesman's place; he sees his own experience as the only valid experience. Because the salesman has not been intimately involved in the interview, he probably has no clear idea why or how the goals were set or the plan was established. Some Q1 sales managers don't bother with plans of action at all; they merely tell the salesman, in effect, "Here's what I want done; you figure out how to do it." The unstated reward for figuring out how to do it is survival on the job. Q1 goals are always those that fill the manager's needs, not necessarily the salesman's.

Q2 SALES MANAGER'S GOAL SETTING

The Q2 establishes goals so vague they are meaningless: "Get out there and do a good job," "Let's show some improvement," "I expect to see some improvement." These statements are worthless. What constitutes a "good job?" What precisely is "some improvement?" In what areas is improvement expected? How can it be achieved? These are the hard but vital questions the Q2 avoids. Because the goals are so vague, it is impossible to assign priorities to them. It is probably too much to say that the Q2 manager develops any plan of action at all. He rarely leaves the salesman with any precise, step-by-step design for getting to the vague goals. The whole interview is without direction and therefore futile.

Q3 SALES MANAGER'S GOAL SETTING

The Q3 either sets vague goals to encourage the salesman ("Keep up the good work") or goals that present no challenge, and therefore no discomfort. He sets easy goals that guarantee no frustration or disappointment. Priorities are vague or nonexistent. Usually, the goals require no new incentives, and no thoroughly worked-out plan of action. (How can anyone develop a plan of action to "Keep up the good work"?) Typically, a salesman leaves a Q3 interview no smarter than he went in. Having no specific plan of action to follow, he is unlikely to get much benefit out of the interview, beyond the pleasant feeling that "the boss is on my side."

Q4 SALES MANAGER'S GOAL SETTING

The Q4 and the salesman jointly set specific goals and realistic priorities ("We agree, then, that you'll shoot for an 8% increase in the next quarter"), outline specific steps for achieving them ("Make 3 to 5 additional calls each week, concentrate on industrial accounts, stop wasting time on nonindustrial users," and so on), assign specific responsibility for achieving the goals ("I'll visit your territory the last week in June for two days of training in the field"), and establish a performance schedule ("Let's take another look at the situation on June 12, and again on July 14"). Although the goals make the salesman stretch, they are practical, achievable, and whenever possible, they are measurable. Definiteness is the rule.

Q4 goals are also challenging; they make the salesman reach out; they require exertion. They are neither overambitious nor discouragingly high, but they do go beyond what the salesman can easily achieve. The Q4 sales manager wants his men to strive, to stretch, even to strain, because otherwise they cannot grow or improve.

REVIEW OF GOALS AND PLAN OF ACTION

Goals and priorities may need to be modified or even completely changed from time to time. If they are, a new plan of action must be developed. Or goals may be retained but the plan of action may need to be revised anyway in the light of experience. The coaching and counseling job is therefore never really finished; it must *continue* with periodic reviews of both goals and plans of action. A review should be a deliberate, painstaking examination of what's happened since the last interview. It should try to answer questions like: Is our goal realistic? Too high? Too low? Is our plan of action working? If not, why? What changes, if any, should we make in our plan of action to make it more effective?

Q1 SALES MANAGER'S REVIEW

The Q1 sales manager does little systematic reviewing. Instead, he uses the review to reassert his authority, to remind the salesman that "I'm still the boss," and to bawl him out or needle him about any recent drawbacks. At the end of the review, little or nothing has changed, although the salesman's fear or resentment has probably been reinforced by new threats. As far as the Q1 sales manager is concerned, the major purpose of the review is to let the salesman know (as if he could ever forget!) that "Big Brother" is watching him.

Q2 SALES MANAGER'S REVIEW

The Q2 sales manager conducts no review unless his superiors insist upon it. If they do, he makes the review short and pointless with statements like "Well, everything seems to be okay, so there's no point in our wasting any time sitting here." Only if the salesman recently has committed a really dangerous blunder will the Q2 manager do anything significant in the review; if he feels threatened, he may use the review as an opportunity to impress the salesman with how disturbed "management" is by his behavior.

Q3 SALES MANAGER'S REVIEW

The Q3 sales manager thinks of the review as a "get-together." In fact, he is likely to conduct the review in a social setting (at lunch, over an after-hours drink). The review, if it can be called that, may begin with a question like "How's it going?" If the salesman answers "Fine," the manager is likely to say "Great, glad to hear it," and move on to other topics. If the answer is "Not so good," he is likely to respond with something like, "Cheer up, things always get better." It is very unusual for a Q3 review to develop into anything more than an amiable exchange of insignificant remarks.

Q4 SALES MANAGER'S REVIEW

A Q4 review is factual and analytic. It focuses on *specifics*. "You were supposed to be at 40% of quota this week, but you're only at 29%. What are the problems? What's wrong with the quota? Or is it the plan of action that isn't working? How are you going about implementing the plan of action?" He then probes for more specific facts. The Q4 sales manager is not satisfied with vague answers. He wants to pinpoint the problem so it can be resolved. To do this, he may refer to call reports or other records, he analyzes carefully, and he takes his time. This is *not* a slapdash process. (If there are no problems, and if the salesman is progressing on schedule, the Q4 review will, of course, be much shorter.)

OUTCOME

Good coaching and counseling should do six things: (*1*) help the salesman understand what is expected of him; (*2*) keep him informed about how he's doing; (*3*) give him understanding of his strengths and weaknesses;

(4) help him set goals and develop plans to achieve them; (5) provide opportunities for systematic reviews of his progress toward his goals; and (6) result in growth and development. It is obvious by now that only the Q4 sales manager does all these things.

Only the Q4 achieves the *understanding* without which maximum growth is extremely difficult, perhaps impossible. Other sales managers achieve mainly *moods*: frustration, resentment, anger, fear, futility, encouragement, complacency, and so forth. But, on the level of understanding and comprehension, they achieve only confusion, doubt, and uncertainty. Q1, Q2, and Q3 counseling largely inhibit growth. Only the Q4 *develops* and *teaches* in any significant sense.

SUMMARY

Coaching and counseling is communication between a salesman and a sales manager leading to maximum results for the company and maximum development for the salesman. The Q1 sales manager believes salesmen will improve only if their security and economic self-interest are threatened; he bases his coaching and counseling on intimidation. The Q2 sales manager doesn't believe he can do anything to help his men improve, so he simply goes through the motions of coaching and counseling (except when he uses the interview to bring one of his men back into line). The Q3 sales manager believes improvement naturally occurs in a warm, supportive environment, so he uses the interview to boost morale and to lend plenty of encouragement. The Q4 sales manager believes men are motivated to grow when they take part in identifying personal improvement areas, setting improvement goals, assigning priorities, and developing a plan of action. He makes the coaching and counseling interview a joint venture in personal discovery.

Because they begin with different assumptions, each sales manager conducts the coaching and counseling interview differently, and each obtains different results. Only the Q4 interview, based on give-and-take and dialogue, usually leads to maximum personal and company growth.

TABLE 13. Coaching and Counseling

	Q1 Sales Manager	Q2 Sales Manager	Q3 Sales Manager	Q4 Sales Manager
Assumptions	Salesmen are lazy; they'll improve only if punished or threatened; threaten their economic security to activate their greed or fear	Salesmen learn only if they want to and if they're ready to learn; I can do little to help them improve; coaching and counseling is really useless as a training device	Salesmen need encouragement from someone they like; I use coaching and counseling to bolster their morale and prove I'm a likeable guy; that's all it takes to get them to improve	Salesmen are motivated to grow when they take part in identifying improvement areas and setting improvement goals based on their own needs and the company's goals
Objectives	Tell the salesman what he's doing right and wrong, but emphasize the wrong Let him know he had better improve or suffer the consequences	Censure the salesman when he messes things up so badly that <u>my</u> security is threatened Insure my survival	Focus on the salesman's strengths to keep him happy and motivate him to do even better in the future	Make the salesman aware of his strengths Help him understand what improvement is needed Demonstrate that his needs can be satisfied by improved performance Help him set priorities and develop plan of action for attaining goals
Skills	Dominance and strength are the most important skills; I let the salesman know I'm strong enough to follow up on my threats	Keep your distance from the salesman; be good at fixing blame when things go wrong	Optimism and goodwill count the most; the manager must be warm, accepting, sociable	Communications skills, problem solving and decision making skills, and goal setting skills count most

318

18

Company Marketing Strategies

PUTTING IT ALL TOGETHER

In this chapter, we describe how company marketing strategies can be categorized by use of the Dimensional model, so that we can speak of four basic company marketing strategies. However, since some people find it difficult to think of company marketing strategies in terms like dominance-submission and hostility-warmth, we have renamed the dimensions.

High Concern for Promotion

Quadrant 1	Quadrant 4
Promotional Strategy	Dynamic Strategy

Low Concern for Product ——————————————— High Concern for Product

Quadrant 2	Quadrant 3
Sit-back Strategy	Product-quality Strategy

Low Concern for Promotion

In the above diagram, the dominance–submission axis has been re-interpreted to mean a high–low concern for promotion (a *high* concern for *promotion* is related to the wish for market dominance; a low concern for promotion is frequently coupled with *submission* or being a *follower* in the market place). The hostility–warmth axis has been re interpreted to mean a low–high concern for product (*concern* for product is related to concern or *warmth* toward customers). As the diagram shows, we have given the following descriptive names to the four quadrants: promotional strategy, sit-back strategy, product-quality strategy, and dynamic strategy.

We shall discover that each of the four basic sales strategies meshes differently with each of the four basic marketing strategies. Before describing how the salesman and marketing strategies mesh, we'll look at the four marketing strategies by themselves. As the charts at the end of the chapter show, each marketing strategy displays different attitudes toward product, service, price, product availability, research and development, market research, communications, packaging, profitability, leadership, and other factors. Let's analyze each marketing strategy and then describe how it meshes with each of the four selling strategies.

THE Q1 COMPANY

Magnetic Specialties Company manufactures, distributes, and sells imprinted advertising specialties ranging from calendars and ballpoint pens to key-rings and balloons. In business for ten years, it has enjoyed a very rapid growth; starting out as a two-man partnership with no salesmen, it now employs eighteen salesmen covering three states. Its factory and warehouse, originally in a storefront, are now housed in a handsome two-story building in an industrial park. To learn more about Magnetic, let's hear from its marketing manager, and from two of its customers.

MARKETING MANAGER: "As one of the founders of this business, I can tell you exactly what accounts for our success. Three things: we hire the toughest, most aggressive salesmen we can find . . . real tigers; we advertise and promote like crazy; and we never let ourselves be beat on price. There's room in this company for only one kind of salesman: the kind that doesn't know the meaning of the word 'no.' We want fast closers who want to make a lot of money. We back them up with plenty of hullabaloo and plenty of razzle-dazzle. We believe you can sell old refrigerators to Eskimos if you promote them right. And we never let our guys be undersold. It's a perfect formula. In ten years, our sales have increased from $25,000 a year to $5,000,000 . . . and they're still climbing."

CUSTOMER A (Sales manager for a small chain of cut-rate service stations): "We use lots of advertising specialties in our business. Over the years, we've given away hundreds of thousands . . . millions, I guess . . . of match books, pencils, drinking glasses. All with our name on them. And we've bought them all from Magnetic . . . for two reasons: first of all, they always let you know about a new idea. The minute they come up with a cheap new gimmick, they send you a flyer on it. They're constantly flooding us with promotional stuff. And, second, they've got the greatest prices around. That's a hard combination to resist. Of course, you've got to be careful when dealing with Magnetic. They usually promise a lot more than they can deliver. Whenever I talk to the Magnetic salesman, I'm as cagey as I can be. I don't want to be taken."

CUSTOMER B (Owner of a large paint store): "I believe in advertising specialties . . . like inexpensive little paint brushes with my store's name and address on them . . . or imprinted paper caps for painters. I buy nearly all my stuff from Magnetic. Their salesman never gives me a chance to buy from anybody else. He camps on my doorstep about once every couple of weeks. He always beats his competitors to the punch. And he's always got the lowest prices in town. He's a pushy guy . . . and I don't think he can be trusted all the time . . . but nobody else in the business can touch his prices. Sure I buy from him . . . once I've made sure that I know what I'm really going to get. I come out okay, as long as I don't let my guard down."

Magnetic Specialties Company has a Q1 marketing strategy. Let's see why.

Q1 Marketing Strategy (Promotional Strategy)

The Q1 company takes a promotional approach to marketing; it assumes that any product can be sold if it is promoted effectively, no matter what its quality or whether a need exists. Promotion becomes more important than the product itself, and heavy emphasis is placed upon the sales force, advertising, packaging, point-of-purchase promotions, and premiums. Little attention is paid to quality control, engineering, research and development, or market research; none of these is considered of basic importance.

Some of the best examples of companies with a Q1 strategy are those run by one or two individuals who control operations tightly. The company is essentially a one- or two-man show, with little delegation of responsibility. If growth forces delegation, the delegation is usually very limited; even as the executive team grows, the company remains highly centralized and unwilling to delegate authority except in trivial matters.

Q1 companies often take a short-range view of things; they want the highest possible profits here and now. The future, they believe, will take care of itself; what counts is to make money today. Long-range goals are slighted in favor of immediate gains.

The leadership of Q1 companies is not particularly interested in product quality; they assume that obsolescence and breakdown will work for them rather than against them. Of course, the product is periodically improved to stay competitive, but it is seldom outstanding. Inventory and delivery techniques are frequently sloppy. Q1 companies try to sell even if they are unable to deliver, on the assumption that it doesn't hurt if production runs behind deliveries. This nonchalant attitude loses some customers, but not enough to offset the volume of business that's usually done.

Not surprisingly, product service is minimal. The company does what it must to maintain good customer relations, but no more. Product manuals are usually brief and uninstructive, with more ballyhoo than technical information. Q1 companies rarely think of themselves as being in business to inform; they are, quite simply, in business to sell.

Naturally, every effort is made to keep prices as low as possible. The management of Q1 companies believes price is the primary reason people buy or fail to buy, so price becomes more important than quality. In fact, Q1 managers cynically contend that people can't readily tell the difference between good quality and bad, but they can instantly tell the difference between high prices and low. Q1 companies will exploit a favorable market situation by keeping prices higher than the product merits, but only when such exploitative pricing is unlikely to damage sales. Their motto is often: "Get it while you can."

Mass distribution is heavily stressed by Q1 companies. They believe people will buy something that's available; the trick is to get your product distributed in enough places. Strenuous efforts are made to obtain as many outlets as possible with good shelf space, displays, window streamers, and so forth, at the retail level. To get shelf space, they often promise lavish returns.

Since Q1 companies have little concern for long-range goals, and since product quality is not considered of major importance, little time or money is spent on research and development of new or improved products. When necessary, research and development are used to counteract competition, but not to build for the distant future. Today's market is emphasized, to the almost complete neglect of tomorrow's needs.

Formal market research is played down or ignored. According to the Q1 company, heavy promotion, good distribution, and low prices lead to sales; there is therefore no need for market research. To find out what is selling, the Q1 company simply checks its orders. If an item is not moving fast enough, word goes out to the sales force to "push" it. Advertising research is also considered unnecessary; the Q1 company feels there's only one way to advertise: with lots of promises and lots of ballyhoo. Research into intangibles like company image is considered completely superfluous, since "company image never sold anything."

Q1 companies hire aggressive salesmen; they want high-pressure men who can hit hard and fast. Salesmen are told, explicitly or implicitly, that it's the sale that counts; customers can be promised almost anything if they'll buy. Little money is invested in public relations, which, like company image, is considered impractical. On the other hand, much is invested in advertising, which is often flamboyant, hard-sell, and not always in the best taste. Direct mail, because it is inexpensive and gets measurable results, is heavily used, as are point-of-purchase displays; often splashy, they emphasize price and premium advantages. The Q1 company's promotional effort is designed to create awareness of its product and move inventory quickly; honesty and integrity are secondary. It would be wrong, however, to imply that such companies always resort to outright trickery or lies; more often, they stretch or bend the truth somewhat, relying largely upon exaggeration and distortion.

A Perspective on the Q1 Company

Many successful small companies start as Q1 organizations, dominated by one (or a small group) of hard-driving, ambitious risk-takers. (This is not necessarily true of all Q1 companies, since some are very big from the outset or as a result of mergers.) They are characterized by intense competitiveness, a compelling desire for rapid and dramatic growth, and a certain measure of ruthlessness. Many Q1 companies behave as if constantly surrounded by enemies against whom they must fight for their lives. Right or wrong (and it is often right), this belief stimulates them to strenuous, and frequently successful, marketing efforts.

Q1 companies place great stress upon "success," a term usually implying the following:

1. High personal income and status. Q1 executives frequently equate

organizational success and personal success, measured by salary, bonuses, stock options, and various symbols of rank (impressive offices, sizable expense accounts, and so on).

2. Dominant position in the industry. Q1 companies are powered by a deep need to be number one. In their tireless striving for supremacy, Q1 executives frequently think of their competitors as the "bad guys," "the enemy," "the other side."

Thus Q1 companies are *power-oriented* and ferociously competitive. This fierce rivalry makes them less concerned about means than ends; whatever leads to success is "good" (or at least "not bad"); whatever hinders success is "bad." In the unending strife for success, anything (or nearly anything) goes.

To sum up, the Q1 company is intent upon dominating its competitors. It sees itself locked in combat with other companies that will destroy it unless it refuses to give quarter. The idea that a growing economy can maintain more than a single company in its field, is considered extremely dangerous. When dealing with other companies or its customers, the Q1 gives no more than it must.

THE Q2 COMPANY

Artistic Wall Plaque manufactures a wide variety of ceramic, wood, and plastic wall plaques which it sells to furniture and department stores and interior decorators in a twelve-state area. In business for nearly twenty-five years, it has experienced virtually no significant growth for the past decade, despite the large expansion of its potential market through new house and apartment construction. Artistic has five salesmen, all of whom have been with it for most of its history. Let's hear more about the company from its Vice President-Sales and from two of its customers:

VICE PRESIDENT-SALES: "We're in a funny business. When you think about all the people who are decorating homes today, and when you think about the tremendous population growth in this country, you'd think a business like ours would be booming. But it isn't. We're getting by . . . but I won't kid you by telling you that we're setting the world on fire. Of course, one big problem is competition; there are an awful lot of companies in the wall plaque business. Too many, I think. But the real problem is that people just don't seem interested in wall plaques. Pictures and prints are the big thing nowadays. And tapestries. But nobody wants to hang wall plaques. The trend is against us, and it has been for years. There's not much we can do about it. After all, people make up their own minds about these things."

CUSTOMER A (Buyer for large department store):   "Yes, I buy some plaques from Artistic, mainly ceramics. They've got a low price on their ceramic plaques, and we can turn a pretty good profit on them. But most of my business goes to other companies. Artistic simply isn't creative enough. They haven't changed their basic designs in five years. And I don't think they've tampered with their production process in twenty years. They're a stodgy company. All the exciting new ideas in wall hangings . . . and there are lots of them . . . come from other companies. You know, interior decoration is like clothing design . . . you've got to keep up with the times. And Artistic hasn't kept up."

CUSTOMER B (Buyer for a small chain of furniture stores):   "Funny thing about Artistic. Twenty years ago, they were in an enviable position. A big boom in home construction was starting, and they were in on it at the outset. But somehow they missed the boat. A lot of their competitors expanded their lines . . . they went into things like prints, picture frames, light-switch covers, small statuary . . . you name it. But not Artistic. They kept on turning out wall plaques and nothing but wall plaques. And not such great ones, either. The first thing anybody knew, Artistic had been left behind . . . way behind. Some of their competitors became rich . . . while Artistic drifted. In fact, if it weren't for their low-price ceramic line, I doubt that Artistic would be in business today."

Let's look closer at the Q2 company, of which Artistic Wall Plaque is one example.

Q2 Marketing Strategy (Sit-Back Strategy)

Q2 companies are characterized by hesitant, foot-dragging marketing. Instead of aggressively designing and promoting their product, they sit back and assume that people will buy it if it is there. Many Q2 companies once enjoyed a unique market advantage that no longer exists; circumstances have changed, but they haven't. Rather than innovate to regain their former position, they rest on their laurels and assume that all will be well.

This satisfaction with the status quo leads to deemphasis of both product and promotion. Advertising and public relations expenditures are low. Salesmen are poorly trained order-takers. Research, product improvement, and quality control are virtually unheard of. Minimal sales are accompanied by minimal growth. Everyone seems content to do just enough to get by. The prevailing slogan is: "Don't make waves." Just enough money is spent on product engineering and quality control to keep the product salable. Basically, the product remains the same, year after year. Enough service is rendered to keep customers from complaining, but more than that is considered superfluous. Product manuals are usually quite complete; the idea is that if customers have a good product manual, they won't have to bother the company for service.

Generally, Q2 companies maintain prices at the same level, or somewhat below, those prevailing in the industry; they assume people buy price rather than quality, and that a low price will move a mediocre product. Distribution is usually slighted, with minimal and spotty efforts to broaden the distribution base. For those Q2 companies selling to retailers, position and point-of-purchase promotion are not considered important enough to justify the expenditure of a great deal of time and effort.

Research and development are virtually nonexistent in many Q2 companies. Management tends to avoid new products, feeling it has enough of a job trying to sell its present line. Formal market research is rare. Q2 managers believe customers are seldom satisfied anyway, so it doesn't pay to get their reactions. "Why pay good money to find out what we already know?" is the typical attitude. As far as company image is concerned, Q2 companies barely recognize that such a thing exists.

Salesmen for Q2 companies are often order-takers who use a "canned" presentation. Thoughtful selling is considered unnecessary, since the customer is expected to buy when he is ready. Salesmen are urged to make lots of calls so that they can be around when the customer finally decides to buy. Good salesmen who enjoy give-and-take with their customers shun Q2 companies. While heavy reliance is placed on sales calls, little attention is paid to other marketing techniques. Advertising is minimal, although direct mail is sometimes used to reduce inventories. Point-of-purchase activities, where they exist at all, are skimpy. Packaging seldom changes. The only promotion that really counts, according to Q2 thinking, is price manipulation at the point of sale.

The Q2 assumption is that "we're sure to get our share as long as we continue to operate as we have in the past. The important thing is to keep plugging." Such companies have no real long-range goals, other than to stay in business. The future is taken for granted; Q2 managers find it hard to believe that their methods may lead to their extinction. They are less concerned with profits than with making enough to get by.

It is no exaggeration to say that Q2 companies are essentially leader-less. No one wants to face the full implications of the present or future. These companies are less interested in making progress than in marking time. In a dynamic, ever-changing world, they often find themselves falling back rather than marking time, and ultimately going out of business.

A Perspective on the Q2 Company

Q2 companies are typically managed by unenthusiastic, weak executives whose primary goal is survival. Content merely to get by, they build conservative organizations that lack initiative. Q2s never lead; they react to conditions created by more assertive companies. Frequently, the reaction is merely a decision to do nothing. Q2s have a deep respect for established ways. Slow-moving and prudent, they lack interest in growth, innovation, or challenge. They want to minimize risk. "Why take chances?" their managers frequently ask. "We're getting as much business as we need. Why spoil a good thing?" Sometimes, these are companies with no apparent need for initiative, companies with lucrative patents or cost-plus contracts. This by no means implies that all or even most such companies are Q2, only that they sometimes lack the *incentives* to go beyond Q2 behavior.

Because the enterprising, aggressive qualities of American business receive so much attention, we easily forget that there are numerous Q2 companies. Many are small or medium size businesses which, by their very nature, fail to get much publicity. Others are large companies in a comfortable rut. Their big cash reserves make it possible to exist without significant growth. The reasons for Q2 indifference vary from company to company. Some are headed by men who are misplaced in business; some by men whose wealth has made them complacent; some by men who lack the skills to guide an organization through change.

For whatever reason, they are unwilling to venture, to undertake risks, to meet the future at least half way. Instead, they rely on proven ideas and tested strategies. The dead hand of the past lies heavy upon Q2 companies, keeping them sluggish, passive, and restrained.

THE Q3 COMPANY

Precision Time Company manufactures watches and clocks. A long-established firm with an excellent reputation, it makes timepieces of remarkable accuracy. The line, very highly priced, is sold only in fine jewelry stores and some major department stores, and is advertised in prestige magazines. In recent years, Precision's sales have increased rather slowly, while a number of competitors, all newer in the industry, have forged well ahead of Precision. Let's find out why by listening to Precision's president and a couple of its customers.

PRESIDENT: "I'm the third generation of my family to head this company. To me, Precision Time is more than a business . . . it's a heritage, a trust. My grandfather started it by making the finest watches in the Western Hemisphere . . . my father continued the tradition . . . and I'm trying to do the same. Our employees feel the same way. We want to make the world's best watches and clocks. When someone buys a Precision product, we want him to know that there's nothing finer. We don't believe in ballyhoo or hard sell or anything like that . . . we believe in quality. We have a legacy of excellence around here . . . and we intend to maintain it. To be perfectly honest with you, I'd rather lose a sale than sell a shoddy watch."

CUSTOMER A (Owner of jewelry store): "Of course I carry Precision products. My customers aren't looking for bargains . . . they're looking for quality, style, reputation. And that's what they get when they buy a Precision timepiece. When I sell a man a Precision watch, I can assure him that the manufacturer will back it up for as long as the customer lives . . . and as long as his heirs live, if he bequeathes it to someone. And that's the truth. Precision stands behind every timepiece it's ever produced . . . and they've been making them now for sixty years. Of course, most of my customers can't afford them, but, for those who want nothing but the best, you can't beat Precision."

CUSTOMER B (Buyer for department store jewelry department): "Yes, I buy Precision watches. For a couple of reasons. One, they're the best on the market. Nothing else compares. And, two, they treat you right. Why, I had a slight delivery problem a few months ago, and . . . would you believe it? . . . one of Precision's Vice Presidents called me long-distance to apologize and to promise me that it wouldn't happen again. And that was just a *small* problem. I don't know a supplier anywhere that treats its customers as royally as Precision. It's too bad they don't make a line of good but less expensive watches, too. They don't seem interested in anything but the top of the market. It's a shame, because they're really wonderful people to work with."

Q3 Marketing Strategy (Product-Quality Strategy)

The Q3 company is characterized by unrealistic optimism. It believes the world will beat a path to its door as long as it makes the best mousetrap. Management is so sure of the value of its product that it seriously believes the product will sell itself. Marketing and promotion are played down, and the product is emphasized. Salesmen are regarded as goodwill ambassadors who do not have to sell hard, since their product will sell itself. The salesman's basic functions are to make friends, take orders, and provide service. Q3 companies are often recognizable by their sparing advertising, which is low-keyed, entertaining, or institutional, and lacking in information related to the full range of customer needs. Q3 advertising is advertising with very little "sell."

Product quality and product improvement are stressed by Q3 managers. The company's tradition of quality is a matter of deep pride. Much money is spent on engineering, quality control, quality improvement, and research and development. Much time is spent on detailed technical manuals and research into customer preferences.

While Q3 companies are deeply concerned with profits, they often naively assume that as long as their product is superior, profits will naturally follow. Their management places great faith in happy employees; every effort is made to treat everyone as part of one big, happy family. Bargaining and compromise are important; if compromises cannot be reached, management prefers to take no action rather than risk open conflict with its personnel. Underlying this attitude is the belief that an excellent product can only be produced by satisfied employees who put their heart into their work.

Q3 companies are very conscious of their image, and do whatever is necessary to maintain it. Since company image is closely related to product reputation, strong efforts are made to keep this reputation high. Everything that reflects on the product—inventories, deliveries, service— is considered important. But nothing is quite as important as the customer. Q3 companies go to great lengths to satisfy their customers. Complaints are handled quickly and efficiently; product manuals are very thorough; service is excellent. But all of this frequently exceeds the customer's real service needs, so that too much time may be spent handling a complaint, a product manual may be too detailed, and service may go well beyond what the customer expects. By exceeding customer needs and expectations, the Q3 may waste large amounts of money.

Q3 managers place a high value on feedback from the field; they are eager to know what their customers think. However, formal market research is usually slighted in favor of information from the sales force; the company's own salesmen and distributors are considered the best possible source of information. What market research is done is usually by the advertising agency; the company itself concentrates on the product. While Q3 companies are usually unwilling to spend large amounts on market research, they happily invest money in building the company image; the whole area of public relations receives heavy emphasis. But emerging or unmet customer needs are frequently ignored.

Q3 companies urge their salesmen to make efforts to be well liked by their customers; a popular salesman and an outstanding product are supposed to equal a sale. Entertainment of customers is considered quite important. Hard selling is avoided; little is spent on direct mail or point-of-purchase advertising. Packaging is dignified and traditional; Q3 companies often have a heavy investment in their packages, which have been handed down over a period of years.

A Perspective on the Q3 Company

Both to employees and outsiders, the Q3 is a "nice place to work." Its personnel frequently say things like: "I like it here. Everyone gets along real well. We're just one, big happy family." Customers say: "They're pleasant people to do business with. They treat their customers right. They take good care of you." Even competitors admit that "They're okay. They play by the rules, don't try to cut your throat, and believe in live and let live." In a phrase, the Q3 is the company everyone likes. Q3 management maintains a personal touch; it tries to stay warm, human, and concerned. Q3 companies see people not as means, but as ends.

As most companies become bigger and more complex, they tend to become somewhat impersonal; Q3 managers struggle against this tendency. They know the importance of system, but dislike having it get in the way of warmth and concern. In some Q3s much time is spent structuring the company to encourage personal interaction; decentralization frequently tempers bigness. (Decentralization is not necessarily a Q3 process. Many Q4 organizations decentralize, but for other reasons. The Q3 decentralizes to maintain warmth between its people and with its customers.)

Q3 management is sometimes mistakenly accused of lacking seriousness or purpose. Work is not neglected in Q3s, and their insistence upon quality is as high as any company's. It can be argued that the Q3 approach is naive, unrealistic, or one-sided, but certainly not that it lacks seriousness.

The real weakness of the Q3 company is that its optimism is frequently unjustifiable. The plain fact is that the world will *not* beat a path to the door of the company that makes the best mousetrap *unless* the mousetrap is intelligently and aggressively marketed. Even then, the mousetrap may far exceed the needs of the marketplace; it may be a better and more expensive trap than anyone requires for catching mice. The problem with the Q3 marketing approach is that it is often out of touch with the real world.

THE Q4 COMPANY

Sterling Battery Corporation manufactures a full line of batteries, ranging from hearing-aid batteries to automobile batteries. It has nationwide distribution through two separate marketing departments, one selling only automotive and truck batteries, the other selling smaller batteries for nonautomotive use. Sales for the entire corporation have increased 8–10% each year for the past five years. Let's try to account for this success by listening to Sterling's general sales manager and two of its customers.

GENERAL SALES MANAGER: "I don't attribute our success to any one thing. It's a combination of factors. First of all, we've got a full product line and a competitive one. Nobody makes better batteries at the same prices. Next, we've got a terrific distribution set-up . . . thanks to the efforts of our sales force. You know, we're an independent manufacturer . . . which makes distribution of our automotive line very difficult. Yet in spite of that, our guys have done a tremendous job of developing new outlets. Then there's the matter of what I call 'competitive savvy.' The truth is that we're smarter . . . or at least we *work* smarter . . . than most of our competitors. Our salesmen provide us with good information on what the competition is doing or is rumored to be doing. Most of the time, we're able to neutralize competitive threats before they happen. Add it all up . . . good product, good distribution, great salesmen, concern with the needs of different segments of our market . . . and you've got the keys to our success."

CUSTOMER A (Service station owner):   "I sure do carry Sterling batteries. They've got a good reputation . . . a lot of people come in here and ask for Sterling by name . . . and Sterling takes good care of its customers. Their salesman's a real pro . . . he's always ready to get me fast delivery if I need it . . . he pays good attention to my inventory

. . . and he's given me lots of good advice on how to increase battery sales. As a matter of fact, I sell more batteries than most dealers, mainly because the Sterling man has taught me how to promote them. I'm a mechanic by trade . . . not a salesman . . . so I really appreciate his help."

CUSTOMER B (Owner of hearing-aid store): "Sterling is a good, competitive line . . . and they've got good, competitive salesmen. The Sterling man really looks after me . . . and he's never made a promise he didn't keep. He's shown me how to use point-of-purchase material to increase battery sales . . . and he's given me some good ideas about using direct-mail with my customers. He's a good man to have around, so naturally I give him the bulk of my business."

Sterling Battery is a Q4 company. Let's learn more about its marketing strategy.

Q4 Marketing Strategy (Dynamic Strategy)

Q4 companies show a high concern for both promotion and product. Time, energy, and money are spent to develop strong salesmen, effective advertising, sound market research, and good public relations, while equal effort is devoted to improving the product and its distribution. Q4 companies are concerned with both short-range profits and long-range goals. They maximize growth and profit by staying tuned in to the needs of the marketplace. They use the marketing concept in its most productive sense.

Q4 leadership is aggressive, forward-looking and committed to success. It believes strongly in purposeful change and adaptation, and readily devises new ideas or new products to meet new customer needs. While they do not ignore experience, Q4 companies are less concerned with how things have been done in the past than with how things should be done in the future. Q4 managers welcome innovation, as long as it is practical and profitable, or will be practical and profitable in the future.

Constantly aware of competitive threats as well as customer needs, Q4 companies pay much attention to product engineering and quality control consistent with customer needs. Every effort is made to gain a competitive edge by outdoing competition. Inventories and delivery schedules are also considered of prime importance; nothing that contributes to customer satisfaction is overlooked. Service after the sale receives much attention, and much time is spent developing useful product manuals.

Q4 companies usually maintain realistic pricing policies. Prices are set only after careful consideration has been given to costs, product quality, nature of the market, and the competitive situation. In their concern with profits, Q4 companies strive for the highest price consistent with customer goodwill, their market position, and their short- and long-range interests.

Distribution is not ignored. The importance of product availability is recognized, but it does not take precedence over other marketing factors. Research and development are highly valued by Q4 managers, who try to anticipate customer wants and needs, and to stay at least one step ahead of the market. Q4 companies try always to be prepared for shifts in the market.

Q4 managers are deeply interested in customer reactions. Much thought is given to maintaining a positive company image; in communications and public relations, the company works closely with its advertising agency in setting advertising goals and methods. Q4 advertising may be entertaining, but it is never *merely* so; it is always informative and clearly related to customer needs.

Salesmen play a key role in the success of Q4 companies. They are expected to be dynamic, well-trained, flexible, and capable of meeting customer needs while contributing to company profits. Advertising and packaging are considered important; advertising is carefully planned and closely related to long-range goals. Direct mail, point-of-purchase displays, and a variety of promotional efforts are used when and as necessary. Packaging is honest and effective; it not only helps sell the product, but also to maintain the company image.

Q4 companies have strong personnel development programs. They continually develop men with the skills and insights needed to stay aware of change and keep abreast or ahead of it. Q4 success is no accident; it is the result of systematic personnel development which insures a steady source of managerial and sales talent.

Q4 companies are usually highly successful because they blend real concern for their customers with an equally real concern for their own progress and profitability. Because they meet customer needs, are flexible and able to change as the market changes, and are led by men who combine short- and long-range goals, they usually lead their industry.

A Perspective on the Q4 Company

Like the Q1, the Q4 organization wants very much to succeed, but it defines success differently. Instead of using the word to mean ascendancy within its industry, it uses it to mean many things: leadership (which is not the same as ascendancy, since leadership can be shared but ascendance cannot) within its industry; high sales and profits; ethical discharge of its obligations to employees, customers, stockholders, suppliers, and the public at large; and a creative or innovative role both in its industry and in the community. This is considerably different than what Q1 companies mean by "success."

If any word characterizes the Q4, it is *dynamic*. The organization constantly seizes the initiative, constantly enterprises. It has a strong sense of *responsibility* to many diverse and often conflicting interests: its own personnel, customers, suppliers, stockholders, the public at large, even *competitors*. Identifying, weighing and balancing these interests so that each is optimally served is one of its chief concerns.

The Q4 tries to align the needs of its people, shareholders, customers, and society with its own goals. It engages in spirited but not destructive competition. It provides liberal employee benefits without forgetting stockholders' claims. It develops a product whose quality is consistent with customer needs (unlike the Q3, which often develops a product whose quality far exceeds customer needs). It undertakes public service projects not to build its image but to fulfill its responsibilities.

Unlike the Q1, the Q4 is competitive but not predatory; it tries to win, but in a fair fight. Unlike the Q2, it values tradition without worshiping it; the past is a guide to the future, not a blueprint. Unlike the Q3, it manifests respect for people in many ways, not only by making them happy; it places growth ahead of contentment. More than any of these companies, the Q4 thrives on change. In a society like ours, its dynamic approach is obviously the one most likely to succeed.

The Q4 company practices enlightened self-interest. It is not a philanthropic organization; its managers quickly reject the Q1 criticism that they are idealistic or impractical. *The Q4 is interested in results.* It believes profit levels can be high while people and principles are served. It believes it shares interests with many groups, and that these shared interests dictate collaboration, not conflict. It believes no company can fulfill its obligations in a dynamic society without itself being dynamic; that adaptability, intelligence, and vision are the most essential ingredients of success in a fast-changing world.

ORGANIZATIONAL BEHAVIOR: AN OVERVIEW

Our descriptions of company marketing behavior are typologies, much simpler than in the real world where most companies are mixtures of all four marketing strategies. In the real world, different people often have different and incompatible impressions of a company's behavior. Let's see why.

Companies, like salesmen, customers, and sales managers, sometimes display secondary or mask strategies. Under severe pressure, any company may shift from its primary marketing strategy to a temporary strategy that is not its typical strategy.

Every company is made up of functional parts, whose behavior is never thoroughly consistent. A company may be basically Q4, but a sales district supervised by a Q1 sales manager may manifest Q1 behavior. A customer coming into contact with this division, and knowing little else about the company, would conclude the whole company was Q1. A management consultant, on the other hand, working with the top marketing staff at the home office, would just as definitely conclude the company was Q4. This kind of difference accounts for much of the disagreement about what a company is "really" like.

Companies sometimes invest large amounts in building "images" that disguise their real behavior. A Q1 company with a long record of plundering competitors, starting price wars, and indulging in unfair labor practices may, through glossy public relations, persuade part of the public that it is responsible and statesmanlike. In effect, companies, like people, sometimes don masks (and sometimes shift to secondary strategies).

Company behavior may change over time. A retired salesman may fondly remember his company as a warm Q3 organization, which it was ten years ago when he worked there. A present-day salesman, working under different management, may correctly think of it as Q2.

Changes in Organization Strategies

The reasons why company strategies change over time are due to economic changes, competitive changes, stockholders, and leadership.

Economic changes. A company in an expanding market, watching sales rise steadily and easily, may function in classic Q3 style, with lavish fringe benefits, a take-it-easy attitude, and managerial unwillingness to push anyone very hard. The same company, in a long market decline, may change its behavior by tightening up on benefits, and stressing tight controls, tough management, productivity, efficiency, and hard work. Eventually, it may fire some salesmen, whereas in better days it retained employees who were not really needed. So an economic change may cause a shift from Q3 to Q1. It is a rare company that never changes its strategy as economic conditions change.

Competitive change. A company with virtually no serious competition may behave in a Q3 way, and may be commended by observers as an "industrial paragon." A few years later, with several scrappy new competitors in the field, with proportionate share of market decreasing, and with pressures intensifying daily, the company may shift to Q1 secondary behavior, which it justifies by the dog-eat-dog conditions in the industry. Competition is always a potent force in shaping strategy. (Our example does not mean, however, that increased competition will always force a company to shift to Q1 marketing behavior. The shift could be to *any* quadrant.)

Stockholders. Stockholders, if sufficiently powerful, well organized, and noisy, sometimes compel changes in an organization's behavior. As a rule, stockholder rebellions cause modifications rather than transformations. A management team widely known for brutish competitive tactics may be forced to moderate those tactics by stockholders who resent the company's reputation and its damaging impact upon sales.

Leadership. Probably most significant in causing change in company behavior is change in leadership. These changes are gradual rather than abrupt, but they can be quite dramatic. A Q4 vice president may, for example, replace a Q3 president. After he solidifies his position and acquires a management team in his own image, significant changes begin to appear in the company. In several years, the strategy may be largely Q4, with only remnants of Q3.

The Evolution of Organizations

Not all companies evolve. Some display the same behavior for many years. But many *do* evolve. While no single route is predominant, three are common: the road to extinction, moving in a circle, and from warfare to dynamic leadership. Let's examine them:

The road to extinction. As the dodo bird attests, not all evolution succeeds. Some, because of a "wrong turn," leads to blind alleys from which there is no escape. The result is usually physical extinction. This pattern is found in companies too. The pattern can be described as Q1–Q2. Many companies begin as Q1 entrepreneurial businesses, organized and led by competitive profit-oriented innovators with a capacity for strenuous work and sacrifice. By refusing to bow to competition, they thrive. But the qualities that built these companies may not continue in the second or third generation. If the business remains a family business, the founder's sons or grandsons may feel little interest in it, may be complacent and self-satisfied, or may simply lack competitive skills. In any event the company may shift from Q1 to Q2. (This is by no means a pattern for family-operated businesses. In some, the second and third generations are as aggressive as the founders; in others, the trend is toward Q4 behavior. No generalizations are possible.) In an economy as vigorous as ours, a Q2 company cannot stay in business indefinitely without very large financial resources (or lucrative patents or cost-plus contracts). Eager competitors entice the Q2's customers, and indifferent or inept management fails to replace them. Ultimately, a more dynamic organization, seeking a patent held by the Q2, or its distribution network or its physical facilities, buys the company, or the Q2 goes out of business. Either way, the change from Q1 to Q2 can lead to extinction, unless dynamic management is brought in to reverse the trend, or more effective strategies are adopted.

Moving in a circle. In another common pattern, a company changes behavior, then shifts back again to its earlier behavior. In this pattern, the Q1 organization in the second or third generation shifts to a Q3 strategy. This commonly happens when the younger generation concentrates its energies on employee benefits and community affairs, or focuses on product development to the exclusion of other matters. Either way, its activities become increasingly impractical, and increasingly remote from operational concerns. No company can survive like this indefinitely. Top management may bring in a crew of professional managers so it can resign from the operation of the company and devote itself to other interests. Or top management may take steps to change itself. The management team may then put a quick end to the drift by resorting to bold Q1 tactics. The company reverts to the behavior that made it successful in the first place, and the circle is complete.

From warfare to dynamic leadership. A third pattern can be described as Q1–Q4. Here, with increasing success and new management, a competitive and exploitative organization realizes it can succeed without lashing out at everyone in sight. This is not an easy change to make; it requires the development of new managerial attitudes and assumptions or new leadership with Q4 characteristics. Either way, the new attitudes must then filter down to various divisions and departments. The change usually requires several years of intensive work. There is nothing inevitable about these patterns, of course. Other patterns can and do occur. Not all organizations start as Q1s and not all Q1s shift to something else. How a company begins and how it changes depend on many factors. The whole truth about any organization is always complex.

Company Marketing Strategies and the Q1 Salesman

Each kind of company prefers a salesman whose selling strategy meshes effectively with its marketing strategy. Where the mesh is not close, the salesman is likely to have serious problems, perhaps even to fail. In part, sales success is the result of effective interaction between the salesman and his company's marketing strategy, just as it is also (in part) the result of effective interaction with his customers and his sales manager.

THE Q1 SALESMAN IN THE Q1 COMPANY

Q1 salesmen in Q1 companies typically make high sales almost immediately. Both salesman and company value quick sales, and neither is very squeamish about *how* the sales are made. Long-range sales are not usually as impressive, since Q1 salesmen often burn out rapidly, become restive in their jobs, or antagonize their customers. As a rule, the Q1 salesman moves on to a better paying or higher position within the company, or he leaves the company entirely. (This is not true if the Q1 salesman is selling a product that does not require repeat or sustained relationships. Such a salesman may stay with the Q1 company for a very long time and be very successful.) Q1 salesmen want quick success, and they realize that if they do not succeed in a Q1 company quickly, they are not going to succeed at all. In spite of their exploitative strategies, the Q1 salesman and the Q1 company suit one another. Their values and actions mesh. The company believes he is the most effective type of salesman; the salesman, while he may not like the company, understands it.

THE Q1 SALESMAN IN THE Q2 COMPANY

Since the Q1 is a fast starter, he shows rapid results in any company, including the Q2. This marketing strategy gives the Q1 salesman the best opportunity to shine, since he seldom stays around long enough for his sales to lag. He usually finds the "do-nothing" atmosphere oppressive, and moves on quickly to another job. Q1 salesmen do not take long to discover that they do not fit into the Q2 company. The conservative Q2 strategy provides no scope for their aggressiveness. In those rare cases in which a Q1 salesman stays with a Q2 company, he often creates too much conflict to be rewarded with a promotion. Q2 firms prefer to promote men who don't rock the boat.

THE Q1 SALESMAN IN THE Q3 COMPANY

The Q1 salesman achieves high sales at the outset. The Q3 company is impressed by his performance. The impression dwindles, however, as he begins to antagonize customers and as sales dwindle. This falling off of sales is largely the result of poor follow-up by the Q1. As his lack of interest in follow-up becomes apparent, the company takes a less favorable view of him, since service after the sale is highly regarded by Q3 companies. Friction also occurs when the Q1 salesman finds his advancement stymied by the leisurely pace at which the Q3 company moves, and he may look for a job in a more aggressive organization. His characteristics are so much at variance with the company's standard method of operation that he sometimes frightens the management; still and all, Q1s do manage to get promoted in Q3 organizations, especially if they're able to maintain a superficial "nice guy" pose.

THE Q1 SALESMAN IN THE Q4 COMPANY

As always, the Q1 salesman gets off to a fast start, then levels off. An attempt is made to get him to change his selling habits, so that he stops using high pressure and stops making promises he cannot fulfill. This restraint makes the Q1 salesman uncomfortable, and his sales may suffer as a result. If the company is successful in its efforts, the Q1 will adopt a less exploitative approach and will fit into the company more comfortably. Or he may resent the attempts, and take a job with a company which will not try to change him. Q1 salesmen do get promoted in Q4 companies, but, when they do, the company makes a strenuous effort to restrain their manipulative behavior. Q1 salesmen seldom go very far in Q4 companies, since it is felt they should always be rather closely supervised. So they usually remain at lower management levels.

Company Marketing Strategies and the Q2 Salesman

THE Q2 SALESMAN IN THE Q1 COMPANY

Sales are poor or mediocre at the start and afterward. The Q1 company demands quick and big results; the Q2 salesman is unable to comply. He is a misfit in a Q1 organization. If he isn't fired first, he is likely to quit, since the pressures are usually more than he can endure. The Q2 is seldom around long enough to be considered for promotion. Even if he were, however, the Q1 company would rarely advance him.

THE Q2 SALESMAN IN THE Q2 COMPANY

At the outset, sales are very poor, but the company is not distressed, since it never expected much. In the long run, sales improve somewhat and level off at a modest level. The Q2 company makes minimal demands upon its salesmen; it expects them to be order-takers, but not much more. The Q2 salesman fits this prescription perfectly. Since he is able to meet the company's minimal goals, and since the company has few goals beyond the minimal, the Q2 salesman manages to hang on, sometimes for many years. In Q2 companies, promotions are often a matter of seniority. As long as the Q2 salesman stays with the company and does nothing that upsets it, he has a good chance of promotion.

THE Q2 SALESMAN IN THE Q3 COMPANY

The Q2 salesman is a slow starter, but the Q3 company never expects too much at first. Over a longer period, he manages to meet the minimum goals set for him, and the company seldom pushes him for more, since he seems to be doing as well as he can. While the Q2 salesman is never an outstanding performer, he does manage to make sales, and the Q3 company has no strong reason to fire him. The easygoing, slow atmosphere of the Q3 organization is comfortable and nonthreatening to the Q2 salesman. Q3 companies promote mainly on seniority, so a Q2 salesman who stays around long enough may be promoted. However, Q3 firms prefer to promote people who are warmer and less aloof than the Q2 salesman. The Q2 salesman is often uncomfortable with the Q3 company's demands for sociability.

THE Q2 SALESMAN IN THE Q4 COMPANY

Q2 salesmen cannot operate in the flexible manner demanded by the Q4 company. Their sales are low. Almost from the beginning, it is obvious that the Q2 does not belong. Where the company expects aggressiveness, he is submissive; where the company encourages warmth, he is hostile. Usually, the company quickly recognizes it has made a mistake in hiring the Q2, and fires him. There is really no such thing as promotability for the Q2 in a Q4 company. If by some quirk he were to stay with the company, promotion would still be out of the question.

Company Marketing Strategies and the Q3 Salesman

THE Q3 SALESMAN IN THE Q1 COMPANY

No matter what kind of company he works for, the Q3 salesman gets off to a slow start. He sells by making friends first, and making friends takes time. After a while, sales are fair, since he adopts the goals of the Q1 company and tries to realize them, although with some modifications. His tenure is average. The Q3 has no desire to change jobs, and the company is satisfied to have him stay, since his sales are not bad and he does promote goodwill among many customers. Q3 salesmen are seldom promoted in Q1 companies. The men who advance in Q1 firms are good at company in-fighting; the Q3 salesman is not. In fact, the Q3 salesman may experience considerable tension in the Q1 company as he finds himself unable to comply with its demands for more aggressiveness.

THE Q3 SALESMAN IN THE Q2 COMPANY

The Q2 company is patient. It makes no stringent demands on the Q3 salesman; as a result, after a slow start, he gets his sales up to average. Q2 companies do not fire people unless they rock the boat, something the Q3 salesman is unlikely to do. Q3 salesmen are usually promoted in Q2 companies as a result of seniority. The Q3 is not the person with whom Q2 management feels most comfortable. Still and all, if he is around long enough, he may become a sales manager.

THE Q3 SALESMAN IN THE Q3 COMPANY

Q3 salesmen blend well in Q3 organizations. Their sales are fairly high, after a slow start. Salesman and company seem made for one another. Both have the same basic outlook, and the same approach to selling. The Q3 salesman in a Q3 company stands an excellent chance of being promoted. In fact, Q3 firms are, as a rule, almost wholly managed by Q3s.

THE Q3 SALESMAN IN THE Q4 COMPANY

There is some conflict between the Q4 and the Q3 approaches to filling customer needs. Because the approaches are not always the same, sales seldom rise above the average level. The Q3 salesman, however, often has no wish to move to another job, and the Q4 company, while it does not consider him an ideal salesman, realizes that his traits fit some of its customers very well. Q3 salesmen are rarely promoted in Q4 companies. Q4 management seeks out practical, aggressive, tough-minded men for promotion, but the Q3 salesman is quite unaware of the hard competitive realities of sales and marketing. Thus the Q3 may enjoy long tenure as a salesman, but he almost never moves into management.

Company Marketing Strategies and the Q4 Salesman

THE Q4 SALESMAN IN THE Q1 COMPANY

The Q4 salesman's beliefs and assumptions conflict with those of the Q1 company. Still and all, he is too good a salesman to do a bad job.

While he does not realize his full potential in a Q1 firm, he is almost always a sound performer. But there is usually some tension between the Q4 salesman and the Q1 company; the company pressures the Q4 to exploit sales situations, and the Q4 resists. Nevertheless, because they are such solid performers, Q4 salesmen are often promoted by Q1 companies. Sometimes, a Q1 company advances so many Q4s into managerial positions that the company begins to change, and a more flexible marketing strategy, resembling the Q4, is adopted.

THE Q4 SALESMAN IN THE Q2 COMPANY

Once again, the Q4 salesman is a sound performer. But the Q2 company's "do-nothing" approach fails to satisfy the Q4 salesman, who wants a more dynamic situation. Once he realizes what kind of company he is with, he begins to look for another job. Q4s are seldom fired, but they usually quit Q2 companies. The Q4 salesman is seldom with a Q2 company long enough to be promoted, but, if he were, promotion would be extremely unlikely, since he would be considered a "boat rocker."

THE Q4 SALESMAN IN THE Q3 COMPANY

Q4s usually do a good job in Q3 companies. Q3 firms allow the Q4 salesman a great deal of latitude, so he is free to operate in his own way. As a result, sales are often quite high. In effect, Q4 salesmen tend to function as their own bosses in Q3 companies, a situation they turn to good advantage. The Q4 usually enjoys working for a Q3 company, but, sooner or later, he realizes that the company is not going anywhere. He may, somewhat reluctantly, then move on to a more aggressive company. A Q4 has only an average chance of being promoted in a Q3 company.

THE Q4 SALESMAN IN THE Q4 COMPANY

The natural meshing of Q4 and Q4 leads to high sales. Q4 salesmen in a Q4 company regard themselves as "career salesmen." Their main desire is to stay with the company and do as good a job as possible, so that they advance as far as their skills can take them. Q4 companies are led almost entirely by Q4 managers.

Why is the Q4 salesman able to sell successfully in *all four* companies? Because his flexibility enables him to cope with a broad range of situations. Less rigid in his behavior than the Q1, Q2, or Q3 salesman, he is also less vulnerable to strategies that do not mesh with his own. This does not mean, however, that he changes his behavior to suit whatever situation he finds himself in. It means that he adapts his behavior to the situation and, *at the same time,* does his best to affect *change* in the company's behavior. As always, he is dynamic; he works hard to get his company to adopt more Q4 tactics and ideas. He does not compromise his ideas; instead, he tries to sell his ideas to his management. If, after a while, it becomes plain to him that he is not succeeding in effecting change, he usually moves to another company.

SUMMARY

Company marketing strategies, like salesmen and sales managers, can be described and analyzed by the Dimensional model. The Q1 company (promotional strategy) assumes any product can be sold if it is promoted effectively; promotion becomes more important than the product itself. The Q2 company (sit-back strategy) apathetically assumes people will buy its product simply because the product is there; they are conservative and dedicated to preserving the status quo. The Q3 company (product-quality strategy) is so sure of the value of its product that it thinks the product will sell itself; it's salesmen function mainly as goodwill ambassadors. The Q4 company (dynamic strategy) has a high but realistic concern for both product and promotion; it tries to develop a product that will satisfy customer needs and to promote it effectively. Most companies display a mixture of all four strategies.

Company marketing strategies very often change as a result of economic changes, competitive changes, stockholder pressures, or new leadership.

Each kind of company prefers a salesman whose selling strategy fits its marketing strategy. Where the fit is poor, the salesman is likely to fail or move on to a more congenial company. Sales success is therefore the result (in part) of interaction between the salesman, his customers, and his company; all three factors must be considered before success or failure can be thoroughly understood.

TABLE 14. Company Marketing Strategies

	Q1-promotional strategy	Q2-sit-back strategy	Q3-product-quality strategy	Q4-dynamic strategy
Product engineering	Doesn't have to be high; product obsolescence works in our favor	Enough to get by	Make it the very best; our tradition and goodwill are at stake	Quality must be consistent with customer needs and competition
Product improvement	Just enough to keep product competitive but not necessarily outstanding	Not really important; we'll always have some market for our product	Improve whenever possible, within the limits of past practices	Product improvement is a constant concern; must be consistent with customer needs and competition
Product delivery	Sell it whether we've got the inventory or not; deliver as fast as you can	Definitely important; must deliver when promised	Must live up to word; keep large inventory to make sure we can deliver	Delivery schedules must meet real customer needs; explore to make sure we really know what those needs are
Product service	It's the customer's responsibility; take care of what you can, but don't over-service	Give just enough service to keep customers off our necks	Be of help to customers; their problems are our problems	Service after sale is essential but varies according to the customer's needs
Product manuals	Skimpy; more like promotional pieces than technical manuals	Put in as much as you can to save us the trouble of servicing complaints	Make them as detailed and helpful as possible	Should be thorough and consistent with customer's capability to use it; not a substitute for service
Product price	Keep it as low as possible; price is more important than quality	Consistency with industry price will sell a mediocre product	Product quality more important than price; don't skimp!	Price consistent with quality and customer needs

344

TABLE 14 (Continued)

	Q1-promotional strategy	Q2-sit-back strategy	Q3-product-quality strategy	Q4-dynamic strategy
Product availability -distribution	Get it out where people can lay their hands on it; availability is essential	Can't get product into every place; wide distribution not important	Quality rather than quantity or breadth of distribution is most important	Distribution consistent with customer needs and quality of outlet; availability is important
-shelf position	Best position in as many places as possible	Can't get the best spots; okay to settle on second or third best	People sell your product, not shelf position	Best shelf position sought when product can be purchased with minimal personal sales influence
Research and development	React to competition; don't spend much on long range	We have enough problems selling what we've got; why ask for trouble?	Horizons limited to present product improvement; visionary research and development is wasteful	Constant concern so emerging customer needs can be fulfilled and marketing opportunities created
Market research -customer satisfaction	Sales will show if customers are satisfied; no need for formal research	Customers are never satisfied; why bother to get feedback?	Your own salesmen and distributors are the best source of this information	All sources of feedback are important; salesmen and distributor information must be periodically supplemented by formal market research
-product improvement	Keep up with trouble spots as revealed by sales; formal research unnecessary	Customers are never satisfied	Your own salesmen and distributors are the best source of this information	(Same as above)

345

TABLE 14 (Continued)

	Q1—promotional strategy	Q2—sit-back strategy	Q3—product-quality strategy	Q4—dynamic strategy
—communica-tion	We know what we should say; formal research is not necessary	Not much to say about product, so why bother to get feedback?	Our advertising agency stays on top of this for us; we trust them	Works closely with ad agency in settling com-munications objectives and researching whether they have been met
—company image	Company image never sold a product; no research is necessary	What is this company image?	Very important since we take pride in our company; may do some formal re-search	Recognizes importance of company image and takes periodic readings
Communications —salesmen	Hit hard and fast; promise anything; the sale is im-portant	Get enough order-taker salesmen with a well-learned spiel; sales will come	Get your customers to like you; friendship plus a fine product will do a fine sales job	Salesmen must diagnose and meet real customer needs; must approach each sales situation well informed and flexibly
—public relations	Like company image —— never sold anything through public relations efforts	What is this public rela-tions business?	We use public relations to show what nice people we are	Public relations is everyone's concern; long-range goals require constant concern over impact on public
—space and time adver-tising	Hard-hitting; sell sizzle and not steak	Don't believe it does much good	Soft sell; entertain the cus-tomer and he'll buy from you	Advertising plays role in creating most favorable product and company images; sets goals in con-junction with agency

TABLE 14 (Continued)

	Q1-promotional strategy	Q2-sit-back strategy	Q3-product-quality strategy	Q4-dynamic strategy
-direct mail	Important because it's cheap and gets fast results	Good way to get rid of occasional oversupply	Don't see much value; it's too direct and hard-hitting	Use direct mail to inform as well as sell; recognize what it can and can't do
-point-of purchase promotion	Make them gaudy and hard-hitting; use price and premiums!	Price will sell it if it can be sold at all; point-of-purchase skimpy	Personal sales and fine reputation sell product; point-of-purchase okay if not too strong	Use point-of-purchase displays and promotional ventures to gain maximum customer acceptance
Package and label	Make sure they attract attention through color, size, etc.	Same package and label as always; not really important, so why change?	Tradition, honesty and quality must be pictured; keep that package and label we've had through the years	Package and label must attract without being deceiving; must communicate desired image objectives
Long-range goals	Not sure the company will be around indefinitely; our objective is to produce now	No long-range goals; no reason to feel this company won't be around, but why worry?	Tradition of product and service must go on and on	Will prosper by adapting to changing customer needs; must constantly look out for new marketing opportunities
Basic assumption	High emphasis on promotion; low emphasis on product	Low emphasis on both promotion and product; "plug along and we'll get our usual share"	Low emphasis on promotion; high emphasis on product; "we've got the best product around, so we don't have to use high pressure"	High emphasis on both promotion and product; "got to have best product and show people how it will benefit them"
Leadership	One man show: top man runs things from hip pocket, delegating very little; if company grows too large for this, is run by rigid and limiting set of strict delegations of authority	No one really wants responsibility for making decisions; policies have been set in the past and we operate on the basis of them; little individual or group initiative	One big happy family; top team meets and compromises: if compromise can't be reached, no action is taken rather than run risk of conflict	Well-formulated leadership utilizes manpower, both managerial and sales, to explore alternatives and arrive at solution best designed to maximize short and long-term sales results

19

A Look Back

SOME REASONS FOR OPTIMISM

In his well-known novel *The Count of Monte Cristo,* Alexandre Dumas wrote that "all human wisdom is summed up in two words—wait and hope." The authors wish it were possible to sum up *this* book in only two words—although we would certainly pick less passive words than Dumas chose. However, we know of no other way to summarize the preceding eighteen chapters—which we hope contain at least a little human wisdom—than in another chapter. No two words will do.

Up to this point, we have discussed a lot of complex ideas. In this chapter we review the most important of these, and try to tie them together. Then, in the last chapter, we talk about the reader's future as a salesman or sales manager, and we impart some wisdom that is just the *opposite* of "wait and hope."

THE BEHAVIORAL SCIENCE PERSPECTIVE ON SELLING AND SALES MANAGEMENT

We began this book by describing some behavioral science insights that are especially important to salesmen and sales managers. Let's review these.

Behavioral science is primarily interested in everyday behavior. As we have seen repeatedly, behavioral science is interested in practical, commonplace activities of the kind that matter to salesmen and sales managers: why people interact as they do, what explains their buying habits, how they communicate with one another.

Behavioral science stresses the importance of human interaction. To understand behavior, we must understand how people act upon one another. As we have seen, selling behavior and buying behavior can only be understood if we analyze what takes place *between* the salesman and the customer. And selling behavior and managerial behavior can only be understood if we analyze what happens *between* the salesman and his sales manager. Ultimately, explanations of behavior must involve more than one person. Any attempt to explain a salesman's behavior without seriously considering his customers' behavior is bound to be at least partly wrong, and vice versa.

Behavioral science is optimistic about people. This optimism is justified by the fact that each of us is capable of growth and change. Salesmen and sales managers (and everyone else) can develop and improve. None of us is permanently frozen into one strategy of behavior. Behavioral science lends very little support to pessimists.

Behavioral science views human behavior as dynamic. Whenever people interact, something happens. The very word *act* means *do*. Salesmen constantly *do* things that advance or retard their success as salesmen. To understand the selling process, we must understand each of the things the salesman does, its impact on the customer, and each of the things the customer does in response. Selling is a matter of constant action, reaction, and interaction. The same is true, of course, of sales management.

Why People Buy

A basic theme of this book has been that people buy for some reason or reasons. Customer behavior is never an accident, although the unaware salesman may think it is. Customers buy because they *think* they'll get some kind of benefit from their purchase. Customers refuse to buy because they *do not* think they will get some kind of benefit by buying. Or, put another way, buying satisfies needs.

Even a customer who buys merely to get rid of a very aggressive Q1 salesman is really filling a need, perhaps a need to get rid of a threatening figure (security need) or perhaps a need to get back to work (self-realization need). Sometimes a purchase satisfies a task need, sometimes a personal need; frequently, it satisfies both.

One reason Q4 selling is so successful is that it is based on identifying and filling both task and personal needs. A salesman who ignores either set of customer needs is really a salesman who relies upon luck.

Persuasive Communication

Persuasion is communication that ties in with needs. Customers are persuaded to buy when they are convinced their purchase will fill a need. But many customers are unsure or unaware of their needs. The Q4 salesman clarifies or crystallizes needs in the customer's mind and then, by using the techniques we have discussed, he communicates to the customer how his product will fill the need. If communication is not concerned with needs, it cannot be persuasive.

Throughout this book, we've emphasized that communication *is* behavior and that *all* behavior communicates. The old notion that a salesman who "talks well" necessarily communicates well is wrong. Eloquence and mastery of language alone do not create understanding and commitment, without which there is no communication. Communication is more than talking. It is inseparable from a salesman's *total behavior*. It depends upon the entire range of behavioral traits.

Any salesman or sales manager who wants to communicate better must understand several points:

1. Not only what a salesman or manager *says,* but everything he *does,* communicates some kind of information. A scowl, a laugh, a grimace all say as much as words, perhaps more. Anthropologist Edward Hall has called this "the silent language." Many times, the silent language is louder than words.

2. Persuasive communication takes place in a climate created by the *interaction* between the salesman and the customer. The *total relationship* between the two determines the results of the communication.

3. A communications climate can be understood only if the basic strategies or *behavior patterns* of the communicators are understood. Communication between a Q1 salesman and a Q3 customer is quite different than communication between a Q2 salesman and a Q2 customer. Neither can be understood without knowledge of the behavioral strategies involved. The same is true, of course, for communication between sales managers and salesmen.

4. The most effective salesmen and sales managers are therefore not merely good talkers who know how to say things clearly and forcefully. *They are students of human behavior,* who know how to cope with their customers' attitudes and emotions as well as with facts. They recognize the irrational as well as the rational barriers that make it difficult for people to get through to one another. They spot communications obstacles, find out why they exist, and remove them.

5. A salesman or manager can *learn* to communicate effectively. This learning must be based upon awareness of the impact of his behavior; understanding of his communications strategy; ability to analyze the interactions between his behavior and the other person's behavior; awareness of the other person's task and personal needs; and knowledge and *practice* of specific communication skills.

Too many salesmen and managers damage their chances for success by believing worn-out notions about communication. They accept at face value such false statements as "a good talker can sell anything," "a good product sells itself," "sell benefits and you'll close lots of sales," or "you can tell a salesman what's wrong with him and force him to change."

What will a "good talker" achieve if he's talking to a man who has tuned him out and is thinking only about leaving the office and going fishing? How can a "good product" be sold if the person who is to be persuaded doesn't understand what it will do for him? What good will "selling benefits" do if the benefits are presented to a man who is hostile or distrustful?

In the last analysis, to communicate persuasively a salesman or manager must understand the other person's task and personal needs and use them to motivate. Unless he does, the noises he makes will fall on deaf ears.

The Sales Manager and Motivation

Let's enlarge upon what has been said above, applying it specifically to sales managers. Salesmen must be communicated with at the level of their needs. The manager must understand what motivates his men just as the salesman must understand what motivates his customers. Communication is communication, no matter what we call the people who do the communicating. In thinking about motivating their salesmen, sales managers will find it useful to keep the following in mind.

1. Motivation is the process by which salesmen are energized to produce sales. The sales manager's job, as the Q4 manager understands, is to create conditions in which his men are energized or activated to work in ways that lead to the achievement of the company's goals and their own as well. In a sense, these conditions exist in any selling job, without help from the sales manager. As long as income is one of the personal

goals of work, and as long as men can earn income only by pursuing company goals, some motivation exists in any sales job. But if a man receives the same fixed income no matter how hard or how well he works, he has no incentive to do more than he must to hold on to his job. On the other hand, if income increases as his performance improves (commissions are a good example) then money alone may spur a salesman to a high level of performance. Put another way, money alone may pressure a salesman to work effectively.

2. However, this is not always the case. Beyond a certain level, the prospect of more money often fails to provide incentive. Money is rarely, like self-realization, an open-ended motivator. Many salesmen reach a standard of living toward which they have been striving and then discover that they are satisfied and have no urge to increase that standard. At that point, money ceases to be the prime motivator. Where the point is located varies, of course, with each man. But it is probably safe to say that our culture imposes certain "ideal" standards of living upon people, and, once these ideal standards are reached, money stops being a strong motivator. This is not to say that salesmen stop working when reaching their ideal income, only that they may stop striving and stretching themselves. They "have it made," and money is no longer the most important incentive.

3. For some salesmen, money provides little incentive in any case. This does not mean that large numbers of salesmen would willingly work without pay, only that pay, *by itself,* does not activate them to very high levels of performance. If pay were all they got from their jobs, their work would probably be unenthusiastic, even apathetic. Many people work with genuine enthusiasm, even fervor, for relatively small incomes, and an increase in income brings no increase in enthusiasm; money alone does not motivate them. We could list endless examples: the dedicated schoolteacher, the passionately curious researcher, the ardent scientist, all come readily to mind. The salesman whose real incentive is to set a new sales record or to get into the "honor club" or to get promoted to sales manager is not motivated primarily by money, and he cannot necessarily be spurred to greater activity by the prospect of more money.

4. As we have said repeatedly, then, the sales manager's job is three-fold: to understand the task and personal needs and aspirations of each salesman, to make sure each salesman understands how he can fill his needs and achieve his aspirations through the pursuit of company goals, and to provide the conditions in which both his and the company's goals can be attained. To do this, the Q4 sales manager relies heavily (but not exclusively) on participation, interplay, and the concept of self-realization.

5. Different salesmen respond to different needs, which give rise to different behavior. Salesmen can be effectively motivated, in great part, on an individual, one-to-one basis. There is no magic psychological prescription that motivates all salesmen; the search for motivational cure-alls is fruitless and wasteful. There is no quick or easy way to motivate people. In recent years, there has been a great deal of talk about the possibility of dispensing prepackaged "motivation" like some kind of wonder drug, an instant remedy for apathy, lethargy, disinterest, and similar afflictions. This is based on faulty understanding of human behavior. Motivation requires careful probing of *individual* needs, patience, and continual reexamination of results.

Alone among sales managers, the Q4 understands this. He *begins* by assuming that, like himself, his salesmen are motivated by needs for growth and independence. But this is only a hypothesis to be tested by experience. If experience proves him wrong, he changes the hypothesis to accord with the facts. Once he discovers, for example, that a salesman's security needs are uppermost, he tries to meet *those* needs, rather than growth and independence needs. He relates to his men on the level of their present needs, realizing that he has a long-range responsibility to help them move up the pyramid if he can. His motivational approach is flexible and adaptable.

6. It does little or no good to label a salesman, since labels by themselves are not very helpful. Nothing significant is accomplished, for instance, by tagging a man "lazy and uncooperative." The meaningful question is *why* he is lazy and uncooperative, and the label does not answer that. Designations like "lazy and uncooperative" can be useful for organizing thinking, but not for much else. Once he identifies a salesman as "lazy and uncooperative," the sales manager must ask pertinent questions: Is he really lazy and uncooperative, or has he withdrawn commitment from the job? If he has, why? Is his withdrawal a manifestation of fear or insecurity? If so, what can be done about it? In other words, is the "lazy and uncooperative" salesman really a Q2 with strong security needs? Or is his laziness and failure to cooperate a manifestation of defiance and resistance toward a Q1 boss? Is he a Q1 who wants to establish his own esteem and sense of independence? If so, what does this behavior say about me, his manager? Does he consider me so weak and ineffective that he can flout my authority openly? If so, what can I do to establish my authority and, at the same time, meet his esteem and independence needs? These are not easy questions to answer. Neither is it always easy to recognize Q1 or Q2 behavior. The descriptions in this book are fairly clear cut, as though each person behaves in one and only one way. But we know that real behavior is more complicated. Real behavior is a mixture of all four quadrants, with one usually predominating over the others. Learning to observe and correctly analyze real behavior is a challenge.

There is *no* simple or easy way to categorize real people on the Dimensional model, nor is there a simple or easy way to discover the needs that underlie behavior. Motivating salesmen is *hard work*. Learning to practice what this book preaches may require months or years of effort.

7. More than that, motivating salesmen is *not* an occasional, sometime activity Once needs are uncovered, it is not sufficient to meet them only periodically. Motivation must be an ongoing, continuing activity *built into* other managerial activities. If a salesman has unfilled security needs, these cannot be gratified by artificial pep talks. The salesman's needs must be bolstered *continuously,* less by what the manager says (any manager, after all, has very limited time in which to talk about these things) than by what he does: by the ways he demonstrates to the salesman that he is valued and important. The salesman's *experiences* must prove to him that his manager is really responding to his needs, not manipulating him. He must feel he is being treated as a human being, not a puppet.

8. The old concept of motivation as something imposed from without, something the sales manager *does* to the salesman, does not stand up in the light of modern behavioral science. Motivation is a drive that exists *within* each person; people are basically goal-seeking. There is, in fact, *no* "unmotivated" person. When a sales manager complains that one of his salesmen "lacks motivation," what he usually means is that the salesman is not motivated in a direction approved by the sales *manager.* Every salesman is motivated because every salesman has task and personal needs; his motivation may conflict with the company's goals, but it is still motivation.

No manager can provide or supply motivation, although many talk as if they can. What a manager can do is help a salesman fulfill his most pressing task and personal needs and thereby redirect his motivation. A man will not be motivated by independence and self-realization until more basic needs (for security, sociability, esteem) have been filled. Nor is fulfillment of his personal needs enough; his need for product knowledge must also be filled. The sales manager cannot always fill all the needs, but he can provide opportunities for the salesman to fill them *himself.* Even a word of encouragement by a manager does not fill a need from outside; the word of encouragement must be perceived *by the salesman* as genuinely encouraging and nonthreatening. In the last analysis, whatever the manager says or does is accepted or rejected *by the salesman.* Motivation is controlled from within, not without.

None of this means that the sales manager is impotent. Far from it. The perceptive and patient manager creates *conditions* in which motivation takes place. Like a skilled physician, he can diagnose, prescribe, even make medicine available. Taking the medicine, however, is up to the patient.

20

A Look Ahead

THE FUTURE IS WHAT YOU MAKE IT

Several important questions remain to be answered before this book is brought to a close: How can the Dimensional analysis help you to become a better salesman or sales manager? How can the ideas in this book be put to practical use? How can Dimensional Selling and Sales Management be tied to your success? Before we answer these questions, it would probably help to restate three points with tremendous *practical* implications.

1. There is no such person as a "born salesman or sales manager." People become good in these fields by *applying* effectively certain well-established principles of the behavioral sciences (and, of course, by mastering the many technical aspects of their jobs). Successful salesmen and sales managers have always done this, usually without realizing it. Either they applied these principles by intuition or learned them the hard way, by trial-and-error, or were taught them by an effective manager. In this book, we have tried to eliminate the need for intuition, which can often mislead, and for trial-and-error, which can be costly.

2. Since a critical factor in successful selling and sales management is *personal self-development,* it is extremely important that salesmen and sales managers become aware of, analyze, and understand their own strategies. Only then can they know their strengths and weaknesses, and

take effective action to reinforce the strengths and overcome the weaknesses. The Dimensional concepts make it possible to become more sensitive to strengths and weaknesses. With a thorough understanding of the Dimensional analysis, a salesman or sales manager can take a knowledgeable look at himself and discover his primary strategy, his secondary strategy, and the masks he most frequently wears. With self-knowledge, a salesman or sales manager can effectively practice the interpersonal and communication skills described in this book. Self-knowledge is the seed from which success grows.

3. Flexibility is tremendously important to sales and sales management success. A salesman who approaches every prospect and customer the same way, who rigidly sticks with one strategy even though it may not work, and who refuses to adapt to varying situations. is doomed either to failure or mediocrity. Like a car with only one gear, he may roll along successfully in easy, downhill situations, but he is sure to run into trouble going up hills. But a salesman who is adaptable, who can size up each selling situation independently, and respond to it intelligently, can, like a car with four gears, manage all kinds of situations. Much the same is true of sales managers. Unyielding inflexibility dooms a manager to mediocrity at best. Management means producing results *through other people,* and this *demands* adaptability. The rigid manager is like a building without sway; both do alright when the weather is calm, but neither can withstand strong winds and raging storms. And, as any sales manager knows, management is frequently stormy.

With these points in mind, we can now ask a crucial question: Is there an ideal selling or sales management strategy? Is there one strategy that recommends itself over all others? Any reader of this book is aware that the authors believe the answer is "yes," although we have not said so explicitly. We are now ready to explain our answer. The best way to do this is to analyze the virtues and defects of each of the four sales and sales management strategies.

THE Q1 SALESMAN

Over the years, many companies have placed a high value on this man, and for good reason. The Q1 salesman produces fast results. If a company wants sales right now, he is the man who can turn the trick. There's one drawback, however, and a serious one. While the Q1 makes sales, he also antagonizes many of his customers, who resent his pushiness and lack of concern for their welfare. While the Q1 does turn in orders, he does not build good long-range relationships. For fast, short-range results, the Q1 salesman is frequently unbeatable. For long-range and long-lasting results, he leaves much to be desired. Long-range success is seldom built on "hit-and-run" selling.

THE Q2 SALESMAN

Successful selling ultimately depends on the salesman's conviction that he *can* make a difference. The Q2 does not believe this. His "whatever will be, will be" attitude cripples him. A salesman who obtains most of his orders by luckily being at the right place at the right time or by evoking sympathy from customers can hardly be expected to build long-lived relationships with his customers.

THE Q3 SALESMAN

Because he is so likable, it is a little painful to find fault with the Q3 salesman. Yet the truth is that he is not very businesslike. He lacks the strength and forcefulness to be a really effective salesman. Within a limited circle of customers, he is usually quite successful. But he is neither tough enough nor adaptable enough to break out of this circle and become generally successful. Unhappily, in the world of selling, love does *not* conquer all.

THE Q4 SALESMAN

This is the "professional" salesman, the salesman nearly all companies are eager to obtain and hold. He sells by effecting a meeting of minds between himself and his customer, so that a commitment by the customer, based on real need and real understanding, results. This produces both immediate sales and sound long-range relationships. Furthermore, the Q4's flexibility enables him to interact effectively with all kinds of customers. He has a better chance of across-the-board success than any other salesman.

We can make a similar analysis of the four sales manager strategies.

THE Q1 SALES MANAGER

Up to a certain point, the Q1 frequently obtains good results. But he seldom gets beyond that point. When he starts reaching for goals that require collaboration, high commitment, and vigorous contributions from others, he is often stymied. He fails to develop a climate in which ordinary salesmen produce in an extraordinary way. By overcontrolling and over-supervising, and by refusing to place any confidence in his salesmen, he takes the enrichment out of work, stifles creativity, and thwarts innovation. By refusing to involve his men in significant goal-setting and decision-making where their own jobs are affected, he fails to develop either understanding or dedication. Men do not extend themselves when they lack commitment, and the Q1 sales manager does not develop committed salesmen. Put another way, his salesmen are committed to their private goals, but not necessarily to the company's goals. As a result, the Q1 sales manager seldom achieves long-range excellence, and his men seldom realize their full potential.

THE Q2 SALES MANAGER

Because he is satisfied merely to get by, the Q2's men usually sell enough to keep their jobs, but seldom more. His apathy, his belief that salesmen cannot be motivated, and his refusal to lead insure that, at best, he will maintain the status quo, which is really all he wants to maintain. He fails to develop a climate in which salesmen extend themselves or gain recognition. As a result, his men rarely develop to their full promise.

THE Q3 SALES MANAGER

He seldom stimulates high performance or creativity because he is unwilling to push hard for sales and because new ideas usually produce some tension, which he prefers to avoid. The Q3's need to avoid tension and conflict of any kind results in a managerial balancing act in which he tries to keep everybody happy at one time. Excellence seldom results in this kind of environment. Management, whether we like it or not, demands hard decisions and willingness to support those decisions, even if some people are made unhappy by them. Loosely organized, easygoing, and not deeply concerned about getting the job done, the Q3 typically generates mediocre results and fails to help his men achieve their potential.

THE Q4 SALES MANAGER

This is the "professional" sales manager, the most effective developer of salesmen. By creating conditions in which his men find fulfillment in their work and an opportunity to exercise independence, by getting them involved in goal-setting, problem-solving, and decision-making, and by stressing genuine participation, he produces a high degree of understanding and commitment which, in turn, leads to high sales results.

The authors consider Q4 selling and Q4 sales management the ideal strategies for today's world, in which more and more successful companies are practicing Q4 marketing strategies. The Q4 salesman's and sales manager's concern for their own success combined with their concern for the welfare of their customers and their companies, create a climate in which personal growth, customer growth, salesman growth, and company growth are all possible.

In spite of our strong bias in favor of the Q4 strategies, it should be stressed that each of the other strategies can be effective in its own way. There are numerous instances in which a Q1 or Q3 salesman can be very successful, and there are even some in which a Q2 can do an effective job. The effectiveness of any salesman or any sales manager, it should be remembered, is determined not only by his own strategy, but by the behavior of the people with whom he interacts, the climate of his company, and the specific demands and expectations of the situation in which he finds himself. These can combine into an infinite number of situations, and in certain of these situations any one of the strategies may have its place. There is no question, however, that the Q4 salesman and sales manager can adapt to more situations than the others. Their flexibility gives them advantages that the others lack.

We do not believe that every reader of this book should strive to become a Q4 salesman or sales manager. In many cases, the attempt would be unrealistic, fruitless, and frustrating. But we do believe that by hard and persistent practice every reader can profitably master some of the skills of the Q4. And we do believe each reader should understand the strengths and weaknesses of each strategy so that, if he chooses to use some strategy other than Q4, he can justify its choice to himself. If you think the Q1 is the best strategy for you, you should know what factors in yourself, your customers, and your company make it the best strategy, and you should be fully aware of the probable consequences of your choice.

As a result of reading this book, you should have a better understanding of your present strategy, what results you can expect from it, and what changes might be desirable. Experimentation and intuition can be largely replaced by knowledge, and knowledge should lead to greater flexibility.

Of course, increased skill in any field seldom results merely from reading a book. The precepts in the book must be practiced. This can be done only by analyzing your own behavior and its impact upon others. You may be able to do this in formal training courses based upon the Dimensional model, or in other training courses in which simulated selling or managing occurs. In any event, every contact with a customer, every sale, every prospecting call, every interaction with a salesman must be analyzed, and a whole series of questions must be answered. How did I behave? What effect did my behavior have? Did I achieve my goal? Why? Or why not? What should I have done differently? How did I probe? Did I present my arguments in a period of high receptivity? How did I respond to the other person's needs? How did I generate a dialogue or a monologue? And on and on. Once this kind of self-analysis becomes routine, greater flexibility is almost sure to result. This point can be expressed as a four-part maxim:

1. All salesman and sales manager development is based upon self-development.

2. Interpersonal self-development comes from awareness of the person-to-person realities with which you deal each day.

3. There can be no significant interpersonal self-development unless you base your *behavior* upon this awareness.

4. There can be no significant interpersonal self-development unless you try out and practice the skills that make for effective interaction.

Of all these points, one is so important it deserves to be repeated: *all sales and managerial development is self-development.* No one but *you* can make you a better salesman or sales manager. Only by *applying* the principles of successful behavior to real-life situations can you improve your skills. This book can point the way, but you must follow the way *by yourself.*

As you do, we hope you will keep in mind the point that we have made repeatedly in the preceding chapters: any salesman or sales manager who diligently and conscientiously applies behavioral science in his daily work *can* achieve significant self-improvement and greater success.

APPENDIX

The behavioral science principles described in this book have been incorporated into two marketing-organization development programs widely used in the United States and abroad. One of these, called Dimensional Sales Training or DST, trains salesmen in the interpersonal skills required for long-range sales success. The other, called Dimensional Sales Management Training or DSM, trains sales managers in the interpersonal skills required for long-range sales-management success. These programs have been conducted in numerous American cities and, with translated materials that have been culturally adapted, on three other continents. A Spanish version has been used in Spanish-speaking Latin America and in Spain; a Portuguese version in Brazil and Portugal; a French version in France, Belgium, and Switzerland; and the English version in Canada, Australia, and the United Kingdom. Work is now in progress on translations into other languages. For the benefit of those readers who would like to know more about DST and DSM they are described in this appendix.

THE "CONTINUING GROWTH" APPROACH

Neither DST nor DSM is a one-time training experience that is supposed to produce instantaneous transformations in behavior. As this book has tried to make clear, behavior change rarely happens very suddenly or spectacularly. In almost every instance, improved sales or sales-management behavior is the result of *continuing* development over a period of time. For this reason, DST and DSM are *continuing* training programs, consisting of a series of seminars. Between each seminar, participants can practice the skills they acquired in the preceding seminar; these in-between periods are as important as the seminars themselves, because in these periods the techniques learned in the seminars are put to use. Thus, a company that begins DST and DSM seminars begins an *ongoing* program of long-range marketing development.

The seminars in this series are:

Dimensional Sales Training: a $4\frac{1}{2}$-day seminar that emphasizes the development of self-awareness in sales situations and of persuasive communication and motivation skills for salesmen.

Dimensional Sales Management Training: a $4\frac{1}{2}$-day seminar that emphasizes the development of self-awareness in sales and sales management situations, and the development of motivation and coaching-and-counseling skills for first-level field sales managers.

DST: Stage II: A $4\frac{1}{2}$-day seminar for both first-level sales managers and the salesmen who report to them, which emphasizes development of the field-level sales team into an effective selling unit.

Spin-Offs: custom seminars designed to fill the continuing training needs of specific companies by applying Dimensional principles to their particular sales and marketing situations.

Thus, the first two seminars, DST and DSM, provide training in fundamental sales and sales-management skills. The third program, DST: Stage II, brings the participants from the first two seminars together and trains them in skills that can weld them into a more effective unit. The spin-off seminars are tailormade programs that apply Dimensional principles to the unique problems of individual companies. The four programs together foster *systematic* long-range growth and marketing-organization development.

DIMENSIONAL SALES TRAINING

DST is concerned with selling as the salesman *experiences* it in real life. The seminar avoids ivory-tower theorizing and concentrates on developing usable skills that will help salesmen succeed in the real world of selling. Three premises underlie this approach:

1. "The" customer is a myth. In the real world, customers differ immensely in their behavior, in their motivation, and in their responses to salesmen.

2. "The" salesman is equally mythical. In the real world, salesmen differ greatly in their behavior, in their beliefs about their jobs, and in the ways they interact with different kinds of customers.

3. Long-range success in selling cannot, therefore, be based on rigid rules that are supposed to cover all selling situations at all times. It must be based on *intelligently flexible* behavior.

The basic purpose of DST is therefore twofold: to help salesmen understand the varieties of customer and salesman behavior (including their own), and to impart skills for coping with a wide variety of customer behaviors intelligently and flexibly. The seminar tries to increase the effectiveness of salesmen by pointing the way to greater adaptability, resilience, and individuality.

What Skills Does DST Impart?

The DST seminar tries to develop four sets of skills: (*1*) diagnostic skills, (*2*) adaptive skills, (*3*) communication skills, and (*4*) specialized selling skills.

DIAGNOSTIC SKILLS

The Dimensional Model of Sales Behavior gives salesmen a scientific system for diagnosing their own behavior and their customers' behavior. The idea is to help salesmen understand the *needs* that underlie various behaviors. Once they do, they can "make sense" out of behaviors that would otherwise seem erratic or incomprehensible.

ADAPTIVE SKILLS

After customer behavior has been diagnosed, it must be adapted to. The DST seminar teaches salesmen *how* to cope with different types of customers. It shows them the penalties they incur by rigid, mechanical, unthinking behavior. By teaching skills in listening, in probing, in analyzing customer needs, and in conveying ideas, the DST seminar develops flexibility and resilience.

COMMUNICATION SKILLS

DST teaches salesmen how to gain understanding and commitment from their customers through dialogue. It gives them an opportunity to practice Q4 communication skills, to get beyond the "I talk, you listen" approach that bedevils so many salesmen and to replace it with two-way communication that generates sales.

The DST seminar imparts techniques for opening the sales presentation, for guiding and controlling it, for developing customer rapport, for managing objections, and for closing successfully. It teaches salesmen how to link product features with customer needs, and how to establish benefits and net gain.

How Does DST Work?

There are two parts to every DST program: the preseminar work and the seminar itself.

PRESEMINAR WORK

Prior to attending the seminar, participants are given approximately twenty hours of preparatory work to complete. They fill out a number of questionnaires which ask them to evaluate and record their own selling strategies as they see them at the time. Then, after reading this book, they complete several tasks which test their understanding of its concepts, and they make their first attempt to apply these concepts to cases of salesman–customer interaction. Finally, they complete a questionnaire which will form the basis of exercises in "real-life" selling in the seminar.

The purpose of the preseminar work. Because each participant has done about twenty hours of preparatory work, the DST seminar begins at a fairly advanced level. There is no need to spend large amounts of seminar time on basic instruction; each participating salesman is familiar with the textbook and with the fundamental Dimensional concepts before he gets to the seminar. Thus, after a brief period on the first day to clarify basic concepts, the seminar can move into the vital area of *skill-formation.* By learning most of their theoretical underpinnings *before* they came to the seminar, participants can devote most of their seminar hours to learning *techniques* and how to implement them in real-life.

THE DST SEMINAR

The seminar starts at 8:00 Monday morning and ends at 11:30 Friday morning. The number of persons attending a seminar usually ranges from ten to thirty. Participants are assigned to teams of five. Teams normally finish their Monday-through-Wednesday activities at 6:45 to 7:30 p.m., and then adjourn for dinner and free time. Thursday evening is open-ended; teams commonly work very late into Thursday night or the early hours of Friday morning. The seminar is wrapped up on Friday morning, with early adjournment so participants can make travel connections home.

The purpose of teamwork. The seminar group is divided into teams for two important reasons. One goal of the seminar is to develop diagnostic skills, and these skills can be developed more rapidly and more thoroughly in small groups in which interaction between the members is sustained and intensive. Small-group activity is especially important in helping a salesman diagnose his *own* behavior; after being keenly observed by his teammates for four days, and after getting candid feedback from them about his behavior, a salesman gets a view of himself *as seen by others* that he could not easily get in any other way. Practically all the seminar activities require teamwork. These activities, which are described on the following pages, are most effectively carried out in small groups marked by close interaction and high candor.

Monday morning. Part of the day is spent clarifying Dimensional concepts. Some of the clarification occurs through lectures, some through team discussions. These discussions not only help to clarify and amplify the men's understanding of the Dimensional Model, but they serve as "icebreakers" for the team.

The purpose of lectures in the DST seminar. Only about 15% of the seminar is taken up by lectures. These are useful for expanding on the basic Dimensional concepts, for clearing up misconceptions, and for giving participants a chance to ask questions. But the lectures do *not* give the seminar its fundamental thrust; this comes from the team activities. The lectures are important, but not nearly so important as the *experience* that each participant gains as he works his way through assigned tasks. Through experience, disembodied concepts become real and believable to the salesman. Throughout, the seminar emphasizes learning through *doing* rather than learning through passivity.

Monday afternoon. Role playing of salesman–customer situations begins. As two men on each team role play, the rest of the team observes, using specially prepared critique-and-feedback forms to guide their observations. At the end of each role play, the observers render a critique of the salesman's role, while the man who played the salesman listens quietly and records the critique on his copy of the critique-and-feedback form. Eventually, each man on each team gets to play a salesman's role and a customer's role, and also gets several chances to observe.

The purpose of role playing. Role playing, or simulated selling, does three things. It lets each participant discover how other people view his behavior. It enables each participant to find out what his strengths and weaknesses as a salesman are, so that he can reinforce the strengths and overcome the weaknesses. It gives each participant an opportunity to experiment with new sales behavior in a supportive, risk-free environment. Role playing is one form of action learning, which is basic to DST.

Behavioral scientists have demonstrated repeatedly that people learn better in active rather than passive situations. Especially in training aimed at behavioral change, lectures are far less effective than was once thought. Salesmen learn more by doing than by merely listening; significant learning occurs when lectures are followed by action which implements the principles of the lectures. A salesman, for example, who hears a description of Q2 customer behavior learns a little, but a salesman who tries to deal with a Q2 customer in a simulated situation learns a great deal.

Another behavioral science principle used extensively in DST is this: people learn best in nonthreatening atmospheres. If a salesman is to improve his behavior, he must experiment with new ways of behaving, and nobody can be expected to experiment willingly if he fears embarrassment, hostile criticism, or ridicule. In the open, supportive atmosphere of a DST seminar, salesmen are encouraged to behave in new ways, to cast off rigidity in favor of flexibility. They know that their fellow team members, who share their experimentation, will be open and candid with them, but not destructive. Equally important, they know they can afford to experiment, since nothing is at risk. If a salesman does a bad job in a role play, he loses nothing, but he gains much from the critique that follows. Few salesmen, of course, will "take a chance" on new behavior when real sales and commissions are at stake. In the risk-free, supportive atmosphere of a DST seminar, learning flourishes as it seldom can in the real world of selling.

The purpose of critique and feedback. A wealth of scientific data proves that people learn best when they know, in unmistakably clear terms, what their mistakes are, so they can start correcting them. A salesman who does not know that his behavior is self-defeating will probably persist in that behavior. This is why constant critique and feedback are an integral part of DST. They give salesmen clear insight into the influence of their behavior upon others; with this insight, they can make changes in their behavior with deliberate speed, before ineffective patterns harden.

The *system* of critique and feedback used in the seminar ties in to the Dimensional Model of Sales Behavior. Through this system, the relevance of the model to real-life situations becomes crystal clear. By using the system repeatedly, the salesmen improve their observational skills; they learn to put a sale under a behavioral microscope, and they learn how to interpret what they see. Before long, they are able to apply the same system of critique and feedback to their *own* behavior.

Tuesday morning. Several video tapes of role plays made on Monday are reviewed, and critique follows. The instructor then gives a lecture on persuasive communication, in which he develops three crucial themes: probing, receptivity, and features, advantages benefit, and net gain.

Tuesday afternoon. More role playing. Typically, the quality of critique and feedback is notably higher on Tuesday than on Monday. Each day, participants sharpen their observational skills, and their increasingly keener observations are reflected in more candid and useful feedback.

An important aid in giving critique and feedback is video tape. A significant number of participants are taped during role playing. Several hours during the week are spent reviewing the tapes and offering critiques of them. These tapes usually produce a spirited exchange of opinions, guided by the instructor. This exchange helps each man clarify his understanding of critical concepts and sharpen his observational skills.

The purpose of video-taping role plays. DST uses closed-circuit TV not as a gimmick, but as an important aid to learning. Taping various simulated situations and then playing them back (using stop-tape and instant-replay when needed) *speeds* the development of self-perception and the learning of communication skills. Video tape enhances *objectivity;* it helps men see themselves as they appear to others. By giving them an "outsider's view, it helps to shatter misconceptions about themselves that many men have carried for years. This is a salutary learning experience.

Video tape is also used early in the seminar to introduce participants to critique and feedback. The salesmen view a taped role-play, and then they view a taped critique by two psychologists on the staff of Psychological Associates. Once they've "seen it done," the salesmen are readily able to render critique on their own.

Wednesday. After hearing a lecture on salesman–customer interaction and reviewing a TV tape, the teams dispense to separate rooms for the Model Sales Strategy task. This is the point at which the seminar moves from the sales process *in general* to the sales process as the men encounter it in their *real* jobs. In this task, the team develops strategies for selling real-life customers whom the men have had no success (or limited success) selling up to this point. The strategies are based on information that each man recorded as part of his preparatory work for the seminar. After each "model" strategy is developed, it is implemented by the salesman, who plays himself, and another member of the team who plays the real-life customer. Critique and feedback are rendered by the team after each presentation.

The purpose of the Model Sales Strategy task. If learning is to "take," it must be relevant to the learner; it must have some significant meaning for him. The Model Sales Strategy provides this meaning. It helps each participant see how the Dimensional principles can help him sell one of his tough customers, how the concepts of the seminar can be related to *his* business.

Why, then, does an activity that is related to a man's real-life situation come only on the third day of the seminar? Why are the role plays on the first two days fictitious? The reason is that each man must understand the *interpersonal processes.* In order to get the men to think in terms of *process* (opening, communication, direction, customer relationship, management of objections, and closing), the seminar begins with fictitious role plays in which the men are not much concerned about the factual details (content) of the product or service they are being asked to sell. If these early role plays involved a man's *own* product, he would probably become enmeshed in questions about pricing, quality, delivery, competition, and so forth, and largely disregard the interpersonal processes. By the third day, participants are almost always ready to focus on *both* process and content.

Thursday morning and afternoon. The application of Dimensional principles to the participants' own business continues. This time, the concepts are applied to an *objection management* task. Each team develops role-playing situations based on real-life objections frequently encountered by its members; the objections are ones that the men have difficulty handling. Each man then role-plays a situation which includes objections that give him trouble whenever he hears them. The team renders critique after each role play. Typically, the team suggests workable ways to handle the objection (besides the one the salesman worked out for himself) and each man thus gets a new and valuable perspective on a frequently heard objection.

Thursday evening. Beginning late Thursday afternoon, the members of each team begin the culminating task of the seminar, the *Summary Feedback* task. In the team rooms, each member of each team receives "summary" critique from the rest of the team. In summary critique, all of the impressions of his behavior that the team has gathered during the seminar are fed back to him. A well-organized written paragraph describing these impressions is developed by the team for each man. Improvement goals are recommended to each man by the team, and a plan-of-action for achieving each goal is discussed with him. No time-limit is set on this task; the critiques run as long as the men feel is useful.

The Purpose of the Summary Feedback Task. Summary critique gives each participant an overall view of himself as other people see him. It helps each man understand what strengths and weaknesses he exhibited during the week, and what changes he should strive to make in his behavior. All of the feedback is about behavior that affects job performance; none is about personal characteristics that have little or nothing to do with sales success. Thus, the Summary Feedback task gives each man information he can *use* and *profit* from.

Summary Feedback is based on the premise that self-development occurs most rapidly in people who are self-aware, alert to their strengths, and conscious of their weaknesses. Self-awareness is the springboard to interpersonal growth. A man who receives candid and constructive feedback in a setting like that of the Summary Feedback task can, it has been estimated, learn as much about himself as he would ordinarily learn in ten or fifteen years of everyday experience.

Friday morning. The participants again fill out the questionnaires they filled out before coming to the seminar, and the two sets of answers are compared so that shifts in attitudes or in self-perception of their sales behavior resulting from the seminar can be spotted. Only total group shifts, not individual shifts, are reported to the group. The questionnaires almost always show that sales attitudes have shifted toward the Q4 quadrant, and sales behavior is now viewed more objectively and realistically; participants typically leave the seminar not only with *greater* belief in the value of Q4 behavior, but also with the realization that their own behavior is *less* Q4 than they had earlier believed. The seminar closes with a lecture on company marketing strategies and their relationship to individual sales strategies.

The purpose of the questionnaires. Generally, the attitude and self-perception questionnaires filled out *before* the seminar reveal that salesmen are somewhat skeptical of the practical worth of Q4 behavior, and that they nevertheless see themselves largely as Q4 salesmen. Or, put another way, they have an idealized view of themselves, but are not sure that the idealized behavior they attribute to themselves is very useful for producing sales. The same questionnaires filled out at the *conclusion* of the seminar generally reveal that the participants are considerably *more* convinced that Q4 behavior "pays," and that they are considerably *less* certain that their own behavior can be described as Q4. In other words their attitudes about selling have changed, and, as a result of the intensive feedback they have received, so have their evaluations of themselves. Their idealized self-image has been at least partly replaced by a truer self-image; they now see themselves more as others see them. With their increased acceptance of Q4 attitudes and their more realistic self-perception, they are ready to *continue* improving their sales behavior.

The basic DST seminar imparts four sets of skills:

1. Diagnostic skills. By repeated observations of simulated sales, participants became adept at spotting various salesmen and customer strategies, and at analyzing the motivation behind these strategies. Virtually every one of the seminar tasks require participants to observe carefully, and to relate their observations to the Dimensional Model. In this way, what might otherwise be disjointed impressions become significant patterns.

2. Adaptive skills. Consistent observation and analysis of sales behavior soon reveals that the inflexible salesman pays a price for his rigidity. He quite often fails to make sales to certain types of customers. Once participants begin to see the merit of adaptability, they begin to try out more flexible behavior in role plays; after a while, some of these new ways of behaving will seem natural and comfortable, and will become part of the salesmen's standard behavioral repertories.

3. Communication skills. In role playing, and in all team interaction, participants practice new or seldom-used communication techniques: probing, spacing, attentive listening, explaining benefits during periods of high receptivity, and so forth. As they begin to learn the value of these techniques, they incorporate them into their primary strategies.

4. Specialized skills. Participants get plenty of opportunity to practice new ways of opening, closing, managing objections, using features, advantages, and benefits, establishing net gain, and so on. And they learn a great deal about specialized selling skills by watching their teammates sell. Both as role players and observers, they acquire new ideas and new viewpoints.

DIMENSIONAL SALES MANAGEMENT TRAINING

DSM is based on premises similar to those that underlie DST:

1. There is no such creature as "the" salesman. Salesmen differ enormously from one another, and a successful sales manager must cope with the differences as well as the similarities.

2. "The" sales manager is as mythical as the unicorn. Like salesmen, sales managers differ from one another.

3. Because of these differences in salesmen and in sales managers, sales management training must develop *intelligently flexible* managers. Rigid rules and unyielding precepts can only cripple a sales manager.

Thus, DSM has two basic purposes: to help sales managers understand the varieties of managerial behavior (especially their *own*), of salesman behavior, and of customer behavior; and to impart the skills that will help them to motivate, train, counsel, guide, and stimulate growth in a wide variety of salesmen *intelligently* and *flexibly*. It tries to free managers from the constricting bonds of mechanical behavior, so that they can develop more successful salesmen and produce more sales.

What Skills Does DSM Impart?

DSM develops in sales managers all the skills that DST develops in salesmen, but it develops them in significantly different ways. In DST, the primary concern is always the salesmen's interaction with *customers*; in DSM, the primary concern is both the salesman's interaction with customers and the sales manager's interaction with salesmen. Accordingly, the DSM seminar develops the same skills as DST and then *adds* to them as follows.

DIAGNOSTIC SKILLS

Managers learn to analyze the behavior of all types of salesmen, from the manipulative Q1 to the compliant Q3. They discover that every salesman's behavior, no matter how puzzling at first, can be explained in terms of the salesman's needs, and that managers can effectively motivate their men only *after* they have analyzed their needs.

ADAPTIVE SKILLS

Many sales managers are baffled by certain kinds of salesmen. They may be unable to control the headstrong Q1, or to pierce the barriers set up by the apathetic Q2, or to stimulate the easygoing Q3. In a word, they lack adaptability. DSM teaches managers how to cope with each type of salesman.

COMMUNICATION SKILLS

Adaptability depends, in large part, upon communication, but many sales managers have limited communication skills. They indulge in long, blustery monologues, they ramble from topic to topic, they communicate in ways that make salesmen defensive or hostile, they gloss over crucial problems, or they are tongue-tied and ill at ease; in each case, they fail to get through to their salesmen. DSM imparts communication skills that enable sales managers to get through, to stimulate and motivate their salesmen.

SPECIALIZED SKILLS

DSM teaches techniques of coaching and counseling, of motivating, and of training salesmen through critique, feedback, and simulated selling.

How Does DSM Work?

DSM requires participants to complete about twenty hours of preseminar work. In the seminar itself, the first two days are devoted to *DST* activities, so that sales managers learn what their salesmen learn in the DST seminar. Concept clarification, critique and feedback, role-playing of sales situations, salesman–customer interaction and the management of objections task are all covered on Monday and Tuesday. On Wednesday morning, activities concerned with sales *management* are introduced, and these fill the next two days, until the Summary Feedback session late Thursday. The wrap-up on Friday is comparable to the wrap-up in the DST seminar. The activities devoted especially to sales management are:

THE SALES MANAGERS' TV CRITIQUE TASK

Early in the seminar, role-plays are recorded on TV tapes. Every participant gets at least one opportunity to be on TV. On Wednesday, the managers (by teams) view these tapes. After each viewing, a member of the team who was *not* one of the role players assumes the role of sales manager and renders critique of the sales performance of the man who played the salesman; the two men (the original salesman and the man who plays his sales manager) engage in a coaching and counseling session. After this session, the other members of the team, who have been observing, render critique to the sales *manager* of his coaching-and-counseling performance. Thus, the manager gets feedback about his managerial skills, and begins to understand his managerial strengths and weaknesses. Each man on the team rotates through this process.

SALES MANAGEMENT "PEOPLE PROBLEMS"

Each manager gives his team a detailed description of a real-life problem he is presently having with either a salesman, a fellow manager, his boss, or someone else in his company. Then, with the manager out of the room, the team develops a role-playing situation based upon the real-life problem. The manager is then called back and required to role-play the situation with a teammate chosen to be the "other" person. The team observes the role-play and afterward renders critique of the manager's performance. Again, the manager receives valuable insight into his interaction with other people; equally important, he acquires useful ideas about how to cope with his real-life problem when he returns home.

The Basic DSM Principles

Selling is not primarily an inborn trait but a learnable skill. This principle gives the manager a larger view of his own role as a trainer and developer. He begins to view coaching and training skills in a new and more significant light. Fatalism is replaced by optimism; the defeatist attitude that "nothing can be done to improve my men" gives way to the knowledge that men *can* learn selling skills. The manager comes to realize that every contact he has with his men should, in some way, further their development. DSM tries to sweep away old myths about selling (which have done untold damage to salesmen and sales managers over the years) and replace them with validated concepts that broaden the manager's perspective on his job.

Managers must understand why salesmen are effective or ineffective. Guesswork and intuition must be superseded by field-tested scientific understanding of selling. Managers must see that sales are an outgrowth of behavioral *interaction*. Selling then begins to seem less mysterious and more subject to the basic principles of human behavior.

The communication chasm that frequently exists between salesmen and their sales managers must be bridged. This can be done if both learn the same vocabulary—the Dimensional vocabulary. This is more than a matter of mere words; this vocabulary helps both men to share ideas, insights, and understanding of sound selling principles. Perhaps most important of all, both men take a giant stride toward a common commitment to skills and goals that they agree upon. Manager and salesmen then come to see themselves not as adversaries fated to work at cross-purposes with one another, not as antagonists constantly viewing one another with suspicion, but as men who agree on how to fulfill shared objectives.

Successful training of salesmen requires a system of critique and feedback based not on guesswork but on thoroughgoing, point-by-point analysis. This feedback should encourage salesmen to try new selling behaviors. Because such feedback is carefully *structured* and not based on spur-of-the-moment conjecture, it is welcomed by salesmen, not resented. Managers can therefore coach their men and set goals with them without generating defensiveness, hostility, indignation, or other barriers. With this kind of manager–salesman interaction, growth and development flourish.

Managers need a method for analyzing and resolving the many "people problems" that are a never-ending part of their jobs. The basic principles of the Dimensional Model apply to a wide variety of behavior and people. Production supervisors, advertising directors, accounting managers, traffic supervisors, people at every level of the company—as well as sales managers and salesmen—can be understood in terms of the four basic behavioral strategies. So the communications skills acquired through DSM can be applied in *any* situation in which the sales manager *interacts* with others. Whether coaching a salesman, managing an outraged customer, explaining a problem to an impatient superior, or trying to get faster delivery from a harassed plant foreman, the sales manager can use communications skills like venting, drawing out, attentive listening, and probing—all of which he learns *through practice* in DSM.

Managers must set goals that elicit both understanding and commitment from their salesmen. Frequently, goals set by management are resisted by salesmen because the goals are not fully understood in terms that count to the salesmen. Unless a salesman realizes *his* personal stake in achieving the goals, he will not feel committed to them. Once again, the vital ingredient in this understanding and commitment is communication skill based upon an understanding of behavioral interaction—a skill provided by DSM.

Managers must learn to interpret their salesmen's behavior in the light of their salesmen's needs. Once these needs are understood, the manager can do a consistent job of motivation, instead of a hit-or-miss one. Motivation must be seen not as a hypodermic needle for emergency use, but as a steady diet. This approach is possible only when managers understand that their salesmen's needs are continuous and fundamental to their day-by-day behavior.

DST: STAGE II

Stage II is a follow-up seminar which applies the concepts and methods of the basic DST and DSM seminars to real-life sales, sales management, and marketing problems confronting the basic field-level selling units. The program places the prime responsibility for solving ongoing sales and sales management problems squarely in the hands of the basic field selling unit. Stage II is thus the "payoff" stage of DST and DSM; it brings behavioral science principles to bear on current real-life sales and marketing challenges. It uses the resources of the basic field selling units to identify and then to resolve their problems and opportunities in a way that achieves maximum benefits for their customers, their company, and themselves.

As with the Basic DST and DSM seminars, no attempt is made to work miracles in a single week. Instead, the field sales manager and his men are provided with techniques they can use continuously to resolve marketing and sales problems in their geographic region. The sales unit is given the means by which it can work *independently* on sales problems as a part of its ongoing activities.

Stage II is distinguished from the earlier seminars in two significant ways. It brings the sales manager and his men together and treats them like what they are in reality: a team. It focuses on *collaboration* in pursuit of common goals, and on *integration* of efforts. It also deals entirely with *real-life* situations. From start to finish, the seminar is concerned with what's *really* going on in the field.

How Does a Stage II Seminar Work?

Stage II should follow Stage I by about six months. This time lapse gives both salesmen and sales manager an opportunity to apply the techniques learned in Stage I to real-life sales and sales management problems. (Stage II need not be conducted in a single $4\frac{1}{2}$-day period. It can be divided into two or three sessions.)

Analysis of marketing barriers and/or opportunities. As part of Stage II preseminar preparation, participants are asked to analyze the marketing barriers and opportunities they are presently facing. Ten major areas, including product quality, pricing, distribution, advertising, and selling efforts are reviewed, and customer needs are tentatively formulated. The team thus comes to the seminar fully prepared to work on solutions to its problems.

Resolving important field sales-management and sales problems. The field sales units are ready, once their marketing barriers and opportunities have been identified, to resolve those problems which can appropriately be resolved at the field level, adhering, of course, to their company's policies and procedures. The full resources of the sales unit are brought to bear on these problems through discussion and role-playing exercises.

Communicating solutions to top marketing management. Once the field sales unit resolves its problems, it compares its solutions with those worked out by other field sales units. Agreements and disagreements are examined, and the best solutions are reported to marketing management for its use in developing marketing strategies. This information is communicated to top marketing management by the field sales manager through existing channels.

Evaluating the field selling unit's effectiveness in dealing with other company functions. As part of the preprogram preparation, participants analyze their typical ways of interacting with company forces outside the basic field unit. For example, they examine their relationship with marketing management, advertising, production, and other sales and nonsales units of the company. During Stage II, the field unit reaches a consensus as to what its typical interactions have been, and what the ideal interactions should be, and then identifies areas in which it can improve. Thus the team analyzes its own past actions, the ideal toward which it should be striving, and the major differences between what it has been doing and what it ought to be doing. It lays the groundwork for moving itself, as a team, into management-by-objectives.

Examining the effectiveness of the field selling unit in its own internal operations. The procedure outlined above is used by the field selling unit to evaluate its internal operations as well. Typical modes of interaction are examined: how the team makes decisions, plans, handles disagreements, coordinates efforts, trains and develops sales unit members, and so forth, first individually and then collectively. The actual is then compared with the ideal and the prime improvement areas spotted.

Examining the field selling unit's effectiveness in meeting the needs of customers. Next, the team, first individually and then collectively, examines the effectiveness of its relationships with its customers. The actual is examined and compared with the team ideal. Specific improvement areas are determined.

Assigning priorities to improvements which would increase the team's effectiveness in working with other company forces, in its internal operations, and in carrying out its sales mandate with customers. The team has by now spent a good deal of time identifying prime improvement areas in its internal and external operations. One of its final activities is to review these improvement areas, to examine their importance, and then to assign priorities to them.

Developing plans of action to effect changes in the designated improvement areas. Once the improvement areas have been assigned priorities, the team develops detailed plans-of-action for achieving improvement. These are not mere New Year's resolutions, glibly made and easily forgotten. They are goals to which the team is intellectually and emotionally *committed* because it has itself taken part in identifying them and analyzing them.

Since not all improvement areas can be covered during the seminar, the team makes plans to develop additional plans-of-action in future meetings. Thus the team has ready-made agendas for future meetings; goal-setting and action-planning can now become a continuing process. A system for reviewing progress on the plans-of-action is established, so that the plans do not languish and ultimately die.

SPIN-OFF PROGRAMS

Because improved behavior is the product of diligent practice over a sustained period of time, the Dimensional programs we have described are not intended as one-shot wonder drugs, but as medicine to be taken in regular doses for a continuing period. The purpose of Dimensional spin-off programs is to give companies *continuing* training in applied behavioral science.

Spin-offs are specialized programs, unique to particular companies, in which Dimensional concepts and techniques are applied to a broad variety of sales and marketing problems. Because spin-offs differ from one another they cannot be described collectively. Their duration and content vary from company to company. Typically, a spin-off requires part or all of one day, and can be conducted in the field by a trainer or field sales manager.

MULTICOMPANY AND SINGLE-COMPANY PROGRAMS

Basic DST and DSM seminars are conducted on both a multicompany basis (with participants from a wide variety of companies and industries) and a single-company basis. Multicompany seminars are often used by companies that want to evaluate Dimensional Training, or by companies whose size makes internal programs impractical. Stage II is, by its very nature, offered on a single-company basis only.

BIBLIOGRAPHY

Readers who want to know more about the behavioral science concepts on which Dimensional Sales and Sales Management are based will find the following books and articles well worth their while.

Allen, Louis A., *The Management Profession,* New York: McGraw-Hill, 1964.

Argyris, C., *Personality and Organization,* New York: Harper and Row, 1957.

Asch, S., *Social Psychology,* Englewood Cliffs, N.J.: Prentice-Hall, 1952.

Bales, R. F., *Personality and Interpersonal Behavior,* New York: Holt, Rinehart and Winston, 1970.

Barnard, C., *Functions of the Executive,* Cambridge, Mass.: Harvard University Press, 1968.

Bavelas, Alex, "Communication Patterns in Task-Oriented Groups," *Journal of the Acoustical Society of America,* 1950.

Bennis, W., *Changing Organizations,* New York: McGraw-Hill, 1966.

Blake, R. and J. Mouton, *The Managerial Grid,* Houston, Texas: Gulf Publishing, 1964.

Cartwright, D., *Studies in Social Power,* Ann Arbor, Mich.: Institute for Social Research, 1959.

Dollard, John and Neal Miller, *Personality and Psychotherapy: An Analysis in Terms of Learning, Thinking and Culture,* New York: McGraw-Hill, 1950.

Drucker, P., *Managing for Results,* New York: Harper and Row, 1964.

Drucker, P., *Age of Discontinuity,* New York: Harper and Row, 1969.

Etzioni, Amitai, *Modern Organizations,* Englewood Cliffs, N.J.: Prentice-Hall, 1964.

Festinger, L., *A Theory of Cognitive Dissonance,* Palo Alto, California: Stanford University Press, 1957.

Fromm, E., *Man for Himself,* New York: Rinehart, 1947.

Gardner, J. W., *Excellence,* New York: Harper and Row, 1961.

Haire, M., *Psychology in Management,* New York: McGraw-Hill, 1964.

Herzberg, F., B. Mausner, and B. Snydeman, *The Motivation to Work,* New York: John Wiley, 1959.

Horney, K., *The Neurotic Personality of Our Time,* New York: Norton, 1937.

Hovland, C. and I. Janis, (Eds.), *Personality and Persuasibility: Vol. 2 Yale Studies in Attitude and Communication,* New Haven, Conn.: Yale University Press, 1959.

Hull, C. L., *Principles of Behavior: An Introduction to Behavior Theory,* New York: Appleton-Century-Crofts, 1943.

Leary, T., *Interpersonal Diagnosis of Personality,* New York: Ronald Press, 1957.

Leavitt, H. J., *Managerial Psychology,* Chicago: University of Chicago Press, 1958.

Likert, R., *New Patterns of Management,* New York: McGraw-Hill, 1961.

Likert, R., *The Human Organization,* New York: McGraw-Hill, 1970.

Maier, N., *Principles of Human Relations,* New York: John Wiley, 1956.

Marrow, A. J., *Behind the Executive Mask,* New York: American Management Association, 1964.

Maslow, A. H., *Motivation and Personality,* New York: Harper and Row, 1954.

Maslow, A. H., *Eupsychian Management,* Homewood, Illinois: Dorsey Press, 1965.

McClelland, D. C., J. W. Atkinson, R. A. Clark, E. L. Lowell, *The Achievement Motive,* New York: Appleton-Century-Crofts, 1953.

McClelland, D. C., J. W. Atkinson, R. A. Clark, and E. L. Lowell, *The Achieving Society,* Princeton, N.J.: Van Nostrand, 1961.

McGeoch, J. A. and A. L. Irion, *The Psychology of Human Learning,* 2nd ed. New York: Longmans Green, 1952, 1953, 1954.

McGregor, D., *The Human Side of Enterprise,* New York: McGraw-Hill, 1960.

McGregor, D., *The Professional Manager,* New York: McGraw-Hill, 1967.

Moreno, Jacob, *Sociometry, Experimental Method and the Science of Society,* Boston: Beacon House, 1951.

Murphy, Gardner, *Personality: A Biosocial Approach to Origins and Structures,* New York: Basic Books, 1966.

Murray, Henry, *Exploration in Personality,* New York: Oxford Press, 1938.

Schien, E. H., *Organizational Psychology,* Englewood Cliffs, N.J.: Prentice-Hall, 1965.

Schutz, William C., *The Interpersonal Underworld (FIRO),* Palo Alto, California: Science and Behavior Books, 1966.

Sherif, Muzafer, *Intergroup Relations and Leadership,* New York: John Wiley, 1962.

Sullivan, H. S., *The Interpersonal Theory of Psychiatry,* New York: Norton, 1954.

Tannenbaum, R., I. R. Weschler, and F. Massorik, *Leadership and Organization: A Behavioral Science Approach,* New York: McGraw-Hill, 1961.

Whyte, W. H., *The Organization Man,* New York: Simon and Schuster, 1956.

Whyte, W., *Money and Motivation,* New York: Harper, Hayser and Row, 1955.

Zaleznik, A. and D. Moment, *The Dynamics of Interpersonal Behavior,* New York: John Wiley, 1964.

INDEX